T0215397

# Pivotal Certified Spring Web Application Developer Exam

A Study Guide

Iuliana Cosmina

Apress®

**Pivotal Certified Spring Web Application Developer Exam**

ISBN-13 (pbk): 978-1-4842-0809-0

ISBN-13 (electronic): 978-1-4842-0808-3

Managing Director: Welmoed Spahr
Lead Editor: Steve Anglin
Technical Reviewer: Manuel Jordan Elera
Editorial Board: Steve Anglin, Louise Corrigan, James T. DeWolf, Jonathan Gennick,
    Robert Hutchinson, Michelle Lowman, James Markham, Susan McDermott, Matthew Moodie,
    Jeffrey Pepper, Douglas Pundick, Ben Renow-Clarke, Gwenan Spearing
Coordinating Editor: Mark Powers
Copy Editor: Kimberly Burton
Compositor: SPi Global
Indexer: SPi Global
Artist: SPi Global

Distributed to the book trade worldwide by Springer Science+Business Media New York, 233 Spring Street, 6th Floor, New York, NY 10013. Phone 1-800-SPRINGER, fax (201) 348-4505, e-mail orders-ny@springer-sbm.com, or visit www.springeronline.com. Apress Media, LLC is a California LLC and the sole member (owner) is Springer Science + Business Media Finance Inc (SSBM Finance Inc). SSBM Finance Inc is a Delaware corporation.

For information on translations, please e-mail rights@apress.com, or visit www.apress.com.

Apress and friends of ED books may be purchased in bulk for academic, corporate, or promotional use. eBook versions and licenses are also available for most titles. For more information, reference our Special Bulk Sales–eBook Licensing web page at www.apress.com/bulk-sales.

Any source code or other supplementary material referenced by the author in this text is available to readers at www.apress.com/9781484208090. For detailed information about how to locate your book's source code, go to www.apress.com/source-code/. Readers can also access source code at SpringerLink in the Supplementary Material section for each chapter.

*To all passionate Java developers, never stop learning and never stop improving your skills.*

*To all my friends for supporting me to make this book happen;*
*you have no idea how dear you are to me.*

# Contents at a Glance

About the Author .................................................................................................. xiii

About the Technical Reviewer ................................................................................. xv

Acknowledgments ................................................................................................ xvii

Introduction ......................................................................................................... xix

■Chapter 1: Introduction ........................................................................................ 1

■Chapter 2: Spring Fundamentals ......................................................................... 17

■Chapter 3: Spring MVC ...................................................................................... 53

■Chapter 4: Spring Portlets ................................................................................ 151

■Chapter 5: Spring RESTful Services ................................................................... 189

■Chapter 6: Spring Web with AJAX ..................................................................... 229

■Chapter 7: Spring Web Flow ............................................................................. 257

■Chapter 8: Spring Boot and WebSocket ............................................................. 367

■Appendix: Resources and Quiz Answers ............................................................ 401

Index ................................................................................................................. 417

# Contents

About the Author ........................................................................................................ xiii

About the Technical Reviewer .................................................................................... xv

Acknowledgments ..................................................................................................... xvii

Introduction ............................................................................................................... xix

■Chapter 1: Introduction ............................................................................................. 1

Spring and What It Does ................................................................................................... 1

The Focus of this Study Guide ......................................................................................... 4

Who Should Use this Study Guide ................................................................................... 5

About the Spring Web Certification Exam ....................................................................... 5

How to Use this Study Guide ........................................................................................... 6

How this Book Is Structured ......................................................................................................... 7

How Each Chapter Is Structured ................................................................................................... 7

Conventions .................................................................................................................................. 8

Downloading the Code .................................................................................................................. 8

Contacting the Author ................................................................................................................... 8

Recommended Development Environment ...................................................................... 8

Recommended Build Tools ............................................................................................................ 9

Recommended IDE ...................................................................................................................... 10

The Project Sample ..................................................................................................................... 11

**■Chapter 2: Spring Fundamentals** ............................................................. **17**

The Basics .......................................................................................... 17

The Spring Core Container .................................................................. 19

Spring Configuration .......................................................................... 21

    XML ................................................................................................. 21

    Annotations ...................................................................................... 25

    Mixed Approach ............................................................................... 26

The Beans .......................................................................................... 27

    Lifecycle and Instantiation ............................................................... 27

    Bean Scopes .................................................................................... 35

    Accessing Beans .............................................................................. 38

Spring AOP ........................................................................................ 41

Testing Spring Applications ................................................................ 44

Summary ........................................................................................... 45

Quick Quiz ......................................................................................... 46

Practical Exercise .............................................................................. 46

**■Chapter 3: Spring MVC** ................................................................... **53**

MVC Basics ........................................................................................ 53

Configuring MVC ................................................................................ 55

    XML Configuration ........................................................................... 56

    Configuration Using Annotations ...................................................... 61

    Configuration Without Using web.xml ............................................... 64

MVC Components ............................................................................... 67

    Infrastructure Beans ........................................................................ 68

    User-Provided Components ............................................................... 94

View Technologies ............................................................................. 109

    Tiles Layouts .................................................................................... 110

    Thymeleaf ........................................................................................ 115

Forms ........................................................................................................... 119

Data Formatting............................................................................................ 125

Data Binding ................................................................................................ 129

Data Validation.............................................................................................. 132

Managing the Form Object .............................................................................. 137

Summary...................................................................................................... 138

Quick Quiz ................................................................................................... 139

Practical Exercise.......................................................................................... 144

■Chapter 4: Spring Portlets ........................................................................ 151

Portlet Basics .............................................................................................. 154

Configuration................................................................................................ 156

The XML Part of the Configuration ................................................................... 157

The Annotation Part of the Configuration .......................................................... 164

Configuration Details and Recommendations ...................................................... 168

The Development and Deployment of a Portlet Application ...................................... 169

Download, Install, Start, and Configure Liferay.................................................... 170

Summary...................................................................................................... 188

■Chapter 5: Spring RESTful Services.......................................................... 189

Core REST Concepts....................................................................................... 189

HATEOAS ..................................................................................................... 195

Advantages of REST ...................................................................................... 197

RESTful Applications Using Spring MVC............................................................. 199

RESTful Clients with Spring.............................................................................. 199

Asynchronous REST Calls................................................................................ 203

Implementing REST with Spring MVC................................................................. 204

Asynchronous REST Services Using @Async Annotated Methods ............................. 213

Using Spring HATEOAS ................................................................................... 216

Summary .................................................................................................... 220

Quick Quiz ................................................................................................ 221

Practical Exercise .................................................................................... 222

■Chapter 6: Spring Web with AJAX .......................................................... 229

What Is AJAX? ........................................................................................... 229

Making AJAX Requests............................................................................. 233

Introducing jQuery .................................................................................. 236

    jQuery HTML DOM Manipulation........................................................................ 240

    jQuery AJAX Calls ........................................................................................... 243

Spring MVC, AJAX, and jQuery................................................................ 245

    Using REST-Style Remoting with JSON ............................................................. 246

Custom Tags ............................................................................................ 250

Summary .................................................................................................. 253

Quick Quiz ................................................................................................ 253

Practical Exercise .................................................................................... 254

■Chapter 7: Spring Web Flow .................................................................. 257

What Is a Flow? ........................................................................................ 257

Web Flow Architecture ............................................................................ 259

Web Flow Internal Logic .......................................................................... 261

Configuration and Infrastructure Beans ................................................ 262

    Configuration Using XML .................................................................................. 263

    Configuration Using Annotations ...................................................................... 267

Create a Flow ........................................................................................... 272

    Flow Definition................................................................................................. 273

    Action States .................................................................................................. 304

Decision States ....................................................................................... 311

Exception Handling.................................................................................. 312

Subflows ........................................................................................................................ 322

Flow Definition Inheritance ........................................................................................ 326

Securing Web Flows..................................................................................................... 327

    Introduction to Spring Security....................................................................................................... 327

    Why Spring Security Is Awesome .................................................................................................... 328

    Spring Security XML Configuration.................................................................................................. 330

    Spring Security Java Configuration ................................................................................................. 343

    Securing Flow Definitions............................................................................................................... 350

Summary....................................................................................................................... 357

Quick Quiz .................................................................................................................... 358

Practical Exercise......................................................................................................... 364

■Chapter 8: Spring Boot and WebSocket.................................................................. 367

What Is Spring Boot?.................................................................................................... 367

Usage and Configuration ............................................................................................. 368

    Customizing Spring Boot ................................................................................................................ 373

    Importing Additional Configuration Elements ................................................................................. 380

    Running Spring Boot Applications ................................................................................................... 381

    Testing Spring Boot Applications .................................................................................................... 383

WebSocket Introduction .............................................................................................. 385

Spring WebSocket Implementation ............................................................................. 386

Spring WebSocket Configuration................................................................................. 390

WebSocket Client Application...................................................................................... 392

    Configure the Server Application to Send Scheduled Messages...................................................... 397

    Monitoring and Debugging ............................................................................................................. 398

■**Appendix: Resources and Quiz Answers** ........................................................ **403**

Study Guide Projects ............................................................................................ 401

    Gradle Configuration Explained ......................................................................... 403

    Building and Troubleshooting ........................................................................... 403

    Deploy on Apache Tomcat.................................................................................. 407

Quiz Answers........................................................................................................ 412

    Quiz Solution for Chapter 2................................................................................ 412

    Quiz Solution for Chapter 3................................................................................ 412

    Quiz Solution for Chapter 5................................................................................ 413

    Quiz Solution for Chapter 6................................................................................ 414

    Quiz Solution for Chapter 7................................................................................ 414

**Index**.................................................................................................................. **417**

# About the Author

**Iuliana Cosmina** is a software engineer and professional developer. She has been programming in Java for more than 10 years. She also taught Java at the Gheorge Asachi Technical University in Iasi, Romania. She has a Bachelor's degree in computer science and a Master's degree in distributed systems from the same university.

She discovered Spring in June 2012 and loved it so much she trained for and passed the exam to become a Certified Spring Professional in November 2012. She trained for and passed the exam to become a Certified Web Application Developer in May 2014.

Her plan is to become a Spring Enterprise Integration Specialist in the near future.

She has contributed to the development of different types of enterprise applications such as search engines, ERPs, track and trace, and banking. During her career in outsourcing she has been a team leader, acting software architect and a DevOps professional. She likes to share her knowledge and expertise via tutoring, teaching, and mentoring, but in the summer of 2014 everything changed because of Steve Anglin, who approached her and gave her a chance to do it by writing this guide. She lives in Sibiu, Romania and works as a software engineer for BearingPoint, a multinational management and technology consulting company.

When she is not programming, she spends her time reading, travelling, hiking, or biking.

- You can find some of her personal work on her GitHub account: https://github.com/iuliana.

- You can find her complete CV on her LinkedIn account: https://ro.linkedin.com/in/iulianacosmina.

- You can contact her at: Iuliana.Cosmina@gmail.com.

# About the Technical Reviewer

**Manuel Jordan Elera** is an autodidactic developer and researcher who enjoys learning new technologies for his own experiments and creating new integrations.

Manuel won the 2010 Springy Award – Community Champion and Spring Champion 2013. In his little free time, he reads the Bible and composes music on his guitar. Manuel is known as dr_pompeii. He has tech reviewed numerous books for Apress, including *Pro Spring, 4th Edition* (2014), *Practical Spring LDAP* (2013), *Pro JPA 2, Second Edition* (2013), and Pro Spring Security (2013).

Read his thirteen detailed tutorials about many Spring technologies and contact him through his blog at http://www.manueljordanelera.blogspot.com and follow him on his Twitter account, @dr_pompeii.

# Acknowledgments

Creating this guide involved a lot of teamwork. It is the first time I've written a technical book and I wouldn't have made it without all the help and advice I received from Mark Powers, Matthew Moodie, and Manuel Jordan. Mark has been very supportive and shared with me his experience on book writing in order to help me and kept encouraging me when I was ready to give up on writing because I thought my work was not good enough.

Matthew and Manuel have been great collaborators; I loved our exchanges of technical ideas and I am very thankful because working with them has helped me grow professionally. Many thanks to Kimberly Burton for her help turning my technical literature into human readable literature.

Most of all I want to thank Steve Anglin for finding me and for trusting me to get this done.

Apress has published many of the books I read and used to improve myself professionally during my studies and even after that. It is a great honor for me to write a book and publish it with Apress. It is great to contribute to the education of the next generation of developers.

I am grateful to all my friends that had the patience to listen to me complain about sleep loss, having too much work to do, and writer's block. Thank you all for being supportive and making sure I still had some fun while writing this book.

And I would also like to add a very special thank you to Levi9 Romania, the company that introduced me to Spring and its country manager Nicu Lazar that supported me to become a Spring Professional.

# Introduction

Three years have passed since I wrote my first Spring project and I regret that this framework grew for ten years without me knowing about it. Four major versions of Spring have been released so far and except for the official study guide required to pass the certification exam, until the conception of this book there was no additional resource such as this.

This study guide provides a complete overview of all the technologies involved in creating a Spring web application from scratch. It guides you step by step into the Spring web world covering Spring 3 and Spring 4. It also covers topics not required for the certification exam, such as Portlets and Thymeleaf, which most developers encounter while in the field.

There are two multi-module projects associated with this book, covering every example presented in the book. As the book was written, new versions of Spring were released, a new version of Intellij IDEA was released, and new versions of Gradle were released. I upgraded to the new versions in order to provide the most recent information and keep this book synchronized with the official documentation. A group of reviewers has gone over the book, but if you notice any inconsistency, please send an email to editorial@apress.com and errata will be created.

The example source code for this book can be found on GitHub and will be maintained, synchronized with new versions of the technologies, and enriched based on the recommendation of the developers using it to learn Spring.

```
http://github.com/iuliana/personal-records
https://github.com/iuliana/book-code
```

I truly hope you will enjoy using this book to learn Spring as much as I enjoyed writing it.

# CHAPTER 1

■ ■ ■

# Introduction

So here you are: you want to learn how to develop web applications using Spring, and you chose this study guide to help you. This might be one of the best decisions that you could make, as this book was written not only to help you to understand Spring Web, but to love it as well. This study guide may even help you pass the certification exam—if you follow all the instructions properly and do all the exercises. This study guide explores more Spring Web topics than those required by the exam; for example, it gives you a short overview of what Spring Web is all about, which you can skip reading, of course; but if you really want to learn Spring to develop web applications like a professional, then it would be wise not to skip this.

## Spring and What It Does

When building a project using Java, a lot of functionality needs to be built from scratch. But a lot of useful functionalities are already built and are free to use because of the open source world we live in. A long time ago, when the Java world was still quite small, you would say that you were using a *library* when you used open source code developed by somebody else, shipped as a *.jar file. But as time passed, the software development world evolved and the libraries grew too. They became *frameworks*. Because they were no longer one *.jar file that you could import, they became a collection of more-or-less decoupled libraries with different responsibilities, and you had the option to import only what you needed.

Released in October 2002 as an open source framework and an inversion of control container developed using Java, Spring was built for the Java platform. It was conceived with the *dependency injection* software design pattern in mind, and its main purpose is to make dependency handling easier. A Java application is basically a group of objects exchanging data and influencing each other's behavior. The Spring Framework simplified the way in which objects talk to each other and the way they depend on each other. This is why Spring evangelists claim that the reason Java was invented was so that Spring would come into existence one day. The development of Java applications became easier when Spring emerged, providing comprehensive infrastructure support. Spring makes it easier to compose disparate components into a fully working application.

Spring comes with a lot of default behaviors already implemented (components called *infrastructure beans* are a default configuration; they can be used to create functional basic applications without extra customization), because the Spring Framework was also built with the *convention over configuration* paradigm as a principle, which seeks to decrease the number of decisions a developer has to make when writing code, but also makes it easier for the developer to customize the behavior of objects, offering increased flexibility.

Spring is currently the VIP of Java frameworks and it has been growing exponentially, especially since 2009, when VMware acquired SpringSource, the company behind Spring. The merger of VMware and the EMC Corporation in April 2013, now known as **Pivotal**, was also advantageous for Spring, as it became one of Pivotal's central elements in its strategy to provide innovative and modern software-driven experiences to its customers. Spring is now a full-blown technology that can be used to build enterprise-ready applications in a very short time, and it comes in 25 flavors.[1] Figure 1-1 shows a diagram of all Spring-released projects. The following list describes these projects.

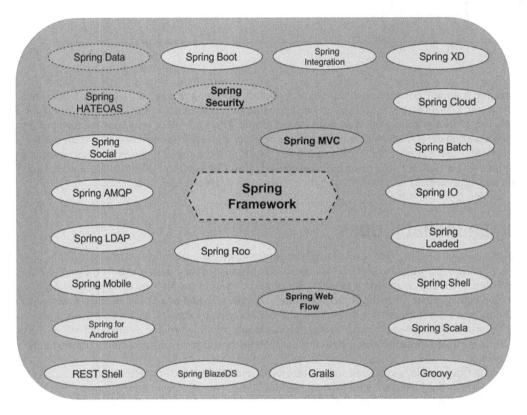

***Figure 1-1.*** *Official Spring projects. The projects drawn with dotted lines are only partially covered in this book or are featured in the source code*

- **Spring Framework** provides core support for dependency injection, transaction management, web applications, data access, messaging, and more.

- **Spring IO** provides a cohesive, versioned platform for building modern applications. It is a modular, enterprise-grade distribution that delivers a curated set of dependencies.

- **Spring Boot** provides compact setups for different types of applications, helping you to focus on your code instead of infrastructure configuration.

- **Spring XD** simplifies the development of Big Data applications.

---

[1]You can read about these projects, as well as other projects that have not been released officially (Spring Session, for example) in detail at http://spring.io/projects.

- **Spring Cloud** provides a set of tools for distributed applications.

- **Spring Data** provides a consistent approach to data access. (This study guide uses a subproject called Spring Data JPA to help us manage data easily.)

- **Spring Integration** supports the well-known Enterprise Integration Patterns via lightweight messaging and declarative adapters.

- **Spring Batch** simplifies and optimizes the work of processing high-volume batch operations.

- **Spring Security** provides tools for authentication and authorization. (Because *web security is one of the subjects of the certification exam*, there is a section about web security in this study guide that you will have to pay close attention to.)

- **Spring HATEOAS** provides some APIs to help the development of REST representations that follow the HATEOAS principle (**H**ypermedia **a**s the **E**ngine of **A**pplication **S**tate, which means that a client interacts with a network application entirely through hypermedia provided dynamically by application servers).

- **Spring Social** provides an API to connect Spring applications to the third-party APIs of social networks like Facebook and Twitter, as well as others.

- **Spring AMQP** provides an API for AMQP-based messaging solutions.

- **Spring Mobile** simplifies the development of mobile applications.

- **Spring for Android** provides key spring components to use in the development of Android applications.

- **Spring Web Flow** supports the building of web application with controlled navigation (Spring Web Flow is another subject in the certification exam.)

- **Spring Web Services** facilitates the development of SOAP-based applications.

- **Spring LDAP** provides tools to develop LDAP applications.

- **Grails**[2] is a powerful open source web framework based on Groovy and inspired by Ruby on Rails. It is used to create web applications that run on the Java Virtual Machine(JVM).

- **Groovy**[3] started as a dynamic language for the Java platform. It brings high-productivity development features to the JVM, and resembles Python, Ruby, Perl, and Smalltalk in regards to syntax and features. SpringSource has taken over its development and maintenance.

- **Spring Scala** mixed up Spring with Scala language features.

- **Spring Roo** helps define application templates that can be built into a full Java application within minutes.

- **Spring BlazeDS Integration** tools integrate Spring with Adobe BlazeDS.

- **Spring Loaded** reloads classes as files change, boosting productivity (similar project to JRebel).

---

[2]Pivotal decided to stop funding this project in March 2015.
[3]Funding for this project also ended in March 2015.

- **Spring Shell** provides the capability to build command-line apps.

- **REST Shell** makes the writing and testing of RESTful application easier with CLI-based resource discovery and interaction.

# The Focus of this Study Guide

As this study guide is being written, the Spring Framework consists of features organized into about 20 modules grouped into the following: Core Container, Data Access/Integration, Web, AOP (aspect-oriented programming), Instrumentation, Messaging, and Test.

The topics covered in this study guide are Spring Framework's support components for the presentation tier (and specifically web-based presentation tiers). A bonus in this book is the Spring WebSocket chapter, which was added to the Spring Framework in version 4 and is also an optional part of the official Spring Web course not featured in the certification exam. In the Figure 1-2 you can see the Spring MVC stack, a tiered representation of the modules commonly used to create Spring web applications.

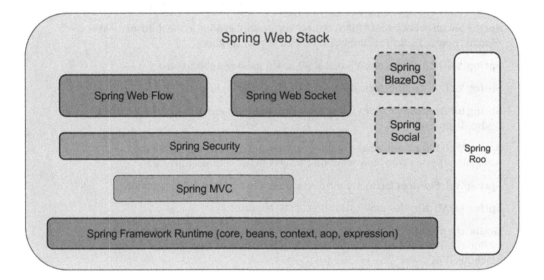

***Figure 1-2.*** *The Spring Web Stack (those with dotted lines will not be covered in this study guide)*

This study guide focuses on helping developers understand how Spring's web infrastructure is designed, and how to write Spring web applications in a few easy steps by maximizing Spring's potential. The study guide's objectives are as follows:

- Use Spring to develop web applications

- Use Spring Web Flow to implement stateful interactions

- Use Spring Security to secure web applications

- Use Spring Test and other test frameworks (JUnit, JMock) to test web applications

- Create Spring web applications using Gradle[4]

---

[4]Gradle is an automated build tool that is easy to configure and use on any type of application. Its build files are written using JSON and Groovy. Gradle combines the power and flexibility of Ant with the dependency management and conventions of Maven into a more effective way to build. Read more about it at https://www.gradle.org.

# Who Should Use this Study Guide

This study guide is designed to help any Spring developer become familiar and comfortable with Spring-associated technologies for web development. It can also be a big help to a developer who wants to become a **Certified Spring Web Application Developer**.[5] That is why every topic in the official VMware Spring Web study guide is given the attention that it deserves.

You do not have to be a Certified Spring Professional to use this study guide; you just need minimal knowledge of Spring. Because this study guide has a full chapter dedicated to the Spring core components, it might be possible for a non-Spring developer to use this study guide too, but the *Spring Framework Reference*[6] official documentation should be consulted to retrieve any missing pieces of information.

In a nutshell, this study guide was written to be used by the following audiences:

- Spring Core developers who want a taste of Spring Web

- Spring developers (Certified Spring Professionals or not) who are looking forward to becoming Certified Spring Web Application Developers

- Java developers who are curious about working with Spring technologies and want to start fast

# About the Spring Web Certification Exam

If you are interested in becoming a **Certified Spring Web Application Developer**, the first step is to go to the VMware official learning site (`http://pivotal.io/training`) and search for the Spring Certification section. There you will find all the details you need regarding the official trainings, including where and when they take place. The training is four days long. There is online training available as well. After creating an account on the VMware site, you can select your desired training. After you make the payment, if you choose an online training, after about a month you will receive (through the mail) an official training kit that consists of the following:

- A pair of conference headphones (usually Logitech) to be used during training to hear your trainer talk and to ask questions.[7]

- A professional webcam (usually Logitech) to be used during training so that your trainer and colleagues can see you, thus simulating a classroom experience.[8]

- A Spring study guide book containing the printed version of the slides your tutor will use during training.

- A Spring study lab book containing explanations and instructions for the practical exercises you will do during training.

- A SpringSource official flash drive containing the following:

    - A JDK installer.

---

[5]Keep in mind that attending a Spring Web training course by Pivotal or at a VMware Authorized Training Center is a prerequisite to becoming a Certified Spring Web Application Developer, as stated on the official site at `http://mylearn.vmware.com/mgrReg/plan.cfm?plan=31111 ui=www_cert`.

[6]The Spring Framework Reference is at `http://docs.spring.io/spring/docs/current/spring-framework-reference/htmlsingle/`.

[7]Depending on the area and the training center, this item is optional.

[8]Depending on the area and the training center, this item is also optional.

- Sources necessary for your training. Each study lab has a small Spring web application with missing configuration and code; the student's task is to complete it to become a working application. The same model is used in the code associated with this book.

- An installer for the most recent stable version of the Spring Tool Suite (STS). The version on the flash drive is mandatory for the course because the installer sets up a local Maven repository with all the needed dependencies, and a full eclipse project configuration with the lab sources. The STS also has an internal tc Server to run the lab applications.

- An HTML or PDF version of the Spring Study Lab.

If you do not choose to do online training, you will not receive the headphones nor the webcam. The training kit and the rest of the materials are given to you when you arrive at the location where the training is taking place. After your training, you receive a free voucher that is required to schedule the certification exam at an approved exam center near you. Basically, this voucher or voucher code is proof that you have attended official Spring Web training.

**!** The exam duration is **90 minutes** and consists of **50 questions**. There are both single-answer and multiple-choice questions. The questions cover (roughly) the following topics:

- Spring overview (Spring core notions)

- MVC essentials (configurations, beans to use, conventions)

- MVC forms and views

- Webflow

- Web security

- REST

The passing score for the exam is **76%**. This means that **38** correct answers are needed to pass. Most of the questions present you with a piece of Java code or configuration and then ask you what it does, so make sure that you understand the code attached to this book and write your own beans and configurations in order to understand the framework better. The good news is that all the code in the exam can be found in the sources that you are given while attending the official training. Other questions present you with affirmations about Spring Web and require you to select the correct or the invalid ones.

If you read this book, understand all the examples, solve the practice exercises, and then attend the official training, the recommendation is to take the certification exam as soon as possible afterward. Do not allow too much time to pass between finishing the training and taking the exam, because we are all human after all, and information can be forgotten. Also, *the certification voucher is only valid for a year*. You can retake the exam if you fail the first time, but it will cost you ~$150.

# How to Use this Study Guide

This study guide follows the same path as the official Spring Web training, and focuses on the topics that are found in the certification exam; but there are a few differences, which are mentioned from now on.

This Spring study guide covers the Spring MVC Portlets. This topic is not in the exam, but you never know when you may need them in your development career, so it is better to have an overview.

The other differences are related to the tools used for the practical examples, which are mentioned in the next section.

# How this Book Is Structured

This study guide has eight chapters. You might think: How is this possible—the official Spring study guide has sixteen chapters, right? It is better to wrap related things together, so in this study guide you have two big chapters that cover 60% of the exam topics: Chapter 3 covers Spring MVC and Chapter 7 covers Spring Web Flow. Also, some topics that have their own dedicated chapter in the official study guide have been included in other chapters, as relevant, in this book. (For example, how to test a web application. There's no need of a separate chapter just for this, as testing is a main portion in the development of an application.)

A list of this study guide's chapters, along with a short description, is presented in Table 1-1.

***Table 1-1.*** *Study Guide Chapters*

| Chapter | Topic | Details |
| --- | --- | --- |
| 1 | Introduction | An introduction to Spring history, technologies, and the tools used for practice in this study guide |
| 2 | Spring Fundamentals | Spring core concepts, components, and configurations |
| 3 | Spring MVC | Spring Web Framework core concepts, components, and configurations |
| 4 | Spring Portlets | What portlets are, how they can be used, and how can Spring make this easier |
| 5 | Spring RESTful Services | Advanced Spring MVC for REST applications |
| 6 | Spring Web with AJAX | Advanced Spring MVC with AJAX web applications |
| 7 | Spring Web Flow | Basic and advanced topics on working with Spring Web Flow |
| 8 | Spring Web Socket | Basic configuration and usage of Spring Web Socket |
| A | Appendix | Two mock exams, answers to review questions, and other comments |

# How Each Chapter Is Structured

The introductory chapter, the one you are reading now, covers the basics of Spring and Spring related-notions that every developer using this study guide should know: what Spring is, how it has evolved, the number of official Spring projects, the Spring Web technologies, the technologies used to build and run the practical exercises, how to register for the exam to become a Certified Spring Developer, and so on. This chapter is the exception; it is structured differently than the others because it is designed to prepare you for what is coming next.

All the other chapters are designed to cover a Spring module and associated technologies, which will help you build a specific type of Spring web application. Each chapter is split into a few sections, but in a nutshell, a chapter could be split as follows:

- Basics

- Configuration

- Components

- Summary

- Quick quiz

- Practical exercise

## Conventions

> **!** This symbol appears in front of paragraphs that you should pay particular attention to.

> **\*\*** This symbol appears in front of a paragraph that is an observation or an execution step that you can skip.

> **?** This symbol appears in front of a question for the user.

> **...** This symbol replaces missing code that is not relevant in the example.

> **CC** This symbol appears in front of a paragraph that describes a convention over configuration practice in Spring, a default behavior that helps a developer reduce his or her work.

[*random text here*] Text surrounded by square brackets means that the text within the brackets should be replaced by a context-related notion.

## Downloading the Code

This study guide comes with code examples and practical exercises. There will be missing pieces of code that you will have to fill in to make applications work and to test your understanding of Spring Web. It is recommended that you go over the code samples and do the exercises, as similar pieces of code and configurations will appear in the certification exam.

The following downloads are available:

- Source code for the programming examples in the book chapters

- Source code for the programming examples in the practice section

You can download these items from the Source Code area of the Apress web site (`www.apress.com`).

## Contacting the Author

More information on Iuliana Cosmina can be found at `http://ro.linkedin.com/in/iulianacosmina`. She can be reached at `iuliana.cosmina@gmail.com`. Follow her personal coding activity at `https://github.com/iuliana`.

# Recommended Development Environment

If you decide to attend the official course, you will notice that the development environment recommended in this book differs quite a lot from the one used for the course—a different editor is recommended, and a different application server, and even a different build tool. The reason for this is to improve and expand your experience as a developer and to offer a practical development infrastructure. Motivation for each choice is mentioned in the corresponding sections.

# Recommended Build Tools

The recommended development environment should be composed of the following technologies:

**Java 8**. Download and install the JDK matching your operating system from `http://www.oracle.com`.

! It is recommended to set the `JAVA_HOME` environment variable to point to the directory where Java 8 is installed (the directory in which the JDK was unpacked) and add `$JAVA_HOME/bin` to the general path of the system. The reason behind this is to ensure that any other development application written in Java will use this version of Java, and prevent strange incompatibility errors during development.

! Verify that the version of Java that your operating system sees is the one you just installed. Open a terminal (Command+Prompt in Windows, or any type of terminal you have installed on Mac OS or Linux) and type the following:

```
java -version
```

You should see something similar to this:

```
java version "1.8.0_40"
Java(TM) SE Runtime Environment (build 1.8.0_40)
Java HotSpot(TM) 64-Bit Server VM (build 25.25-b02, mixed mode)
```

**Grade 2.x**

** The sources attached to this book can be compiled and executed using the Gradle Wrapper, which is a batch script on Windows, or by using a shell script on other operating systems. When you start a Gradle build via the wrapper, Gradle is automatically downloaded and used to run the build, thus you do to need to install Gradle as stated previously. Instructions on how to do this can be found on the public documentation at `www.gradle.org/docs/current/userguide/gradle_wrapper.html`.

It is a good practice to keep code and build tools separate, but this study guide uses the Wrapper to easily set up the practice environment by skipping the Gradle installation step, and also because the recommended source code editor uses the Wrapper internally.

If you decide to use Gradle outside the editor, you can download the binaries only (or, if you are more curious, you can download the full package, which contains binaries, sources, and documentation) from the official site (`https://www.gradle.org`), unpack it and copy the contents somewhere on the hard drive. Create a `GRADLE_HOME` environment variable and point it to the location where you have unpacked Gradle. Also add `$GRADLE_HOME/bin` to the general path of the system.

Gradle was chosen as a build tool for the sources of this book because of the easy setup, small configuration files, flexibility in defining execution tasks, and the fact that the SpringSource team currently uses it to build all Spring projects.

! Verify that the version of Gradle that your operating system sees is the one that you just installed. Open a terminal (Command+Prompt in Windows, any type of terminal you have installed on Mac OS or Linux) and type gradle -version. You should see something similar to this:

```
------------------------------------------------------------
Gradle 2.3
------------------------------------------------------------
Build time: 2014-11-24 09:45:35 UTC
Build number: none
Revision: 6fcb59c06f43a4e6b1bcb401f7686a8601a1fb4a
Groovy: 2.3.9
Ant: Apache Ant(TM) version 1.9.3 compiled on December 23 2013
JVM: 1.8.0_40 (Oracle Corporation 25.25-b02)
OS: -- whatever operating system you have --
```

The preceding text shows a confirmation that any Gradle command can be executed in your terminal; Gradle was installed successfully.

**Jetty 9** is an open source web server that is free to use and easy to install; that's why it was chosen to be used in this study guide instead of the SpringSource tc Server. No need to download and install this web server, though, because there is no need to. There is a Gradle plugin called Getty that will be used to download the Jetty web server and deploy your *.war artifact on it. If you want to read more about Jetty, you can do so at http://eclipse.org/jetty/.

## Recommended IDE

The recommended IDE to use in this study guide is Intellij IDEA. The reason for this is that it is the most intelligent Java IDE. IntelliJ IDEA offers outstanding framework-specific coding assistance and productivity-boosting features for Java EE. Spring also includes support for Maven and Gradle. It is the perfect choice to help you focus on learning Spring, rather than how to use an IDE. It can be downloaded from the JetBrains official site (https://www.jetbrains.com/idea/). It is also quite light on your operating system and quite easy to use.

Because the web applications developed as practice in this study guide are deployed on Jetty, the community edition of Intellij IDEA can be used because we do not need the server plugin. The main disadvantage of the community edition, though, is that it does not come with the Spring plugin, which is very useful in creating Spring configuration files because it adds the bean namespace by default. But solving the exercises in this book won't require that, so you can still consider IDEA an option. If you are curious about the full power of this IDE, you can download the Ultimate Edition, which has a trial period of 30 days. And you can even try to deploy the code samples on a Tomcat instance from within IDEA. You will find an example of how to do this in the appendix.

If you are already familiar with a different Java editor, you can use it—as long as it supports Gradle.

# The Project Sample

Most of the code used in this study guide, except the book code modules, makes up a project named **Personal Records Manager**. This is a proof of concept application that aspires to manage the personal information of a group of people. The application is multimodular and each module is duplicated. The projects suffixed with **practice** are missing pieces of code and configuration, and are the ones that need to be solved by you to test your understanding of Spring Web. The projects suffixed with **solution** are proposal resolutions for the tasks. You can see the project structure and the modules in Figure 1-3.

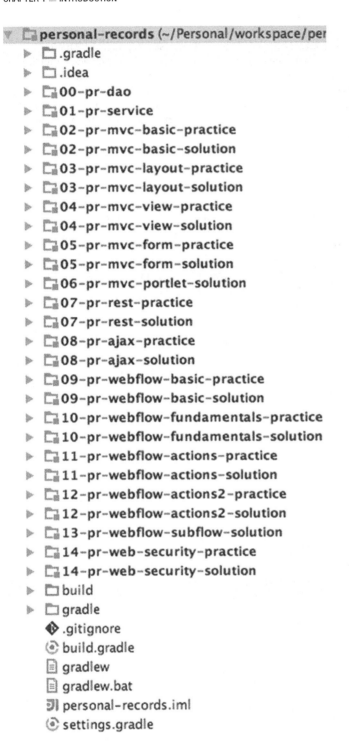

*Figure 1-3.* *The Personal Records Manager Application diagram*

The foundation module is the **00-pr-dao**, which handles all database operations by using Hibernate and Spring Data JPA. All other modules are client web applications, which will help the end user introduce new data, modify existing data, and perform searches. Each module is specific to a part of a chapter. Each module name is prefixed with a number, so no matter what IDE you use, you will always have the modules in the exact order that they were intended to be used.

The general functionality of each web application is described in Figure 1-4.

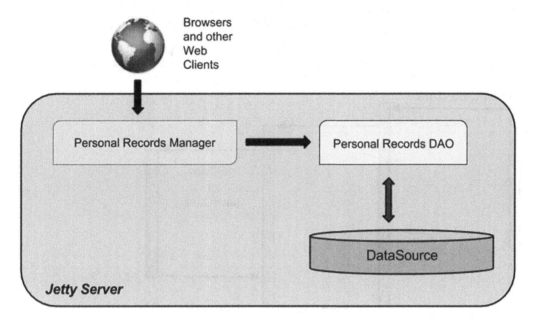

**Figure 1-4.** *The Personal Records Manager Application structure*

The foundation of this application is its DAO (data access objects) module, which contains entities classes that are mapped on database tables, and classes used to handle entities, called *repositories*. The web projects use the DAO project to manipulate data according to user requests. The UML diagram in Figure 1-5 describes the general behavior of our application. In some chapters, however, diagrams that describe a more detailed behavior are presented.

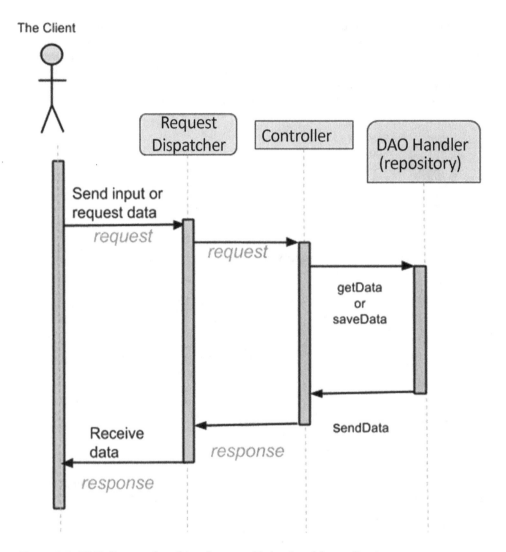

*Figure 1-5. UML diagram describing the general behavior of the application*

The entities have common fields used by Hibernate to uniquely identify each entity instance (id) and the fields used to audit each entity instance (createdAt and modifiedAt) and keep track of how many times an entity was modified (version). These fields have been grouped in the AbstractEntity class to avoid having duplicated code. The class hierarchy can be analyzed in Figure 1-6.

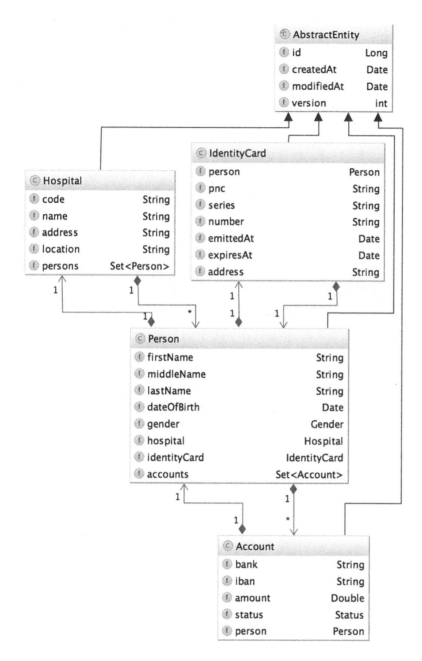

**Figure 1-6.** *This diagram shows the relationships between entity classes and the relationships between tables in the database. (The **pnc** is a personal numerical code that uniquely identifies a person and will be used to test some Spring validations on it. The **iban** is an alphanumeric code that uniquely identifies a bank account.)*

This chapter does not have any practice and sample code attached to it, so more information regarding the setup of the project, and how it is built and executed, is provided in upcoming chapters.

# CHAPTER 2

■ ■ ■

# Spring Fundamentals

This chapter is necessary for building a Spring background, which will be very helpful in the upcoming chapters. This chapter will help you get familiar with the Spring container, context, beans, and most Spring core modules and how they work together to allow developers to focus on solving problems instead of building up support.

## The Basics

Any application system is made of components that work together to solve a problem. In object-oriented design they are called *classes*. Figure 2-1 depicts the sequence of operations necessary to create a Person instance. Because this chapter is about Spring Core, a web application is not needed, so requests to manipulate Person instances will be directed to implementations of the PersonManager interface. Implementations of this interface will provide access to the database using an implementation of PersonRepository interface. The operation is pretty simple and the setup to write and execute the code should be too. This is where Spring comes in—providing a way to build an application using plain old Java objects (POJOs)[1] and applying enterprise services (transaction execution, remote execution) noninvasively.

---

[1] A software term introduced by Martin Fowler, Rebecca Parsons, and Josh MacKenzie in September 2000 to refer to ordinary Java objects not bound by any restriction.

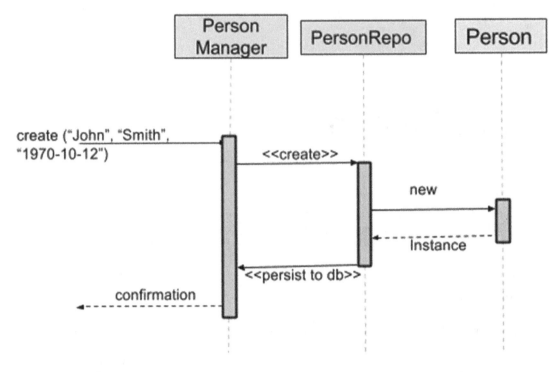

***Figure 2-1.*** *UML sequence of operations necessary to create a Person instance*

The components making up an application interact and depend on one another. Defining how these objects are composed is quite difficult using plain Java. Even with the help of all the design patterns defined by experts in the software industry, the work is still cumbersome, as the pattern components still have to be implemented before being used. The Spring *inversion of control* (IoC) container was designed to help developers compose objects into fully working applications, ready to use.[2]

The Spring container is responsible for the creation of components, resolving their dependencies and providing them to other components. It does this by reading the configuration of an application from `*.xml` files or annotated configuration classes, and internally constructs a graph of dependencies between the objects. It then proceeds to traverse the graph, and creates and injects dependencies according to the configuration. The result of this initialization is an `ApplicationContext`, which provides access to application components, resource loading, internationalization support, and other features that won't be mentioned in this guide because it is out of scope.[3] Figure 2-2 depicts the process of creating an `ApplicationContext` using the Spring IoC container.

---

[2]The process through which an object is provided its dependencies, whether it is using a constructor or properties which are set using setter methods, is called *dependency injection. inversion of control* is the concept through which an external component has control over what is provided as a dependency to an object.

[3]For more information, see the public reference documentation at `http://docs.spring.io/spring/docs/current/spring-framework-reference`.

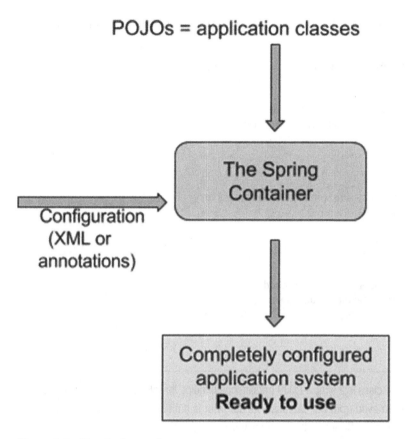

**Figure 2-2.** *How Spring works*

# The Spring Core Container

The Spring core container is made of the following modules:

- `spring-beans`

- `spring-core`

- `spring-context` and `spring-context-support` (provides support classes that help integration of third-party libraries for caching, mailing, scheduling, and template engines)

- `spring-expression`

The `spring-core` and `spring-beans` modules provide the fundamental part of the framework: the IoC and dependency injection features, which the container needs to solve and inject dependencies as specified in the configuration. The `spring-context` module extends the previous two modules, adding support for internationalization, resource loading, event propagation, and transparent creation of contexts. The core component of this module is the `ApplicationContext` interface. The `spring-expression` module provides a powerful Expression Language for querying and manipulating an object graph at runtime, and for operations like setting and getting property values, property assignment, and others.

Considering the diagram in Figure 2-1, the classes needed to support implementing the operation to save a Person instance look like this:

```
public class PlainPersonManagerImpl implements PersonManager {
    PersonRepository repo;

    //injecting a dependency using the constructor
    public PlainPersonManagerImpl(PersonRepository repo) {
        this.repo = repo;
    }
...
}
public class PlainPersonRepository implements PersonRepository {
    private DataSource dataSource;
    @Override
    public int save(Person person) {
        ..
    }
    //injecting a dependency using a setter method
    public void setDataSource(DataSource dataSource) {
        this.dataSource = dataSource;
    }
}
```

---

■ ! The PlainPersonRepository class is a simple POJO persistence handler. Its sole responsibility is to ensure Person instances are saved and retrieved from the database. Its behavior is built on a javax.sql.DataSource implementation. This is different from the Spring Data JPA repositories used in the Personal Records Manager project, which will be presented later. The approach specific to this chapter is Spring Core–based, which is more "old-style," before Spring Data JPA existed; this is to best introduce the Spring core modules and possibilities.

---

To implement that functionality in plain Java language, you have to write something like this:

```
PersonRepository repo = new PlainPersonRepository();

DataSource dataSource = new com.oracle.jdbc.pool.OracleDataSource();
dataSource.setUrl("jdbc:oracle:thin:@localhost:1521:orcl");
//set other dataSource properties
    ...
repo.setDataSource(dataSource);
PersonManager personManager = new PlainPersonManagerImpl(repo);
Person person = new Person("John", "Smith","1980-04-13");
// Use the manager
personManager.save(person);
```

As you can easily see, except the last line, everything else is setup code—the preparation before the execution of the method. It is a lot of code. What would happen if you decided to change method signatures or to use a different DataSource implementation? A big part of this code would have to be changed too.

In the next section, let's see how Spring does the same thing.

# Spring Configuration

There are three ways to define the configuration of an application using Spring:

- Special XML configuration files that allow usage of elements described in the associated namespaces

- Java-based configuration classes (classes annotated with @Configuration can be used by Spring IoC as a source for bean definitions)

- Mixed configuration: XML and annotations

All three types of configurations are covered in the following sections. The code sources attached to this chapter will help you test your understanding of each.

## XML

The following code is the XML content of a file named app-simple-config.xml, which is the configuration file for a simple Spring application:

```
<beans>
        <bean id="personManager" class="com.book.plain.PlainPersonManagerImpl">
                <constructor-arg ref="personRepository" />
        </bean>
        <bean id="personRepository" class="com.book.plain.PlainPersonRepository">
                <property name="dataSource" ref="dataSource" />
        </bean>
        <bean id="dataSource" class="com.oracle.jdbc.pool.OracleDataSource">
                <property name="URL" value="jdbc:oracle:thin:@localhost:1521:orcl" />
                ...
        </bean>
</beans>
```

And here is how the code to save a Person instance looks with Spring:

```
// Create the application from the configuration
ApplicationContext context =
                new ClassPathXmlApplicationContext("app-simple-config.xml");
// Look up the application manager interface
PersonManager manager = (PersonManager) context.getBean("personManager");
// Use the manager
manager.save(new Person("John", "Smith","1980-04-13"));
```

As you can see, the code is a lot smaller, because all the preparation of the environment was moved into the XML configuration file. And the configuration file can be manipulated more easily. If an external property file is used as entry for some of the values in it, in some simple cases, the application doesn't even have to be recompiled to change behavior. The DataSource configuration can be separated from the general configuration file, which can later allow you to easily switch between DataSource implementations—depending on the context in which a code should run.

```
<util:properties id="dbProp" location="classpath:datasource/db.properties"/>

<bean id="dataSource" class=
            "org.springframework.jdbc.datasource.DriverManagerDataSource">
    <property name="driverClassName" value="#{dbProp.driverClassName}"/>
    <property name="url" value="#{dbProp.url}"/>
    <property name="username" value="#{dbProp.username}"/>
    <property name="password" value="#{dbProp.password}"/>
</bean>
```

In the previous example, the property values that look like #{value} are loaded from the db.properties file, which contains the following:

```
driverClassName=org.h2.Driver
url=jdbc:h2: ~/prod
username=prod
password=prod
```

The values for the properties are loaded into a java.util.Properties instance with an id of dbProp using a functionality offered by the util namespace in the first line of the configuration, and then their values are accessed using the SpEL (Spring Expression Language) syntax and injected into the dataSource bean. (There is another way to do this using a component named PropertyPlaceholderConfigurer, which is covered in the "How Bean Factory Post Processors Work" section.) Spring knows how to do this because configuration files are constructed using XML namespaces.

```
<beans xmlns="http://www.springframework.org/schema/beans"
       xmlns:xsi="http://www.w3.org/2001/XMLSchema-instance"
       xmlns:util="http://www.springframework.org/schema/util"
       xsi:schemaLocation="
       http://www.springframework.org/schema/beans
       http://www.springframework.org/schema/beans/spring-beans.xsd
       http://www.springframework.org/schema/util
       http://www.springframework.org/schema/util/spring-util.xsd">
          ...
</beans>
```

The underlined values in the previous example show how a prefix is assigned to a namespace and how a namespace is associated with an XSD schema that contains the XML elements that can be used in the configuration file. Usually, each namespace contains definitions for all XML tags for a specific spring module, or a group of tags with related responsibilities.

As everything in Spring is a bean, most commonly used configuration styles use the bean's root element, and the namespace for it is declared using the xmlns attribute. When additional namespaces are used, the elements defined by them need to be used inside the current element (beans). They need to have a prefix associated so that the Spring IoC knows in which namespace to look for those element definitions; notations such as xmlns:[prefix]="[namespace URL]" are used.

■ !   The running code in this example can be found in 02-chapter-solution project. This is a module of the book-code project, which was designed to gradually test your knowledge acquired while reading this book. The book-code contains one or more modules for each chapter. Some module names are postfixed with **-practice** and contain a series of TODO tasks that the developer should be able to complete after reading a chapter.

The modules prefixed with **-solution** contain the completed tasks and are meant to be used for comparison with the developer's own solution. Sometimes a solution module might contain extra code that is meant simply to show the developer other situations that he might encounter in Spring projects.

For example, by splitting up the configuration file to isolate the DataSource configuration, you could have the following configuration for a production environment:

```
ApplicationContext context =
                new ClassPathXmlApplicationContext("application-config.xml","db-config.xml");
```

And this configuration could be for a test environment:

```
ApplicationContext context =
                new ClassPathXmlApplicationContext("application-config.xml","test-db-config.xml");
```

The two environments are completely decoupled, and the tests are very easy to write. Figure 2-3 displays a typical structure for a Spring Maven project with a split configuration for production and a test environment.

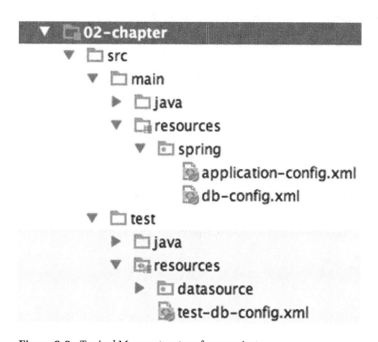

***Figure 2-3.***  *Typical Maven structure for a project*

■ ! In this example, the configuration files were created under a directory named spring to emphasize that these are Spring configuration files, because in a more complex project there could be XML configuration files for other purposes (for example, logging or caching stored outside of the spring directory). The code in this book intentionally skips the spring directory from the path to reduce the size of the quotes and to make the list of configuration files more readable.

In the configuration files, and when instantiating contexts, resources are usually prefixed with a word that tells the Spring container where they are located. These prefixes can be used for any type of resources needed in an application. Consider a standard Maven setup for a project like the one in Figure 2-3; Table 2-1 shows the paths where a Spring container would look for resource files depending on the prefix.

**Table 2-1.** *Prefixes and Corresponding Paths*

| Prefix | Location | Comment |
| --- | --- | --- |
| no prefix | In root directory where the class creating the context is executed. | In the main or test directory. The type of the resource being loaded depends on the ApplicationContext instance being used. (A detailed example is presented after this table.) |
| classpath: | The resource should be obtained from the classpath. | In the resources directory; the resource is of type ClassPathResource. |
| file: | In the absolute location following the prefix. | The resource is loaded as a URL from the filesystem and is of type UrlResource. |
| http: | In the web location following the prefix. | The resource is loaded as a URL and is of type UrlResource. |

The following is an example of resource loading without using a prefix:

```
Resource template = ctx.getResource("application-config.xml");
```

Depending on the context class used, the resource loaded can have one of the following types:

- If ctx is a ClassPathXmlApplicationContext instance, the resource type is ClassPathResource

- If ctx is a FileSystemXmlApplicationContext instance, the resource type is FileSystemResource

- If ctx is a WebApplicationContext instance, the resource type is ServletContextResource

# Annotations

Spring also supports configuration via annotations. The previous XML configuration can be replaced by a class annotated with @Configuration, and looks like this:

```
@Configuration
@PropertySource(value = "classpath:datasource/db.properties")
public class AppConfig {

    @Autowired
    Environment env;

    @Bean(name="personManager")
    public PersonManager getPersonManager(){
        return new PlainPersonManagerImpl(getPersonRepository());
    }

    @Bean(name="personRepository")
    public PersonRepository getPersonRepository(){
        PersonRepository repo = new PlainPersonRepository();
        repo.setDataSource(getDataSource());
        return repo;
    }

    @Bean(name="dataSource")
    public DataSource getDataSource(){
        DriverManagerDataSource dataSource = new DriverManagerDataSource();
        dataSource.setDriverClassName(env.getProperty("driverClassName"));
        dataSource.setUrl(env.getProperty("url"));
        dataSource.setUsername(env.getProperty("username"));
        dataSource.setPassword(env.getProperty("password"));
        return dataSource;
    }
}
```

All the code to save a Person instance looks like this:

```
@RunWith(SpringJUnit4ClassRunner.class)
@ContextConfiguration(classes = {AppConfig.class})
public class SecondAnnotationPersonSaveTest {

    @Autowired
    PersonManager personManager;

    @Test
    public void savePerson() {
        personManager.save(new Person("John", "Smith", "1980-04-13"));
    }
}
```

When annotations are used, XML configuration files are no longer needed, nor namespaces. Specific annotations are used to mark configuration classes (@Configuration) and to mark methods as bean definitions (@Bean); this is not covered because it is outside the scope of this book. What you need to remember is that the @Bean annotation makes sure that every time the annotated method is called the same bean is returned. Without it, the method will return a newly created instance each time.

---

■ **CC**   In the previous code example, each @Bean annotation has the attribute name populated with a value to name the bean created by the method. This attribute is neither mandatory nor necessary. When it is not specified, the Spring IoC determines a name for the bean based on the method name by removing the *get* and lowercasing the first letter of the remaining string.

---

## Mixed Approach

XML and annotations can be mixed. You could have the bean classes annotated with @Component (or any annotation extending @Repository for DAO repository classes, @Service for service classes, or @Controller for MVC handler classes) and one or more XML files, which define just the DataSource configuration and specifies where the beans are located. In the following code sample, the DataSource configuration is separated in another file (as shown in the "How Bean Factory Post Processors Work" section) to decouple configurations for production and test environments.

```
<beans xmlns="http://www.springframework.org/schema/beans"
       xmlns:xsi="http://www.w3.org/2001/XMLSchema-instance"
       xmlns:context="http://www.springframework.org/schema/context"
       xsi:schemaLocation="
       http://www.springframework.org/schema/beans
       http://www.springframework.org/schema/beans/spring-beans.xsd
       http://www.springframework.org/schema/context
       http://www.springframework.org/schema/context/spring-context.xsd"

       <context:component-scan base-package="com.book.beans"/>
       ...
</beans>
```

In XML configuration files, bean definitions describe the way a dependency should be provided to them: using either constructors or setters. This is called **autowiring**. When using annotations, the way a dependency should be provided is described using the @Autowire annotation on a constructor or setter.[4] But you need to tell the Spring IoC container to look for that type of annotation, and the declaration <context:component-scan ...> does exactly that.

When using annotations, <bean> declarations are no longer needed because each bean type is annotated with @Component, or an extension of it, and the <context:component-scan..> declaration tell the Spring IoC container to look for those types of annotations in the specific file. The process of identifying annotated bean types is called **autodiscovery**.

---

[4]The @Autowiring annotation can also be used on the field directly, called *field injection*; but this approach is discouraged because it makes testing difficult. As the field is usually private, to test the containing bean, a full Spring context must be set up or reflection must be used to access the field.

Thus what the following configuration element does is enable bean autowiring and autodiscovery anywhere in the classpath in packages (and subpackages) named as the value of the attribute base-package.

```
<context:component-scan base-package="com.book.beans"/>
```

The `<context: ..>` declarations are Spring's way of compacting the declaration of infrastructure beans named *PostProcessor, which take care of interpreting annotations into beans definitions.

- `<context:annotation-config/>` registers the following:

  - `AutowiredAnnotationBeanPostProcessor` (supports @Autowired, @Value, @Inject)
  - `CommonAnnotationBeanPostProcessor` (supports @Resource, @PostConstruct, @PreDestroy)
  - `PersistenceAnnotationBeanPostProcessor` (supports @PersistenceUnit, @PersistenceContext)
  - `RequiredAnnotationBeanPostProcessor` (supports @Required)

- `<context:component-scan base-package="com.book.beans"/>` implicitly enables the functionality of `<context:annotation-config>` and adds support for more annotations (@Repository, @Service, @Controller, which are specializations of @Component, @Configuration, etc.)

If you want to extend your knowledge about this, you can always read the Spring Reference Documentation.[5] More detailed information is outside the scope of this book.

# The Beans

The beans are the objects handled by the Spring IoC container. The following section will cover all you need to know about how beans are created, how the beans are categorized, how they are accessed, and how they are destroyed when they are no longer needed.

## Lifecycle and Instantiation

The beans are created in order of dependency. If a bean of type B, needs a bean of type A for its creation, the Spring container will know to first create bean A and then inject it into bean B. If an application has multiple configuration files, the Spring container first reads all of them, internally creates a dependency tree of bean definitions, and then starts traversing the tree, starting with its lowest level where the simplest bean definitions are. In the cases mentioned in previous sections, the order for bean creation (instantiation) is dataSource, personRepository, and personManager. The steps are described in Figure 2-4.

---

[5]The Spring Reference Documentation can be accessed at `http://docs.spring.io/spring/docs/current/spring-framework-reference/htmlsingle/`.

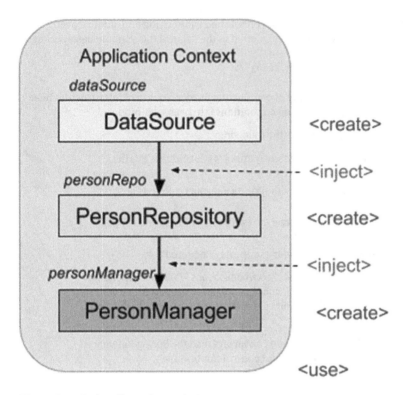

**Figure 2-4.** *Order of bean instantiation*

A bean cannot be created if its required dependencies do not exist; an exception is thrown in case of missing dependencies. But how does the Spring container know which dependencies are required? There are a few ways. One is the type of injection. Spring supports two types of injection: via constructor and via setter. The constructor injection is when the constructor of a bean is defined as having an argument of type another bean. In the previous example, the PersonManagerImpl constructor definition requires a PersonRepository instance as an argument, and thus the PersonManagerImpl requires a bean of type PersonRepository to be created before its creation.

```
<!- Constructor injection ->
<bean id="personManager" class="com.book.PersonManagerImpl">
      <constructor-arg ref="personRepository" />
   </bean>

   <!- Setter injection->
   <bean id="personRepository" class="com.book.JdbcPersonRepository">
      <property name="dataSource" ref="dataSource" />
</bean>
```

Any object that has a constructor with arguments cannot be constructed without passing in arguments. This restriction does not apply for the setter injection, but it can be enforced in two ways:

- By annotating the setter method with @Required. If the property is not set, a BeanInitializationException is thrown.

- By annotating the setter method with @Autowire the Spring IoC container tries to inject a bean with the specific type. If such a bean is not found, a BeanCreationException is thrown.

One of the advantages of using the setter injection is that you can create hierarchical beans, and setters will be inherited. In a setter injection, bean creation and dependency injection are two separate steps; for constructor injection there is only one step. So basically, setter injection makes your configuration more flexible.

For a bean to "come to life" and become available to be used for a purpose, it has to go through the steps shown in Figure 2-5.

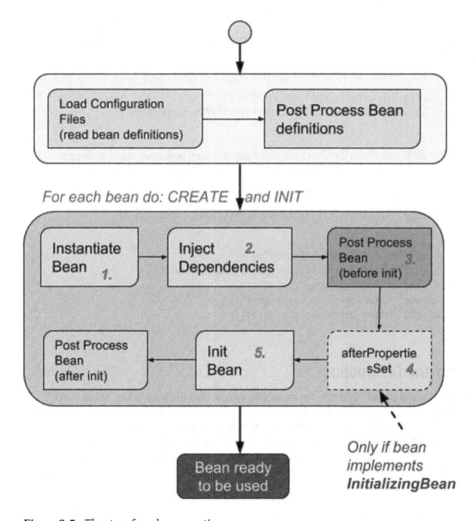

*Figure 2-5. The steps for a bean creation*

## How Bean Factory Post Processors Work

A bean definition can be modified before instantiating the bean, and this is done by beans called *bean factory post processors*. They are defined as classes implementing the BeanFactoryPostProcessor interface and are recognized by an application context and instantiated before any other beans in the container. The most used and known in the Spring world is the PropertyPlaceholderConfigurer.

```
<bean id="dataSource" class=
            "o.s.jdbc.datasource.DriverManagerDataSource">

    <property name="driverClassName" value="${driverClassName}"/>
    <property name="url" value="${url}"/>
    <property name="username" value="${username}"/>
    <property name="password" value="${password}"/>
</bean>

<context:property-placeholder location="classpath:datasource/db.properties"/>
```

The last line in this example is a simplified version of defining a PropertyPlaceholderConfigurer using the Spring context namespace; it is equivalent to the following:

```
<bean class=
   "o.s.beans.factory.config.PropertyPlaceholderConfigurer">
        <property name="location" value="classpath:datasource/db.properties"/>
</bean>
```

This bean reads those properties from the db.properties file and then populates the dataSource source bean with their values. Of course, the easier way to do this is to use SpEL expressions and the util namespace:

```
<util:properties id="dbProp" location="classpath:datasource/db.properties"/>

<bean id="dataSource" class=
    "o.s.jdbc.datasource.DriverManagerDataSource">
  <property name="driverClassName" value="#{dbProp.driverClassName}"/>
  <property name="url" value="#{dbProp.url}"/>
  <property name="username" value="#{dbProp.username}"/>
  <property name="password" value="#{dbProp.password}"/>
</bean>
```

## Bean Initialization and Destruction

An ApplicationContext instantiates all singleton (bean scopes are covered in detail in the "Bean Scopes" section) beans by default and also destroys them at the end of their lives. After a bean has been created and its dependencies injected, it can be initialized automatically by telling the context to execute a specified method. Before a bean ends its life, a different method might be called to do some resource cleanup. The context can be told to automatically do that too. These methods must have a void no-argument signature. There is no restriction on the accessor used for them. In the official documentation, the lifecycle methods given as example are all public. But there are opinions that state they should be protected or private (obviously, it does not apply to InitializingBean's afterPropertiesSet and DisposableBean's destroy) to prevent direct calls of these methods from the application code, as these methods should be called only once and only by the Spring IoC container.

There are multiple options for bean initialization:

- Using @PostConstruct from JSR 250

- Using @Bean's initMethod attribute

- Implementing InitializingBean and providing implementation for the afterPropertiesSet method *(not recommended because it couples the application code with Spring infrastructure code)*

- Using the init-method attribute on a <bean/> XML definition

When a bean ends its life, some cleanup operations might be necessary; to implement this kind of behavior, there are also multiple options:

- Using @PreDestroy from JSR 250

- Using @Bean's destroyMethod attribute

- Implementing DisposableBean and providing implementation for the destroy method *(not recommended, as it couples the application code with Spring infrastructure code)*

- Using the destroy-method attribute on a <bean/> XML definition

In the code sample there is a bean in the com.book.spring.components package that was implemented in such a way to clarify the Spring bean lifecycle. The bean is called CompleteLivingBean and has @PostConstruct and @PreDestroy annotated methods, implements InitializingBean and DisposableBean, and has methods in which names are used as values for attributes init-method and destroy-method. This bean was implemented using a *combined lifecycle strategy* to clearly show when each initializer/destruction method is called by the Spring IoC and to clearly display the bean creation steps in Figure 2-5.

This is the configuration:

```
<context:component-scan base-package="com.book.beans"/>

<bean id="livingBean" class="com.book.beans.CompleteLivingBean"
      init-method="initMethod"
      destroy-method="destroyMethod">
      <property name="internal" value="testValue"/>
</bean>
```

This is the definition of the bean class:

```
public class CompleteLivingBean implements InitializingBean, DisposableBean {
    public String internal;

    public CompleteLivingBean() {
        logger.info("1. Constructor.");

    }

    public void setInternal(String internal) {
        logger.info("2. Setter.");
        this.internal = internal;
    }

}
```

```java
    @PostConstruct
    public void postConstruct(){
        logger.info("3. @PostConstruct.");
    }

    @Override
     public void afterPropertiesSet() throws Exception {
        logger.info("4. afterPropertiesSet.");
    }

    public void initMethod(){
        logger.info("5. init-method.");

    }

    @PreDestroy
    public void preDestroy(){
        logger.info("6. PreDestroy.");

    }

    @Override
    public void destroy() throws Exception {
        logger.info("7. destroy.");

}

    public void destroyMethod() throws Exception {
        logger.info("8. destroy-method.");

    }

}
```

Also, there is no restriction on method names used as values for init-method and destroy-method attributes; initMethod and destroyMethod were used in this example to make their purpose really obvious.

---

■ ! In the certification exam, you might be asked which method is executed first—the one annotated with @PostConstruct or the one mentioned by the init-method; so the CompleteLivingBean helps clear up when methods are executed and why.

---

When executing the test for the com.book.beans.BeanLifecycleTest bean, you will see the following output:

```
INFO c.b.b.CompleteLivingBean - 1. Constructor.
INFO c.b.b.CompleteLivingBean - 2. Setter.
INFO c.b.b.CompleteLivingBean - 3. @PostConstruct.
INFO c.b.b.CompleteLivingBean - 4. afterPropertiesSet.
```

```
INFO c.b.b.CompleteLivingBean - 5. init-method.
...
INFO c.b.b.CompleteLivingBean - 6. @PreDestroy.
INFO c.b.b.CompleteLivingBean - 7. destroy.
INFO c.b.b.CompleteLivingBean - 8. destroy-method.
```

As represented in Figure 2-5, when a bean is created, the following succession of actions happens:

1. The constructor is called first to create the bean.

2. The dependencies are injected (setters are called).

3. The pre-initialization BeanPostProcessors are consulted to see if they want to call anything from this bean. The @PostConstruct annotation is registered by the CommonAnnotationBeanPostProcessor, so this bean will call this annotated method. This method is executed right after the bean has been constructed and before the class is put into service,[6] before the actual initialization of the bean (before afterPropertiesSet and init-method).

4. The InitializingBean's afterPropertiesSet is executed right after the dependencies were injected.

5. The init-method attribute value method is executed last, as this is the actual initialization method of the bean.

When a bean is destroyed:

1. The @PreDestroy method is executed, as this has to be executed before a destroy method, if one exists. The PreDestroy annotation is used on methods as a callback notification to signal that the instance is in the process of being removed by the container.[7]

2. The DisposableBean's destroy method is executed next, as the Spring standard order defines it so.

3. The destroy-method attribute value method is executed last, as this is the actual destroy method of the bean, and the Spring standard order defines it so.

This is the simplified and more natural explanation of the bean lifecycle; in most cases, this is all you will need. If you want to view the full picture with full plumbing details and other things the context does, you can read the official JEE and Spring documentation.[8]

---

■ ! The main reason for init-method and destroy-method creation was to give the developer a little control over beans definitions from third-party libraries, which have classes that cannot be modified or extended. This way, the developer can decide what gets executed after creation and what executes before destruction by using XML configuration.

---

[6]A snippet from the JEE official Java doc at http://docs.oracle.com/javaee/7/api/javax/annotation/PostConstruct.html.
[7]A snippet from the JEE official Java doc at http://docs.oracle.com/javaee/7/api/javax/annotation/PreDestroy.html.
[8]http://docs.spring.io/spring/docs/current/javadoc-api/org/springframework/beans/factory/BeanFactory.html.

# How Bean Post Processors Work

A BeanPostProcessor allows the developer to process a bean instance created by the IoC container after its instantiation, and then again after the initialization lifecycle event has occurred on it. BeanPostProcessors are defined as classes implementing the BeanPostProcessor interface, and are recognized by an application context and instantiated before any other beans in the container, because after their instantiation, they are used to manipulate other beans instantiated by the IoC container. The @PostConstruct and @PreDestroy annotations are processed by a bean called CommonAnnotationBeanPostProcessor. This is not a default infrastructure bean for the Spring IoC container, so to use it you have to specify it in the configuration of the application. You would expect to need something like this in the mvc-config.xml file:

```
<bean class="o.s.c.a.CommonAnnotationBeanPostProcessor"/>
```

And this could work, but there will be some issues because configuring the bean like that overrides the Spring defaults, which might lead to unexpected behavior. Fortunately, this bean configuration is one of those included in the following line, a Spring shortcut based on the context namespace:

```
<context:component-scan base-package="com.book.beans"/>
```

Or in this one:

```
<context:annotation-config/>
```

The BeanPostProcessor beans wrap other beans into AOP proxies that add extra behavior (more details on AOP in the "Spring AOP" section). The Spring Framework has different types of BeanPostProcessors that can be used for caching, transactions, security, and so forth. The CommonAnnotationBeanPostProcessor scans for methods annotated with @PostConstruct and @PreDestroy, and calls those methods at the appropriate time.

The code samples use logback to display logs. By increasing the granularity of the log for the Spring Framework to DEBUG, you can see what is happening "behind the scenes," and what CommonAnnotationBeanPostProcessor is actually doing. In the following configuration snippet, you are shown how to modify the granularity of the log by editing the logger element for the Spring Framework in the logback.xml file:

```
<logger name="org.springframework" level="DEBUG" additivity="false">
    <appender-ref ref="STDOUT" />
</logger>
```

After modifying the log file when running the BeanLifecycleTest, you can see the behavior of the CommonAnnotationBeanPostProcessor[9]:

```
INFO CompleteLivingBean - 1. Constructor.
DEBUG CABPP - Found init method on class
    CompleteLivingBean: private void CompleteLivingBean.postConstruct()
DEBUG CABPP Found destroy method on class
    CompleteLivingBean: protected void CompleteLivingBean.preDestroy()
```

---

[9]CABPP is the acronym for CommonAnnotationBeanPostProcessor. It is used to fit a log quote nicely on a page.

```
DEBUG CABPP Registered init method on class CompleteLivingBean:
    InitDestroyAnnotationBeanPostProcessor$LifecycleElement@64e17f36
DEBUG CABPP Registered destroy method on class CompleteLivingBean:
    DestroyAnnotationBeanPostProcessor$LifecycleElement@a27dd7d7
INFO c.b.b.CompleteLivingBean - 2. Setter.
DEBUG CABPP - Invoking init method on bean 'livingBean':
    private void CompleteLivingBean.postConstruct()
INFO c.b.b.CompleteLivingBean - 3. @PostConstruct.
INFO c.b.b.CompleteLivingBean - 4. afterPropertiesSet.
...
DEBUG CABPP - Invoking destroy method on bean 'livingBean':
protected void CompleteLivingBean.preDestroy()
INFO c.b.b.CompleteLivingBean - 1. @PreDestroy.
```

The previous section mentioned that there are annotation attributes equivalents for the init-method and destroy-method. If you were to define CompleteLivingBean using a class annotated with @Configuration, it would look like this:

```
@Bean(initMethod = "initMethod", destroyMethod = "destroyMethod")
public CompleteLivingBean getCompleteLivingBean() {
    return new CompleteLivingBean();
}
```

And would be equivalent to this XML definition:

```
<bean id="livingBean" class="com.book.beans.CompleteLivingBean"
           init-method="initMethod" destroy-method="destroyMethod"/>
```

# Bean Scopes

When the Spring IoC instantiates beans, it creates a single instance for each bean—unless a property is set on the bean definition specifying otherwise. The property in question is called *scope* and the default scope for a bean is singleton. The scopes are defined in Table 2-2.

***Table 2-2.*** *Bean Scopes*

| Scope | Description |
| --- | --- |
| singleton | The Spring IoC creates a single instance of this bean and any request for beans with an id or ids matching this bean definition results in this instance being returned. |
| prototype | Every time a request is made for this specific bean, the Spring IoC creates a new instance. |
| request | The Spring IoC creates a bean instance for each HTTP request. Only valid in the context of a web-aware Spring ApplicationContext. |
| session | The Spring IoC creates a bean instance for each HTTP session. Only valid in the context of a web-aware Spring ApplicationContext. |
| global-session | The Spring IoC creates a bean instance for each global HTTP session. Only valid in the context of a web-aware Spring ApplicationContext. |

So when a bean is created without a scope attribute, the scope of the bean is singleton:

```
<bean id="personRepository" class="com.book.JdbcPersonRepository">
    <property name="dataSource" ref="dataSource"/>
</bean>
```

Otherwise, the scope of the bean is the one specified by the value of the scope attribute:

```
<bean id="personRepository" class="com.book.JdbcPersonRepository"
          scope="prototype">
    <property name="dataSource" ref="dataSource"/>
</bean>
```

There is an annotation equivalent to this that can be used on @Component (and other stereotype annotations) annotated beans:

```
@Component
@Scope(value = ConfigurableBeanFactory.SCOPE_PROTOTYPE)
public class PrototypeBean {

    private Logger logger = LoggerFactory.getLogger(PrototypeBean.class);
    private static int instanceCounter = 0;
    public PrototypeBean() {
        logger.info("-> Constructing instance no: " + (++instanceCounter));
    }
}
```

---

■ ! @Scope(value = ConfigurableBeanFactory.SCOPE_PROTOTYPE) is equivalent to @Scope(ConfigurableBeanFactory.SCOPE_PROTOTYPE) and @Scope("prototype") because constant SCOPE_PROTOTYPE is of type string and has the "prototype" value. Using Spring constants eliminates the risk of misspelling the scope value.

---

The @Scope annotation can also be used on a bean definition annotated with @Bean to specify the scope of the resulting bean.

```
@Bean(name="personManager")
@Scope("prototype")
//or @Scope(ConfigurableBeanFactory.SCOPE_PROTOTYPE)
public PrototypeBean getPrototypeBean(){
    return new PrototypeBean();
}
```

If you were to execute the following test, the test would pass:

```
@Test
    public void testPrototype() {
        // Create the application from the configuration
        ClassPathXmlApplicationContext context =
          new ClassPathXmlApplicationContext("classpath:test-app-config.xml");
        PrototypeBean pb1 = (PrototypeBean)context.getBean("prototypeBean");
        assertNotNull(pb1);
        //the bean is requested by type
        PrototypeBean pb2 = context.getBean(PrototypeBean.class);
        assertNotNull(pb2);
        assertNotEquals(pb1,pb2);
}
```

And this is what would be seen in the log file:

```
DEBUG - Creating instance of bean 'prototypeBean'
INFO -> Constructing instance no: 1
DEBUG - Finished creating instance of bean 'prototypeBean'
DEBUG - Creating instance of bean 'prototypeBean'
INFO -> Constructing instance no: 2
DEBUG - Finished creating instance of bean 'prototypeBean'
```

A special case of bean scope is the scope of an **inner bean**. An inner bean is defined within the scope of another bean. The reason for doing this is because the bean does not need to be shared with other beans, but is needed only for the creation of the enclosing bean. The scope attribute has no meaning for an inner bean and is ignored; so are the attributes id and name, as the bean is anonymous. When using Java Configuration, the inner bean is just a local variable in a method. The following code snipped declares the DataSource bean as an inner bean:

```
<util:properties id="dbProp" location="classpath:datasource/db.properties"/>

<bean id="personRepository" class="com.book.JdbcPersonRepository">
    <property name="dataSource">
        <bean id="dataSource" class=
        "org.springframework.jdbc.datasource.DriverManagerDataSource">
            <property name="driverClassName" value="#{dbProp.driverClassName}"/>
            <property name="url" value="#{dbProp.url}"/>
            <property name="username" value="#{dbProp.username}"/>
            <property name="password" value="#{dbProp.password}"/>
    </bean>
    </property>
</bean>
```

## Accessing Beans

Beans can be identified in three ways: by type, by name, and by id. The following subsections explain these in detail; examples are provided for each case. How to access beans configured with annotates is covered too.

## Bean Identification by Type

A bean can be identified by its type if there is only one definition of a bean with that type in the Spring configuration file.

The BeanPostPrecessor classes registered by <context:annotation-config/> that scan for annotations are singleton infrastructure beans instantiated by the Spring IoC container, when that configuration line is present in a Spring configuration file. At any time during the life of an application only one instance of each of those beans will exist. Basically, this configuration file:

```
<beans xmlns="http://www.springframework.org/schema/beans"
      xmlns:xsi="http://www.w3.org/2001/XMLSchema-instance"
      xmlns:context="http://www.springframework.org/schema/context"
      xsi:schemaLocation="
      http://www.springframework.org/schema/beans
      http://www.springframework.org/schema/beans/spring-beans.xsd
      http://www.springframework.org/schema/context
      http://www.springframework.org/schema/context/spring-context.xsd">

      <context:annotation-config/>

</beans>
```

Is equivalent to this:

```
<?xml version="1.0" encoding="UTF-8"?>
<beans xmlns="http://www.springframework.org/schema/beans"
      xmlns:xsi="http://www.w3.org/2001/XMLSchema-instance"
      xsi:schemaLocation="http://www.springframework.org/schema/beans
        http://www.springframework.org/schema/beans/spring-beans.xsd">
<!--the org.springframework. package was shortened to o.s.
  for this code to fit the page better -->
<bean class="o.s.beans.factory.annotation.AutowiredAnnotationBeanPostProcessor"/>
<bean class="o.s.context.annotation.CommonAnnotationBeanPostProcessor"/>
<bean class="o.s.orm.jpa.support.PersistenceAnnotationBeanPostProcessor"/>
<bean class="o.s.beans.factory.annotation.RequiredAnnotationBeanPostProcessor"/>

</beans>
```

Considering the following bean definition:

```
<bean class="com.book.sandbox.SimpleBean" />
```

If there is no other bean definition with the same class attribute value, the bean can be accessed like this:

```
SimpleBean sb = context.getBean(SimpleBean.class);
```

Or can even be injected as a dependency via autowiring:

```
@Autowired
SimpleBean simpleBean;
```

---

■ ! In the `book-code/02-chapter` project, there is a class called `BeanIdentificationTest` that tests various scenarios of bean identification.

---

## Bean Identification by Name

The `<bean/>` element has an attribute called name. The value assigned to this attribute in a bean definition can be used to access this bean. A duplicate bean name will invalidate a configuration file. The name is flexible and can be used to define more than one name when the values are separated by a comma (",") or a semicolon (";"). The bean is defined as follows:

```
<bean name="sbb0" class="com.book.sandbox.SimpleBean"/>
```

Can be accessed as follows:

```
// the old way
SimpleBean sb0 = (SimpleBean)context.getBean("sb0");
  // or the Spring 3.0 way
SimpleBean sb0 = context.getBean("sb0", SimpleBean.class);
```

And can also be injected as a dependency via autowiring using the @Qualifier annotation:

```
@Autowired
@Qualifier(value = "sb0")
SimpleBean simpleBean;
```

The @Bean annotation has a name attribute too, so an equivalent annotation configuration can be created:

```
@Bean(name="simpleBean")
public SimpleBean getSimpleBean(){
  return new SimpleBean();
}
```

# Bean Identification by id

The <bean/> element has an attribute called id. The value assigned to this attribute in a bean definition can be used to access the bean. This attribute uniquely identifies a bean, so a duplicate bean id will invalidate a configuration file. This attribute can appear alongside the name attribute, and both can be used to access the bean. The id and the name attributes serve the same purpose: they are both used to define bean identifications. The difference between them is that the value of the id attribute must conform to XML standard id, which means no weird characters like a comma (",") or semicolon (";") can be contained in it.

Basically, the following bean definition is valid:

```
<bean name="sb0" id="id0" class="com.book.sandbox.SimpleBean"/>
```

And the following test will pass, as both calls will return the same bean:

```
@Test
public void testBeans() {
    ...
    SimpleBean sb01 = context.getBean("sb0", SimpleBean.class);
    SimpleBean sb02 = context.getBean("id0", SimpleBean.class);
    assertTrue(sb01 == sb02);
}
```

# Accessing Annotated Beans

The beans defined using @Component and extensions of it can be autowired by name or by type without any extra configuration.

---

■ **CC**   When using annotation configuration—beans annotated with @Component or extensions of it—the Spring IoC container also creates a logical name for these beans by lowercasing the first letter of the class name.

---

```
@Component
@Scope(value = ConfigurableBeanFactory.SCOPE_PROTOTYPE)
public class PrototypeBean { ... }
...
\\ requesting bean by name
PrototypeBean pb1 = (PrototypeBean)context.getBean("prototypeBean");
assertNotNull(pb1);
\\Requesting bean by type
PrototypeBean pb2 = context.getBean(PrototypeBean.class);
assertNotNull(pb2);
assertNotEquals(pb, pb2);
```

# Spring AOP

AOP is an acronym for **a**spect-**o**riented **p**rogramming and represents a programming paradigm that aims to simplify code by grouping repetitive operations in units called *aspects*. AOP helps managing common functionality that spans across the application, like logging, security, and transactionality. AOP complements OOP (**o**bject-**o**riented **p**rogramming) by providing a more advanced way of decoupling the code and modularizing an application.

The AOP framework complements the Spring IoC container. The container can be used without it in small applications that do not require the use of security or transactions, because these are the key crosscutting concerns for enterprise applications.

In Spring, an aspect is class annotated with @Aspect. It contains methods called *advices* that are annotated with aspect-specific annotations that intercept the execution of other beans' methods and performs specific operations before and/or after their execution, and can prevent the execution of an intercepted method if necessary.

The AOP framework makes this possible by scanning all aspects when the application context is started, and creates AOP proxy objects that wrap around existing beans to implement aspect contracts. When the target beans are requested for usage or injection, the proxy object is injected or returned instead. From a developer's point of view, it looks like the intended object is used, but the Spring IoC container works with the proxy object that is wrapped around it.

Let's see how AOP can make things easier when you want to save a Person instance to the database using the PersonManagerImpl mentioned at the beginning of the chapter.

The following is what the code looks like in Spring without AOP. Figure 2-6 shows the UML diagram.

```xml
<!-- configuration will contain this element -->
<bean id="txManager" class=
      "org.springframework.jdbc.datasource.DataSourceTransactionManager">
    <property name="dataSource" ref="dataSource"/>
</bean>
```

```java
// PersonManagerImpl.java
...
@Autowired
@Qualifier("txManager")
PlatformTransactionManager transactionManager;
@Autowired
@Qualifier("personRepository")
PersonRepository repo;

public int save(Person person) {
    TransactionDefinition def = new DefaultTransactionDefinition();
    TransactionStatus status = transactionManager.getTransaction(def);
    int result = repo.save(person);

    transactionManager.commit(status);
    return result;
}
```

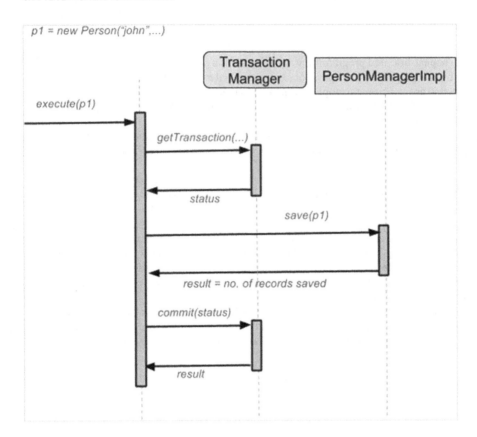

**Figure 2-6.** *Diagram in non-AOP mode*

And here is how it looks using AOP (the UML diagram is presented in Figure 2-7):

```
<!-- configuration will contain this element needed to switch on
the transactional behaviour -->
<tx:annotation-driven transaction-manager="txManager"/>
// PersonManagerImpl.java
@Component("personManager")
@Transactional
public class PersonManagerImpl implements PersonManager {
    @Autowired
    @Qualifier("personRepository")
    PersonRepository repo;

    public int save(Person person) {
        return repo.save(person);
    }
}
}
```

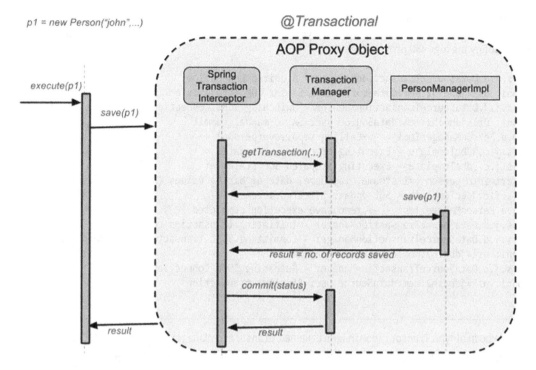

**Figure 2-7.** *Diagram in AOP mode*

The <tx:annotation-driven/> configuration element is defined in the Spring tx namespace, which has to be added to the configuration file:

```
<beans xmlns="http://www.springframework.org/schema/beans"
      xmlns:xsi="http://www.w3.org/2001/XMLSchema-instance"
      xmlns:context="http://www.springframework.org/schema/context"
      xmlns:tx="http://www.springframework.org/schema/tx"
      xsi:schemaLocation="
      http://www.springframework.org/schema/beans
      http://www.springframework.org/schema/beans/spring-beans.xsd
      http://www.springframework.org/schema/tx
      http://www.springframework.org/schema/tx/spring-tx.xsd">
      ...
</beans>
```

And in order to run the methods of a bean in a transactional environment, you also have to specify the TransactionManager instance used to handle the transactions. In a test environment, the annotation @TransactionConfiguration is used:

```
@RunWith(SpringJUnit4ClassRunner.class)
@ContextConfiguration(locations = {"classpath:app-aop-cfg.xml",
      "classpath:spring/test-db-config.xml"})
@TransactionConfiguration(transactionManager = "txManager")
public class PersonSaveTest {
...
}
```

To verify that the test method is running in a transaction environment, you can switch the Spring Framework log to DEBUG, as explained in the "Lifecycle and Instantiation" section, and run the test. In the console, the following logs will prove this:

```
DEBUG o.s.j.d.DataSourceTransactionManager - Acquired Connection
    conn1: url=jdbc:h2:mem:dataSource user=SA for JDBC transaction
DEBUG o.s.j.d.DataSourceTransactionManager - Switching JDBC Connection
    conn1: url=jdbc:h2:mem:dataSource user=SA to manual commit
INFO c.b.a.PersonManagerImpl - -> Calling repo.save(person)
DEBUG o.s.j.c.JdbcTemplate - Executing prepared SQL update
DEBUG o.s.j.c.JdbcTemplate - Executing prepared SQL statement
    insert into person (firstname, lastname, date_of_birth) values (?,?,?)
DEBUG o.s.j.c.JdbcTemplate - SQL update affected 1 rows
INFO c.b.a.PersonManagerImpl - -> repo.save execution completed.
DEBUG o.s.j.d.DataSourceTransactionManager - Initiating transaction commit
DEBUG o.s.j.d.DataSourceTransactionManager - Committing JDBC transaction on Connection
    conn1: url=jdbc:h2:mem:dataSource user=SA
DEBUG o.s.j.d.DataSourceTransactionManager - Releasing JDBC Connection
    conn1: url=jdbc:h2:mem:dataSource user=SA after transaction
```

---

■ **CC**   If the bean of type `TransactionManager` is named `transactionManager` when in a transactional environment, the Spring IoC container will detect it automatically and there is no need to specify it as an argument for the `@TransactionConfiguration` annotation. Even more, `@TransactionConfiguration` can be replaced with `@Transactional`, and the test methods will still be executed in a transactional environment.

The `transaction-manager` attribute from the `<tx:annotation-driven/>` can be omitted too.

Also, `@Qualifier("transactionManager")` is not needed when the `transactionManager` is autowired and the bean of type `TransactionManager` has the default name.

In the code samples presented here, a bean of type `TransactionManager` with a different name was used to show the developer the configurations needed to work in cases other than the default one, because in bigger applications, multiple beans of type `TransactionManager` might be needed.

---

# Testing Spring Applications

When it comes to writing code, there are two types of testing that matter: unit testing and integration testing.

- **Unit testing** is used to test small units of code, thus its naming. Unit testing is easy to do—not much setup is necessary, and since JUnit[10] has introduced @Test annotation writing, unit tests have become a breeze.

---

[10]The most commonly used Java testing framework (see `http://junit.org`).

- **Integration testing** is used to test bigger chunks of code made up of objects interacting together in a given context, and the focus is set on business logic and object integration with each other. The context is usually made up of mocks or stubs that replace the objects, which are not the focus of the tests. You can imagine that creating a testing context is not a simple job.

The Spring Framework includes a testing module called spring-test that makes integration testing really practical to implement. The tests that have been used throughout this chapter use the spring-test module.

- The SpringJUnit4ClassRunner, as the names says, is a Spring class used to tell JUnit that the tests in this class are executed in a Spring test context.

- The @ContextConfiguration receives one or more configuration files as parameters that are used to initialize the test context.

- The @TransactionConfiguration is the annotation that injects the transactionManager instance used to run tests in a transactional environment. As mentioned earlier, this can be skipped, and @Transactional can be used when the TransactionManager bean has the default name.

---

■ **CC**   When using @ContextConfiguration to annotate a test class, the configuration file path can be skipped, and then Spring IoC container will look for a file named [TestClassName]-context.xml in the same location where the test class is defined. When the project has a Maven structure, the configuration is placed in the resources directory, and the directories matching the package name for the test class are created so the file will have the same relative path as the test class.

So if you have test class com.book.simple.SimpleTest annotated with @ContextConfiguration, then resources will have com/books/simple/SimpleTest-context.xml to provide the test context configuration, which is automatically discovered and used by the Spring IoC container.

---

# Summary

After reading this chapter, you should have a basic knowledge of how Spring does its magic and understand the following:

- Two flavors of configuration can be mixed: XML-based (decoupled from classes code) and Java annotation–based (bean definitions are mixed in the class code)

- The lifecycle of a bean

- How to access a bean

- What AOP is and how and where Spring can apply it

- How to test Spring applications

# Quick Quiz

**Question 1:** What is a bean?

    A.    a plain old Java object

    B.    an instance of a class

    C.    an object that is instantiated, assembled, and managed by a Spring IoC container

**Question 2:** What is the default scope of a bean?

    A.    default

    B.    singleton

    C.    protected

    D.    prototype

**Question 3:** What types of dependency injection are supported by Spring IoC container?

    A.    setter injection

    B.    constructor injection

    C.    interface-based injection

    D.    field-based injection

**Question 4:** What is true about @PostConstruct and @PreDestroy ?

    A.    they are JSR-250 annotations

    B.    they are supported by AutowiredAnnotationBeanPostProcessor

    C.    they are registered by the <context:component-scan/> element

*Detailed answers are in the Appendix.*

# Practical Exercise

The practice module for this chapter is in the book-code project; it is named 02-chapter-practice. The solution is in the 02-chapter-solution module. You are given the code for a few related beans. Your task is to complete the existing configuration files, to create test contexts, and to make sure that the tests pass.

The book-code project is a gradle multimodule project. It can be built from the command line by running gradle build under the book-code directory. This will build all modules of the project. The build will fail when run for the first time because of the unresolved tasks in the -practice projects. If you do it this way, you will have something similar to the following output in your console:

```
$ gradle build
..
:02-chapter-practice:compileJava UP-TO-DATE
:02-chapter-practice:processResources UP-TO-DATE
:02-chapter-practice:classes UP-TO-DATE
:02-chapter-practice:jar UP-TO-DATE
:02-chapter-practice:assemble UP-TO-DATE
:02-chapter-practice:compileTestJava UP-TO-DATE
:02-chapter-practice:processTestResources UP-TO-DATE
```

```
:02-chapter-practice:testClasses UP-TO-DATE
:02-chapter-practice:test

com.book.plain.PlainPersonSaveTest > savePerson FAILED
java.lang.AssertionError at PlainPersonSaveTest.java:31

..
BUILD FAILED
Total time: 4.096 secs
```

If you decided to use the Intellij IDEA editor on the Gradle tab, you already have available all the predefined Gradle tasks and you can just double-click the one you are interested in. In the following image, the selected task is the build task for the project book-code; but if you scroll down in that view, you will see the modules in the project and you can choose to build a specific module. So double-click under the :02-chapter-practice on the build task and execute it. The build will fail, but this is expected. This task will succeed because it does not execute the tests. In Figure 2-8 you can see how your IDE should look.

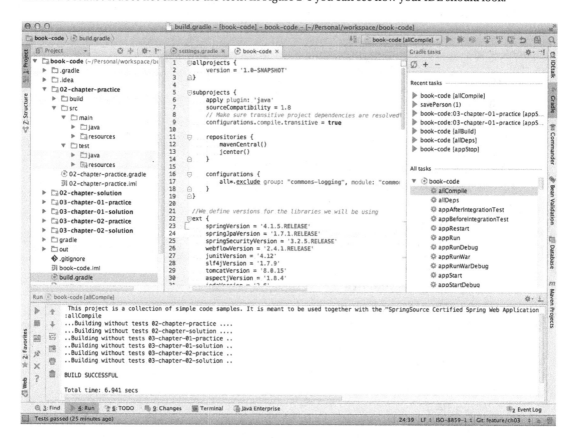

*Figure 2-8.* *Intellij IDEA Gradle run*

---

■ ! To compile projects without failing (due to tests in practice projects that are not fixed yet), you can use the allCompile task, which was created this purpose.

---

On the left in the Project view, you can see the book-code project and the component modules. Each module has the typical Maven structure mentioned earlier in the chapter (see Figure 2-3). Expand the 02-chapter-practice and look in the com.book.base package. In it you will notice the implementation of the Person class. The instances of this class are used in the test examples and are handled by instances of classes that implement PersonManager.

The PersonManager interface defines the int save(Person person) method, which should return the number of records that were affected. In this case, it can be only 1 (one Person instance was saved) or 0 (no Person instance was saved).

The PersonRepository interface will be implemented by the repository classes used in this example. Some repositories will actually save Person instances into a test database, but most of them will just print a log message to tell the developer that the method was executed correctly. The code for this chapter was created to show how a Spring application is configured, so more complex functionality is not covered. Classes and methods are commented properly, so using them is very straightforward.

Every time a project or module is built with gradle, a directory named build is created containing the detailed results of the build for that project or module. This can be seen in Figure 2-9.

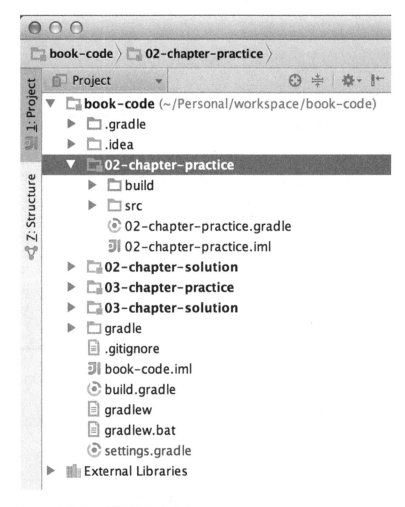

***Figure 2-9.*** *Intellij IDEA Project view*

What is relevant when working with these sources is the `reports\tests\index.html` file. When opened in a browser, it displays all the failing tests in that module. This page can be refreshed during development to track, step by step, the number of tests that have to be fixed. When accessed after the first `gradle build`, it should display what is depicted in Figure 2-10.

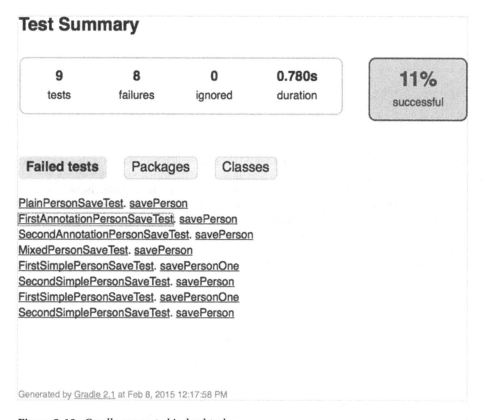

*Figure 2-10.* *Gradle-generated index.html*

There are eight tests failing, and they do so because the implementation for them is incomplete. Completing them has been left as practice for you, the developer reading this book. Click the TODO label in the bottom-left corner. A view will open that should look like what is shown in Figure 2-11. Click and expand everything. Every TODO task has a number attached. Start resolving the tasks in ascending order.

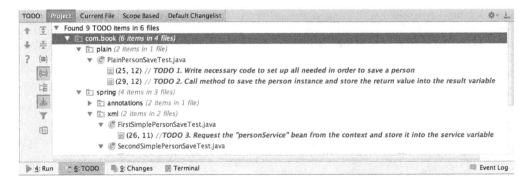

*Figure 2-11.* *Intellij IDEA TODO tab*

The root package is called com.book. Under this package all packages will group classes with a common purpose. For example, the plain package contains classes that implement the functionality for saving a Person instance by using plain Java—no Spring beans or configuration files, as was shown in the beginning of the "The Spring Core Container" section. As Maven convention requires, the test classes are placed in the same package as the classes being tested, but under the test directory. The first exercise is to complete the plain Java implementation to save a Person instance and make the com.book.plain.PlainPersonSaveTest. After you have written the code, run the test.

Just right-click anywhere in the file and choose Run and the class name in the menu, similar to what you see in Figure 2-12.

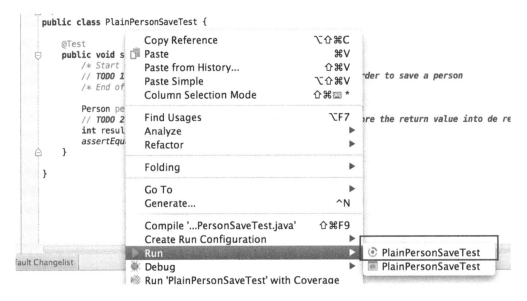

*Figure 2-12.* *Intellij IDEA— running a Gradle test*

If the test does not pass, go back and re-read the beginning of this chapter to refresh your memory on how dependency injection is handled in plain Java. After you are done and you have a successful build for 02-chapter-practice, you can compare your solution to the one in 02-chapter-solution.

Also, you should take a look at the sources, test sources, and resources under packages aop, noaop, and sandbox.

The book.code.spring.noaop package contains classes that implement a transactional bean used to save a Person instance, but opening and committing a transaction are done manually.

The book.code.spring.aop package contains classes that implement a transactional bean used to save a Person instance using Spring AOP.

Both implementations are tested in a test context that uses a H2 in-memory database to perform the actual save of a Person instance. The configuration of the test database is in the test-db-config.xml file, and you will notice that the Spring jdbc namespace is used. As JPA is not used, you need some *.sql initialization files, which can be found under the test/resources/datasource directory.

```xml
<jdbc:embedded-database id="dataSource" type="H2">
    <jdbc:script location="classpath:datasource/db-schema.sql"/>
    <jdbc:script location="classpath:datasource/db-test-data.sql"/>
</jdbc:embedded-database>
```

The com.book.spring.sandbox contains classes and tests designed to help you understand how bean identification works.

When you have passed all the tests and you feel confident that you have a solid grasp of the Spring fundamentals, you can continue to the next chapter.

# CHAPTER 3

■ ■ ■

# Spring MVC

This chapter was written with the intention of teaching a developer how to create a simple Spring web application and understand how the background *plumbing* can be modified according to the desired approach. Think of Spring infrastructure components as LEGO pieces. You can connect them in different ways to get the final result: a working web application. After going through this chapter, you should be able identify and use the main components of Spring MVC to create a web application in a few easy steps.

Aside from describing and giving examples on how Spring Web MVC works, this chapter also teaches you how to integrate it with different view technologies, like JSP, Apache Tiles, and Thymeleaf.[1]

## MVC Basics

Spring Web MVC is a popular request-driven framework based on the model-view-controller software architectural pattern, which was designed to decouple components that by working together make a fully functional user interface.

The typical model-view-controller behavior is displayed in Figure 3-1.

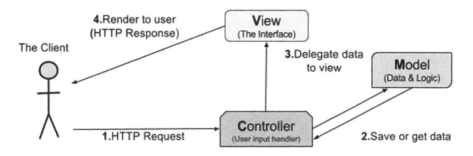

*Figure 3-1.* *Typical MVC behavior*

---

[1]Thymeleaf is the new sheriff in Web town. It is an XML/XHTML /HTML5 template engine that works both in web and non-web environments. It is really easy to integrate it with Spring. If you want to read more about it before using it in the practice code for this chapter, go to the official site at http://www.thymeleaf.org/.

The Spring Web MVC provides preconfigured beans for the implementation of this behavior. These beans are contained in two main libraries:

- spring-web.jar

- spring-webmvc.jar

These libraries are the core of all Spring-related modules. At the center of the Spring Web MVC framework sits the `DispatcherServlet` class, which is the entry point for any Spring web application. Before any HTTP request reaches the specific controller, it has to go through `DispatcherServlet` for that controller to be identified.[2] In a nutshell, the `DispatcherServlet` coordinates all request-handling operations using other infrastructure components defined in Spring and user-defined components. And it acts as a front controller, an entry point for the web application. The Spring components mentioned earlier can be categorized as follows:

- Spring MVC infrastructure components
  - handler mappings
  - handler adapters
  - view resolvers
  - personalization beans
  - exception resolvers
- User-provided web components
  - handler interceptors
  - controllers

Thus, the Spring MVC functional flow can be sketched somewhat like in Figure 3-2.

---

[2]If it looks as if Spring MVC resembles Struts, you are definitely not imagining things. The Spring Web MVC was inspired by Struts, which was one of the first MVC-based frameworks. The `DispatcherServlet` in Spring has the same responsibilities as the `ActionServlet` in Struts, as both are implementations of the Front Controller Pattern. You can read more about this software design pattern at `http://www.martinfowler.com/eaaCatalog/frontController.html`.

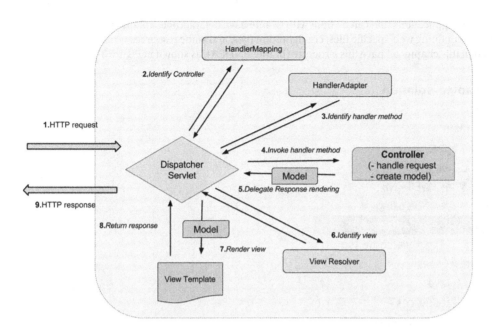

**Figure 3-2.** *Spring MVC functional flow*

Briefly put, to configure a Spring web application, you need to do the following:

- Define the `DispatcherServlet` as the main servlet handling all requests to the application in `web.xml` and link it to the Spring configuration, or configure this servlet programmatically by using a class implementing `WebApplicationInitializer` (only possible in a Servlet 3.0+ environment)

- Define the application configuration (usually in a Spring configuration file named `mvc-config.xml` or a Java configuration class), which should do the following:

  - Define the MVC context used (handler adapter, handler mapping, and other infrastructure beans)

  - Define a view resolver (or more)

# Configuring MVC

Spring Web MVC can be configured just like any other Spring application, via XML (using mostly the `<mvc/>` namespace), Java configuration annotations, or by mixing these. A Spring web application can be configured in two ways:

- **All-in-one configuration**: `web.xml` (part of JEE specification) or a `WebApplicationInitializer` implementation and Spring application configuration files. Back-end and front-end configurations are coupled and the `DispatcherServlet` is the *only entry point* to the application.

- **Separate configuration**: Used for more complex applications when the `DispatcherServlet` is not the only entry point (usually applications that require the back end to be accessed via REST or SOAP requests/web services, and in this case, the back end needs a separate listener).

Typical Java web applications that can be built with Gradle have the internal structure consecrated by Maven. The folder containing web-specific files, configuration files, and static resources is named webapp. The projects used in this chapter all have this structure (in Intellij IDEA), as shown in Figure 3-3.

***Figure 3-3.*** *Typical Java web application structure with web.xml configuration file*

# XML Configuration

Spring XML configuration for core applications was covered in the previous chapter. But XML namespaces can be used for declaring web-specific infrastructure beans too. There are multiple ways to configure a web application; multiple files can be used for web-specific beans to be grouped together based on their purpose. In this chapter, multiple ways to create a configuration are presented, and after getting familiar with all of them, you will be able to "mix and match" to create configurations for the types of applications that you will develop.

## All-in-One Configuration

This is the simplest way to configure a web application. The Spring configuration files are all referred to in the web.xml file as a value for the contextConfigLocation parameter.

```
<servlet>
    <servlet-name>admin</servlet-name>
    <servlet-class>
    org.springframework.web.servlet.DispatcherServlet
    </servlet-class>
    <init-param>
        <param-name>contextConfigLocation</param-name>
        <param-value>
        /WEB-INF/spring/mvc-config.xml
        /WEB-INF/spring/app-config.xml
        </param-value>
    </init-param>

</servlet>
```

```
<servlet-mapping>
    <servlet-name>admin</servlet-name>
    <url-pattern>/</url-pattern>
</servlet-mapping>
```

In the preceding case, the mvc-config.xml contains the Spring configuration for the front-end (controllers and MVC infrastructure beans) of the application, and the app-config.xml contains the back-end configuration (service beans). In this case, all Spring configuration files are loaded by the DispatcherServlet and a web context is created.

## Separate Configuration

The proper way to configure a more complex web application to make it more extensible and flexible is to decouple the front-end configuration the back-end configuration. Such an implementation provides web services access to the back end. This can be done by having a separate listener for the back-end configuration. This complicates the content of web.xml a bit, and the configuration looks similar to the next one:

```
<context-param>
    <param-name>contextConfigLocation</param-name>
    <param-value>/WEB-INF/spring/app-config.xml</param-value>
</context-param>

<listener>
    <listener-class>
        org.springframework.web.context.ContextLoaderListener
    </listener-class>
</listener>

<servlet>
    <servlet-name>admin</servlet-name>
    <servlet-class>
        org.springframework.web.servlet.DispatcherServlet
    </servlet-class>
    <init-param>
        <param-name>contextConfigLocation</param-name>
        <param-value>/WEB-INF/spring/mvc-config.xml</param-value>
    </init-param>
</servlet>
<servlet-mapping>...</servlet-mapping>
```

▧ **CC**   When the back-end Spring configuration file is named applicationContext.xml, there is no need to specify the <context-param> element in your configuration. The Spring IoC container accepts the previously mentioned file name as a default name for the backed configuration file and it will load it automatically.

The web.xml file is transformed to this:

```
<listener>
    <listener-class>
        org.springframework.web.context.ContextLoaderListener
    </listener-class>
</listener>
<!-- The backend configuration file is named applicationContext.xml -->
<!-- The <context-param> is no longer needed.-->

<listener>
    <listener-class>
        org.springframework.web.context.ContextLoaderListener
    </listener-class>
</listener>

<servlet>
    <servlet-name>mvc-dispatcher</servlet-name>
    <servlet-class>
        o.s.web.servlet.DispatcherServlet
    </servlet-class>
    <init-param>
        <param-name>contextConfigLocation</param-name>
        <param-value>/WEB-INF/spring/mvc-config.xml</param-value>
    </init-param>
</servlet>
<servlet-mapping>...</servlet-mapping>
```

---

■ !   Throughout this book, package names may not be presented fully: or.springframework. usually becomes o.s. The reason for this is to fit the configuration and code samples better in the page to make them more readable.

---

■ CC   If the Spring MVC configuration file is named [servletName]-servlet.xml, there is no need to specify the <init-param> element either. The Spring IoC container accepts the previously mentioned file name template (replace servletName with the name given to the servlet) as a default name for the front-end configuration file and it will load it automatically.

---

The separate configuration can be simplified like this:

```
<context-param>
    <param-name>contextConfigLocation</param-name>
    <param-value>/WEB-INF/app-config.xml</param-value>
</context-param>
```

```
    <listener>
        <listener-class>
            org.springframework.web.context.ContextLoaderListener
        </listener-class>
    </listener>

    <servlet>
        <servlet-name>mvc-dispatcher</servlet-name>
<!-- The frontend configuration file is named mvc-dispatcher-servlet.xml -->
 <!-- The <init-param> is no longer needed.-->
        <servlet-class>
            o.s.web.servlet.DispatcherServlet
        </servlet-class>
        <load-on-startup>1</load-on-startup>
    </servlet>
    <servlet-mapping>
        <servlet-name>mvc-dispatcher</servlet-name>
        <url-pattern>/</url-pattern>
    </servlet-mapping>
```

Customizing the configuration is easy. All rules from Spring core configuration apply. Wildcards are supported. Different resource prefixes can be used. The DispatcherServlet can even be configured to a different url-pattern. In this case, the requests to the application must contain the value of the url-pattern value, otherwise they won't be handled by the DispatcherServlet. This approach is suited when the application uses multiple DispatcherServlet instances.

```
<init-param>
        <param-name>contextConfigLocation</param-name>
        <param-value>
            /WEB-INF/spring/*-beans.xml
            classpath:com/book/app-config.xml
        </param-value>
    </init-param>
...
<servlet-mapping>
    <servlet-name>admin</servlet-name>
    <url-pattern>/admin/*</url-pattern>
</servlet-mapping>
```

In the previous example, the DispatcherServlet handles the request with the URL matching [server:port]\[application-name]\admin\*.

---

■ !  Throughout this book and in all code examples, the Spring MVC configuration file is named mvc-config.xml to emphasize that only Spring MVC components are defined in it; otherwise, this configuration file can be named in any other way. The contents of this file are used for view, locale, and time zone resolution and for customizing handler mappings and other Spring MVC infrastructure beans.

---

The controllers can be defined in the mvc-config.xml configuration file using the bean tag element, just like any other bean, but starting with Spring 3.0, the preferred way to define controllers is using the @Controller annotation, which is why the Spring MVC is often referred to as @MVC.

The main component of an MVC XML configuration is the <mvc:annotation-driven/> element that registers all necessary default infrastructure beans for a web application to work: handler mapping, validation conversion beans, and many others.

Another component that is important is the <mvc:default-servlet-handler/>. Usually in Spring web applications the default servlet mapping "/" is mapped to the DispatcherServlet. This means that static resources have to be served by it too, which might introduce a certain lag in providing a response as the DispatcherServlet has to find the resources that the request URL is mapped to. The <mvc:default-servlet-handler/> configures a DefaultServletHttpRequestHandler with a URL mapping of "/*" and the lowest priority relative to other URL mappings. Its sole responsibility is to serve static resources.

You can see some user-defined beans needed for configuring a Spring MVC application in the following example. Configurations might differ, depending on the types of resources used.

```
<!-- Defines basic MVC defaults (handler mapping, date formatting, etc) -->
<mvc:annotation-driven/>

<!-- Configures a handler for serving static resources by forwarding to the
     Servlet container's default Servlet.-->
<mvc:default-servlet-handler/>

<!-- ResourceBundle bean used for internationalization -->
<bean name="messageSource"
      class="o.s.context.support.ReloadableResourceBundleMessageSource"
      p:basename="classpath:messages/global"/>

<!-- View resolver bean used to render a *.jsp page -->
<bean id="jspViewResolver"
    class="o.s.web.servlet.view.InternalResourceViewResolver">
    <property name="prefix" value="/WEB-INF/"/>
    <property name="suffix" value=".jsp"/>
</bean>
```

---

■ ! Before continuing to the next section, take a look at the module project 03-chapter-01-practice under the book-code project. This is a simple project focusing on the XML-based configuration; it can be used to test your understanding of this section. It uses the minimum number of Spring infrastructure beans required to start a web application and display a simple JSP page.

To run a project that is a web application from the command line, execute the gradle *appRun* task.

To run a project in IntelliJ IDEA, use the appStart task to start the application and *appStop* to stop the application.

Make sure to execute the tasks from under the specific module in the Gradle task tree. Figure 3-4 can help you identify the task you need to run the application within IntelliJ IDEA.

▼ ⊚ :03-chapter-01-practice
    ⚙ appAfterIntegrationTest
    ⚙ appBeforeIntegrationTest
    ⚙ appRestart
    ⚙ appRun
    ⚙ appRunDebug
    ⚙ appRunWar
    ⚙ appRunWarDebug
    ⚙ appStart
    ⚙ appStartDebug
    ⚙ appStartWar
    ⚙ appStartWarDebug
    ⚙ appStop

*Figure 3-4. Gretty plugin special tasks to start and stop web applications*

---

```
2015-03-01 15:48:36.834 WARN  -  03-chapter-01-practice runs at:
2015-03-01 15:48:36.834 WARN  -  http://localhost:8080/03-chapter-01-practice
```

Open that location in your browser. If you see the page shown in Figure 3-5, the project is working properly. Run gradle *appStop* to stop the server.

---

## Welcome to the most simple page of Spring MVC!

**If you see this page, then your first Spring Web application is working as intended and your XML configuration is correct.**
**Congratulations!**

*SpringSource Certified Spring Web Application Developer Exam - Sample application*

*Figure 3-5. Practice Spring MVC application welcome page*

## Configuration Using Annotations

An equivalent configuration using Java configuration can be created, but there are a few additional details needed for the configuration class to work properly. The configuration class has to also be annotated with the @EnableWebMvc annotation and has to either implement WebMvcConfigurer or extend an implementation of this interface, for example: WebMvcConfigurerAdapter, which gives the developer the option to override only the methods he or she is interested in.

Annotating a configuration class with @EnableWebMvc has the result of importing the Spring MVC configuration implemented in the WebMvcConfigurationSupport class; it is equivalent to <mvc:annotation-driven/>. This class registers a lot of Spring infrastructure components that are necessary for a web application (covered later in this chapter).[3]

To tell the DispatcherServlet that the configuration will be provided by a configuration class instead of a file, the following changes have to be made in web.xml:

- Define an initialization parameter named contextClass with the full name of the Spring class used to create an annotation-based context as the value.

- The initialization parameter named contextConfigLocation should have the full name of the configuration class written by the developer as the value.

```
<servlet>
        <servlet-name>admin</servlet-name>
        <servlet-class>
                        org.springframework.web.servlet.DispatcherServlet
        </servlet-class>
        <init-param>
            <param-name>contextClass</param-name>
            <param-value>
            o.s.web.context.support.AnnotationConfigWebApplicationContext
            </param-value>
        </init-param>
        <init-param>
            <param-name>contextConfigLocation</param-name>
            <param-value>
                com.book.config.WebConfig
        </param-value>
        </init-param>
</servlet>
```

The configuration class for what was configured with XML in the previous chapter looks like this:

```
@Configuration
@EnableWebMvc    // equivalent with <mvc:annotation-driven/>
@ComponentScan(basePackages = {"com.book.controllers"})
// equivalent with <context:component-scan base-package="com.book.controllers"/>
//used to scan only web components
public class WebConfig extends WebMvcConfigurerAdapter {
    ...

    @Bean(name = "messageSource")
    MessageSource getMessageSource() {
        ReloadableResourceBundleMessageSource
                    messageSource = new ReloadableResourceBundleMessageSource();
        ...
        return messageSource;
    }
```

---

[3]If you want, you can look in the API documentation for detail information about this class, which is available at http://docs.spring.io/spring/docs/current/javadoc- api/.

```
// <=> <mvc:default-servlet-handler/>
@Override
public void configureDefaultServletHandling(
        DefaultServletHandlerConfigurer configurer) {
    configurer.enable();
}


@Bean
 InternalResourceViewResolver getViewResolver(){
    InternalResourceViewResolver resolver = new InternalResourceViewResolver();
    resolver.setPrefix("/WEB-INF/");
    resolver.setSuffix(".jsp" );
    return resolver;
}
}
```

The @ComponentScan annotation is the equivalent of <context:component-scan />. It is used to find all the classes annotated with @Controller in the package com.book.controllers.

---

■ ! Before continuing to the next section, take a look at the module project 03-chapter-02-practice under book-code. This is a simple project focusing on the Java configuration–based configuration and can be used to test your understanding of this section. It uses the minimum number of Spring infrastructure beans required to start a web application and display a simple JSP page.

The Gradle running instructions are the same as the instructions for the previous section.

---

## Mixed Configuration

---

■ ! There are Spring-specific annotations like @Controller, @Service, @Component, and @Repository, which can be used to configure a Spring application without the need to use a Java configuration class; instead, an XML file is used, containing context or MVC namespace element definitions. This is called a *mixed configuration*, because it uses annotations to define the beans, and XML to define the context.

---

In practice, most common and frequently used Spring configurations imply a combination of XML and annotations. The primary reason for this is legacy code, as XML configuration was the first and only way to configure a Spring application prior to Spring 2.5. Migration to a more recent version of Spring is usually a slow process, and projects remain stuck between worlds for some periods of time. And there are also developers that still prefer XML because it seems easier to separate configurations for the back end, front end, security, web services, and so on, in separate files (although this can just as easily be done with Java configuration classes). It is also intuitive and very readable when it comes to dependency injection. It is more practical to have the definition of the relationship between the beans decoupled from the bean implementation. Because it is more practical to implement transaction management using annotations, it is very visible which method is executed in a transaction.

Annotations should be applied when they provide functionality and/or visibly mark the annotated classes or methods for a specific purpose. Annotations should not tie the code down to some specific process, so the code should function normally without them. The most obvious case here is the @Controller annotated classes for the web side of an application. In the back end, @Repository and @Service annotations are used for the same purpose. When looking at the code of a controller class, you see the annotation and you can easily infer what the purpose of that class is. All annotation mentioned earlier are Spring stereotype annotations, which are used to denote the roles of types in the overall architecture.

A typical Spring web application configuration uses an mvc-config.xml file to declare the infrastructure beans and @Controller annotated classes.

## Configuration Without Using web.xml

Starting with Servlet 3.0+, the web.xml file is no longer needed to configure a web application. It can be replaced with a class implementing the WebApplicationInitializer (or a class extending any of the Spring classes that extend this interface). This class is detected automatically by SpringServletContainerInitializer (an internal Spring supported class, which is not meant to be used directly or extended). The SpringServletContainerInitializer class is bootstrapped automatically by any Servlet 3.0+ container.

The SpringServletContainerInitializer[4] extends javax.servlet.ServletContainerInitializer and provides a Spring-specific implementation for the onStartup method. This class is loaded and instantiated, and the onStartup is invoked by any Servlet 3.0–compliant container during container startup, assuming that the Spring-web module JAR is present on the classpath.

Considering you have a web.xml file that looks like this:

```
<servlet>
    <servlet-name>admin</servlet-name>
    <servlet-class>o.s.w.s.DispatcherServlet</servlet-class>
    <init-param>
        <param-name>contextConfigLocation</param-name>
        <param-value>
            /WEB-INF/spring/mvc-config.xml
        </param-value>
    </init-param>
    <load-on-startup>1</load-on-startup>
</servlet>
<servlet-mapping>
    <servlet-name>admin</servlet-name>
    <url-pattern>/</url-pattern>
</servlet-mapping>
```

---

[4]The code for this class is at https://github.com/spring-projects/spring-framework/blob/master/spring-web/src/main/java/org/springframework/web/ SpringServletContainerInitializer.java.

The most obvious way to implement WebApplicationInitializer is this:

```
public class WebInitializer implements WebApplicationInitializer {
    @Override
    public void onStartup(ServletContext servletContext) throws ServletException {
        ServletRegistration.Dynamic registration =
                    servletContext.addServlet("dispatcher", new DispatcherServlet());
        registration.setLoadOnStartup(1);
        registration.addMapping("/");
        registration.setInitParameter("contextConfigLocation",
                    "/WEB-INF/spring/mvc-config.xml");
    }
}
```

The class does not need to be annotated or linked to any other configuration file existing in the application. You can easily notice which lines from XML turned into which lines in the code, right?

But there is another way, which involves constructing the application context first and then injecting it into the DispatcherServlet:

```
XmlWebApplicationContext appContext = new XmlWebApplicationContext();
appContext.setConfigLocation("/WEB-INF/spring/mvc-config.xml");
ServletRegistration.Dynamic registration =
    servletContext.addServlet("dispatcher", new DispatcherServlet(appContext));
registration.setLoadOnStartup(1);
registration.addMapping("/");
```

And there is an even simpler way—by extending AbstractDispatcherServletInitializer, an abstract implementation of the WebApplicationInitializer:

```
public class WebInitializer extends AbstractDispatcherServletInitializer {

    @Override
    protected WebApplicationContext createRootApplicationContext() {
//there is no root application context for the web application context to inherit
    return null;
}

    @Override
    protected WebApplicationContext createServletApplicationContext() {
        XmlWebApplicationContext cxt = new XmlWebApplicationContext();
        cxt.setConfigLocation("/WEB-INF/spring/mvc-config.xml");
        return cxt;
    }

    @Override
    protected String getServletMappings() {
        return new String { "/" };
    }
}
```

Java-based annotation configurations are supported too—in multiple ways. Consider that you have a WebConfig class and a web.xml that looks like this:

```
<servlet>
    <servlet-name>admin</servlet-name>
    <servlet-class>
        o.s.web.servlet.DispatcherServlet
        </servlet-class>
    <init-param>
        <param-name>contextClass</param-name>
        <param-value>
            o.s.web.context.AnnotationConfigWebApplicationContext
        </param-value>
    </init-param>
    <init-param>
        <param-name>contextConfigLocation</param-name>
        <param-value>
            com.book.config.WebConfig
        </param-value>
    </init-param>
    <load-on-startup>1</load-on-startup>
</servlet>

<servlet-mapping>
    <servlet-name>admin</servlet-name>
    <url-pattern>/</url-pattern>
</servlet-mapping>
```

This is the most obvious way to implement WebApplicationInitializer's onStartup() method:

```
ServletRegistration.Dynamic registration =
    servletContext.addServlet("dispatcher", new DispatcherServlet());
registration.setLoadOnStartup(1);
registration.addMapping("/");
registration.setInitParameter("contextConfigLocation", "com.book.config.WebConfig");
registration.setInitParameter("contextClass",
    "o.s.w.c.s.AnnotationConfigWebApplicationContext");
```

But wait, there's more! You can create the application context and inject it into the DispatcherServlet as you did before:

```
AnnotationConfigWebApplicationContext context =
    new AnnotationConfigWebApplicationContext();
context.register(WebConfig.class);

ServletRegistration.Dynamic registration =
    servletContext.addServlet("dispatcher", new DispatcherServlet(context));
registration.setLoadOnStartup(1);
registration.addMapping("/");
```

And the easiest way to do it is with AbstractAnnotationConfigDispatcherServletInitializer, which extends AbstractDispatcherServletInitializer, an abstract implementation of the WebApplicationInitializer. Spring provides them to help you eliminate some of the code writing. By extending the AbstractAnnotationConfigDispatcherServletInitializer template and using customization methods offered by the AbstractDispatcherServletInitializer, the developer is only required to provide concrete implementations for three methods: getRootConfigClasses, getServletConfigClasses, and getServletMappings.

```
public class WebInitializer extends
        AbstractAnnotationConfigDispatcherServletInitializer {
    @Override
    protected Class<?> getRootConfigClasses() {
    //there is no root application context for the web application context to inherit
        return null;
    }

    @Override
    protected Class<?> getServletConfigClasses() {
        return new Class { WebConfig.class };
    }

    @Override
    protected String getServletMappings() {
        return new String { "/" };
    }
}
```

■ ! Before continuing with this chapter, take a look at the 03-chapter-03-practice and 03-chapter-04-practice and try to make the projects run. The first requires you to configure a Spring web application using a Spring XML–based configuration and without a web.xml file. The second requires you to configure a Spring web application using a Java-based configuration and without a web.xml file. Be creative, read the Spring API if necessary, and then you can even compare your solution to the ones provided in the solution projects.

The Gradle running instructions are the same as in the previous section.

# MVC Components

The configuration of a Spring web application integrates quite a few infrastructure beans.

The DispatcherServlet looks for implementations of type: HandlerMapping, HandlerAdapter, ViewResolver, and HandlerExceptionResolver. Out-of-the-box implementations for the previously mentioned interfaces are provided by Spring. The default configuration can be found in the DispatcherServlet.properties, which is in the spring-webmvc.jar in package org.springframework.web.servlet.[5]

---

[5]The contents can be accessed directly on GitHub at https://github.com/spring-projects/ spring-framework/ blob/master/spring-webmvc/src/main/resources/org/springframework/web/ servlet/DispatcherServlet. properties.

■ !   You can find the jar in your local maven repository. It is recommended to open the file and study it, because in the exam you might be asked about the default components configured in Spring for some MVC bean types. Some of them are deprecated in the current API—DefaultAnnotationHandlerMapping, for example—and the file will suffer some changes in future versions.

The infrastructure beans mentioned earlier can be configured manually, but this is rarely done and is recommended to be avoided, as the explicit configuration cancels the default configuration for that bean type. In Spring 4.0, <mvc:annotation-driven/> and the equivalent @EnableWebMvc do just that—override the default configuration to provide the new features, so you don't have to struggle with the configuration yourself.

A Spring web application can use more than one infrastructure bean of a specific type. In this case, the beans can be chained and have an associated priority value specified using the order property. For example, you can have multiple HandlerMapping implementations:

```
<bean
    class="o.s.web.servlet.handler.SimpleUrlHandlerMapping">
    <property name="order" value="0"/>
</bean>
```

```
<bean
    class= "o.s.web.servlet.mvc.support.ControllerClassNameHandlerMapping">
    <property name="order" value="1"/>
</bean>
```

When <mvc:annotation-driven/> or @EnableWebMVC is used in the application configuration, the RequestMappingHandlerMapping implementation is registered internally with Spring MVC. This class was added in Spring 3.1; it allows RequestMappings for the same URL to be in different controller classes. It is meant to replace the DefaultAnnotationHandlerMapping implementation. It was introduced to make the annotation controller support class more customizable and open for extension. When using the RequestMappingHandlerMapping, the actual handler is an instance of HandlerMethod, which identifies the specific controller method that will be invoked. Starting with Spring version 4.0, the DefaultAnnotationHandlerMapping was marked as deprecated.

The following sections cover each of the infrastructure bean types in detail.

# Infrastructure Beans

Spring MVC offers developers a lot of support when it comes to building the *plumbing* of a web application, so developers can focus on implementing the actual service a web application is expected to provide. The beans provided by Spring MVC are often called *infrastructure beans*, which have default configurations that work out of the box. Each of these infrastructure beans are presented in detail in the following sections.

# HandlerMapping

This HandlerMapping Spring interface is implemented by classes that map parts of URL for the incoming requests to the appropriate handlers and a list of pre- and post-processor interceptors (AOP is used for this). Prior to Spring 3.1, it was necessary to specify one or more HandlerMapping beans in the application context, but after the introduction of annotated controllers, there is no need to do so. All HandlerMapping implementations are used by the DispatcherServlet to identify the handler (controller class) of a request.

In the `DispatcherServlet.properties`, you find the following default `HandlerMapping` implementations configured:

```
org.springframework.web.servlet.HandlerMapping=
org.springframework.web.servlet.handler.BeanNameUrlHandlerMapping,\
org.springframework.web.servlet.mvc.annotation.DefaultAnnotationHandlerMapping
```

The `BeanNameUrlHandlerMapping` class maps URLs to beans with names that start with "/". So a request incoming with URL `http://localhost:8080/persons` maps to bean:

```
@Controller("/persons")
public class PersonsController {
    ...
}
```

---

■ ! The `DefaultAnnotationHandlerMapping` is deprecated in Spring 4.0 as it was replaced by `RequestMappingHandlerMapping`.

---

The `RequestMappingHandlerMapping` class maps URLs to classes annotated with @RequestMapping. So a request coming from URL `http://localhost:8080/persons/list` is handled by the following controller:

```
@RequestMapping("/persons")
@Controller
public class PersonsController {

    @RequestMapping(value="/list")
    public void list(Model model){
        ...
    }
}
```

In the preceding example, the @RequestMapping at method level is used to narrow the mapping expressed at class level, if one is present. The annotation is not really necessary at method level when it is present at class level, because narrowing can be done using other criteria too; for example, the request method type.

```
@RequestMapping("/persons")
@Controller
public class PersonsController {
    //End user requests to see data for a certain person.
    @RequestMapping(method = RequestMethod.GET)
    public void getPerson(Model model){
        ...
    }

    //End user sends data to save for a certain person.
    @RequestMapping(method = RequestMethod.POST)
    public void savePerson(Person person, Model model){
        ...
    }
}
```

It is mandatory for any HTTP request path to be uniquely mapped onto a specific handler. It is recommended to keep all related handler methods in the same bean, and not span them across multiple handler beans in order to improve code readability.

Another implementation worth mentioning is ControllerClassNameHandlerMapping, which was introduced in the spirit of convention over configuration. This implementation offers the possibility to generate URL path mappings from the class names and method names of registered or annotated controller beans. The convention is to take the short name of the class, remove the Controller suffix, lower case the first letter of the remaining text, prefix it with "/", and then add the method name used to handle the request. Using this implementation, the PersonsController mentioned earlier is mapped to "/persons*" and the @RequestMapping("/persons") annotation is no longer needed.

In the book-code project, there is a sample module named 03-chapter-05-solution, which contains a simple controller with the following implementation.

```
@Controller
public class WelcomeController {

    @RequestMapping
    //maps to /welcome/sayhi
    public String sayhi(Model model){
        model.addAttribute("salute", "Hi!");
        return "welcome";
    }

    @RequestMapping
    //maps to /welcome/sayhello
    public String sayhello(Model model){
        model.addAttribute("salute", "Hello!");
        return "welcome";
    }
}
```

In order for a request to be solved correctly using the ControllerClassNameHandlerMapping, a HandlerAdapter implementation needs to be configured. AnnotationMethodHandlerAdapter will do, even if it is deprecated in Spring 4.0.

```
...
    <context:component-scan base-package="com.book"/>
    <bean
        class="o.s.web.servlet.mvc.support.ControllerClassNameHandlerMapping"
        p:caseSensitive="true"/>

    <bean id="annotationMethodHandlerAdapter"
        class="o.s.web.servlet.mvc.annotation.AnnotationMethodHandlerAdapter" />
...
```

■ **!** An example of how to configure the `ControllerClassNameHandlerMapping` bean and how it works is implemented in the `03-chapter-05-solution` module in the `book-code` project. This project does not have a practice project associated with it because there is no need for one.

The Gretty plugin is quite flexible and can be configured to start a web application on a different context or port. When working locally, the URL of the application looks like this: `http://localhost:8080/03-chapter-05-solution`. The context is the string after the port, and Gretty automatically takes the name of the project and uses it as context for the web application, if not configured to do otherwise. Also, the default port is 8080, which is the default port used by most of application servers for web applications.[6]

As the name of the modules in `book-code` are quite long, Gretty was configured to use a different context, which can also emphasize the purpose of the application.

```
gretty {
    port = 8080
    contextPath = '/mvc-handling'
}
```

# HandlerAdapter

The `HandlerAdapter` interface is internal and is not intended for application developers. It must be implemented by each handler to be able to handle a request. The `DispatcherServlet` uses this interface to invoke handler methods because the interface is taking care of solving various annotations inside a controller class and identifies which method should be called.

In the `DispatcherServlet.properties` you find the following default `HandlerAdapter` implementations:

```
org.springframework.web.servlet.HandlerAdapter=
org.springframework.web.servlet.mvc.HttpRequestHandlerAdapter,\
org.springframework.web.servlet.mvc.SimpleControllerHandlerAdapter,\
org.springframework.web.servlet.mvc.annotation.AnnotationMethodHandlerAdapter
```

These are the out-of-the-box defaults if `<mvc:annotation-driven/>` is not specified.

When `<mvc:annotation-driven/>` or `@EnableWebMVC` is used in the application configuration, `RequestMappingHandlerAdapter` is used. Introduced in Spring 3.1, the scope of this class is to work with `RequestMappingHandlerMapping` to make this class the only place where a decision is made about which method should handle a request. This actually means that every handler method is a unique endpoint that can be identified from class and method-level `RequestMapping` information. Prior to Spring 3.1, identifying and calling a handler method involved two steps: identifying a controller (handler) using a `HandlerMapping` implementation and identifying the method (handler method) using a `HandlerAdapter` implementation. Starting with Spring 3.1, everything is done in one step, with the two classes working together.

So Figure 3-2 is not an accurate representation for Spring >=3.1; when using `<mvc:annotation-driven/>` or `@EnableWebMVC`, Figure 3-6 is more accurate.

---

[6]The full list of configuration options for Gretty can be found at `http://akhikhl.github.io/gretty-doc/Gretty-configuration.html`.

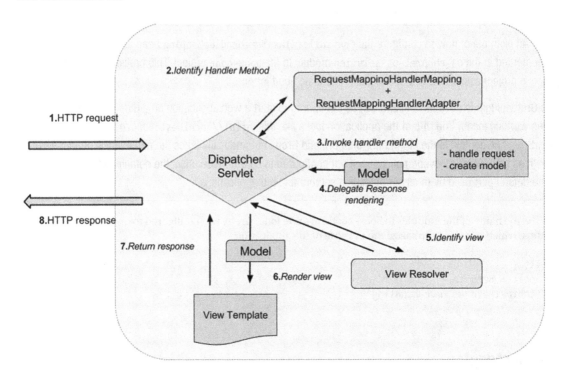

**Figure 3-6.** *@MVC Spring >= 3.1*

The old implementations were kept in the Spring MVC library, but it is recommended to use the ones introduced in Spring 3.1 and enabled by the MVC namespace or @EnableWebMVC because these ensure a simpler configuration and faster identification of a handler method, and take advantage of other new features introduced in Spring 3.1. Here is a list of some of the changes introduced by this approach:

- It is no longer possible to use SimpleUrlHandlerMapping or BeanNameUrlHandlerMapping to identify a controller and then identify the handler method by narrowing the method choice with @RequestMapping.

- It is no longer possible to have a single method without explicit mapping to solve all requests mapped to a controller. The new support classes will throw a Not Found 404 error.

- HandlerInterceptor and HandlerExceptionResolver (covered later in the chapter) can now expect the object-based handler to be a HandlerMethod. They can examine its parameters and annotations.

- Custom argument and return types are supported for handler methods.

- @PathVariable annotated parameters (covered later in the chapter) are automatically added to the model, so it's not necessary to manually add them if you are providing them as part of forwarding or redirecting.

- Supports parameterized URI template on redirect strings.

- RequestMappings now support consumes/produces, so it's not necessary to specify h eaders="ContentType=application/json". This is a little closer to the JAX-RS style of specifying @Consumes/@Produces annotations. This helps in producing the correct error code if unsupported media types are referenced on REST requests.

The preceding list is not complete. If you want a full read of all the advantages of using the new handler support classes, you can find it in the official documentation.[7] Some are also mentioned in the following sections; those are the ones you should focus on for the exam.

When the web application starts, if the logger of the application is configured properly, you should be able to see all the beans used in the application, including the infrastructure beans. The following is a snippet from a debug log printed when 02-pr-mvc-basic-solution starts. Run the project yourself to analyze the console output in more detail.

```
INFO Initializing Spring FrameworkServlet 'mvc-dispatcher'
...
DEBUG o.s.b.f.s.DefaultListableBeanFactory - Pre-instantiating singletons ...,
accountRepo,hospitalRepo,personManager,identityCardRepo,transactionManager,
entityManagerFactory, ..., o.s.w.s.m.m.a.RequestMappingHandlerMapping#0,
... ,o.s.w.s.m.m.a.RequestMappingHandlerAdapter#0,
o.s.w.s.m.m.a.ExceptionHandlerExceptionResolver#0,...,
org.springframework.web.servlet.view.InternalResourceViewResolver,
,messageSource,localeResolver,themeResolver,
...
```

# ViewResolver

The HTTP response returned to the client after the execution of a handler method is constructed using a model and a view. The model contains the data that is used to populate a view. Spring provides view resolvers to avoid ties to a specific view technology. Out of the box, Spring supports JSP, Velocity templates, and XSLT views. The interfaces needed to make this possible are ViewResolver and View. The first provides a mapping between view names and actual views. The second takes care of preparing the request and forwards it to a view technology.[8]

---

[7]http://docs.spring.io/spring/docs/current/spring- framework-reference/htmlsingle/#mvc-ann-requestmapping-31-vs-30, http://docs.spring.io/spring/docs/current/spring- framework-reference/htmlsingle/#mvc-config-enable.
[8]http://docs.spring.io/spring/docs/4.1.x/spring- framework-reference/htmlsingle/#mvc-viewresolver.

All handler methods must resolve to a logical view name that corresponds to a file, either explicitly by returning a `String`, `View`, or `ModelAndView` instance or implicitly based on internal conventions. The core view resolver provided by Spring is the `InternalResourceViewResolver`, which is the default view resolver, as you can see in the `DispatcherServlet.properties` file:

```
org.springframework.web.servlet.ViewResolver=
        org.springframework.web.servlet.view.InternalResourceViewResolver
```

## View Resolver Chaining

A web application can have more than one `ViewResolver` configured and the `DispatcherServlet` discovers them by type. In this case, the default view resolver configuration is overridden, meaning the `InternalResourceViewResolver` is not the default resolver anymore, so if this bean is needed, it has to be configured explicitly. In this case, the available view resolvers can and should be chained to have a fixed sequence of resolvers trying to obtain a view. The next example shows how two view resolvers can be chained together to resolve JSP and Excel views:

```
<!-- in mvc-config.xml -->

<bean name="persons/list.xls" class="com.book.persons.PersonsExcelView"/>

<bean
  id="xlsViewResolver"
 class="...web.servlet.view.BeanNameViewResolver"
    p:order="0"/>

<bean
    class="org.springframework.web.servlet.view.InternalResourceViewResolver"
    p:order="1" />
```

---

■ !  Defining bean properties using the `p: ...` syntax is possible by using **the p namespace** that offers a way to contract bean definitions in XML configuration files to reduce their size and make them more readable.[9]

---

Chaining view resolvers is also possible using a Java configuration class:

```
\\ in @Configuration annotated class
@Bean(name="persons/list.xls")
public View excelView(){
        return new PersonsExcelView();
}

@Bean(name="xlsViewResolver")
public ViewResolver xlsViewResolver(){
    BeanNameViewResolver resolver = new BeanNameViewResolver();
```

---

[9]You can read more about it in the official documentation at http://docs.spring.io/spring/docs/current/ spring-framework-reference/html/beans.html#beans- p-namespace.

```
    resolver.setOrder(0);
    return resolver;
}

@Bean
  public ViewResolver jspViewResolver() {
    InternalResourceViewResolver resolver = new InternalResourceViewResolver();
...
    resolver.setOrder(1);
    return resolver;
}
```

When a view resolver does not result in a view (usually null is returned, but there are view resolvers that throw exceptions), Spring examines the application context for other view resolver beans and inspects each of them until a view is obtained. If this is not possible, a ServletException is returned. When resolver beans are chained, the inspection is done based on the value of their order property; the lower the value of the property, the higher the priority when resolving view names.

---

■! The InternalResourceViewResolver resolves the view no matter what view name is returned. It throws an exception if it cannot resolve a view name, so this bean always has to be placed last in the chain; otherwise, Spring skips looking for other view resolver beans in the context. XSLT and JSON are also resolvers that must be last in the chain. Tiles, Velocity, and FreeMarker can appear anywhere in the chain.

---

In the case just presented, if the BeanNameViewResolver does not return a view (a request method has returned a logical view name different than "persons/list.xls"), the next resolver is called to do that.

The InternalResourceViewResolver is the most important implementation provided by Spring. It is a specialization of UrlBasedViewResolver (so they cannot be used together in a configuration, chained or not) and inherits the behavior of interpreting view names as a URL, supports the **"redirect:"** prefix and the **"forward:"** prefix. And supports InternalResourceView(Servlets and JSPs) and JstlView.

---

■! The "redirect:" and "forward:" prefixes are appended to the logical view name to tell the servlet container what to do.

With "forward:", the servlet container just forwards the same request to the target URL, and the browser is not involved and does not know the URL has changed. A forward should be used for safe operations when reloading the page won't result in corrupt data (usually for requesting data to display in the page).

With "redirect:", the response status is set to 302 and the URL to redirect to is set in a Location header, then the response is sent to the browser. The browser then makes another request to the new URL. Redirect is a two-step operation; it is recommended to be used when the first request is a data manipulation request, and the browser must then be redirected to a confirmation page to prevent data duplication.

---

The "redirect:" prefix can be returned together with a view name to delegate the creation of the response to another handler. The most suitable for such behavior is when a POST request was received and the possibility to resubmit the same form data has to be eliminated. The browser sends an initial POST, receives a response to redirect to a different URL, and then performs a GET request for the URL received as a response. This sequence of actions matches a web development design pattern named `Post-Redirect-Get` that prevents duplicate form submissions. In Figure 3-7, the `Post- Redirect-Get` process is displayed using the `PersonsController`.

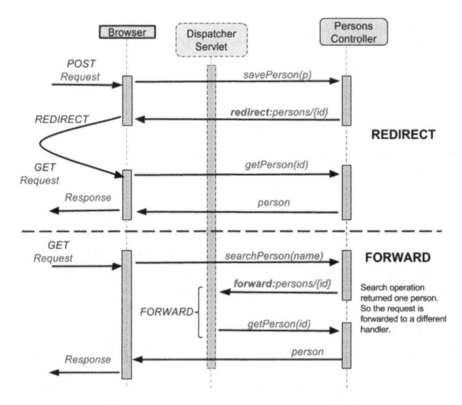

***Figure 3-7.*** *Post-Redirect-Get in Spring using the "redirect:" prefix compared to "forward:"*

"`redirect:`" and "`forward:`" are recognized by the `UrlBasedViewResolver` and all its subclasses. They treat them accordingly and consider the view name after the prefix as the redirect/forward URL.

---

■ **!**  You will have the occasion to work with "`redirect:`" and "`forward:`" in the `05-pr-mvc-form-practice` project.

---

All view file templates are stored under /WEB-INF for security reasons. They cannot be accessed directly via a manually introduced URL and they require a model in order to be rendered. The previously mentioned view implementations supported by `InternalResourceViewResolver` have the following characteristics:

- `InternalResourceView` exposes the model attributes as request attributes and forwards the request to the specified resource URL using a `RequestDispatcher`.

- `JstlView` is a specialization of `InternalResourceView` that exposes request attributes specifying the locale and the resource bundle for JSTL's formatting and message tags, using Spring's locale and `MessageSource` ( the JSTL library is required in the classpath for this View technology to be available).

More about this topic is covered later in this chapter.

This is an example of how a view is resolved using the chained resolvers configured earlier:

```
/* 1 */
@RequestMapping("/persons.htm")
public String listHtml(HttpServletRequest rq, Model model) {
   model.addAttribute(personManager.getAllPersons());
   return "accounts/list";
}

/* 2. */
@RequestMapping("/persons.xls")
public String listExcel(HttpServletRequest rq, Model model) {
   model.addAttribute(personManager.getAllPersons());
   return "persons/list.xls";
}
```

The first method has `InternalResourceViewResolver` resolve the view, and the second is taken care of by `BeanNameViewResolver` and a `PersonsExcelView` is rendered.

As you can see, the implementation for the two methods is almost identical. The URL and the logical view name returned are different, however. And there's a programming principle called **D**on't **R**epeat **Y**ourself! that those two methods do not respect. Let's try and respect that principle by merging the two methods into one:

```
/* 1 */
@RequestMapping("/persons")
public String list(HttpServletRequest rq, Model model) {
   model.addAttribute(personManager.getAllPersons());
   if (rq.getRequestURL().toString().endsWith("xls")) {
       return "persons/list.xls";
   } else {
       return "persons/list";
   }
}
```

But this is not an acceptable solution either. What if the application is requested to support PDF views too? That means more `if-else` instructions have to be added. Right now you are probably telling yourself: "There's gotta be a better way of doing this!" And there is. Worry not, this shall be covered in the next section.

---

■ ! Take a look at the `03-chapter-06-solution` project. It has been set up to work with the chained resolver configuration mentioned in this chapter. The data can be viewed in a web page, an Excel document or a PDF. Run it and take a look at the implementation before moving on to the next section.

---

## Content Type Negotiation

Another way of organizing the view resolver beans and making sure that the view name is always resolved correctly is to use content-type negotiation. The previous approach, resolver chaining, works only when each resource is associated with one view type. But clients might request different content-types for the same resource via extension, request header, request parameter, and so forth. In this case, chaining won't work, as the type of view returned depends on some parameters that have to be taken into consideration and then a matching view resolver must be selected to do the job. The bean that does that is the ContentNegotiatingViewResolver, which was introduced in Spring 3.0. This bean does not resolve views but delegates the job to the view resolver implementations defined in the application configuration, selecting the view matching the content-type in the client request.

There are two strategies for a client to request a view from the server:

- Use a distinct URL for each resource by using a different extension in the URL (example: http://localhost:8080/persons/list.xls requests an Excel view containing a list of persons, while http://localhost:8080/persons/list.pdf requests a PDF view containing a list of persons)

- Use the same URL but set the Accept HTTP request header to the desired resource type (example: a request coming from http://localhost:8080/persons/list having the Accept header set to application/pdf requests a PDF view containing a list of persons)

---

■ ! The problem with the Accept header is that it cannot be used when the client is a browser, as most browsers force its value to text/html. Because of this, web applications are always built to use the first approach and each view type is mapped to its own URL (taking the extension into consideration; for example: /persons/list.html, /persons/list.xls). The Accept header approach is most useful for REST web services and similar automation scenarios.

---

The ContentNegotiatingViewResolver implements the Ordered interface, so it can be used alongside other resolvers, it can be part of a view resolver chain, and it has to have the highest priority in the chain. This is due to its behavior; if theContentNegotiatingViewResolver cannot select a View, it returns null, and Spring examines the application context for other view resolver beans and inspects each of them until a view is obtained. Usually the ContentNegotiatingViewResolver is configured to pick up view resolvers automatically from the application context, so it should always resolve to a View. The next resolvers in the chain can be considered a fallback solution, to make sure that a View is provided.

The ContentNegotiatingViewResolver can be configured in a similar way, as shown in the following example:

```
<bean class="o.s.web.servlet.view.ContentNegotiatingViewResolver"
  p:order="-1">
    <property name="mediaTypes">
        <map>
            <entry key="html" value="text/html"/>
            <entry key="xls" value="application/vnd.ms-excel"/>
            <entry key="pdf" value="application/pdf"/>
            <entry key="json" value="application/json"/>
        </map>
    </property>
```

```
    <property name="viewResolvers">
        <list>
            <bean class="o.s.web.servlet.view.BeanNameViewResolver"/>
            <bean class="o.sweb.servlet.view.tiles3.TilesViewResolver" />
            <bean class="com.book.resolver.JsonViewResolver"/>
        </list>
    </property>
    <property name="defaultViews">
        <list>
            <bean class="o.s.web.servlet.view.json.MappingJackson2JsonView" />
        </list>
    </property>
    <property name="defaultContentType" value="text/html"/>
     <property name="ignoreAcceptHeader" value="true"/>
      <property name="favorParameter" value="false"/>
    <property name="favorPathExtension" value="true"/>
</bean>

<!-- Fallback Resolver: If no extension matched, use JSP view -->
<!-- Resolves view names to protected .jsp resources within the
        /WEB-INF directory -->
<bean class="o.s.web.servlet.view.InternalResourceViewResolver"
    p:prefix="/WEB-INF/"
    p:suffix=".jsp"
    p:order="0"/>
```

Here is the meaning of each property used in the previous configuration:

- mediaTypes: Map containing extension to content-type correspondences. This property is not mandatory and it does not have to be set in the application when the JavaBeans Activation Framework is used, in which case the types are determined automatically.[10]

- viewResolvers: The list of view resolvers to delegate to. This property is not mandatory and when it is not set, all view resolver beans in the context are detected and used, but they have to be ordered.

- defaultViews: The default view to use when a more specific view could not be obtained.

  The property is not mandatory.

- defaultContentType: The type to render in case a match was not found. The property is not mandatory.

- ignoreAcceptHeader: Indicates that the HTTP Accept header should be ignored if true, and taken into consideration if false. The property is not mandatory, and if not set, it defaults to false.

---

[10]By default, strategies for checking the extension of the request path and the Accept header are registered. The path extension check performs lookups through the ServletContext and the JavaBeans Activation Framework (if present) unless media types are configured. In order to use the JavaBeans Activation Framework, the activation.jar has to be in the classpath of the application.

- favorParameter: Indicates if a request parameter named format should be used to determine the requested content-type. The property is not mandatory, and if not set, it defaults to false.

- favorPathExtension: Indicates if the extension of the request URL should be used to determine the requested content-type. The property is not mandatory, and if not set, it defaults to true.

Starting with Spring 3.2, ContentNegotiationManagerFactoryBean and ContentNegotiationManager were introduced in order to encapsulate all content-type related configurations for the ContentNegotiatingViewResolver.

ContentNegotiationManagerFactoryBean provides access to a ContentNegotiationManager configured with one or more ContentNegotiationStrategy. An equivalent configuration to the preceding, after Spring 3.2, looks like this:

```xml
<bean class="o.s.web.servlet.view.ContentNegotiatingViewResolver">
    <property name="viewResolvers">
        <list>
            <bean class="o.s.web.servlet.view.BeanNameViewResolver"/>
            <bean class="o.sweb.servlet.view.tiles3.TilesViewResolver"/>
            <bean class="com.book.resolver.JsonViewResolver"/>
        </list>
    </property>
    <property name="defaultViews">
        <list>
            <bean class="o.s.web.servlet.view.json.MappingJackson2JsonView" />
        </list>
    </property>
<!-- All content-type related configuration is now done by this bean
        since Spring 3.2 -->
    <property name="contentNegotiationManager">
        <bean class="o.s.web.accept.ContentNegotiationManagerFactoryBean>
            <property name="mediaTypes">
                <map>
                    <entry key="html" value="text/html"/>
                    <entry key="json" value="application/json"/>
                    <entry key="pdf" value="application/pdf"/>
                    <entry key="xls" value="application/vnd.ms-excel"/>
                </map>
            </property>
            <property name="defaultContentType" value="text/html"/>
            <property name="ignoreAcceptHeader" value="true"/>
            <property name="favorParameter" value="false"/>
            <property name="favorPathExtension" value="true"/>
        </bean>
</property>
```

■ !   The problem with using JavaBeans Activation Framework is that if the extension is not recognized, it sets the content-type to `application/octet-stream` by default. This means that the `Views` configured with the `defaultViews` property are not taken into consideration and the `ContentNegotiatingViewResolver` will return null. That's why in Spring 3.2, the `useJaf` property was introduced; it can be set to `false` to disable the JavaBeans Activation Framework. This property has been added to `ContentNegotiationManagerFactoryBean` too.

Considering the previous configuration, the following code displays how a view is resolved using content negotiation type:

```
// In PersonsController.java
@RequestMapping("/persons")
public String list(Model model) {
        model.addAttribute(personManager.getAllPersons());
        return "persons/list";
}
<!-- In mvc-config-->
<bean class="com.book.persons.PersonsExcelView"/>
```

As you can see, there is no need for the bean name to be `persons/list.xls`, because the `ContentNegotiatingViewResolver` does the match without it.

■ !   In the following XML configuration, the `util` namespace is introduced to simplify the configuration. The `util` namespaces allows you to define and use collections in the same way that beans are defined and used in a configuration file.

This configuration can be simplified by using the p and `util` namespaces, which allow the `ContentNegotiatingViewResolver` XML bean definition to be simplified, as follows:

```
<beans xmlns="http://www.springframework.org/schema/beans"
       xmlns:xsi="http://www.w3.org/2001/XMLSchema-instance"
       xmlns:context="http://www.springframework.org/schema/context"
       xmlns:mvc="http://www.springframework.org/schema/mvc"
       xmlns:p="http://www.springframework.org/schema/p"
       xmlns:util="http://www.springframework.org/schema/util"
       xsi:schemaLocation="http://www.springframework.org/schema/mvc
          http://www.springframework.org/schema/mvc/spring-mvc.xsd
          http://www.springframework.org/schema/beans
          http://www.springframework.org/schema/beans/spring-beans.xsd
          http://www.springframework.org/schema/context
          http://www.springframework.org/schema/context/spring-context.xsd
          http://www.springframework.org/schema/util
          http://www.springframework.org/schema/util/spring-util.xsd">
...
```

```
<!-- sample usage of the util namespace to declare a map -->
    <util:map id="mediaTypesMap">
        <entry key="html" value="text/html"/>
        <entry key="xls" value="application/vnd.ms-excel"/>
        <entry key="pdf" value="application/pdf"/>
        <entry key="json" value="application/json"/>
    </util:map>

 <!-- sample usage of the util namespace to declare a list -->
    <util:list id="defaultViewsList">
        <!-- Excel view-->
        <bean class="com.pr.views.PersonsExcelView"/>
        <!-- JSON View -->
        <bean class="o.s.web.servlet.view.json.MappingJackson2JsonView"/>
    </util:list>

    <util:list id="resolverList">
        <bean class="com.pr.resolver.JsonViewResolver"/>
        <bean class="o.s.web.servlet.view.BeanNameViewResolver"/>
        <!-- Resolves logical view names to Tiles 3 definitions -->
        <bean id="tilesViewResolver"
            class="o.s.web.servlet.view.tiles3.TilesViewResolver"
            p:requestContextAttribute="requestContext"/>
    </util:list>
    <bean class="o.s.web.servlet.view.ContentNegotiatingViewResolver"
        p:order="-1"
        p:defaultViews-ref="defaultViewsList"
        p:viewResolvers-ref="resolverList">

        <property name="contentNegotiationManager">
            <bean class="o.s.web.accept.ContentNegotiationManagerFactoryBean"
                p:defaultContentType="text/html"
                p:ignoreAcceptHeader="true"
                p:favorParameter="false"
                p:favorPathExtension="true"
                p:mediaTypes-ref="mediaTypesMap"/>
        </property>
    </bean>

<beans>
```

Of course, this means taking out the defaultViewsList and the mediaTypesMap outside the declaration of the ContentNegotiatingViewResolver, which is the only place that they are needed. In this configuration, they can be used by other beans, although this is rarely needed. The choice belongs to the developer, depending on what configuration approach he is most comfortable with.

---

■ !   When the p namespace is used, the p:[property-name]-ref means this property is a reference to an existing bean in the context, with the id specified as the value.

---

That's mostly it when it comes to content-type negotiation. What is left to add is some sample code for the Java configuration:

```
@Configuration
@EnableWebMvc
public class WebConfig extends WebMvcConfigurerAdapter {
// Configures the contentNegotiationManager bean
@Override
public void configureContentNegotiation(ContentNegotiationConfigurer configurer) {
            configurer
                .ignoreAcceptHeader(true)
                .defaultContentType(MediaType.TEXT_HTML)
                .favorParameter(false)
                .favorPathExtension(true);
}

//Configure ContentNegotiatingViewResolver
@Bean
public ViewResolver contentNegotiatingViewResolver
                (ContentNegotiationManager manager) {
  ContentNegotiatingViewResolver resolver = new ContentNegotiatingViewResolver();
  resolver.setContentNegotiationManager(manager);

  // Define all possible view resolvers
  List<ViewResolver> resolvers = new ArrayList<>();
        resolvers.add(beanNameViewResolver());
        resolvers.add(tilesViewResolver());
        resolvers.add(jsonViewResolver());
        resolver.setViewResolvers(resolvers);

        List<View> defaultViewList = new ArrayList<>();
        defaultViewList.add(jsonView);
        resolver.setDefaultViews(defaultViewList);

        resolver.setOrder(0);
        return resolver;
}
@Bean
public ViewResolver jsonViewResolver() {
    return new JsonViewResolver();
}

@Bean
public MappingJackson2JsonView jsonView(){
    return new MappingJackson2JsonView();
}
```

```
@Bean
InternalResourceViewResolver getViewResolver(){
    InternalResourceViewResolver resolver = new InternalResourceViewResolver();
    resolver.setPrefix("/WEB-INF/");
    resolver.setSuffix(".jsp" );
    resolver.setOrder(1);
    return resolver;
}

 // other bean definitions ...
}
```

In the Java-annotated configuration there is no need to create a ContentNegotiationManager using the ContentNegotiationManagerFactoryBean. Spring does it automatically if you provide a configuration for it by overriding the implementation for the configureContentNegotiation method.

## JSON View Resolver

In this section, in the code samples, the MappingJackson2JsonView is an example of a default View. This is a Spring MVC View implementation that renders JSON content by serializing the model for the current request using the Jackson 2.x ObjectMapper. By default, everything serializable (classes that implement the Serializable interface) in a model map is being serialized, except for framework-specific classes and classes or fields annotated with @JsonIgnore. The configuration for the view is provided by Jackson2ObjectMapperBuilder.

The only tiny issue is that there is no view resolver provided by Spring, which could resolve this type of view. So a developer has to create one; but worry not— it's quite easy:

```
@Component
public class JsonViewResolver implements ViewResolver {

    @Override
    public View resolveViewName(String viewName, Locale locale) throws Exception {
        MappingJackson2JsonView view = new MappingJackson2JsonView();
        //make JSON output readable using proper indentation
        view.setPrettyPrint(true);
        return view;
    }
}
```

When using Java configuration classes, all that is needed is a @Bean annotated method:

```
@Bean
public ViewResolver jsonViewResolver() {
    MappingJackson2JsonView view = new MappingJackson2JsonView();
    view.setPrettyPrint(true);
    return view;
}
```

The Jackson library provides a set of annotations designed to be used when implementing classes subjected to JSON serialization to customize what is serialized and in which format. This way of working is similar to JPA and JAXB.

■ **!** The project 03-chapter-07-solution has a view resolver configuration that uses a ContentNegotiatingViewResolver. The data can be viewed in a web page, Excel document, PDF document, or JSON. Run it and take a look at the implementation before moving on to the next section.

## Personalization Beans

Most web applications are created to provide a certain service to users from different places in the world, so the application needs to adapt to the language used by those customers (a process called *internationalization*). Some web applications offer their users the ability to customize the application's interface based on a number of available themes. Spring offers the ability to easily customize the locale and look-and-feel of a web application via a couple of infrastructure beans.

## MessageSource

To support internationalization, a Spring application must have in its context a bean named messageSource. The class of this bean must implement the MessageSource interface and provides access to localized messages. This class provides concrete implementations for localization methods named getMessage(...). When an ApplicationContext is loaded, it automatically searches for this bean in the context and all calls to getMessage(...) methods are delegated to this bean.

Spring provides two out-of-the-box implementations for the MessageSource interface: ResourceBundleMessageSource and StaticMessageSource. The second one allows messages to be registered programmatically and it is intended to be used in testing. The first implementation relies on JDK's ResourceBundle implementation. Reloading a resource bundle during execution is not possible, as ResourceBundle caches loaded bundles files forever, so the implementation usually used in a web application is ReloadableResourceBundleMessageSource, which is a Spring-specific implementation that accesses bundles using specified base names, participating in the Spring ApplicationContext's resource loading. This class supports reloading properties files containing the internationalization information; it is usually slightly faster than ResourceBundleMessageSource. Another advantage is that it can read properties files with a specific character encoding.

In the following, you can see a simple XML configuration of this bean:

```
<bean id="messageSource"
    class="o.s.context.support.ReloadableResourceBundleMessageSource">
    <property name="basenames">
        <list>
            <value>/WEB-INF/messages/global<value/>
        </list>
    </property>
    <property name="cacheSeconds">1</property>
</bean>
```

When only one resource bundle and the p-namespace are used, the previous definition becomes this:

```
<bean id="messageSource"
    class="o.s.context.support.ReloadableResourceBundleMessageSource"
    p:basename="/WEB-INF/messages/global"
    p:cacheSeconds="1"/>
```

When Java-based configuration is used, the bean definition looks like this:

```
@Bean
public MessageSource getMessageSource(){
    ReloadableResourceBundleMessageSource messageSource =
        new ReloadableResourceBundleMessageSource();
    messageSource.setBasename("/WEB-INF/messages/global");
    messageSource.setCacheSeconds(1);
    return messageSource;
}
```

The cacheSeconds property is used to set the number of seconds to cache the loaded property files. Internationalization messages are loaded from properties files under /WEB-INF/messages/; they are named global_[locale].properties.

To use the messageSource bean to retrieve internationalized resources inside handler methods, simply inject the bean in the controller and call the desired getMessage(...) method. The Spring type library is used for this purpose too. The fmt tag library, which is a component of JSTL, can be used too. The syntax is a little different, as you can see in the following example:

```
<!-- JSTL fmt way -->
<fmt:message key="menu.home"/>
 <!-- Spring way -->
<spring:message code="menu.home"/>
```

When using the spring:message tag, the MessageSource classes can be integrated with the Spring context. The spring:message- tag works with the locale support that comes with Spring. If the "code" attribute isn't set or cannot be resolved, the "text" attribute is used as the default message. And spring:message supports dynamic names for internationalization codes, so a message code can be an expression:

```
<spring:message code="myPrefix.${account.state}"/>
```

ReloadableResourceBundleMessageSource is able to load messages from properties files with a specific encoding. In order for those messages to be successfully incorporated in a view, Spring provides a class called CharacterEncodingFilter, which is used to apply character encoding to requests. It can work in two modes to do the following:

- Enforce the encoding
- Apply the encoding if one is not already defined

This bean is added to the web.xml file like this:

```
<filter>
    <filter-name>characterEncodingFilter</filter-name>
    <filter-class>o.s.web.filter.CharacterEncodingFilter</filter-class>
    <init-param>
        <param-name>encoding</param-name>
        <param-value>UTF-8</param-value>
    </init-param>
```

```
    <init-param>
        <param-name>forceEncoding</param-name>
        <param-value>true</param-value>
    </init-param>
 </filter>
<filter-mapping>
    <filter-name>characterEncodingFilter</filter-name>
    <url-pattern>/*</url-pattern>
</filter-mapping>
```

Equivalent Java-based configuration looks like in the following code snippet:

```
\\in class implementing WebApplicationInitializer
 @Override
protected Filter getServletFilters() {
    CharacterEncodingFilter characterEncodingFilter = new CharacterEncodingFilter();
    characterEncodingFilter.setEncoding("UTF-8");
    characterEncodingFilter.setForceEncoding(true);
    return new Filter { characterEncodingFilter};
}
```

# LocaleResolver

In order for the messageBean to solve the messages, a locale must be defined for a web application. The value for the locale is taken from the browser. The bean resolving the locale must be named localeResolver and it must implement the LocaleResolver interface, because the DispatcherServlet looks for such a bean to use. A LocaleResolver can also store a different locale defined by the user. In Spring, there are three types of locale resolvers defined:

- AcceptHeaderLocaleResolver: Reads the locale from the request

- CookieLocaleResolver: Reads/writes the locale from/to a cookie named org. springframework.web.servlet.i18n.CookieLocaleResolver.LOCALE (unless named otherwise in the bean definition using property cookieName)

- SessionLocaleResolver: Reads/writes the locale from/to an HTTP session

---

■ !   The default name of the cookie can be confusing because it looks like a full name for a static variable, but no such variable exists. The same applies to the theme cookie mentioned in the next section.

---

When a specific LocaleResolver is not defined, AcceptHeaderLocaleResolver is used as default. When users select language, CookieLocaleResolver or SessionLocaleResolver can be used. CookieLocaleResolver is most often used in stateless applications without user sessions; this bean is defined in the mvc-config.xml file. The following definition is quite common:

```
<bean id="localeResolver" class="o.s.w.s.i18n.CookieLocaleResolver"
        p:defaultLocale="en"
        p:cookieMaxAge="3600"/>
```

The cookieMaxAge sets the maximum age in seconds for the cookie. If set to –1, the cookie is deleted only when the client shuts down.

In order for Spring to be notified of the changes in the locale, a bean of type LocaleChangeInterceptor needs to be configured. This ensures that the locale interceptor will be applied to all handler mappings.

```
<mvc:interceptors>
    <bean class="org.springframework.web.servlet.i18n.LocaleChangeInterceptor" />
    </mvc:interceptors>
```

An equivalent Java configuration for this bean can be used by providing an implementation for the addInterceptors method when implementing WebMvcConfigurer or overriding the same method when extending WebMvcConfigurerAdapter:

```
\\in the @Configuration and @EnableWebMvc annotated class
    @Override
    public void addInterceptors(InterceptorRegistry registry) {
        registry.addInterceptor(localeChangeInterceptor());
        \\other interceptors can be added here
    }

  @Bean
public LocaleChangeInterceptor localeChangeInterceptor(){
    return new LocaleChangeInterceptor();
}
```

This interceptor detects requests to change the locale by looking for a request parameter named locale by default. The LocaleResolver bean is used to store the value of this parameter. A different name can be set by using a different value for the parameterName property. Request URLs to change the locale are expected to contain the parameter name and a value in the URL: http://myapp.com/?[parameterName]=[locale_name] (under /WEB-INF/messages/ a [filename]_[locale_name].properties files is defined).

## ThemeResolver

If the web application has a customizable look and feel, the different themes can be managed using a bean named themeResolver. The bean resolving the theme has to implement the ThemeResolver interface, because the DispatcherServlet looks for such a bean to identify the resources needed for creating a response.

To use a ThemeResolver, you have to do the following:

1.  Create a [theme].properties file on the classpath (under /WEB-INF/classes/). The "theme" term can be replaced with any word describing that theme. In it, add the properties specific to that theme. In the code samples attached to this chapter, you have a file named blue.properties that contains the following theme properties:

    ```
    style.css=/styles/decorator-blue.css
    banner.image=/images/banner-blue.png
    ```

2. Use the Spring theme tag to resolve theme properties.

```
<%@ taglib prefix="spring" uri="http://www.springframework.org/tags" %>
...
<spring:theme var="styleCss" code="style.css"/>
<c:url var="styleCssUrl" value="${styleCss}"/>
<link type="text/css" type="stylesheet" href="${styleCssUrl}" />
```

To access the current theme in a view, you can use the RequestContext; but first you need to expose a requestContext attribute:

```
<bean class="org.s.web.servlet.view.InternalResourceViewResolver">
    <property name="requestContextAttribute" value="requestContext"/>
</bean>

<c:if test="${requestContext.theme.name eq 'blue'}">
...
```

In Spring there are three types of theme resolvers defined:

- FixedThemeResolver: The default implementation uses a configured default theme

- CookieThemeResolver: Reads/writes the theme attribute from/to a cookie named org.springframework.web.servlet.theme.cookieThemeResolver.THEME (unless named otherwise in the bean definition using property cookieName)

- SessionThemeResolver: Reads/writes the theme attribute from/to a HTTP session

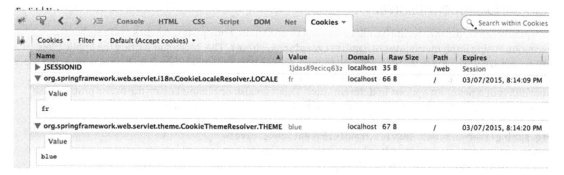

*Figure 3-8.* *List of cookies for the Personal Records Manager application*

You can view the two cookies using the Firebug extension for Firefox by opening the console and looking in the Cookies tab. You should see a cookie listing similar to the one shown in Figure 3-8.

For Spring to be notified of the changes in the theme, a bean of type ThemeChangeInterceptor needs to be configured. This ensures that the theme interceptor is applied to all handler mappings:

```
<mvc:interceptors>
    <bean class="org.springframework.web.servlet.theme.ThemeChangeIntcrceptor" />
</mvc:interceptors>
```

An equivalent Java configuration for this bean can be used by providing an implementation for the addInterceptors method when implementing WebMvcConfigurer or overriding the same method when extending WebMvcConfigurerAdapter:

```
\\in the @Configuration and @EnableWebMvc annotated class
    @Override
    public void addInterceptors(InterceptorRegistry registry) {
        registry.addInterceptor(themeChangeInterceptor());
        \\other interceptors can be added here
    }

    @Bean
public ThemeChangeInterceptor themeChangeInterceptor(){
    return new ThemeChangeInterceptor();
}
```

This interceptor detects requests to change the theme by looking for a request parameter named theme by default. The ThemeResolver bean is used to store the value of this parameter. A different name for it can be set by using a different value for the parameterName property. Request URLs to change the theme are expected to contain the parameter name and a value defined in the application: http://[parameterName]?theme=[theme_name] (under /WEB-INF/classes/ a [theme_name].properties files is defined).

## HandlerExceptionResolver

Exceptions can be thrown during handler mapping or execution. Spring MVC catches and handles the exceptions using implementations of HandlerExceptionResolver. The developer writing the application can customize the beans provided by Spring or provide his own implementation. The typical way to treat an MVC exception is to prepare a model and select an error view. Multiple exception resolvers can be used to treat different types of exceptions in different ways. They can also be chained using the order property like any other infrastructure bean. Spring MVC supports the following default resolvers:

```
org.springframework.web.servlet.HandlerExceptionResolver=
o.s.w.s.m.a.AnnotationMethodHandlerExceptionResolver,\
o.s.w.s.m.a.ResponseStatusExceptionResolver,\
o.s.w.s.m.s.DefaultHandlerExceptionResolver
```

An exception resolver provides information related to the context in which the exception was thrown, which handler method was executing, and which arguments it was called with.

Spring MVC also provides some implementation of its own, which you can configure and use instead of writing a full implementation. The preferred ways to handle exceptions are by using the SimpleMappingExceptionResolver bean and annotating methods with @ExceptionHandler. SimpleMappingExceptionResolver can be used to map exception classes to different views. The SimpleMappingExceptionResolver provides the following options:

- Maps exception classes to view names

- Specifies a default error page for any exception that is not handled

- Logs a message if configured to do so by setting a logger name for the warnLogCategory property

- Sets the name of the exception attribute to add to the model so it can be used inside a view

The following is an example on how to configure a SimpleMappingExceptionResolver bean to map exception types to error views, depending on the class name:

```
<bean class="o.s.web.servlet.handler.SimpleMappingExceptionResolver">
    <property name="exceptionMappings">
        <map>
            <!-- No need for package name, any package name will match. If you have
            two exceptions with the same name in different packages, you need to use
            the full class name to implement the proper behaviour -->
            <entry key="DataAccessException" value="databaseError"/>
            <entry key="InvalidPncException" value="pncError"/>
            <!-- The databaseError and pncError are logical view names -->
        </map>
    </property>
    <property name="defaultStatusCode" value="500"/>
    <property name="defaultErrorView" value="error"/>
</bean>
```

An equivalent Java configuration can be obtained by defining the bean programmatically:

```
\\in the @Configuration and @EnableWebMvc annotated class
@Bean(name="simpleMappingExceptionResolver")
    public SimpleMappingExceptionResolver createSimpleMappingExceptionResolver() {
        SimpleMappingExceptionResolver resolver =
                new SimpleMappingExceptionResolver();

        Properties mappings = new Properties();
        mappings.setProperty("DatabaseException", "databaseError");
        mappings.setProperty("InvalidPncException", "pncError");

        resolver.setExceptionMappings(mappings); // None by default
        resolver.setDefaultStatusCode(HttpStatus.INTERNAL_SERVER_ERROR.value());
        resolver.setDefaultErrorView("error");
        return resolver;
    }
```

■ !   Views returned from @ExceptionHandler methods do not have access to the exception, but views defined to SimpleMappingExceptionResolver do. This means that when using SimpleMappingExceptionResolver, the @ExceptionHandler methods must construct and return a ModelAndView instance. (See example in the 02-pr-mvc-basic-solution module.) In order to return a logical view name from a method annotated with @ExceptionHandler, ExceptionHandlerExceptionResolver must be extended.

To provide a custom implementation, the SimpleMappingExceptionResolver can be extended; its methods can be overridden to provide the desired functionality.

Methods annotated with @ExceptionHandler can be used to handle exceptions inside a single controller or they may apply to many when defined inside a class annotated with @ControllerAdvice.

Annotated exception handler methods are automatically called when controller methods throw an exception, and the method does not treat it itself. Method signatures are as flexible for an exception handler method as the controller handler methods (this is discussed in the "Controllers" section). Next you see an exception handler method used to handle database exceptions for the PersonsController class:

```
@Controller
public class PersonsController {
...
    @ExceptionHandler
    public String handleException(DataAccessException ex) {
        return "databaseError";
    }
}
```

The @ExceptionHandler can be set to treat a specific type of exception, using the annotation parameter, thus rendering the exception argument of the method unnecessary.

```
@Controller
public class PersonsController {
...
    @ExceptionHandler(DataAccessException.class)
    public String handleException() {
        return "databaseError";
    }
}
```

But using a parameter gives access to the exception, which can be treated or logged. Of course, the two approaches can be mixed.

The @ExceptionHandler can be set to treat an array of exceptions. If an exception is thrown that matches one of the types in the list, then the method annotated with the matching @ExceptionHandler is invoked. The same can be done by setting the array as an argument for the annotated method. By using different @ExceptionHandler annotated methods for each type of exception, the code can become crowded. So exceptions can be grouped by different criteria; for example, an @ExceptionHandler method can handle a group of database access exceptions, another can treat security exceptions, and so on. The chosen approach depends on the exception handling specifications of a project and developer preference.

Spring MVC internal exceptions raised while processing a request are translated by a class named DefaultHandlerExceptionResolver to specific error codes: a client error (4xx) or a server error (5xx), which is set on the response. This class is registered by default with the MVC namespace and @EnableWebMVC.

But when writing your own exceptions, you can set the status code on the exception class, like this:

```
@ResponseStatus(value= HttpStatus.NOT_FOUND, reason="Requested item not found")
public class NotFoundException extends Exception {
...
}
```

A class annotated with @ControllerAdvice allows you to use the same exception handling techniques across the whole application, not just a single controller. Three types of methods are supported inside a class annotated with @ControllerAdvice:

- Methods annotated with @ExceptionHandler that are used to handle exceptions

- Methods annotated with @ModelAttribute that are used to add data to the model

- Methods annotated with @InitBinder that are used for configuring form-handling

A controller advice class used only for exception handling could look like in the following example, which depicts a global default exception handler:

```
@ControllerAdvice
public class GlobalExceptionHandler {

    @ExceptionHandler(value = Exception.class)
    public ModelAndView defaultErrorHandler(HttpServletRequest req, Exception e)
                                    throws Exception {
        if (AnnotationUtils.findAnnotation(e.getClass(),
                                    ResponseStatus.class) != null){
            // we test to see if the exception is annotated with @ResponseStatus
            // if it is, we will re-throw it and let Spring handle it.
            throw e;
        }

        ModelAndView mav = new ModelAndView();
        //set exception details to be displayed in the page
        mav.addObject("exception", e);
        //set request URL to be displayed in the page, so the request causing
        //the problem can be identified
        mav.addObject("url", req.getRequestURL());
        mav.setViewName("error");
        return mav;
    }
}
```

■ **!** Notice in the previous example that the exception handler method returns a `ModelAndView` instance that is created inside the method body. The reason for this is that the methods in classes annotated with `@ControllerAdvice` are methods that apply to a group of controllers in the application. This can be customized via `annotations()`, `basePackageClasses()`, and `basePackages()` methods. But the methods are not part of the controller, so a model cannot be automatically injected by Spring. Also, a global exception handler like this one uses the same view to display all exception-specific messages in the application, so the view must be linked to the model, which in this case can only be done by creating a `ModelAndView` instance that is handled appropriately by the `DispatcherServlet`.

If you want to analyze the full capabilities of treating exceptions with Spring MVC, you can take a look at tutorials posted on their official site.[11] For passing the certification exam, all that was presented here should suffice.

## User-Provided Components

Although Spring MVC offers a lot of ready-to-use components for creating web applications (all that is required are small customizations), there are components that need to be implemented by the developer. Such components are controllers and interceptors. Controllers include and are the focus object of everything that has been presented so far. Controllers are the handlers identified by handler mappings; their methods handle application requests and return views. They can use message source to populate models with internationalized data and can contain methods for exception handling. If until now it was hard to connect all the infrastructure beans and picture what exactly they did, this mystery will be solved in the "Controllers" section, which puts every LEGO piece in its proper place. The handler interceptors are not really a big thing compared to it, but they are useful too.

## Controllers

Controllers are POJOs—simple beans annotated with the `@Controller` annotation—that are used to handle requests. Each controller class contains methods that are mapped to a request URL via the `@RequestMapping` annotation. These methods are used to handle different requests. Each method executes three steps:

1. Invoke services.

2. Populate a model.

3. Select a view.

---

[11]A detailed explanation of exception handling using Spring MVC is at `https://spring.io/blog/2013/11/01/exception-handling-in-spring-mvc`.

Here is a simple controller example. Notice the syntax for @RequestMapping annotation.

```
@Controller
@RequestMapping("/persons")
public class PersonsController {

    private PersonManager personManager;

    @Autowired
    public PersonsController(PersonManager personManager) {
        this.personManager = personManager;
    }

    // Handles requests to list all persons.
    @RequestMapping(value="/", method = RequestMethod.GET)
    public String list(Model model) {
        model.addAttribute("persons", personManager.findAll());
        return "persons/list";
    }

     //Handles requests to shows detail about one person.
    @RequestMapping(value="/{id}", method = RequestMethod.GET)
    public String show(@PathVariable Long id, Model model) {
        model.addAttribute("person", personManager.findOne(id));
        return "persons/show";
    }
}
```

When @RequestMapping is used to annotate a controller class, the path that the controller is mapped to is a part of the request's URL. The previous methods handle requests looking like this:

```
# handled by the list menthod
http://localhost:8080/persons/

# handled by the show menthod
http://localhost:8080/persons/144
```

All handling methods are relative to the path set by the @RequestMapping at class level. This means that the class mapping is solved first, and then the request mapping.

---

■ ! A controller can have methods that are not annotated with @RequestMapping. These methods are not used to solve requests. They are practically ignored, processing a user request.

---

The methods of a controller can be mapped using @RequestMapping with the following URI templates:

- By URL only:

```
@RequestMapping("persons/list")
public String list(Model model) {
...
}
```

- By URL and request method:

```
@RequestMapping("persons/list", method = RequestMethod.GET)
public String list(Model model) {
...
}
```

- By URL with request parameters:

```
@RequestMapping(value="/persons/show", params={"id"})
public String show(@RequestParam("id") Long id, Model model) {
...
}
```

- By URL with a parameter and a specific value for it:

```
@RequestMapping(value="/persons/show", params={"id=1123"})
public String show(@RequestParam("id") Long id, Model model) {
...
}
```

- By URL with a path variable:

```
@RequestMapping(value="/persons/{id}")
public String show(@PathVariable("id") Long id, Model model) {
...
}
```

- By URL with a path variable and a regular expression that the value must match:

```
@RequestMapping(value = "/{id:[\\d]*}")
//the regular expression [\\d]* insures the id to be numeric,
//made of one or more digits.
public String show(@PathVariable("id") Long id, Model model) {
...
}
```

The preceding are simple examples of URIs onto which controllers methods are mapped. The options do not stop here and any of these can be mixed, depending on the developer's needs. For example, you can do something like this in web applications:

```
@RequestMapping(value="/persons/{id}/?dateOfBirth=1983-08-18")
public String show(@RequestParam("dateOfBirth") Date date,
    @PathVariable Long id, Model model) {
...
}
```

The controller methods can have very flexible signatures. The following can be used as arguments in any combination or order:

- Model

- HttpServletRequest

- HttpServletResponse

- HttpSession

- Locale

- Principal

In the body of a controller method, path variables and request parameters must be accessed to process the request. If the URI template is a RESTful URI,[12] then the variable is part of the URI, called a *path variable*, and can be accessed using @PathVariable:

```
@RequestMapping(value="/persons/{id}")
public String show(@PathVariable("id") Long identifier, Model model) {
...
}
```

---

■ **CC**    When the method argument has the same name with the path variable, the value for the @ PathVariable annotation is no longer required.

---

So the preceding method becomes:

```
@RequestMapping(value="/persons/{id}")
public String show(@PathVariable Long id, Model model) {
...
}
```

---

[12]A RESTful URI identifies a domain resource (like a book, or a person, in this case) rather than an application resource like a web page or a form. URI is the acronym for Uniform Resource Identifier. URL is the acronym for Uniform Resource Locator. REST services work only with URIs and @PathVariable.

And handles requests similar to: `http://localhost:8080/persons/144`.

There is a special case when the @PathVariable is not even needed and the default is the argument name; this happens when the application is compiled with debug symbols enabled. It is rarely used because the result is an unoptimized/debuggable byte code. This is mentioned here because the official course mentions it too, and it might be useful to know that this possibility exists in case you ever need it.

When the URI is non-RESTful, the variable is provided as a parameter in the request URL. The request parameter can be accessed using the @RequestParam annotation.

```
@RequestMapping(value="/persons/show", params={"id"})
public String show(@RequestParam("id") Long identifier, Model model) {
...
}
```

Type conversion is applied, and if the parameter value is missing or has the wrong type, an exception is thrown.

---

■ **CC** When the method argument has the same name with the request parameter, the value for the @RequestParam annotation is no longer required. The `params` property is no longer needed for the @RequestMapping either.

---

So the preceding method becomes this:

```
@RequestMapping(value="/persons/show")
public String show(@RequestParam Long id, Model model) {
...
}
```

The request parameter can be set as optional if it is not a primitive type; in this case, it defaults to null and must be handled in the method body.

```
@RequestMapping(value="/persons/show", params={"id"})
public String show(@RequestParam(value="id", required=false) Long identifier,
Model model) {
if(identifier == null) {
//return a specific view
}
...
}
```

The request parameter can also be set as optional when the request parameter is a primitive type and a fallback default value is provided.

```
@RequestMapping(value="/persons/show", params={"id"})
public String show(@RequestParam(value="id", required=false,
                defaultValue = "2") long identifier, Model model) {
    if(identifier == null) {
        //return a specific view
    }

    ...

}
```

Request parameters can have any type, including Date and Number, and these types can be formatted by using the following annotations:

```
//matches http://localhost:8080/persons/1983-08-18
@RequestMapping(value="/persons/{birthDate}")
public String list(@PathVariable
        @DateTimeFormat(pattern = "yyyy-MM-dd") Date birthDate,
            Model model) {

...
}
```

```
//matches http://localhost:8080/accounts/?minAmount=$5000.50
@RequestMapping(value="/accounts" params={"minAmount"})
public String list(@RequestParam
        @NumberFormat(style = NumberFormat.Style.CURRENCY) Double minAmount,
            Model model) {

...
}
```

To generate a Spring-parametrized URI in a JSP file, a combination of <spring:url> tag and <spring:param/> is used:

```
<%@ taglib prefix="spring" uri="http://www.springframework.org/tags" %>
...
 <spring:url var="showUrl" value="{id}">
     <spring:param name="id" value="${person.id}"/>
</spring:url>
 <a href="${showUrl}">${person.id}</a>
```

The first three lines of the preceding example generate a URI similar to http://localhost:8080/person/123 by using the current context of the application and the person attribute in the model. The generated URI is stored as a value for the showUrl attribute in the model. In the next line, that attribute is used to populate the HTML link element.

After the execution of the code in a mapping method, the controller selects a view for the resulting data to be rendered in. The controller's responsibility includes populating a model map with the data to display in the view. There are multiple ways of specifying the resulting view too, but the default is for the mapping method to return a string, which is the **logical view name**. (By default, a path to a JSP file is expected, unless some view resolver is used, such as TilesResolver, for example). Also, the controller can directly write to the response stream and complete the request (when handling AJAX calls or REST services, cases that are presented in detail in the following chapters). The process to identify which view is being used is called **view resolution**, which is performed by one view resolver class or a chain of view resolver classes.

# Accessing Model Data

Accessing Model data instances is simple, especially when the model is used as an argument of the request method, and Spring takes care of injecting it:

```
@RequestMapping("/persons")
public String list(Model model) {
    model.addAttribute("persons", personManager.findAll());
     return "persons/list";
}
```

All model attributes are available in the JSP for rendering.

Attributes can be added to the model without specifying a name. There are convention-over-configuration rules applied by Spring to infer the name of an attribute based on the type of the attribute value set. For example:

- Person person = personManager.getById(id);

  ```
  model.addAttribute(person);
  //added as "person" as the reference type is Person
  ```

- List<Person> persons = personManager.findAll();

  ```
  model.addAttribute(persons);
  // added as "personList" as reference type is List<Person>
  ```

---

■ **CC**  When objects are added to a model without specifying an attribute name, this is inferred by lowercasing the first letter of the reference type. If the attribute is a collection of objects, the attribute name is composed from the reference type with first letter lowercased and suffixed with the specific collection suffix (a simple name of the Collection interface implemented): "Set" for Set<?>, "List" for List<?>, etc.

---

When only one object needs to be added to the model, the object can simply be returned by the method and it is automatically added to the model. This obviously does not work with objects of type String, because Spring assumes the returned String value is a logical view name. When the following approach is used, the returned object is added to the model as an attribute and the name is inferred based on the conventions mentioned earlier.

```
@RequestMapping("/persons/list")
public List<Person> list() {
      return personManager.findAll();
      //model name attribute convention will be used
}
```

But the attribute name can be specified by annotating the method with @ModelAttribute and specifying a different attribute name.

```
@RequestMapping("/persons/list")
@ModelAttribute("persons")
public List<Person> list() {
    return personManager.findAll();
}
```

■ **CC**   When the handler method returns an object, the `DispatcherServlet` has to infer the view to render the model. The logical view name is extracted from the mapping URL by stripping the first "/" and the extension if present. In the preceding examples, the logical view name used is `"persons/list"`.

## Selecting a View

A controller method selects a view by returning its name, and `DispatcherServlet` takes care of the rest using the ViewResolvers in the context. But there are conventions over configurations in place that allow a controller method to return null and a view is still selected, like the convention mentioned right before this section.

The logical view name can be extracted from the request URI by removing the leading slash and extension. This is done by the `RequestToViewNameTranslator`.

```
@RequestMapping("/persons/list.html")
public String list(Model model) {...}
// logical view name is: "persons/list"
```

■ **CC**   The same view name "persons/list" is inferred if you have a `@RequestMapping` `("/persons")` on the controller class and `@RequestMapping` `("/list.html")` on the method.

When `<mvc:annotation-driven/>` or `@EnableWebMVC` is used in the application configuration for simple views that do not require a model being populated with data can be defined without controllers. The following sample code shows how to configure such views using XML and Java configuration.

```
<!-- in mvc-config.xml -->
<mvc:view-controller path="/" view-name="welcome"/>

//in class annotated with @Configuration and @EnableWebMvc
// and implementing WebMvcConfigurer
@Override
public void addViewControllers(ViewControllerRegistry registry) {
    registry.addViewController("/").setViewName("welcome");
}
```

## Redirecting

Controller methods can also make redirect requests instead of selecting a view. This is done by returning a string representing a view name prefixed with `"redirect:"`. Redirecting implies a new HTTP request being created and usually some request attributes need to be passed from one request to the other. Until Spring 3.1, this was done using `@ModelAttribute` on a controller method, or `@SessionAtributes` on the controller class.

The `@ModelAttribute` makes sure that the annotated method is always invoked before a request handling method, thus adding the person instance to the model as an attribute with the name `"person"`:

```
@ModelAttribute
public Person getPerson(@PathVariable Long id) {
    return personManager.getPerson(id);
}
```

The object is not added to the HttpServletRequest to fulfill this purpose, but to the model; the reason for this is that Spring MVC wants to keep the view usage as generic as possible, which means not forcing the application to use only view technologies based on HttpServletRequest.

The @SessionAttributes is used on a controller class to designate which model attributes should be stored in the session.

```
@SessionAttributes("person")
@Controller
@RequestMapping("/persons")
public class PersonsController {

    @RequestMapping("/{id}", method = RequestMethod.GET)
    public Person show(@PathVariable Long id, Model model) {
        model.add("person", personManager.getPerson(id));
        return "persons/show";
    }
}
```

Starting with Spring 3.1, there is another way: using **flash attributes**, which are saved in an object model implementing the RedirectAttributes interface. Flash attributes provide a way for one request to store attributes intended for use in another. Flash attributes are supported by default; no extra configuration is needed. They are automatically added to the model after the redirect, but they must be added to the redirectAttributes object before the redirect call.

```
@Controller
@RequestMapping("/persons")
public class PersonsController {

    @RequestMapping(method = RequestMethod.POST)
     public String edit(@Valid Person person,
     final RedirectAttributes redirectAttributes,
     BindingResult result, Model model) {
         if (result.hasErrors()) {
             return "persons/edit";
         }
         personManager.update(person);
         redirectAttributes.addFlashAttribute("person", person);
         return "redirect:/persons/show";
         }
    }

    @RequestMapping("/show", method = RequestMethod.GET)
     public String show(@ModelAttribute("person") Person person) {
        // because the attribute is already in the model,
        //the only thing left to do is return the view name
           return "persons/show";
    }

}
```

The object added to the `redirectAttributes` model is added to the model at redirect time with the same attribute name. So if the parameter name is different in the method being called at redirect time, a value representing the attribute name for the `@ModelAttribute` has to be set. In the previous example, this was done anyway just to make it obvious, but because of the Spring convention over configuration is in place, the value for the verb|@ModelAttribute| can be skipped, as the name of the argument is considered.

---

■ ! A sample of what controller methods look like and a sample of "redirect:" usage are found in the `03-pr-mvc-layout-solution` module. The equivalent practice module is covered at the end of this chapter.

---

## Testing Controllers

When testing controllers, the focus is to check that handler methods return the expected logical view name and that the expected data has been placed in the model as an attribute. When doing unit testing, the manager does not need to be involved, as saving data to the database defeats the purpose of testing a small unit. So managers used in the controllers can be replaced with skeleton objects with simulated functionality. This can be done by creating skeleton objects, called *stubs*, or mocking libraries can be used, to pass to them the responsibility of implementing the objects according to the desired functionality. The library used to mock the managers used in the code samples for this book is called Mockito.[13] The tests have to be run with `MockitoJUnitRunner` for the mock objects to be treated accordingly.

Assuming you have a controller that looks like this...

```java
public class PersonsController {

    private PersonManager personManager;

    @Autowired
    public PersonsController(PersonManager personManager) {
        this.personManager = personManager;
    }

    @RequestMapping(value="/list", method = RequestMethod.GET)
    public String list(Model model) {
        model.addAttribute("persons", personManager.findAll());
        return "persons/list";
    }
}
```

A test method for the `list` handler method will look like this:

```java
@RunWith(MockitoJUnitRunner.class)
public class PersonsControllerTest {
    private PersonsController personsController;

    @Mock
    private PersonManager managerMock;
```

---

[13]More information about it is at `http://mockito.org`.

```
    @Before
    public void setUp(){
        personsController = new PersonsController(managerMock);
    }

    @Test
    public void list() {
    // setting up a mock manager that returns an empty list when
    // findAll() is called
        when(managerMock.findAll()).thenReturn(new ArrayList<>());

    //a model object is "manually" constructed to pass as argument
    // to the controller method
        Model model = new BindingAwareModelMap();
        String view = personsController.list(model);
        assertEquals("persons/list", view);

        //this tests if the handler method has added
        //the "persons" attribute to the provided model.
        assertNotNull(model.asMap().get("persons"));
    }
}
```

The @Mock annotation makes sure that the object is treated as a mock object by the library and a skeleton implementation is provided transparently. Statements beginning with calls to the when method define the behavior of the respective object when its mock methods are called. The syntax is quite intuitive and really easy to use. The statement underlined in the preceding code sample can be translated as: "When the findAll() method is called on the mock object, return an empty list of persons."

Integration testing of the controllers can be done by creating a test context for their execution, and it has the advantage of testing the integration of application layers with each other. The test class looks like this:

```
@RunWith(SpringJUnit4ClassRunner.class)
@WebAppConfiguration
@ContextConfiguration({
        "file:src/main/webapp/WEB-INF/spring/mvc-config.xml",
        "classpath:spring/app-dao-config.xml",
        "classpath:spring/test-db-config.xml"
    })
public class AllControllerTest {

    @Autowired
    private PersonsController personsController;

    @Before
    public void setUp(){
        //we are making sure the controller was initialized correctly
        assertNotNull(personsController);
    }
```

```
    @Test
    public void list() {
        Model model = new BindingAwareModelMap();
        String view = personsController.list(model);
        assertEquals("persons/list", view);
        assertNotNull(model.asMap().get("persons"));

        // test to see id the manager returned the expected result
        assertTrue(((List<Person>) model.asMap().get("persons")).size() == 16);
    }
}
```

The WebAppConfiguration annotation makes sure that the context in which the test methods in this class are run is WebApplicationContext. The root path of the web application is set using this annotation, and the default value for it is the one consecrated by Maven "src/main/webapp". There are other ways of initializing a test web context or even for mocking one using MockMvc, which is the main entry point for server-side Spring MVC test support. Other test libraries can be used to fully test a controller and all objects involved in handling a request. For example, Hamcrest, a testing library that offers a lot of useful methods named *matchers* test the type of expected params, attribute values, results, and so forth.[14]

```
@RunWith(SpringJUnit4ClassRunner.class)
@WebAppConfiguration
@ContextConfiguration({"file:src/main/webapp/WEB-INF/spring/mvc-config.xml",
        "classpath:spring/app-dao-config.xml", "classpath:spring/test-db-config.xml"})
public class HospitalsControllerTest {

    @Autowired
    private WebApplicationContext wac;

    private MockMvc mockMvc;

    @Before
    public void setUp() {
        assertNotNull(wac);
        this.mockMvc = MockMvcBuilders.webAppContextSetup(this.wac).build();
    }

    @Test
    // test all aspects handling a request to "/hospitals/
    public void list() throws Exception {
        mockMvc.perform(get("/hospitals/"))
                // test if response status is 200
                .andExpect(status().isOk())

                // test if the attribute "hospital" was added to the model
                .andExpect(model().attributeExists("hospitals"))
```

---

[14]Read more about it on the official site at http://hamcrest.org/.

```
                //when using Tiles, we can test the forward of the request to
                //the template for the page
                .andExpect(forwardedUrl("/WEB-INF/templates/layout.jsp"));
    }
    @Test
    //test a method returning "redirect:/persons/list"
    // (all persons born at the hospital with code =134181)
    public void listp() throws Exception {
        mockMvc.perform(get("/hospitals/134181"))
        // test if response status is 302
        .andExpect(status().isFound())

        //test if the "persons" attribute was added to the redirectAttributes model
        .andExpect(flash().attributeExists("persons"))

        // test if the redirect request is sent to the expected URL
        .andExpect(redirectedUrl("/persons/list"));
    }
}
```

These are the Spring MVC flavors presented in the book; choose whichever you feel most comfortable with.

# Handler Interceptors

Handler interceptors are very useful for adding common functionality for all controllers inside an application. For example, a handler interceptor in an application could be used to audit requests, or to monitor the execution time of handler methods, or to generate performance reports. The most obvious examples for the use of an interceptor are internationalization, validation of data in the request, and request data convertors. Security checks could also be executed by a handler interceptor to give or restrict access to a handler method.

When using REST, a special interceptor of type JsonViewResponseBodyAdvice can be used to customize the response before the JSON serialization with MappingJackson2HttpMessageConverter.

The handler interceptors are beans in the application context. A handler interceptor class must implement the HandlerInterceptor interface and provide concrete implementation for any of the methods that the user is interested in:

- preHandle: Called after the HandlerAdapter has identified the handler method and before its invocation. This method controls the execution of other interceptors in the chain and the handler method by returning a Boolean value.

- postHandle: Called after the HandlerAdapter invokes the handler method and before the DispatcherServlet renders the view (can add extra objects to the model).

- afterCompletion: Called after the request has processed and the view has rendered.

This method is called regardless of the outcome of the handler method call; it can be used for resources cleanup (behavior similar to a finalize method).

The interceptors that modify the response before serialization must implement ResponseBodyInterceptor and provide an implementation for the beforeBodyWrite method. (This is covered in more detail in Chapter 5.)

When personalizing the application with locale and theme, the LocaleChangeInterceptor and ThemeChangeInterceptor are configured like this:

```
<!-- XML -->
 <mvc:interceptors>
        <bean class="o.s.web.servlet.i18n.LocaleChangeInterceptor"/>
        <bean class="o.s.web.servlet.theme.ThemeChangeInterceptor"/>
 </mvc:interceptors>

//Java Configuration
//in the @Configuration and @EnableWebMvc annotated class
@Override
public void addInterceptors(InterceptorRegistry registry) {
    registry.addInterceptor(localeChangeInterceptor());
    registry.addInterceptor(themeChangeInterceptor());
}

@Bean
public LocaleChangeInterceptor localeChangeInterceptor(){
    return new LocaleChangeInterceptor();
}

@Bean
public ThemeChangeInterceptor themeChangeInterceptor(){
    return new ThemeChangeInterceptor();
}
```

Both interceptors use their preHandle method to set locale and theme values on the appropriate resolvers.[15]

Users can also create their own interceptors; in 02-pr-mvc-basic-solution the AuditInterceptor is given as an example.

```
@Component
public class AuditInterceptor extends HandlerInterceptorAdapter {
@Override
public boolean preHandle(HttpServletRequest request,
    HttpServletResponse response, Object handler)
throws Exception {
    // custom implementation here
      return true;
}
```

---

[15]You can take a look at these interceptors' code on GitHub at https://github.com/spring-projects/spring-framework/blob/master/spring-webmvc/src/main/java/org/springframework/web/servlet/theme/ThemeChangeInterceptor.java and https://github.com/spring-projects/spring-framework/blob/master/spring-webmvc/src/main/java/org/springframework/web/servlet/i18n/LocaleChangeInterceptor.java.

```
@Override
public void postHandle(HttpServletRequest request,
     HttpServletResponse response, Object handler, ModelAndView modelAndView)
         throws Exception {
     // custom implementation here
}

@Override
public void afterCompletion(HttpServletRequest request,
     HttpServletResponse response, Object handler, Exception ex)
        throws Exception {
     // custom implementation here
}
}
```

To enable this interceptor, you have to configure it in the context. The following snippets show how this can be done in XML and using Java configuration:

```
<!-- XML -->
<mvc:interceptors>
   <bean class="com.pr.interceptor.AuditInterceptor"/>
</mvc:interceptors>

//Java Configuration
//in the @Configuration and @EnableWebMvc annotated class
@Override
public void addInterceptors(InterceptorRegistry registry) {
    registry.addInterceptor(auditInterceptor());
}

@Bean
public AuditInterceptor auditInterceptor(){
    return new AuditInterceptor();
}
```

The schema in Figure 3-9 displays what happens "behind the scenes" when a handler interceptor is used in a Spring MVC application.

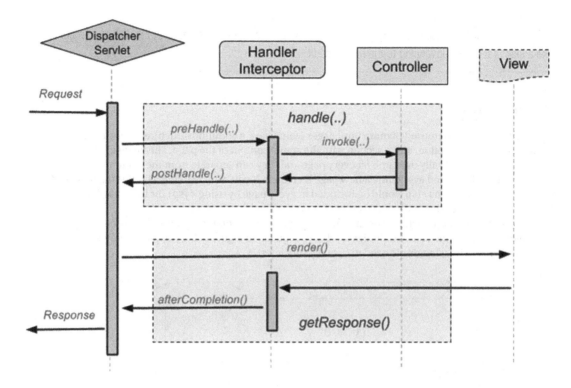

**Figure 3-9.** *Handler Interceptor methods and places where invoked*

# View Technologies

Again, Spring MVC was designed to be as *view agnostic* as possible. Most web applications generate HTML content. The "ViewResolver" section mentions how a Spring web application can generate other types of content, such as PDF, Excel, or JSON. The complete list of view technologies that Spring supports is far longer than this. To put it in perspective, anything that provides a ViewResolver and a View implementation is compatible with Spring.

Based on the type of content being generated, the views can be categorized as follows:

- **Display views**: The response is an HTML page generated using a template: JSP, Tiles, Thymeleaf, FreeMarker, or Velocity.

- **File-generating views**: The response is an output file when rendered and it is automatically downloaded by the browser: Apache POI, JExcelApi (Excel), IText (PDF), JasperReports, or XSLT transformation.

- **Data-delivery views**: The response is actually just data and it is meant to be used with AJAX and web services: JSON, Java-XML Marshalling, Atom, and RSS.

This book covers Tiles and Thymeleaf. Tiles is in the official certification course. Thymeleaf is a bonus section that was added because it is the newest template engine in the web development world (its "birth" year was 2014) and it is quite a promising technology. Its goal is to provide templates that are easy to use and extend. It works in web and non-web environments.

■ ! The book-code module 03-chapter-07-solution covers all three categories of the views mentioned. Take a look at it before advancing to the next section.

## Tiles Layouts

A web application of composed of more html pages which have a common structure, typically a header/ footer, a menu for navigation, and a section with the actual content of the page. The header, footer, and navigation menu are usually the same on every page and they can separate from the contents of a page in their own files to be reused every time a new page is created. If you were working with JSP, the files header. jsp, footer.jsp, and menu.jsp would be included in every page by using `<jsp:include page=..."/>`. This means three repetitive include statements in every page.

A more practical approach is to create a page template that contains common page elements and placeholders for dynamic content, similar to what is depicted in Figure 3-10. The placeholders are replaced at rendering time with whatever is needed (usually subviews).[16]

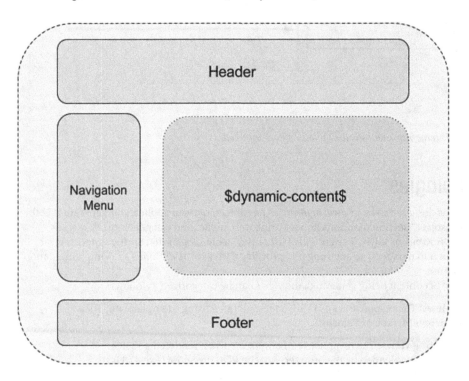

*Figure 3-10.* *Reusable page template*

---

[16]This approach is described by the Composite View pattern that introduces the notions of composite and atomic views. A **composite view** is a tree structure of atomic views. An **atomic view** can be included dynamically and it changes based on the context.

Doing this with only plain JSP is not an option. There are currently multiple ways available to do it. But the one that was interesting for the Spring creators is Apache Tiles.

Apache Tiles is an open source template engine framework that was a part of the currently deceased Apache Struts 1. It is based on the Composite View pattern and was built to simplify the development of user interfaces. To use tiles in a Spring web application, you have to do the following:

1. Define template layout for the pages.

2. Configure tiles definitions in `tiles.xml` file(s).

3. Configure the tiles resolver bean.

Apache Tiles 3.0.5, which is the version used for the code samples, is the most recent stable release at the time this book was written.

## Define Page Templates

A simple template layout, matching the page representation in Figure 3-10, is as simple as this:

```
...
<%@ taglib prefix="tiles" uri="http://tiles.apache.org/tags-tiles" %>
...
<!-- /WEB-INF/templates/layout.jsp -->
<head>
        <tiles:insertAttribute name="pageTitle"/>
</head>
<body>
        <div class="header">...</div>
        <div class="menu">...</div>
        <div class="content">
                <tiles:insertAttribute name="content"/>
        </div>
        <div class="footer">...</div>
</body>
```

## Configure Tiles Definitions

The `tiles.xml` files are Tiles configuration files, which define the structure of a page using XML. One or more tiles definitions can be in the same file; it is recommended to store the configuration file and the pages configured in the same directory, as shown in Figure 3-11.

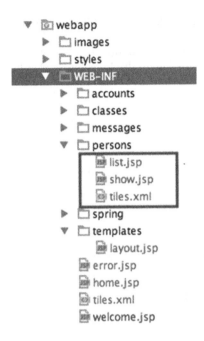

*Figure 3-11. Tiles configuration files and templates positioning in the application structure*

Tiles definitions are reusable fragments consisting of a template and attributes. Inheritance is possible using the extends attribute. A tile definition element looks like this:

```
<!DOCTYPE tiles-definitions PUBLIC
        "-//Apache Software Foundation//DTD Tiles Configuration 3.0//EN"
        "http://tiles.apache.org/dtds/tiles-config_3_0.dtd">

<tiles-definitions>
    <definition name="layout" template="/WEB-INF/templates/layout.jsp"/>
</tiles-definitions>
```

This example is called a *base tile* because every other definition extends it. Without this tile definition, every other tile definition in your project has to be configured with the template attribute, underlined in the preceding example.

The extended version of the layout.jsp is quite big, and some parts are replaced by "..". To view its real and full content, please see the 03-pr-mvc-layout-practice project.

```
...
<%@ taglib prefix="tiles" uri="http://tiles.apache.org/tags-tiles" %>
...
<!-- /WEB-INF/templates/layout.jsp -->
<head>
...
```

```
    <title>
        <spring:message>
            <tiles:insertAttribute name="pageTitle"/>
        </spring:message>
    </title>
</head>
...
<div class="page">

    <!-- The header is actually a png image banner,
        that will be loaded depending on the chosen theme-->
    <div class="banner"></div>

    <!-- section to select Locale and Theme -->
    <div class="themeLocal"> ...</div>

    <!-- section with the navigation menu, dynamic data
    The menu item is modified to display the current page
    based on the value for the menuTab attribute -->
    <div class="menu">
     <ul>
            <li><c:if test="${menuTab eq 'home'}">
                <strong>
                  <a href="<c:url value="/"/>"><spring:message code="menu.home"/></a>
                </strong>
             </c:if>
                <c:if test="${menuTab != 'home'}">
                    <a href="<c:url value="/"/>"><spring:message code="menu.home"/></a>
                </c:if>
            </li>
            ...
     </ul>
    </div>

    <!-- Dynamic data - body of the page -->
    <div class="content">
        <tiles:insertAttribute name="content"/>
    </div>

    <div class="footer">
        <p><spring:message code="footer.text"/></p>
    </div>
```

This is what a simple tile definition that extends the base tile looks like:

```
<definition name="home" extends="layout">
    <put-attribute name="pageTitle" value="home.title"/>
    <put-attribute name="content" value="/WEB-INF/home.jsp"/>
    <put-attribute name="menuTab" value="home" />
</definition>
```

The tiles attributes are the placeholders for dynamic data; the gaps in the template need to be filled. The following can be an attribute:

- A *string* that will be rendered or used as it is.

- A *template* with or without attributes that need to be filled to render the page.

- A *tile definition* with all (some) attributes filled.

---

■ **?**    In the code sample, can you identify which of these types of tiles attributes were used?

---

Accessing tiles attributes in JSP is done using the tag provided by tiles:

- `<tiles:insertAttribute/>`: The standard approach to insert the value of an attribute into a page[17]

- `<tiles:importAttribute/>`: This is used to add attributes to model (it works only with Spring)[18]

In the following example, the `menuTab` attribute is used for navigation in the application. Each tile definition sets a different value for that attribute. The value is tested and the menu navigation option matching the current page is displayed in bold text.

```
...
<tiles:importAttribute name="menuTab" />
<c:if test="${menuTab eq 'home'}">
   <!-- show the home menu option with bold text -->
</c:if>
```

## Configure the Tiles Resolver Bean

Spring MVC provides out-of-the-box support for Apache Tiles. There is a `TilesView` to interpret logical view names as tiles definitions. There is a `TilesViewResolver` bean to resolve views and a class named `TilesConfigurer` to bootstrap Tiles with a set of configuration files.

```
<!-- Resolves view names to Tiles 3 definitions -->
<bean id="tilesViewResolver"
      class="org.springframework.web.servlet.view.tiles3.TilesViewResolver"/>

<!-- Configures Tiles 3 -->
<bean id="tilesConfigurer"
      class="org.springframework.web.servlet.view.tiles3.TilesConfigurer">
        <property name="definitions">
```

---

[17]Detailed API information on `tiles:insertAttribute` is at https://tiles.apache.org/framework/tiles-jsp/tlddoc/tiles/insertAttribute.html.
[18]Detailed API information on `tiles:importAttribute` is at https://tiles.apache.org/framework/tiles-jsp/tlddoc/tiles/insertAttribute.html.

```
        <list>
            <value>/WEB-INF/tiles.xml</value>
            <!-- add more tiles definition files if present -->
        </list>
    </property>
</bean>
```

The equivalent Java configuration looks like this:

```
// In the @Configuration and @EnableMvc annotated class
@Bean
    TilesViewResolver tilesViewResolver(){
        return new TilesViewResolver();
    }

    @Bean
    TilesConfigurer tilesConfigurer(){
        TilesConfigurer tilesConfigurer = new TilesConfigurer();
        tilesConfigurer.setDefinitions("/WEB-INF/tiles.xml");
        // add more tiles definition files if present
        return tilesConfigurer;
    }
}
```

This code sample replaces the InternalResourceViewResolver with TilesViewResolver. The InternalResourceViewResolver can be configured for plain *.jsp files too, but do not forget to set the order property and/or configure a content negotiating resolver.

---

■ ! The module 03-pr-mvc-layout-practice of the Personal Records Manager project covers Tiles definitions and their usage with Spring MVC. Further details are presented in the practice section of this chapter, but you can take a look at the 03-pr-mvc-layout-solution if you cannot wait to see the Tiles in action.

---

# Thymeleaf

When asked why he decided to create another template engine, because there were already quite a few available, co-creator Daniel Fernandez said this on the Thymeleaf official forum:[19]

> In my humble opinion, Spring MVC 3 is a fantastic web framework tied to a horrible, extremely old and spaghetti-code-loving template engine: JSP. That's why I wanted the combination of Spring MVC with Thymeleaf to really shine. In some ways I suppose I wanted to give Spring MVC the template engine it deserved. Not from the performance point of view (matching the speed of JSPs, which run in specialized containers, would be very difficult), but more from the points of view of code elegance, readability, and design/coding separation of concerns. Also, I wanted to provide first-class support for the emerging HTML5 standard.

---

[19]A full discussion is at http://forum.thymeleaf.org/why-Thymeleaf-td3412902.html.

The underlined text in Fernandez's reply should interest any developer. **Thymeleaf is not a certification exam subject**, so it can be skipped. But Thymeleaf is nevertheless a practical alternative to JSP, and the SpringSource team fancies it quite a bit, so knowing how to configure it and use it could be useful in the future.

Both Spring and Tiles come with an attribute set that you can use to write your page templates. Thymeleaf is more flexible because it allows you to define a set of template attributes or even tags with the names that you want and with the logic that you want. So it is not just a template engine, it is a framework. Something called *standard dialects* are offered: **Standard** and **SpringStandard**, which contain all you might need to create a page template. You can recognize them in a page because they are prefixed with `"th:"`. The two dialects are almost identical, but the one created for Spring has additional capabilities for integrating into Spring MVC applications (it supports SpEl , the Spring expression language).

Most Thymeleaf attributes allow their values to be set as or containing expressions called **Standard Expressions**, which can be of the following types:

- **Variable expressions**

  ```
  <td th:text="${person.firstName}"></td>
  <!-- or -->
  <tr th:each="person : ${personList}">
  ```

- **Selection or asterisk expressions**: These are executed on a previously selected object instead of the entire context variables map.

  ```
  <div th:object="${person}">
                  <p th:value="*{firstName} *{lastName}"></p>
  </div>
  ```

- **Text externalized expressions** (internationalization expressions) used to retrieve locale specific messages from external sources (*.properties files). They even accept parameters.

  ```
  <tr>
      <td th:text="#{person.label.firstname} & #{person.label.lastname}</td>
      <!-- or -->
      <td th:text="#{person.created(${id})}"</td>
  </tr>
  ```

- **URL expressions** used to generate session- and context-specific URIs (equivalent to `<spring:url/>` and `<c:url/>`).

  ```
  <img alt="Simple tymeleaf application" title="logo"
                      th:src="@{/images/banner.png}"/>
  <form th:action="@{/createPerson}">
  <a href="show.html" th:href="@{/persons(id=${person.id})}">
  ```

Thymeleaf allows HTML attributes so that templates can link to each other nicely when opened directly in a browser, outside the context of the application, in the same way that Thymeleaf attributes link to each other when executed in the context of a web application. In the previous example, if you want to view your template before deploying the application, you can open the file in a browser and the `th:href` will be replaced by the values of the static `href`.

Considering the following Thymeleaf template:

```
...
<h4>
    Welcome to the sample page with Spring MVC and Thymeleaf!
    <br/>
    Here is a list of random persons:
</h4>

<div class="content" th:if="${not #lists.isEmpty(personList)}">
    <table>
        <thead>
        <tr>
            <td>Cnt.</td>
            <td>First Name</td>
            <td>Last Name</td>
        </tr>
        </thead>
        <tbody>
        <tr th:each="person,iterationStatus : ${personList}">
            <td><a th:text="${iterationStatus.count}" href="show.html"
                    th:href="@{/persons(id=${person.id})}">1</a></td>
            <td th:text="${person.firstName}">John</td>
            <td th:text="${person.lastName}">Smith</td>
        </tr>
        </tbody>
    </table>
</div>
...
```

In Figure 3-12 you can see what the page looks like when opened in the browser outside the application context.

Simple tymeleaf application

**Welcome to the sample page with Spring MVC and Thymeleaf!**
**Here is a list of random persons:**

Cnt. First Name Last Name

<u>1</u>    John         Smith

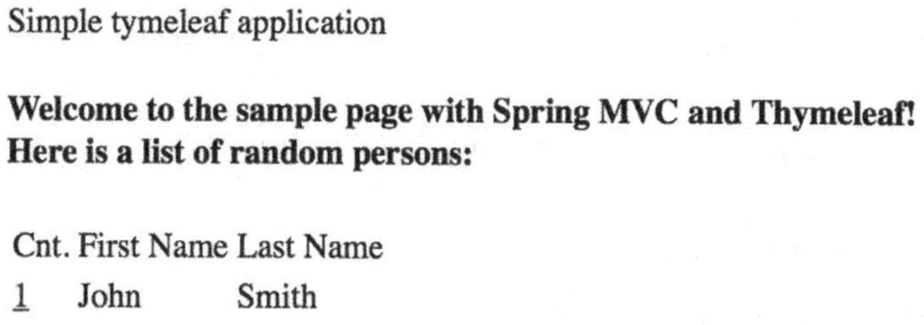

**Figure 3-12.** *Thymeleaf template page opened in the browser outside the application context*

In the application context, all the Thymeleaf expressions are resolved and the resulting page looks like the one shown in Figure 3-13.

**Welcome to the sample page with Spring MVC and Thymeleaf!**
**Here is a list of random persons:**

| Cnt. | First Name | Last Name |
|------|------------|-----------|
| 1 | John | Smith |
| 2 | Jane | Doe |
| 3 | Jason | Bourne |
| 4 | Evelyn | Salt |

***Figure 3-13.*** *Thymeleaf template page opened in the browser in the application context*

The URL expression `th:href="@{/persons(id=${person.id})}"` turns into a URL with a request parameter; for example, `.../persons?id=4`. To generate a URI, `.../persons/4` the expression has to be modified to this:

`th:href="@{/persons/ ${person.id}__}"`.

The notions presented here are the minimum necessary to create a Thymeleaf simple template. The `03-chapter-08-solution` module in the `book-code` project is a perfect example of how simple it is to create a Thymeleaf template to display a list of persons. All that is left now is to explain how Thymeleaf can be integrated with Spring.

Thymeleaf integrates with both Spring 3.x and Spring 4.x and uses two separate libraries, which are packaged in separate `*.jar` files: `thymeleaf-spring3-{version}.jar` and `thymeleaf-spring4-{version}.jar`. As this book is being written, the most current version of Thymeleaf is 2.1.4.RELEASE. The library corresponding to the Spring version used needs to be added to the classpath together with the `thymeleaf.jar`. Thymeleaf offers a set of Spring integrations equivalent to the ones in JSP:

- Spring SpEl can be used in Thymeleaf templates

- It creates forms in templates that are completely integrated with form-backing beans and result hidings

- It displays internationalization messages from message files managed by Spring via `MessageSource`

To integrate Thymeleaf with Spring, you need to define the following:

- The view resolver bean of type `ThymeleafViewResolver`

- The Thymeleaf engine bean of type `SpringTemplateEngine` used to handle the Thymeleaf expressions

- The template resolver bean of type `ServletContextTemplateResolver` used to configure the location and type of templates that the other beans are expected to work with

```
<bean id="templateResolver"
        class="org.thymeleaf.templateresolver.ServletContextTemplateResolver">
        <property name="prefix" value="/WEB-INF/persons/" />
        <property name="suffix" value=".html" />
        <property name="templateMode" value="HTML5" />
        <!-- Template cache is true by default. Set to false if you want -->
        <!-- templates to be automatically updated when modified. -->
        <property name="cacheable" value="true" />
</bean>
 <bean class="org.thymeleaf.spring4.view.ThymeleafViewResolver">
        <property name="templateEngine" ref="templateEngine" />
        <property name="order" value="1"/>
</bean>

<bean id="templateEngine" class="org.thymeleaf.spring4.SpringTemplateEngine">
        <property name="templateResolver" ref="templateResolver" />
</bean>
```

And this is all. If you would like to use Thymeleaf in your future projects, you can find all the information you need on their official site at http://www.thymeleaf.org. Also, before continuing to the next section, you might want to run and take a look at the 03-chapter-08-solution module.

# Forms

Starting with version 2.0, Spring provides a set of specialized tags for handling form elements when using JSP and the Spring Web MVC. Each tag provides support for a set of attributes matching the ones in the corresponding HTML element, which makes Spring quite easy for the user. The Spring tag library is integrated into Spring MVC, which allows the tags to have access to the command object and model.

The Spring tag library is inside the spring-webmvc.jar. To use the tags in a JSP page, the following directive must be added on top of the JSP page:

```
<%@ taglib prefix="sf" uri="http://www.springframework.org/tags/form" %>
```

The "sf" prefix is short for *spring form*. Any prefix can be used, but in this book, "sf" was chosen because it is short and its meaning is quite obvious. The "spring" prefix will be used for Spring-specific tags that are not related to forms (internationalization and URL generation).

In the examples attached to this chapter, you create forms to edit and to search for a person. A form for editing a person is depicted in Figure 3-14.

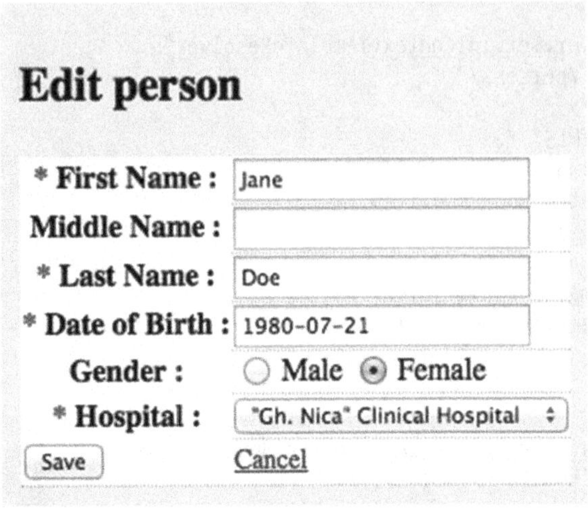

# Edit person

|  |  |
| --- | --- |
| * First Name : | Jane |
| Middle Name : |  |
| * Last Name : | Doe |
| * Date of Birth : | 1980-07-21 |
| Gender : | ○ Male ⦿ Female |
| * Hospital : | "Gh. Nica" Clinical Hospital ⬍ |
| Save | Cancel |

**Figure 3-14.** *Form used to edit a Person*

The Spring form tag library provides equivalent elements for the HTML elements needed to design a form, annotations for data binding and data validation, and tools for error processing. The code that creates form follows Figure 3-14.

```
...
<%@ taglib prefix="sf" uri="http://www.springframework.org/tags/form" %>
<%@ taglib prefix="spring" uri="http://www.springframework.org/tags" %>
...
<div class="person">
    <spring:url value="/persons/{id}" var="editUrl">
        <spring:param name="id" value="${person.id}"/>
    </spring:url>
    <sf:form modelAttribute="person" action="${editUrl}" method="POST">
        <table>
            <tr>
                <th>
                    <label for="firstName">
                        <span class="man">*</span>
                        <spring:message code="label.Person.firstname"/> :
                    </label>
                </th>
                <td><sf:input path="firstName"/>
                <sf:errors cssClass="error" path="firstName"/></td>
            </tr>
            ...
            <tr>
                <th>
                    <label for="dateOfBirth">
                        <span class="man">*</span>
                        <spring:message code="label.Person.dob"/> :
                    </label>
                </th>
```

```
    <td><sf:input path="dateOfBirth"/>
    <sf:errors cssClass="error" path="dateOfBirth"/></td>
</tr>

<tr>
    <th>
        <label for="gender">
            <spring:message code="label.Person.gender"/> :
        </label>
    </th>
    <td>
        <sf:radiobutton path="gender" value="MALE"/>
         <spring:message code="label.Person.male"/>
        <sf:radiobutton path="gender" value="FEMALE"/>
        <spring:message code="label.Person.female"/>
    </td>
</tr>
<tr>
    <th>
        <label for="hospital">
            <span class="man">*</span>
            <spring:message code="label.Hospital"/> :
        </label>
        </th>
        <td>
            <sf:select path="hospital">
                <c:choose>
                    <c:when test="${person == null}">
                        <sf:option value="">
                        <spring:message code="label.choose"/></sf:option>
                    </c:when>
                    <c:otherwise>
                        <sf:option value="${person.hospital.id}">
                                      ${person.hospital.name}
                        </sf:option>
                    </c:otherwise>
                </c:choose>

                <sf:options items="${hospitalList}"
                    itemValue="id" itemLabel="name"/>
            </sf:select>

        </td>
    </tr>
    <tr>
        <td>
            <button id="saveButton" type="submit">
                <spring:message code="command.save"/>
            </button>
        </td>
```

```
                    <td>
                        <a href="${editUrl}">
                            <spring:message code="command.cancel"/>
                        </a>
                    </td>
                </tr>
            </table>
        </sf:form>
</div>
```

In the previous code there are a few elements that are underlined. They are Spring form tags equivalent to HTML form tags. The only difference is that they are fully integrated with Spring MVC and their content is populated from the modelAttribute and other Spring form–specific objects, which are covered a little bit later.

The behavior of a Spring form can be described using this succession of steps:

1.   An initial GET request causes the form object to be created and presented to the user.

2.   The user inserts data in the form and sends a POST request to submit the form. In this step, the data inserted is evaluated, validated, and stored in the form object.

3.   POST-Redirect-GET if the operation is successful (if the objective of the POST request has succeeded, a GET request is created to present a confirmation message to the user).

Without the POST-Redirect-GET behavior, an application will behave incorrectly, because subsequent POST requests could lead to duplicate data and/or data corruption. The forms used for search operations do not need a POST request, because submitting a search query has no side effects and it redirects to the results page.

When working with forms, all the fields in a form should map to the fields of an object called a *data transfer object* (DTO). In the example, this is done for the Search Person form, which is covered later. When editing a person, it is more suitable to use a Person object as a data transfer object. The Person object is an instance of an @Entity class, and maps to a row in the person table in the database. These types of objects are called *domain objects*. This requires that the object used for this purpose should have a default constructor, getters, and setters for all the fields used in the form. Although using a domain object as a form object welcomes the undesired possibility that some web logic–specific operations might creep in, it is practical to use when the objects handled are simple[20] and entity fields are annotated with specific validation annotations (example: @NotEmpty, NotNull, etc.), because implementing a validator class at the web layer may no longer be necessary.

Form-specific data transfer objects are also required when the information from a form is aggregated from multiple domain objects. This allows the form object to encapsulate only what is needed to be displayed on the screen: web layer logic, validation logic, logic for information transfer between the form object, and domain object.

Figure 3-15 shows the correspondence between the form tags and the fields in the CriteriaDto object.

---

[20]Adam Bien, one of the most respected Java developers in the world, has named DTOs objects "anemic in general and do not contain any business logic" on his blog at http://www.adam-bien.com/roller/ abien/entry/ value_object_vs_data_transfer.

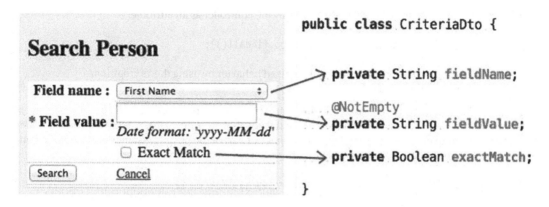

**Figure 3-15.** *Form to search a Person*

The following can be said when using Spring forms:

- The CriteriaDto object is linked to the form via modelAttribute="criteriaDto" and it corresponds to the @ModelAttribute annotated object in the controller class.

- The Spring form has a method attribute the same as an HTML form, and the value of this attribute is the type of request being sent to the server.

  ```
  <sf:form action="${personsUrl}" modelAttribute="criteriaDto" method="get">
      ....
  </sf:form>
  ```

- The Spring form has an action attribute the same as an HTML form, and the value of this attribute is the URL of the request.

  ```
  <spring:url value="/persons/go" var="personsUrl"/>
   <sf:form action="${personsUrl}" modelAttribute="criteriaDto" method="get">
   ....
  </sf:form>
  ```

- <sf:input path="fieldName"/> is rendered into an HTML input field that is populated with the value of the field named fieldName in the criteriaDto object. Each of the fields defined in a Spring form specifies a path attribute that corresponds to a getter/setter method of the model attribute (in this case the CriteriaDto object). When the page is loaded, Spring calls the getter of each field to populate the form view. When the form is submitted, the setters are called to save the values submitted by the user using the form to the model attribute fields.

- <sf:select/> elements are rendered into HTML select elements and can be constructed using domain object lists:

  ```
  <sf:select path="hospital" itemValue="id" itemLabel="name"
             items="${hospitalList}"/>
  ```

The hospitalList has to be added to the model by the controller as an attribute:

```
model.addAttribute("hospitalList", hospitalRepo.findAll());
```

- `<sf:select/>` elements can have customized behavior by using the `<sf:option/>` and `<sf:options/>` tag.

For example, if the same form is used for editing and creating a person instance, when a new person is created, you might want to display a default option in the hospital drop-down list, making it obvious for the user that a value has to be selected. That default option is not part of the hospital list model attribute. When a person is edited, you want to select the hospital where that person was born.

```
<%@ taglib prefix="c" uri="http://java.sun.com/jsp/jstl/core" %>
....
<sf:select path="hospital">
    <c:choose>
        <!-- no person attribute, form is used to create a person -->
        <c:when test="${person == null}">
            <sf:option value="">
                <!-- default option not in the hospital list model attribute -->
                <spring:message code='label.choose'/>
            </sf:option>
        </c:when>
         <!-- form is used to edit a person, person model attribute is set -->
        <c:otherwise>
            <sf:option value="${person.hospital.id}">
                ${person.hospital.name}
            </sf:option>
        </c:otherwise>
    </c:choose>
    <!-- Dynamic list of options -->
    <sf:options items="${hospitalList}" itemValue="id" itemLabel="name"/>
</sf:select>
```

The preceding example is rendered as an HTML select element containing all hospitals in the hospitalList model attribute and an extra static **Choose hospital** option when the form is used to create a person. The names of the hospitals are used as labels for the available options in the select element. The JSP c taglib is used for conditional operations.

- The Spring JSP tag library integrates nicely with other JSP libraries, like Tiles and JSTL.

- The `<sf:errors/>` is a Spring special tag for displaying errors. The error messages can be internationalized; this is covered in the "Data Validation" section.

When it comes to using Spring forms, three key subjects must be well understood to use them like an expert: formatting, data binding, and validation; each of these is given the proper coverage in its own section.

# Data Formatting

In the Person edit form, you need to display and eventually edit a java.util.Date instance and a Hospital instance. These are complex types and the Spring tag library does not know how to handle them on its own. The developer must provide implementations for the org.springframework.format.Formatter<T> interface for the specific type of object handled in the form. Formatter classes parse text data, turn them into objects, and transform beans into text data ready for rendering. In the 05-pr-mvc-form-solution module, which is the project specific to this section, two formatters are used in the **Edit person** form; where they are used is shown in Figure 3-16.

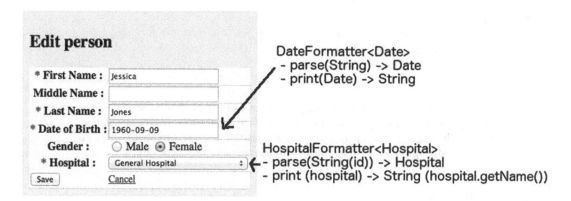

***Figure 3-16.*** *Formatters used in the form to edit a person*

Formatters can be used in four places in the application:

- On the field using annotations (all JSPs pages displaying this annotation use this formatter)

  ```
  @DateTimeFormat(pattern = "yyyy-MM-dd")
  private Date dateOfBirth;
  ```

- In the JSP tags (used when multiple JSP pages need to display data differently)

  ```
  <fmt:formatDate value="${person.dateOfBirth}" pattern="yyyy-MM-dd" />
  ```

- Registered in the application using the FormattingConversionServiceFactoryBean bean

  ```
  <mvc:annotation-driven conversion-service="typeConversionService" />

  <!-- Define a custom ConversionService -->
  <bean id="typeConversionService"
        class="o.s.format.support.FormattingConversionServiceFactoryBean">
      <property name="formatters">
          <set>
              <bean class="com.pr.util.DateFormatter"/>
              <bean class="com.pr.util.HospitalFormatter"/>
          </set>
      </property>
  </bean>
  ```

The DateFormatter implementation used in the personal-records project looks like this:

```
public class DateFormatter implements Formatter<Date>{
    public static final SimpleDateFormat formatter =
                            new SimpleDateFormat("yyyy-MM-dd");

    @Override
    public Date parse(String s, Locale locale) throws ParseException {
        return formatter.parse(s);
    }

    @Override
    public String print(Date date, Locale locale) {
        return formatter.format(date);
    }
}
```

- On the controller or service method arguments by using implementation of the org.springframework.validation.Validator interface and the @Validated annotation. In the following example, the URI path variable used to request data about a person is of type String and it has to be checked for whether it represents a valid id.

```
@Component
public class IdValidator implements Validator {

    @Override
    public boolean supports(Class<?> clazz) {
        return String.class.equals(clazz);
    }

    @Override
    public void validate(Object target, Errors errors) {
        String id = (String) target;
        if(!id.matches("/{id:\\d*}")) {
            errors.reject("id.malformed");
        }
    }
}
```

The controller method to retrieve a person's data and using that validator looks like this:

```
@RequestMapping(value = "/{id}", method = RequestMethod.GET)
public String show(@Validated(IdValidator.class)@PathVariable String id,
  Model model) throws NotFoundException {
    Long theId = Long.parseLong(id);
    Person person = personManager.findById(theId);
    if(person == null) {
        throw new NotFoundException(Person.class, theId);
    }
    model.addAttribute("person", person);
    return "persons/show";
}
```

In the examples in this book, only Date and Hospital formatters are covered because they are the only ones needed in the associated projects, but any complex field type can have a formatter. For example:

- formatting numbers:

```
@NumberFormat(style=Style.NUMBER, pattern="#,###.###")
private final BigDecimal amount;
```

- formatting currencies:

```
@NumberFormat(style=Style.CURRENCY)
private final BigDecimal amount;
```

When field values are formatted inside a JSP page, formatting annotations are no longer needed. When formatters are registered using the FormattingConversionServiceFactoryBean bean, the specific types are automatically converted without another annotation or tag.

The <mvc:annotation-driven/> and @EnableWebMVC registers default formatters for Numbers and Dates by offering support for specific annotations: @NumberFormat and @DateTimeFormat. If Joda Time is in the classpath, support for it is also enabled.

Java configuration to register custom formatters can be done in two ways: by defining a @Bean of type ConversionService, or by implementing the addFormatters method defined in WebMvcConfigurer (or by overriding it when implementations of this interface are used).

The second way is easier:

```
\\in the @Configuration & @EnableWebMvc annotated class
@Override
    public void addFormatters(FormatterRegistry formatterRegistry)
    {
        formatterRegistry.addFormatter(getDateFormatter());
        formatterRegistry.addFormatter(getHospitalFormatter());
    }

    @Bean
    public DateFormatter getDateFormatter(){
        return new DateFormatter();
    }

    @Bean
    public HospitalFormatter getHospitalFormatter(){
      return new HospitalFormatter();
    }
}
```

The first way is more complicated. The following is an example of an annotated ConversionService bean definition:

```
\\ in the @Configuration annotated class
    public ConversionService conversionService() {
        FormattingConversionServiceFactoryBean bean =
                new FormattingConversionServiceFactoryBean();
        bean.setFormatters(getFormatters());
        bean.afterPropertiesSet();
        ConversionService object = bean.getObject();
        return object;
    }
```

```
    private Set<Formatter> getFormatters() {
      Set<Formatter> formatters = new HashSet<>();
       formatters.add(dateFormatter);
      formatters.add(dateFormatter);
      return formatters;
    }
```

```
// definition for formatter beans as in the previous example
```

Now you have the conversionService bean. Let's look at the equivalent for <mvc:annotation-driven conversion-service="conversionService" />:

```
@FeatureConfiguration
class MvcFeatures {



        @Feature
        public MvcAnnotationDriven annotationDriven(
                    ConversionService conversionService) {
            return new MvcAnnotationDriven().conversionService(conversionService)
        }
        ...
}
```

MvcAnnotationDriven provides the same options as the XML elements using a conveniently chained method API. But who needs a complicated way to do this when there is an easier way, right?

HospitalFormatter is a custom formatter specifically created to be used in projects attached to this book. It basically transforms a Hospital instance into its name so that it can be rendered in a view. And it takes a hospital id and retrieves the Hospital instance from the database to be returned to the controller, where it is used further. As the HospitalFormatter is a bean like any other, the HospitalManager bean can be injected into it to make this happen. So the custom implementation looks like this:

```
public class HospitalFormatter implements Formatter<Hospital> {

    @Autowired
    HospitalManager hospitalManager;

    @Override
    public Hospital parse(String text, Locale locale)
                            throws ParseException {
        Long id = Long.parseLong(text);
        return hospitalManager.findOne(id);
    }

    @Override
    public String print(Hospital hospital, Locale locale) {
        return hospital.getName();
    }
}
```

# Data Binding

Form objects, data transfer objects, and domain objects have been mentioned so far. But how are they linked together? How does the information from a form object get transferred to a data transfer object or to a domain object? How does Spring MVC know how to do this? The answer to these three questions is a process named **data binding**.

Spring MVC binds the request to the form object. When a form is submitted, string data is transformed into objects that are injected into the form object using getters and setters. A POST request or form submission means setters for the form model attribute are called. A GET or page/form load means getters are called upon the form model attribute to populate the view. Each object is identified using the path attribute value in the corresponding Spring element tag. The form object it tightly bound to the JSP page, and if the form object cannot be created, the JSP page won't be rendered correctly. The form object is linked to the JSP page using the modelAttribute attribute in the <sf:form/> tag:

```
<sf:form modelAttribute="person" action="${editUrl}" method="POST">
...
</sf:form>
```

In the controller, the form object can be accessed in multiple ways. It can be received as an argument to the method mapped to the ${editUrl}.

```
@Controller
public class PersonsController {

    @RequestMapping(method=RequestMethod.POST)
    public String update(Person person) {
    ...
}
```

In this case, data is copied automatically into the object, and the object is re-created on every request. You can annotate the form object with the @ModelAttribute annotation.

```
@Controller
public class PersonsController {

    @RequestMapping(method=RequestMethod.POST)
    public String edit(@ModelAttribute("person") Person person) {
    ...
}
```

---

■ **CC** When the name of the modelAttribute is the same as the name of the argument in a handler method, the value for @ModelAttribute can be skipped. So in the previous case, public String update (@ModelAttribute("person") Person person) is equivalent to public String update(@ModelAttribute Person person).

---

This annotation was mentioned in the "Redirecting" section; it can be used the same way for forms too, because in this case, you have a controller that handles the edit and show requests for a person instance. @ModelAttribute annotated methods are executed before the chosen @RequestMapping annotated handler method. They effectively pre-populate the implicit model with specific attributes, in this case, the person instance to be displayed or edited.

So you can simplify the controller like this:

```
@Controller
@RequestMapping("/persons/{id}")
public class PersonsController {

    @ModelAttribute
    public Person findPerson(@PathVariable Long id) {
        return personManager.findOne(id);
    }

    @RequestMapping(method = RequestMethod.GET)
    public String show() {
        return "persons/show";
    }

    @RequestMapping(value="/edit", method = RequestMethod.GET)
    public String edit(Model model) {
        //we add the hospitalList to show in the Hospital drop-down list
        model.addAttribute(hospitalRepo.findAll());
        return "persons/edit";
    }
@RequestMapping(method = RequestMethod.POST)
public String save(Person person, BindingResult result, Model model) {
    if (result.hasErrors()) {
        // we need to add this here as the dropdown list
        // has to be populated correctly
        // and "hospitalList" is not a model attribute
        model.addAttribute(hospitalRepo.findAll());
        return "persons/edit";
    }
    personManager.save(person);
    return "redirect:/persons/".concat(person.getId());
  }

}
```

In this implementation, you do not have to concern yourself with the existence of the form object because the methods of this controller are only accessible when the URL is constructed with a valid person id.

By default, all fields in a form are binded to the form object, but Spring MVC offers the possibility to modify the default behavior by customizing a WebDataBinder object. Some fields can be blacklisted or whitelisted for the binding process:

```
@InitBinder
public void initBinder(WebDataBinder binder) {
    //allowed fields
    binder.setAllowedFields("firstName", "lastName");
    //disallowed fields
    binder.setDisallowedFields("pk", "*Pk");
}
```

The recommended behavior is to whitelist only the necessary fields, even if there might be a lot of them to minimize the security holes.

The validation errors are binded to the form object too using a `BindingResult` object.

```
@RequestMapping(method = RequestMethod.POST)
    public String save(@Valid Person person, BindingResult result, Model model) {
        if (result.hasErrors()) {
            return "persons/edit";
        }
    ...
}
```

If you look at the beginning of this section, where the **Edit person** form code is, you see that some elements look like this:

```
<sf:errors cssClass="error" path="dateOfBirth"/></td>
```

They are right next to their analogue elements:

```
<sf:input path="dateOfBirth"/>
```

And they have the exact path attribute value. These elements are used to display validation errors when the POST handler method returns back to the edit view because the `BindingResult` object was populated by an existing validator bean. When returning to the form, the submitted data is still there, but there is extra information about the state and condition of the submitted data, something more or less like what you see in Figure 3-17.

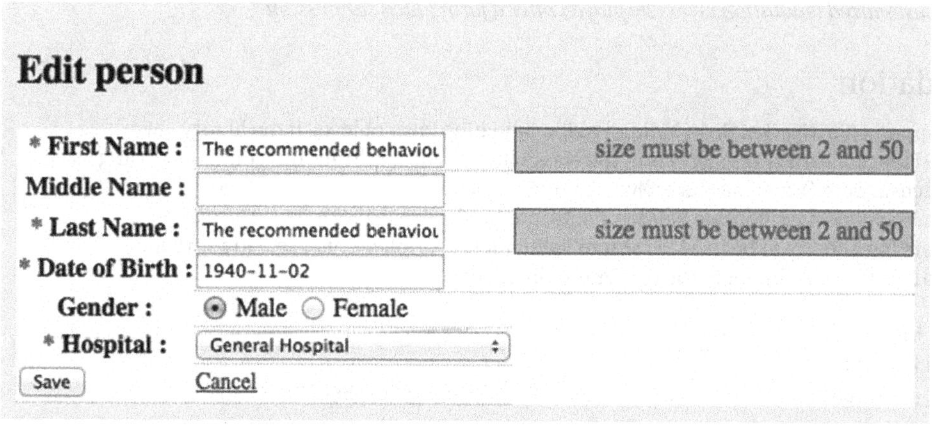

*Figure 3-17. Spring default validation errors displayed after a form failed submission*

Spring MVC has its own validator messages, but supports externally provided validator messages too. Data binding error messages can be customized and internationalized. The following are some examples; depending on the validation library used, the message keys could be different:

```
NotEmpty.person.firstName=Please insert First Name Value
Size.person.firstName=Length must be between {2} and {1}
typeMismatch.dateOfBirth=Invalid format, should be \'yyyy-mm-dd\'
typeMismatch.amount=Incorrect amount
```

And after the customization, when a submit fails, the invalidated form looks like what's shown in Figure 3-18.

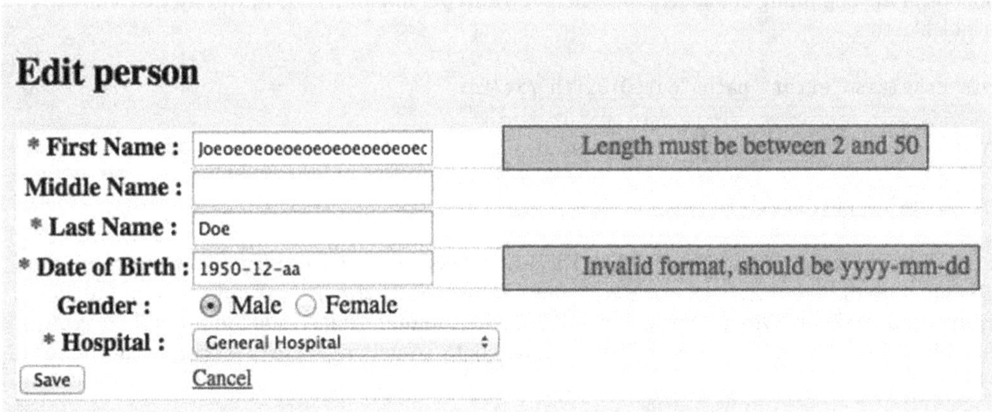

***Figure 3-18.*** *Customized validation errors displayed after a form failed submission*

## Data Validation

Spring MVC supports JSR 303/349 Bean Validation for validating form objects. If the library `javax.validation:validation-api:[version]` is in the classpath and the application is configured using `<mvc:annotation-driven/>` or `@EnableWebMvc`, it is automatically detected and enabled.

Spring 4+ also supports Hibernate Validator 4.3+, but for the `org.hibernate:hibernate-validator:[version]` library to be used, a custom validator that implements `org.springframework.validation.Validator` must be set in the configuration; for example:

```
<!-- Enables hibernate validator -->
<bean id="validator"
    class="o.s.validation.beanvalidation.LocalValidatorFactoryBean"/>

<!-- Defines basic MVC defaults (handler adapter, mapping,
            date formatting, etc) -->
<mvc:annotation-driven validator="validator"/>
```

The Hibernate Validator is an extension of the default set of validation annotations provided by the `validation-api` library, that's why when using Hibernate Validator, `validation-api` is enabled by default, as `validation-api` is a dependency of the Hibernate Validator.

■ !  To depict this, a special Gradle task was created for you in the oo-pr-dao module: allCompileDeps. When executed, Gradle prints the dependency tree for the oo-pr-dao module in the Intellij IDEA console. If you analyze the output, you will find the following snippet.

```
+--- org.hibernate:hibernate-validator:5.1.3.Final
|    +--- javax.validation:validation-api:1.1.0.Final
|    +--- org.jboss.logging:jboss-logging:3.1.3.GA
|    \--- com.fasterxml:classmate:1.0.0
```

The following are examples of validation annotations:

- @NotNull: Field cannot be null

- @Size (min, max): File must have a length in the range (min, max)

- @Pattern: String not null and matching

- @NotEmpty: String must not be empty (Hibernate)

- @Min(val), @Max(val): String must be of length at least minimum, or maximum in size

They are used on the fields of interest in the domain object or data transfer object:

```
public class Person extends AbstractEntity {

    @Size(min=2, max=50)
    public String firstName;

    @Size(min=2, max=50)
    public String lastName;

    @NotNull
    // comment the following if a custom formatter is registered
    @DateTimeFormat(pattern = "yyyy-MM-dd")
    private Date dateOfBirth;
...
}
```

The validation is invoked by annotating the form object with @Valid and the errors are registered in the BindingResult object too, alongside the binding errors.

In the JSP form, the way the errors are displayed can also be customized. In the previous section, each error was mapped to its field, but you can also print all the errors in the same place by using the following syntax:

```
<sf:form modelAttribute="person">
        <form:errors path="*"/>
...
</sf:form>
```

This approach is not recommended for big forms. It is also quite annoying for the user to have to search for the form field he has to correct. By linking the error to the form field, it becomes quite obvious where the correction must be applied.

The Hibernate Validator contains its own set of internationalization files with default internationalized messages. The Resource bundle is named `ValidationMessages`; it is located in the `hibernate-valdiator.jar` under the `org.hibernate.validator` package. You can expand the `hibernate-validator.jar` and look at it contents in Intellij IDEA, as shown in Figure 3-19.

**Figure 3-19.** *Contents of the hibernate-validator.jar*

The message keys in the `ValidationMessages.properties` files are the message keys set by default in the definition of each annotation. For example, the following is a snippet of code for the `@NotEmpty` annotation:

```
@Constraint(validatedBy = { })
@Target({ METHOD, FIELD, ANNOTATION_TYPE, CONSTRUCTOR, PARAMETER })
@Retention(RUNTIME)
@ReportAsSingleViolation
@NotNull
@Size(min = 1)
public @interface NotEmpty {
    String message() default "{org.hibernate.validator.constraints.NotEmpty.message}";
        ...
}
```

For every field that fails, the `@NotEmpty` validation has the default error message printed next to it (if configured so), read from the Hibernate Validator resource bundle files. These messages can be overridden by creating your own `ValidationMessages` resource bundle in the classpath of the project. Also, the message keys can be customized by making the new message key a parameter for the message property when using the annotation; this allows specific messages to be displayed when the same annotation is used on different fields:

```
// in the Person entity class
@NotEmpty(message="lastname.notempty")
public String lastName;

#in the ValidationMessages.properties
lastname.notempty=Lastname cannot be empty!
```

When using Spring forms, the error messages can be part of the application resource bundle under WEB-INF\messages; the message keys usually respect the following template:

constraintName.modelAttributeName.propertyName

Each part of the Spring message key is linked to elements in the application, as depicted in Figure 3-20.

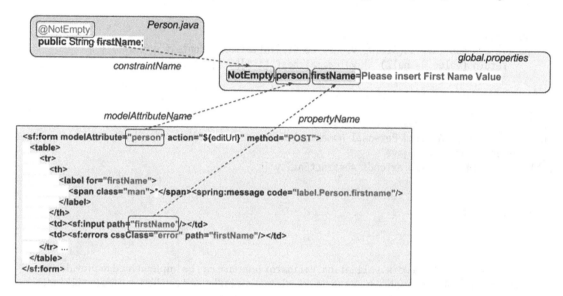

***Figure 3-20.*** *Spring message keys and linked elements*

The message samples at the end of the previous section include customized validation messages, used in the 05-pr-mvc-form-practice and solution modules.

Spring also supports the JEE @Constraint[21] annotation, which can be used to define customized validation annotations.

```
// Pnc.java
@Constraint(validatedBy = [PncValidator.class])
@Target( { ElementType.METHOD, ElementType.FIELD })
@Retention(RetentionPolicy.RUNTIME)
public @interface Pnc {
    //using specific message key
    String message() default "{pncFormatExpected}";
    Class<?>[] groups() default {};
}
```

---

[21]See http://docs.oracle.com/javaee/7/api/javax/validation/Constraint.html.

```java
//In PncValidator.java
public class PncValidator implements
                        ConstraintValidator<Pnc, String> {
    @Override
    public void initialize(Pnc constraintAnnotation) {
        // nothing to initialize
    }

    @Override
    public boolean isValid(String value, ConstraintValidatorContext context) {
        return (value == null) || value.matches("[1-2][0-9]*");
    }
}


// In Resouce bundle global.properties files
pncFormatExpected= A valid Personal Numerical Code is required!
// Usage in IdentityCard.java
public class IdentityCard extends AbstractEntity {
...
@Pnc
private String pnc;
...
}
```

Or the org.springframework.validation.Validator interface can be implemented to provide a custom validator implementation, which can be specific to a controller and can be set using @InitBinder:

```java
class PncValidator extends Validator {
    public void validate(Object target, Errors errors) {
        if ((Person)target)
                        .identityCard.pnc.matches("[1-2][0-9]*") )
            errors.rejectValue("pnc", "pncFormatExpected");
    }

    public boolean supports(Class<?> clazz) {
        return clazz instanceof Person.class;
    }
}


@InitBinder
public void initBinder(WebDataBinder binder) {
    binder.setValidator(new PncValidator());
}
```

Or a validation method can be implemented directly into the data transfer object and called from the controller:

```
public class CriteriaDto {
    public void validate(Errors errors) {
    if (fieldValue == null || fieldValue.isEmpty())
            errors.rejectValue("fieldValue", "valueExpected");
    }
}
...

@RequestMapping(method=RequestMethod.Get)
public String search(CriteriaDto criteriaDto, BindingResult result) {
    criteriaDto.validate(result);
    // process failure or success normally ...
}
```

## Managing the Form Object

Using a form implies multiple requests, which means that the form object has to be the same across two or more requests (when validations fail, for example). There are more ways to manage the form object:

- **The object is created on every request.** This strategy is recommended when creating a new object and the form contains all required data for it.

- **The object is retrieved on every request using a @ModelAttribute annotated method.** This strategy works best for editing existing objects. It scales well and it is very simple. The disadvantage is that before every request, the method to retrieve the object is called; thus Spring MVC must bind the request parameters to it. For big forms using data transfer objects representing an aggregation of domain objects, this process can introduce a certain latency because domain objects have to be retrieved from the database and then aggregated.

- **The object is stored in the session between requests.** This strategy works for both creating and editing objects. It performs better, but it does not scale because it crowds the session.

- **The object is managed by using flash attributes.** This is the best solution for both scenarios, as the object is passed from one request to another by Spring MVC.

In the first case, the object is created in the initial GET request, and then Spring MVC takes care of creating it again and binding all request parameters to it.

```
@Controller
@RequestMapping("/persons/{id}")
public class PersonsController {

    //1. object is being created on every request
    // initial GET request, object is created
    @RequestMapping(value="/new", method=RequestMethod.GET)
    public String new(Model model) {
        model.add(new Person());
    }
```

```
//2. object is being retrieved
@ModelAttribute
 public Person findPerson(@PathVariable Long id) {
     return personManager.findOne(id);
 }

// the POST request - Spring MVC takes care of creating the object and binding
 @RequestMapping(method=RequestMethod.POST)
 public String save(Person person) {
     ...
 }
}
```

In the second case, the object is retrieved by a manager (service class) before every request and @ModelAttribute annotation on a method is used for this; you can see this in the code sample at the beginning of the "Data Binding" section. The last two cases were covered in the "Redirecting" section.

# Summary

After reading this chapter, you should have a wide understanding of Spring Web MVC and all it has to offer. Here is a simple list of topics that you should keep handy when reviewing your new knowledge:

- What is the DispatcherServlet and what is its role in Spring Web MVC applications?

- What is the controller programming model?

- How do you configure Spring MVC applications using XML, Java configuration, mixed cases, and Servlet 3.0 with no web.xml configurations?

- What are the Spring MVC infrastructure beans and how are they configured?

- What is the difference between a URL and a URI?

- How you can create a reusable layout using Tiles for a Spring web application?

- How do you personalize a Spring MVC application?

- What types of views does Spring MVC support? What must be provided to do so?

- How do you chain ViewResolvers to support multiple view types in a single application?

- How do you configure a ContentNegotiatingViewResolver to support multiple view types for the same resource?

- How do you create a Spring form?

- Spring MVC provides a JSP tag library for form rendering. How do you format and validate data handled by the form?

- How does data binding work?

- How do you write unit and integration tests to test controllers logic?

# Quick Quiz

**Question 1:** Considering the following configuration in `web.xml`, what is the name of the parameter that holds the location of the Spring MVC configuration file?

```
<servlet>
    <servlet-name>mvc-dispatcher</servlet-name>
    <servlet-class>o.s.web.servlet.DispatcherServlet</servlet-class>
    <init-param>
        <param-name>?????</param-name>
        <param-value>
            /WEB-INF/spring/mvc-config.xml
        </param-value>
    </init-param>
    <load-on-startup>1</load-on-startup>
</servlet>
<servlet-mapping>
    <servlet-name>mvc-dispatcher</servlet-name>
    <url-pattern>/</url-pattern>
</servlet-mapping>
```

       A.   contextListener

       B.   configurationLocation

       C.   contextConfigLocation

**Question 2:** Considering the following configuration in `web.xml`, what is the name of the parameter that points to the Spring infrastructure bean that enables Java configuration?

```
<servlet>
<servlet-name>mvc-dispatcher</servlet-name>
<servlet-class>o.s.web.servlet.DispatcherServlet</servlet-class>
<init-param>
    <param-name>???</param-name>
    <param-value>
      o.s.web.context.support.AnnotationConfigWebApplicationContext
    </param-value>
</init-param>
<init-param>
    <param-name>contextConfigLocation</param-name>
    <param-value>
        com.book.config.WebConfig
    </param-value>
 </init-param>
 <load-on-startup>1</load-on-startup>
</servlet>

<servlet-mapping>
    <servlet-name>mvc-dispatcher</servlet-name>
    <url-pattern>/</url-pattern>
</servlet-mapping>
```

    A.   contextClass

    B.   configClassLocation

    C.   contextConfigLocation

    D.   contextClassName

**Question 3:** In `web.xml`, the servlet name has been configured to `mvc-dispatcher`. What is the default name of the MVC configuration file that Spring looks for?

    A.   mvc-config.xml

    B.   mvc-dispatcher.xml

    C.   mvc-dispatcher-servlet.xml

**Question 4:** As a developer, what do you need to do to configure Spring Web MVC application without using an `web.xml` file ?

    A.   Extend the `AbstractDispatcherServletInitializer` class and override at least `createServletApplicationContext` and `getServletMappings`.

    B.   Extend the `AbstractAnnotationConfigDispatcherServletInitializer` class and override at least `getServletConfigClasses` and `getServletMappings`.

    C.   Implement `WebApplicationInitializer`.

    D.   Extend `WebApplicationInitializer` and annotate the class with @`EnableWebMvc`.

**Question 5:** Which of the following are Spring MVC infrastructure components?

    A.   `Validator` implementations

    B.   `HandlerAdapter` implementations

    C.   `HandlerMapping` implementations

    D.   `ControllerAdvice` implementations

**Question 6:** The purpose of `HandlerMapping` implementations is to map incoming requests to the appropriate handlers and a list of pre- and post-processor interceptors. Is this statement true?

    A.   Yes

    B.   No

**Question 7:** `RequestMappingHandlerMapping` is registered by default when the following configuration style is used for a Spring web application:

    A.   XML configuration using the MVC namespace specific element `<mvc:annotation-driven/>`

    B.   Java configuration using a configuration class annotated with @EnableWebMVC

**Question 8:** What are the key interfaces used by Spring to render responses without tying itself to a specific view technology?

    A.   `View`

    B.   `ViewResolver`

    C.   `ViewConfigurer`

**Question 9:** Which of the following is an out-of-the-box view technology supported by Spring?

    A.   JSP

    B.   Thymeleaf

    C.   Velocity templates

    D.   XSLT

    E.   Tiles

**Question 10:** What is the default ViewResolver implementation configured by Spring?

    A.   InternalResourceViewResolver

    B.   JspResourceViewResolver

    C.   UrlBasedViewResolver

    D.   BeanNameViewResolver

**Question 11:** What is the difference between chaining ViewResolver beans and content-type negotiation?

    A.   There is no difference.

    B.   View Resolver chaining allows supporting multiple view types in a single application.

    C.   Content-type negotiation allows support for multiple view types for the same resource.

**Question 12:** What is true about the HTTP `Accept` header?

    A.   It can be used in a Spring Web MVC application to decide the view type for a resource only when the client is a browser.

    B.   It is used for REST web services.

    C.   It is useless when the client is a browser.

    D.   It can be taken into consideration by setting a value for the `ignoreAcceptHeader` property in the `ContentNegotiatingViewResolver` bean.

**Question 13:** From the following list, select the Spring infrastructure bean types responsible with application personalization:

    A.   `MessageSource` implementations

    B.   `LocaleChangeInterceptor`

    C.   `LocaleResolver` implementations

    D.   `ThemeResolver` implementations

**Question 14:** What is true about the @ExceptionHandler and @ControllerAdvice annotations?

    A.    They are used for handling exceptions thrown by controller methods.

    B.    When a method inside a controller is annotated with @ExceptionHandler, this method handles the exceptions thrown only in that controller.

    C.    @ControllerAdvice is used at class level; in addition to @ExceptionHandler annotated methods, this class can define other types of methods.

**Question 15:** Given the following controller, to what request will the call method be mapped to?

```
@Controller
 @RequestMapping("/persons")
public class PersonsController {

    @RequestMapping("/list")
    public String call(Model model,HttpServletRequest rq) {
    ...
    }
}
```

    A.    http://localhost:8080/persons

    B.    http://localhost:8080/persons/list

    C.    http://localhost:8080/persons/call

**Question 16:** Given the following controller, is the declaration of the show method correct?

```
@Controller
 @RequestMapping("/persons")
public class PersonsController {

    @RequestMapping("/{id}")
    public String show(@PathVariable String number, Model model) {
    ...
    }
}
```

    A.    Yes

    B.    No

**Question 17:** What of the following is something that a Spring MVC handler method could not return?

    A.    a string

    B.    a Model

    C.    a ModelAndView

    D.    a JstlView instance

    E.    a null value

**Question 18:** Which of the following statements regarding annotation-based configuration are true?

    A.    Annotating a class with `Controller` is not enough for that class to handle requests; the class also has to extend Spring's `AbstractController` class.

    B.    `@RequestMapping` is both used at class and method level.

    C.    To enable auto-detection of controller classes, you have to enable component scanning in your configuration.

    D.    `@ModelAttribute` can only be used to annotate controller method arguments.

**Question 19:** What is true about `@ModelAttribute` ?

    A.    This annotation is used to bind a method parameter or method return value to a named model attribute, exposed to a web view.

    B.    If a method is annotated with it, that method will be executed before handling any request.

    C.    This annotation is used to bind a form object to a controller.

**Question 20:** What is `@InitBinder` used for?

    A.    To initialize a controller.

    B.    To mark a method that initializes the WebDataBinder, which is used to populate command and form object arguments of annotated handler methods.

    C.    To mark a method for execution before handling any request.

**Question 21:** Which is true when a new view technology is added to a Spring web application?

    A.    The view technology in question must provide a class implementing Spring's View interface.

    B.    The view technology in question must provide a class implementing Spring's ViewResolver interface.

    C.    The view technology must require specific configuration beans to be defined.

**Question 22:** When working with Spring forms, which is the recommended workflow?

    A.    A GET request is made to display the form, a POST request is made to submit the data, and a GET request is made to display a confirmation page and prevent multiple resubmissions.

    B.    A GET request is made to display the form, and a POST request is made to submit the data.

**Question 23:** Given the following Spring form definition, what is wrong with it?

```
<%@ taglib prefix="sf" uri="http://www.springframework.org/tags/form" %>
...
  <sf:form action="${personsUrl}" method="GET">
  ...
</sf:form>
```

    A.   The method of a form cannot be GET.

    B.   The `modelAttribute` is missing.

    C.   The `<%@ taglib prefix="spring" uri="http://www.springframework.org/tags" %>` is missing

**Question 24:** Does Spring MVC support validation of form data?

    A.   Yes

    B.   No

**Question 25:** Which of the following are validation annotations used on form object fields?

    A.   @NotNull

    B.   @Size

    C.   @Valid

    D.   @NotEmpty

    E.   @Constraint

    F.   @Required

    G.   @Pattern

# Practical Exercise

This chapter is quite big, so it has four module projects associated with it and each of the modules covers a specific section. Figure 3-21 depicts the eight module projects attached to this chapter: four practice projects and four proposed solutions for them. You are welcome to analyze the proposed solutions and compare them to your solutions to test your understanding of Spring MVC.

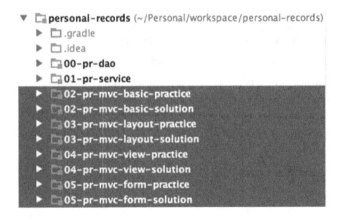

*Figure 3-21.* *Practice projects for Chapter 3*

All web modules depend on the 01-pr-service module. This project contains the @Service classes and the repositories used to manage data. The 01-pr-service depends on the 00-pr-dao module that contains entity classes and common classes (formatters, enums, and utility classes) used by all other modules. The service module was created to respect the standardized three-tiered software architecture pattern, depicted in Figure 3-22. Each tier has a specific responsibility:

- The **data tier** is the data access layer that usually encapsulates persistence mechanisms and exposes the data. It should provide an application programming interface (API) to the logic tier that exposes methods of managing the stored data without exposing or creating dependencies on the data storage mechanisms.[22]

- The **logic tier** (also known as the *service layer*) controls an application's functionality by performing detailed processing. This tier is needed when the application needs to be accessed by different type of clients (browsers, web services, etc.).

- The **presentation layer** is the topmost level of the application that users can directly access, such as a web page or a desktop GUI.

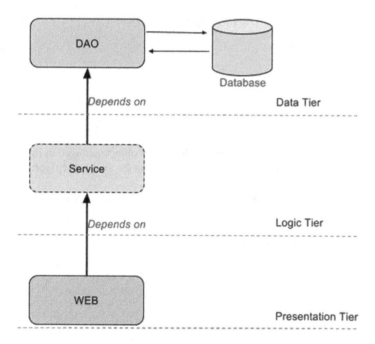

**Figure 3-22.** *Typical standardized three-tiered architecture*

---

[22]In the PErsonal REcords Manager project, because Spring DATA JPA is used, the implementation of the repositories API is reduced to interfaces extending the **JpaRepository** interface. They are placed in the logic tier/service layer.

Because the Personal Records Manager is quite a small project, the service classes do not do much besides calling analogous methods form repository beans.

The HospitalFormatter is part of the 01-pr-service module because it needs a manager instance to retrieve the hospital instance from the repository.

The DBInitializer class is also located in the service class; it is used to populate the database with some sample entries when a web application starts. This class is a simple bean with access to all the service components used in the application, and with a @PostConstruct annotated method that uses those service classes to insert data. This is the most practical way to initialize a small test-scoped database that does not require external configuration files or additional libraries in the classpath. The bean is annotated with @Component and it is automatically discovered, created, and initialized at application boot time.

The @Service annotated classes are organized in the hierarchy depicted in Figure 3-23.

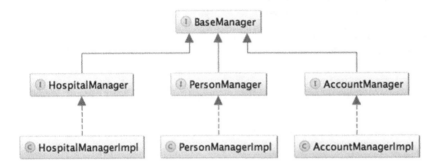

**Figure 3-23.** *Service classes hierarchy*

They are all named [EntityType]ManagerImpl, where EntityType is the type of object managed by the class. The Impl suffix is used to emphasize that the class is a concrete implementation for the [EntityType]Manager interface.

The BaseManager interface contains all the basic method skeletons common to all service classes.

```
@Transactional
public interface BaseManager<E extends AbstractEntity> {

    @Transactional(readOnly = true)
    List<E> findAll();

    @Transactional(readOnly = true)
    E findById(Long id);

    E save(E e);

    void delete(E e);

    void deleteById(Long id);
}
```

The manager interfaces extending it add method skeletons specific to each managed entity-type.

The repository components are created using Spring Data JPA and are in fact interfaces extending the JpaRepository interface. This interface extends CrudRepository, which provides sophisticated CRUD functionality for the entity class being managed. All other method definitions that are needed, but not provided, are defined in the interface extending JpaRepository. They are annotated with the @Query annotation, and the query to be executed is set through it; for example:

```
@Query("select p from Person p where p.lastName = :lastName")
List<Person> getByLastname(@Param("lastName") String lastName);
```

For Spring to provide proxy repositories with the configured implementation for the interfaces that extend JpaRepository, the following line has been added to the app-dao-config.xml configuration file:

```
<beans xmlns="http://www.springframework.org/schema/beans"
    ...
    xmlns:jpa="http://www.springframework.org/schema/data/jpa"
    xsi:schemaLocation="http://www.springframework.org/schema/beans
    ...
    http://www.springframework.org/schema/data/jpa
    http://www.springframework.org/schema/data/jpa/spring-jpa.xsd
    ...">
  <jpa:repositories base-package="com.pr.repos"/>
</beans>
```

The equivalent Java configuration makes use of the @EnableJpaRepositories annotation:

```
@Configuration
@EnableJpaRepositories("com.pr.repos")
class ApplicationConfiguration {

  @Bean
  public EntityManagerFactory entityManagerFactory() { ... }
  @Bean
  public DataSource dataSource() {...}

...
{
```

The basic configuration *.gradle file for each web module project looks like this:

```
(1) apply plugin: 'war'
apply from: 'https://raw.github.com/akhikhl/gretty/master/pluginScripts/gretty.plugin'

dependencies {
    (2) compile project(':01-pr-service')
    compile misc.slf4jApi, misc.slf4jJcl, misc.logback,
            hibernate.ehcache, hibernate.em, hibernate.core, hibernate.validator,
            spring.jdbc, spring.orm, spring.contextSupport, spring.data,
            spring.webmvc,
            misc.dbcp, misc.h2, misc.joda, misc.jstl, misc.tilesJsp,
            misc.tilesReqApi, misc.javaxEl
    testCompile tests.junit, tests.mockito, spring.test,
        tests.hamcrestCore, tests.hamcrestLib
}
```

```
gretty {
    port = 8080
(3) contextPath = '/mvc-layout'
}
```

1. This line is where the Gretty plugin is defined to run this module.

2. This is the line where the dependency from the 01-pr-service project is defined. This line ensures that before compiling the web application, the 01-pr-service is compiled first.

3. This is the line where the Gretty plugin is configured to start the application with a different context than the name of the project. In the case presented here after starting the application, the web interface can be accessed at http://localhost:8080/mvc-layout This was necessary for practical reasons, because by default the module name is used, and the names of the modules in this chapter are quite long.

All the projects can be built without the tests by running the allCompile task, as mentioned earlier in the book. In case you forgot, the task can be found directly under the project root, in this case the personal-records project, in the Intellij IDEA Gradle task tab, as you can see in Figure 3-24.

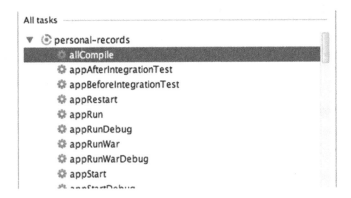

*Figure 3-24.* *The Gradle allCompileTask*

The other two tasks you need to use are the appStart and appStop under the module-project name in the Intellij IDEA Gradle task tab; they start and stop the web application, as depicted in Figure 3-25.

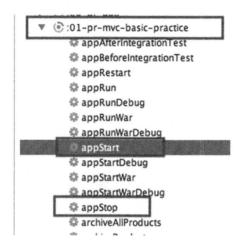

**Figure 3-25.** *The Gerry start and stop web application tasks*

All the modules in `personal-records` can be built and run separately when using Gradle outside of Intellij IDEA, by using the command line in a terminal and running specific Gradle tasks:

```
$ cd personal-records
$ gradle :02-pr-mvc-basic-practice:build
$ gradle :02-pr-mvc-basic-practice:run
```

In the previous examples, the `:02-pr-mvc-basic-practice` is the name of the submodule, and `:build` and `run` are Gradle tasks to be run for the modules.

---

■ ! When running examples in the command line, the `run` task is used instead of `appStart` to run the web modules in Gretty, so the execution can be ended by pressing any key in the terminal.

---

Each of the projects suffixed with `-practice` is incomplete, missing either a bean definition or a configuration. In its place there is a TODO comment explaining what you have to do to make the project build. Each project covers a specific topic from the chapter, as follows:

- `02-pr-mvc-basic-practice` is a simple Spring web application project that displays a list of persons from the applications. It should contain proper definitions for all the personalization beans you read about in the chapter; it is what the TODOs are all about: configuring the personalization beans properly. It has only one controller, the `PersonsController`, which is used to populate the `list.jsp` and `show.jsp` views. This controller also has an `@ExceptionHandler` method that handles cases when a link is manually created with a non-existing person id. (Test the exception handling method by manually accessing `http://localhost:8080/mvc-basic/persons/99`.)

- `03-pr-mvc-layout-practice` is a simple Spring web application project that uses the Tiles engine to create views. Some configuration is missing and some methods have to be added for the project to work correctly. The Tiles template for the application is found under `webapp/WEB-INF/templates`; it is called `layout.jsp`. You can see the full path within the project in Figure 3-26.

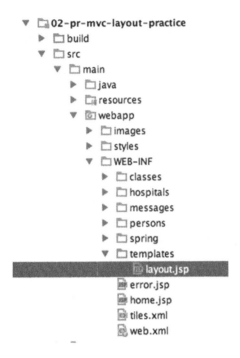

**Figure 3-26.** *Path of the Tiles layout template*

There are two controllers defined PersonsController and HospitalsController. Each of the controllers has the responsibility of populating the corresponding list.jsp views and the HospitalsController has a method that uses redirect: and redirectAttributes. This project also contains unit and integration tests designed to test you controllers.

- 04-pr-mvc-view-practice is a simple Spring web application project that uses content view negotiation to present the data to the user in a specific view format for the persons/list URL. All it is missing is a proper configuration for the ContentNegotiatingViewResolver bean.

- 05-pr-mvc-form-practice is a simple Spring web application project that presents the user with a form to edit users and one to search for users. The TODO tasks require the user to place the correct annotation on methods to enable validation and finish implementing the person search form. The part of the application managing Hospital entries has been removed for the purpose of simplicity, but if you want to practice your Spring form skills, you are welcome to try to create an edit form for a Hospital entry after you have solved the existing TODOs.

All the applications are internationalized and themed. There are two languages available—English and German, and two colored themes—blue and green.

When all the tests pass, all the applications start successfully and provide the expected functionality, and you feel confident that you have a solid grasp of the Spring Web MVC, you can continue to the next chapter.

# CHAPTER 4

■ ■ ■

# Spring Portlets

Although not required for the certification exam, spring portlets are covered in this book because a lot of medium-sized companies tend to favor portal applications, which come with a set of modules already implemented. Companies may also hire developers to provide the customized functionality via pluggable components. Usually, these portal applications are licensed and supported, which is an advantage when things do not go exactly as planned, because you have direct contact with a team of experts that can help you with problems specific to the software.

Portlets are pluggable web components used when creating a **portal**, which is a complex web-based application that provides personalization, authentication, and customizable content aggregation from multiple sources. A **portlet** is a Java-based web component; its lifecycle is managed by a portlet container, which processes requests and generates dynamic content.[1] Each portlet produces a fragment of markup that is combined with the markup of other portlets in the context of a composite portal page. On enterprise application servers, a new *war* archive is deployed on a server, either manually by copying it into a deployment directory, or by uploading it using a manager application. A standard Java portlet should be deployable on any portlet container[2] that complies with the standard.

The advantage of using portlets is that the developer has to only handle the implementation of the logic inside a portlet; the portal server takes care of the rest, such as building and securing the page. Although this seems restrictive, the value of a portal application is the control that is given to administrators and users.

A portlet (or a collection of portlets) behaves as a web-based application per-se, and it can be aggregated to build more complex web applications—portals. Portal applications are as widely used as servlet applications and the design of such applications comes in two flavors:

- Portlets provide small units of functionality and are aggregated by the portal server into a larger application (see Figure 4-1).

---

[1]This definition is given in the official Java portlet specification at https://jcp.org/en/jsr/detail?id=286.
[2]A *portlet container* is an application that runs portlets and provides the appropriate context. Examples of well-known and widely used portal applications that can be customized using portlets include IBM WebSphere Portal; Liferay Portal, an enterprise web platform for building business solutions; GateIn Portal (formerly JBoss Portal), an open source web site framework; and the Blackboard learning management system.

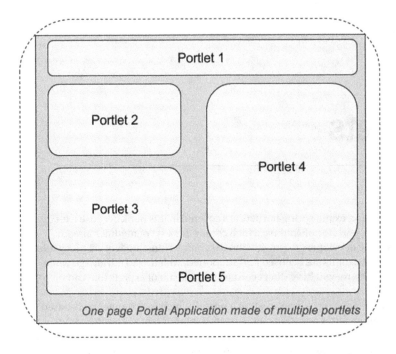

*Figure 4-1. Diagram of portlets as units of a single-page portal application*

- Whole applications can be written to reside in only one or a few portal pages (see Figure 4-2).

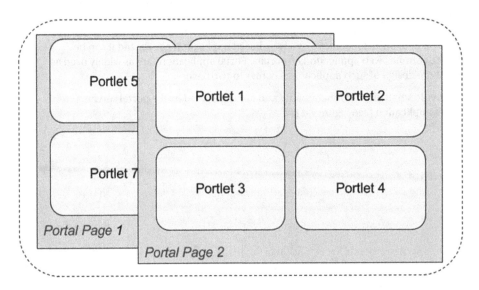

*Figure 4-2. Diagram of a multipage portal application*

Choosing which approach to use depends on the requirements of the application and the number of different functionalities that the application must provide. For example, a university's portal application is made of multiple pages, and each of those is made of multiple portlets with functionality related to a common domain. But a smaller application—a blog, for example—does not need multiple pages; the whole application can fit into one portal page.

**Liferay Community Edition version 6.2-ce-ga4**[3] is used to run the examples in this chapter (Figure 4-3 shows the official Liferay site to help you easily see what you need to download). Choices are made by taking compatibility with Spring into consideration, as well as how practical development and deployment will be. Every portal application requires specific configurations, but Liferay allows high decoupling between portal and application configuration, which is quite an important feature, as you will soon discover.

# Community

- Core Liferay Portal platform
- Community-supported features
- Good for smaller, less critical deployments
- Used for contributing to Liferay development

Bundle with Tomcat

See our list of third party software.

Download

*Figure 4-3. Liferay Portal version to download: Community Edition Bundle with Tomcat*

Spring provides an MVC framework for the JSR-168 and JSR-268 portlet development. This framework tries, as much as possible, to mirror the Web MVC framework, and also uses the same underlying view abstractions and integrations technology to make portlet development more practical.

---

[3]Download the Liferay Community Edition from http://www.liferay.com/downloads/liferay-portal/available-releases.

# Portlet Basics

Portlet workflow is different from servlet workflow because it involves two distinct phases: an **action** phase and a **render** phase. The action phase is executed only once; this is the phase where backend logic is executed. During the render phase, the response that gets sent back to the user is produced. So there is a separation between activities that affect the state of the system and the activities that generate data to be displayed.

Figure 4-4 depicts the difference between MVC servlet handling and MVC portlet handling when using Spring.

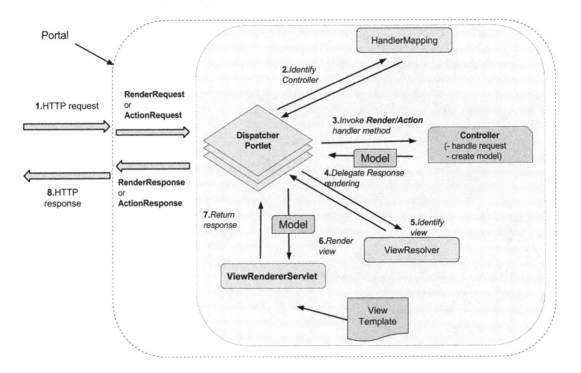

***Figure 4-4.*** *Spring MVC portlet handling*

In the early versions of Spring MVC framework, implementing a controller class in a servlet-based application meant extending the o.s.web.servlet.mvc.AbstractController class (or implementing the org.springframework.web.servlet.mvc.Controller interface) and overriding the handleRequest() method, which is called by DispatcherServlet. Starting with Spring 3.0, this was no longer necessary, because annotations (@Controller and @RequestMapping) are used to provide a more flexible and practical way of working with controllers.

There is an equivalent Spring class for portlets that should be extended to create a portlet: the org.springframework.web.portlet.mvc.AbstractController class (and an equivalent interface org.springframework.web.portlet.mvc.Controller).

The handleActionRequest() and the handleRenderRequest() methods should be overridden; the org.springframework.web.portlet.DispatcherPortlet handles their invocation.

Since Spring 3.0, annotations have made things easier for development of portlets too. @Controller is used to annotate a portlet controller, @RenderMapping is used to annotate a render method, and @ActionMapping is used to annotate an action method.

The advantage of annotations is that multiple render and action methods can be defined, and they can be called depending on the request parameters.

The DispatcherPortlet uses a few special infrastructure beans to process requests and render appropriate views; they are implementations of interfaces analogous to MVC servlet interfaces. So when it comes to portlets, handler mappings are used to map requests and portlet modes with controllers, multipart resolvers, and handler exception resolvers. Data binding, command object usage, model handling, and view resolution are the same as in the servlet framework, and they are performed by the same classes. An intermediary servlet bridge class, called ViewRendererServlet, is used for rendering views; it transforms a portlet rendering request to a servlet request and the view can be rendered using the servlet infrastructure specific beans (view resolvers, messageSource, etc.). The only things not available are the usage of the redirect: prefix and RedirectView, because these kinds of operations are linked to the URL of the request, which in this case is generated by the portal and the results would be unexpected.

Most portal applications expect the result of rendering a portlet to be an HTML fragment, so any view technologies like JSP/JSTL, Velocity, FreeMarker, and XSLT are allowed. This also means that Spring taglib and Spring form taglib are supported.

Each portlet has a javax.portlet.PortletMode defined, which indicates the function the portlet is performing in the render method. A portlet can change its portlet mode programmatically when processing an action request. The portlet specification defines three portlet modes: VIEW, EDIT, and HELP. Depending on the security restrictions, a user can have access only to specific portlet modes; unauthenticated users can only use VIEW and HELP, whereas authenticated users can also use EDIT.

Portlets are required to support VIEW mode; and this is the only mode needed—even in complex applications. EDIT and HELP are not mandatory. Portal applications can define their own custom portlet modes. For example, the Liferay Portal has additional portlet modes:

- ABOUT

- CONFIG

- PRINT

- PREVIEW

- EDIT_DEFAULTS

- EDIT_GUEST

Liferay also allows its users to create their own portlet modes.

Spring also acts as a portlet container, providing portlets with a runtime environment and managing their lifecycle. Spring receives requests from the portal and decides which portlet to execute. The portal is responsible with aggregating the resulted content.

The following is the typical flow of events for using a portal application:

1. The user gets authenticated by the portal.

2. The user makes an HTTP request to the portal.

3. The request is received by the portal.

4. The portal determines if the request contains an action targeted to any of the portlets associated with the portal page.

5. Using the portlet container, the portal invokes portlets to obtain content to be displayed in the resulting portal page.

6. The portal aggregates the output of the portlets in the main page, and then sends the results back to the client.

As seen in this example, even if the request is directed to a single portlet in the page, the whole page is being reconstructed and rendered. This can be avoided by using AJAX components in the portlet pages, and instead of action requests, resource requests can be used (methods will be annotated with @ResourceMapping), but this implies adding a lot of resource handling logic for conversion and validation, which otherwise can be done by Spring automatically.

A portal page can be made of one or more portlets, as seen in Figure 4-5.

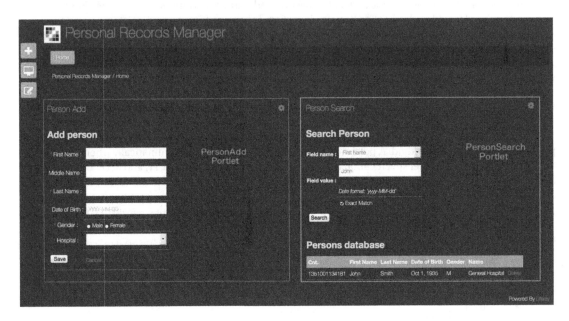

***Figure 4-5.*** *Liferay Portal page with various portlet components*

# Configuration

Spring Portlet is a request-driven web MVC framework designed around the DispatcherPortlet, which is the entry point for a portlet application. It plays the same role as a front controller as DispatcherServlet does for servlet applications. Because each portlet behaves as a stand-alone application, a DispatcherPortlet is defined for each portlet. Each DispatcherPortlet has its own WebApplicationContext, which inherits everything defined in the root WebApplicationContext. Everything inherited can thus be overridden in the portlet-specific scope. A context inheritance diagram example is depicted in Figure 4-6.

Portal
Context

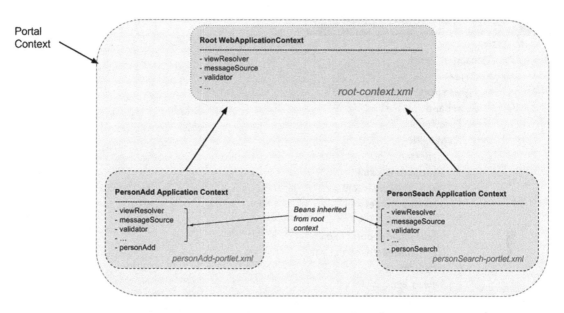

**Figure 4-6.** *Context inheritance diagram in this chapter's application sample*

Configuring a portlet application can be done by using only XML files, but when working with Spring MVC portlet, it is practical to use annotations to reduce the size of XML configuration files and make them more readable.

In the source code attached to this chapter, two portlets are defined: PortletSearch and PortletAdd. Snippets of code from the content of one or the other are used in this book to provide examples for the terms and definitions being mentioned.

# The XML Part of the Configuration

The DispatcherPortlet(s) is/are declared in a configuration file name portlet.xml, which resides under the WEB-INF directory. *This file must exist with the mentioned name and in the mentioned location in any web archive containing portlet definitions.* It is the configuration file for the portlet applications. You can consider it the equivalent of web.xml for portlets.

A portlet application has the same structure as a normal web application, but the necessary configuration files depend on the portal application. How to use Liferay in this case will be discussed shortly; you can see the application structure provided in Figure 4-7.

**Figure 4-7.** *The structure and configuration files for a Liferay portlet application*

Each file under WEB-INF has a specific purpose that will be discussed in detail later in this chapter. A short description of these files and their purposes can be seen in Table 4-1.

**Table 4-1.** *Message Converters Table*

| File Name | Purpose | Observation |
|---|---|---|
| app-config.xml | Application configuration | Spring, part of the root context |
| liferay-display.xml | List of portlets available | Liferay |
| liferay-portlet.xml | Portlets configuration in the portal | Liferay |
| mvc-config.xml | Web infrastructure configuration | Spring, part of the root context |
| personAdd-portlet.xml | PersonAdd portlet configuration file | Spring, inherits root context |
| personSearch-portlet.xml | PersonSearch portlet configuration file | Spring, inherits root context |

The following list describes what every configuration file contains.

- app-config.xml and mvc-config.xml are the typical Spring configuration files that contain the user-defined application beans and web infrastructure beans that are inherited by portlet contexts:

```
<!-- app-config.xml -->
    <context:component-scan base-package="com.pr">
        <context:include-filter type="annotation"
                    expression="o.s.stereotype.Service"/>
        <context:include-filter type="annotation"
                    expression="o.s.stereotype.Repository"/>
    </context:component-scan>
```

```
<!-- Import configuration for the datasource and the dao project -->
<import resource="classpath:spring/app-dao-config.xml"/>
<import resource="classpath:spring/db-config.xml"/>

<!-- mvc-config.xml -->
    <bean id="viewResolver"
          class="o.s.web.servlet.view.InternalResourceViewResolver"
          p:viewClass="org.springframework.web.servlet.view.JstlView"
          p:prefix="/WEB-INF/person/" p:suffix=".jsp"/>

<bean id="messageSource"
      class="o.s.context.support.ReloadableResourceBundleMessageSource"
      p:basename="classpath:localization/global"
      lazy-init="true"/>
```

- `liferay-display.xml` is a Liferay Portal configuration file, which contains the list of portlets available to add in the pages of a site and a category that groups them together. This file is not mandatory, but it is recommended to create it to shorten the deployment process. Having this file in the war (alongside `liferay-display.xml`) allows you to install a portlet war application using the App Manager in Liferay, without any additional operations (see Figure 4-8).

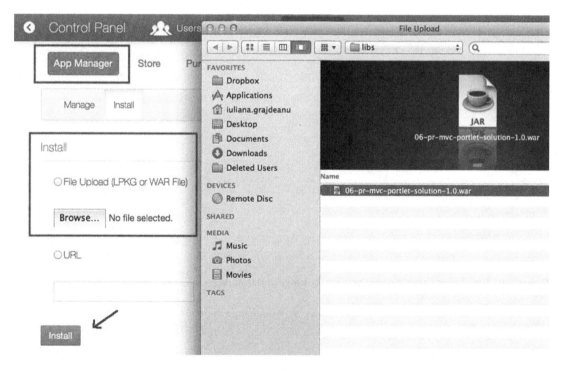

*Figure 4-8.* *The App Manager in Liferay*

- This is the syntax of the file:

```
<display>
        <category name="Personal Records">
                <portlet id="personAdd" />
                <portlet id="personSearch" />
        </category>
</display>
```

- And when creating a site or a site template, Liferay provides user portlets (see Figure 4-9).

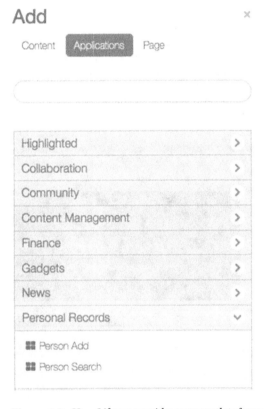

***Figure 4-9.*** *How Liferay provides user portlets for usage in portal pages*

- `liferay-portlet.xml` is a Liferay configuration file that contains typical settings for user created portlets in the context of the web application: portlet names, if they can be used more than once in a page,[4] additional JavaScript files, CSS files,[5] and so forth.

```
<liferay-portlet-app>
    <portlet>
        <!-- The canonical name of the portlet, it has to be unique -->
        <portlet-name>personSearch</portlet-name>
        <!-- Indicates if multiple instances of this portlet
            can appear on the same page -->
        <instanceable>false</instanceable>

        <!-- not used in the example, but can appear in a configuration -->
        <footer-portlet-javascript>/js/main.js</footer-portlet-javascript>
        <header-portlet-css>/styles/general.css</header-portlet-css>
        <requires-namespaced-parameters>false</requires-namespaced-parameters>
    ...
    </portlet>
</liferay-app>
```

As these settings are Liferay specific, they won't be covered in detail here. If you are interested in working with Liferay, you can find more details on the official site at www.liferay.com.

---

! Starting with Liferay 6.2, the `requires-namespaced-parameters` parameter must be specified for a portlet. It must be set to `false` for parameter values to be read correctly. When not specified, the default value is `true` and the portal associates a unique name to each HTML element in the page to prevent name collisions between different portlets in the page.

---

- `personSearch-portlet.xml` and `personAdd-portlet.xml` are portlet application configuration files. A configuration file for each portlet must be created. All beans used by the portlet controller bean (except the beans inherited from the root context) are declared in it. The name must match the `<portletName>-portlet.xml` template, where `<portletName>` is the name of the portlet as declared in `portlet.xml`. In our example, only the definition of the portlet controller bean can be specified. This file is loaded by the `DispatcherPortlet`:

```
<bean id="personSearch" class="com.pr.search.PersonController"
    p:personManager-ref="personManager"/>
```

---

[4]Portlets behave as stand-alone applications, so it is possible to add the same portlet multiple times to a page, unless configured differently.

[5]Liferay and other portlet containers provide a context for the portlets to run in. This context contains theme elements defined in CSS files, and additional functionality in the interface via JavaScript. But the user can override or complement Liferay by providing custom CSS and JavaScript files.

But if you want to use annotations as much as possible, you could do so:

```
<!-- in personSearch-portlet.xml -->
    <context:component-scan base-package="com.pr.search"/>
    <mvc:annotation-driven/>
```

```
<!-- in personAdd-portlet.xml -->
      <context:component-scan base-package="com.pr.add"/>
      <mvc:annotation-driven/>
```

The scanned package contains the portlet controller class and all the
components involved in defining the functionality of a portlet. Although the `<mvc:annotation-driven/>`
declaration seems redundant, it is actually needed because portlets are independent applications, even if
they inherit the same root context and they reside in the same portal application context.

As mentioned, each portlet behaves as a standalone application, and that's why these configuration files
are needed. The root Spring configuration is defined in the
`app-config.xml` and `mvc-config.xml`. Without these configuration files, the deployment will fail, because
the Spring MVC portlet expects a configuration file for each portlet. Here is what happens at deploy time if the
`personSearch-portlet.xml` file is missing:

```
o.s.w.p.c.XmlPortletApplicationContext - Refreshing PortletApplicationContext
for namespace 'personSearch-portlet'...
o.s.b.f.x.XmlBeanDefinitionReader - Loading XML bean definitions from
PortletContext resource /WEB-INF/personSearch-portlet.xml
ERROR o.s.w.p.DispatcherPortlet - Context initialization failed
o.spring.beans.factory.BeanDefinitionStoreException: IOException parsing XML
document from PortletContext resource /WEB-INF/personSearch-portlet.xml;
nested exception is java.io.FileNotFoundException:
Could not open PortletContext resource /WEB-INF/personSearch-portlet.xml
...
```

- `portlet.xml` is the configuration file that defines settings for the portlet(s), such
  as the portlet request handler (the portlet class). When working with Spring only,
  DispatcherPortlet, supported modes, supported locales, supported MIME types,
  and the resource bundle are used. This file contains multiple portlet elements—one
  for each portlet defined in the application.

  ```
  <portlet-app ...>
  <portlet>
        <portlet-name>personSearch</portlet-name>
        <portlet-class>o.s.web.portlet.DispatcherPortlet</portlet-class>
            <supports>
                  <mime-type>text/html</mime-type>
                  <portlet-mode>view</portlet-mode>
            </supports>
            <resource-bundle>localization.global</resource-bundle>
            <portlet-info>
                  <title>Person Search</title>
            </portlet-info>
  </portlet>

  <portlet>
  ```

```
    <portlet-name>personAdd</portlet-name>
    ...
    <!-- configuration is analogous to the one for personSearch -->
</portlet>
<!-- More settings for other portlets -->
</portlet-app>
```

- web.xml contains the deployment descriptor for the web resources, and this is
  where the ViewRendererServlet is declared and the connection to the Spring MVC
  configuration is made. There is no DispatcherServlet defined, because portlet
  applications run in a portlet context, which is different form a servlet context.
  According to Portlet Specification 1.0, every portlet application is also a Servlet
  Specification 2.3–compliant web application, and thus it needs a web application
  deployment descriptor, meaning a web.xml file:

```
<web-app ...>
    <context-param>
      <param-name>contextConfigLocation</param-name>
      <param-value>/WEB-INF/root-context.xml</param-value>
    </context-param>
    <listener>
        <listener-class>o.s.web.context.ContextLoaderListener</listener-class>
    </listener>

        <servlet>
                <servlet-name>ViewRendererServlet</servlet-name>
                <servlet-class>o.s.web.servlet.ViewRendererServlet</servlet-class>
                <load-on-startup>1</load-on-startup>
        </servlet>

        <servlet-mapping>
                <servlet-name>ViewRendererServlet</servlet-name>
                <url-pattern>/WEB-INF/servlet/view</url-pattern>
        </servlet-mapping>
</web-app>
```

The ViewRendererServlet is the bridge servlet for portlet support. During the render
phase, DispatcherPortlet wraps PortletRequest into ServletRequest and forwards control to
ViewRendererServlet for actual rendering. This process allows the Spring Portlet MVC framework to use the
same View infrastructure as that of its servlet version; that is, the Spring Web MVC framework. The /WEB-
INF/servlet/view is the default value available for internal resource dispatching. The ViewRendererServlet
bridge servlet can be mapped to a different URL pattern by using the viewRendererUrl property.

! As mentioned at the beginning of the chapter, the controllers can be created without annotations by extending the |o.s.web.portlet.mvc.AbstractController class. This is the old way of doing things, before the introduction of the @Controller annotation. It is still supported, but not recommended, and it is not as practical as using an annotated controller. In this case, the <portletName>-portlet.xml looks a little different. The HelloWorldController in the book-code/04-chapter-solution module has a configuration file that looks like this:

```
<bean id="helloWorldController" class="com.book.HelloWorldController"/>
<bean id="portletModeHandlerMapping"
 class="o.s.web.portlet.handler.PortletModeHandlerMapping">
 <property name="portletModeMap">
   <map>
     <entry key="view">
       <ref bean="helloWorldController"/>
     </entry>
   </map>
 </property>
</bean>
```

The PortletModeHandlerMapping class is an implementation of the o.s.web.portlet.HandlerMapping interface used by Spring to map from the current PortletMode to request handler beans.

# The Annotation Part of the Configuration

At the time this book is being written, a full annotation configuration for a portlet-based application is not possible. A combination of XML and annotations can be used, because Spring MVC annotations are available for usage in portlet controllers too. For example, in the PersonAddController, the @ModelAttribute is used in a similar manner as for a servlet container. The PersonAddController is a simple controller that allows the user to create a person instance.

```
import org.springframework.stereotype.Controller;

...

@Controller("personAdd")
@RequestMapping("VIEW")
public class PersonAddController {
...
@RenderMapping
    public String render(Model model) {
    model.addAttribute(new Person());
    return "add";
  }
```

```
@ModelAttribute
private List<Hospital> getHospitals() {
    return hospitalManager.findAll();
}


@ActionMapping("add")
public void addPerson(@Valid @ModelAttribute Person person,
    BindingResult result, ActionRequest actionRequest,
    ActionResponse actionResponse,
    SessionStatus sessionStatus, Model model) {
    if (!result.hasErrors()) {
        logger.info("ACTION: action saving person = " person);
        try {
                personManager.save(person);
                model.addAttribute("message",
                    messageSource.getMessage("label.Person.saved", null,
                        actionRequest.getLocale())));
                sessionStatus.setComplete();
        } catch (Exception e) {
            logger.error("Unexpected error when saving person.", e);
            model.addAttribute("error", "Internal Error.
                Contact Administrator.");
        }
    } else {
        logger.info("Validation failed");
        model.addAttribute("errors", result);
    }
  }
 }
}
```

The model attribute defined by getHospitals() is used to populate the hospital drop-down list in the view fragment in add.jsp. The view fragment is basically normal JSP code; any taglibs can be used, and the portlet taglib is used to define the render and action URLs that will be mapped to methods in the controller responsible for populating and managing data for the JSP fragment.

```
(1) <%@ taglib prefix="portlet" uri="http://java.sun.com/portlet_2_0"%>
<%@ taglib prefix="c" uri="http://java.sun.com/jsp/jstl/core" %>
<%@ taglib prefix="fn" uri="http://java.sun.com/jsp/jstl/functions" %>
(2) <%@ taglib prefix="sf" uri="http://www.springframework.org/tags/form" %>
<%@ taglib prefix="spring" uri="http://www.springframework.org/tags" %>

(3) <portlet:defineObjects />

<h3>
  <spring:message code="persons.add.title"/>
</h3>

(4) <portlet:actionURL var="addPersonUrl">
    <portlet:param name="javax.portlet.action" value="add"/>
</portlet:actionURL>
```

```
(5) <portlet:renderURL var="cleanPersonUrl">
    <portlet:param name="action" value="clean" />
</portlet:renderURL>

<div class="person">
...
<sf:form name="person" modelAttribute="person"
              action="${addPersonUrl}"
              method="POST">
    <table>
        <tr>
            <th>
            <label for="firstName">
                <span class="man">*</span>
                <spring:message code="label.Person.firstname"/>
            </label>
        </th>
        <td><sf:input path="firstName"/></td>
        <td><sf:errors cssClass="error" path="firstName"/></td>
        </tr>
        <tr>
            <th>
                <label for="middleName">
                    <spring:message code="label.Person.middlename"/>
                </label>
            </th>
            <td><sf:input path="middleName"/></td>
            <td><sf:errors cssClass="error" path="middleName"/></td>
        </tr>
        ...
        <!-- other form elements -->
        <tr>
            <td>
                <input type="submit"
                              value=" <spring:message code='command.save'/>">
            </td>
            <td>
                <a href="${cleanPersonUrl}">
                    <spring:message code="command.cancel"/>
                </a>
            </td>
        </tr>
    </table>
</sf:form>
</div>
```

The previous sample code is a snippet from the definition of the add.jsp fragment. A few lines are marked with numbers in parentheses; here is why those lines are important:

- (1) The portlet taglib definition for JRS 286. (A portlet container that supports JSR 286 should also support JSR 168.)

- (2) The Spring form taglib definition.

- (3) Needed to use renderRequest, renderResponse, and portletConfig variables.[6]

- (4) An element used to define an action URL for a portlet. The javax.portlet.action parameter value must match the value of the @ActionMapping annotation placed on the action method in the controller. Other parameters with different names can be used and the {name,value} pairs, must appear as a value for the @ActionMapping annotation params attribute to correctly identify the action method to use. In the case described in the preceding snippet, the following method will be mapped to the addPersonUrl:

```
@Controller("personAdd")
@RequestMapping("VIEW")
public class PersonAddController {
...
@ActionMapping("add")
        public void addPerson(...){
        ...
        }
    ...
}
```

- (5) An element used to define a render URL. This element has a parameter, and its name and value appears in the @RenderMapping annotation params attribute to correctly identify the render method to use. In the case described in the preceding snippet, the following methods will be mapped to the cleanPersonUrl:

```
@Controller("personAdd")
@RequestMapping("VIEW")
public class PersonAddController {
...
  @RenderMapping(params = "action=clean")
    public String renderNew(Model model) {
    //the model attribute is removed from the model and a new on is added
    //causing the form to be emptied of data
        model.asMap().remove("o.s.validation.BindingResult.person");
        model.addAttribute(new Person());
        return "add";
    }
...
}
```

---

[6]https://blogs.oracle.com/deepakg/entry/jsr286_defineobjects_tag.

# Configuration Details and Recommendations

If you paid enough attention to the example configuration files presented in the previous sections, you might have noticed that there are some common elements between the configuration files; portlet names and portlet ids have to respect some strict rules in order for the portlets to be deployed correctly. Figure 4-10 is a mashup of all files used in defining a portlet. In this image, only configuration elements specific to the PersonAdd portlet are depicted. Analogous elements are also defined for the PersonSearch portlet in this book's code samples. If you decide to experiment with the provided code and create your own portlet, the configuration should be done similarly to what is presented in Figure 4-10 for the PersonAdd portlet.

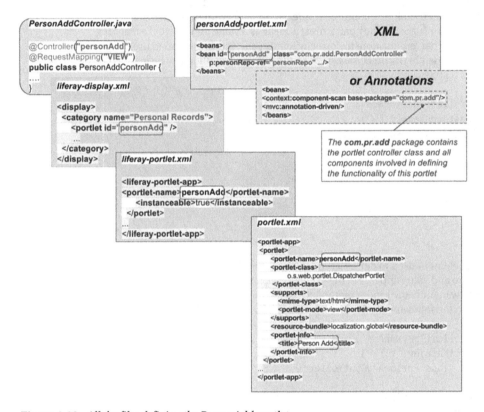

**Figure 4-10.** *All the files defining the PersonAdd portlet*

When developing a portlet, it is important to keep a standard for naming beans and configuration items; make it as global as possible, because when elements are not found, Spring reports these as errors in the portal application. Spring is quite clear in telling you what is missing, but portal application exceptions can be quite confusing, especially when you are working with a portal application for the first time. So if you want your portlet development to go flawlessly, try to follow these recommendations:

1. Try to start development by writing the controller. Name the controller appropriately. A controller name should be made of the following:

    a. The name of object type being manipulated

    b. The type of manipulation (list, search, edit, add)

    c. The Controller suffix

For example, a controller that handles requests for searching for a person would be named PersonSearchController. The name of the controller bean should be the object type name + manipulation type. So the PersonSearchController name is annotated with @Controller("personSearch").

2. The second file is the Spring portlet configuration type. It is named as follows:

    a. The name of the object type being manipulated

    b. The type of manipulation (list, search, edit, add)

    c. The -portlet suffix

So, a file to configure a portlet that performs a person search would be called personSearch-portlet.xml. Inside this file, a bean defines the controller type that you previously created, and dependencies are injected when XML configuration is used. The bean id is the name of the controller bean defined in the previous step.

```
<bean id="personSearch">
    <property name="personManager" ref="personManager"/>
</bean>
```

When annotations are used to configure the necessary components, only the package that you are interested in is scanned, and the <mvc:annotation-driven/> is added:

```
<context:component-scan base-package="com.pr.search"/>
<mvc:annotation-driven/>
```

3. The liferay-display.xml is next. Set the portlet id as object type name + manipulation type.

4. In the liferay-portlet.xml, set the portlet name as object type name + manipulation type too.

So, for the portlet that displays a list of people, the portlet id and portlet name should be personList.

5. In portlet.xml, use the same portlet name as you did in the previous step.

6. Another recommendation is to make portlets that display data instanceable and the portlets that alter data non-instanceable. The reason for this is as follows: if a portlet that displays data is placed twice in the page, both portlets will always display the same data, because they share the request. The same happens with portlets that alter data; so basically, two action requests are made with the same parameters, even if the input parameters have been populated in only one of them. This leads to exceptions at the database level if the database is properly designed. If not, this leads to data duplications, and sometimes data corruption.

7. If you have only one portlet, the root-context.xml is not necessary and all Spring infrastructure beans can be declared in the <portletName>-portlet.xml.

# The Development and Deployment of a Portlet Application

Since this chapter does not cover topics required for the certification exam, no quiz or practical exercises are in it; instead, a short step-by-step tutorial explains how to install, start, and configure Liferay, and deploys the code samples offered to you. After you understand the process and create some portal pages with the given portlets, you can try to create your own portlet by following the recommendations from the previous section.

# Download, Install, Start, and Configure Liferay

As mentioned in the beginning of this chapter, Liferay can be downloaded from www.liferay.com/downloads/liferay-portal/available-releases. The following examples use the Community Edition, bundled with Tomcat, because it is free and can be downloaded directly. Also, Tomcat is really easy to use.

After you click the **Download** button a *.zip file is saved onto your computer. The file is usually named liferay-portal-tomcat-[version]-ce-ga[index]-[date+build_number].zip. Unpack the archive in a desired location. And this is the end of the install process.

If you open the directory, you will see the content depicted in Figure 4-11.

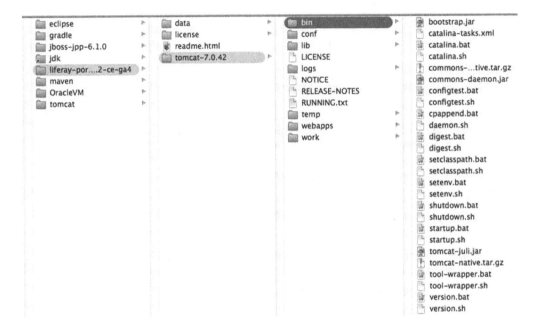

*Figure 4-11.* *The Liferay installation archive*

The tomcat-[version] is the version of Tomcat that Liferay is based upon. It has the normal structure and functionality of a Tomcat application server, but it contains some extra jars and configuration files for the Liferay Portal application.

---

! Currently, Liferay is based on Tomcat 7, so a configuration without a web.xml file is not possible.

---

To start Liferay, you have to open a shell terminal or a **Command Prompt** instance. Go to the tomcat/bin directory inside the Liferay installation. Start the server as you would start Tomcat.

```
Windows / Command Prompt
C:\{directory}\liferay-{version}\omcat-{version}\bin catalina.bat run
# you also have the option to "double-click" on startup.bat

Linux / MacOs shell terminal
cd /{directory}/liferay-{version}/tomcat-{version}/bin ./startup.sh
```

You can look in `tomcat-[version]/logs/catalina.out` to see when the server is up and whether exceptions were thrown due to incompatibilities between the Java version and Liferay. There could be other tomcat `*.log` files in the directory, but the `catalina.out` file is the one you should be interested in, because it is the main logging file for Tomcat and logs are written into it in real time when the server is up. Liferay 6.2 is compatible with Java 8, however, so no such problem should arise. When the server is started, a window is opened in your default system browser at the address `http://localhost:8080`.

This page asks you to insert a few settings details. For the examples in this book, the default configuration can be used. The page should look like the one shown in Figure 4-12.

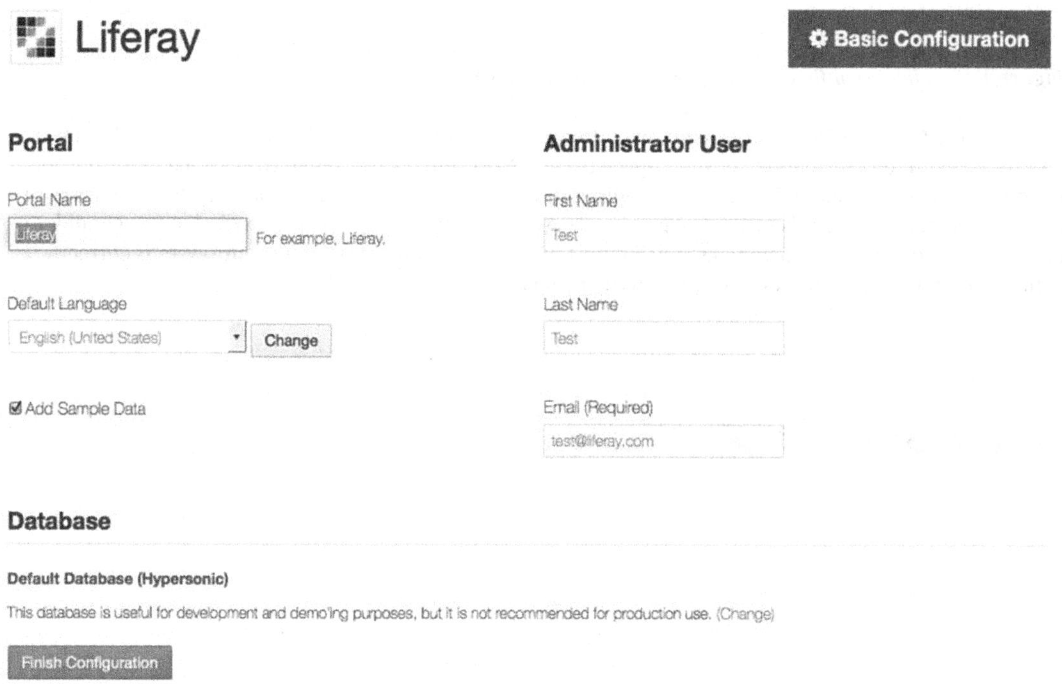

**Figure 4-12.** *The Liferay welcome page*

Click the **Finish Configuration** button on the bottom-left corner of the page. The default settings are saved in an internal in-memory database. You should see a confirmation page that looks like the shown one in Figure 4-13.

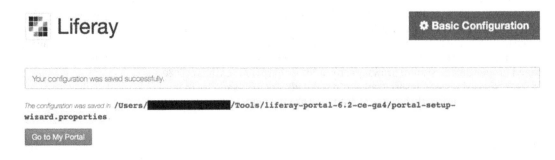

*Figure 4-13.* *Liferay configurations saved confirmation page*

Click the **Go to my Portal** button in the bottom-left corner of the page. The next page is the **Terms of Use** page. Just scroll down and click the **I Agree** button. Next, you are presented with a page requiring you to add a password reminder. Just insert something simple and click the **Save** button. The default password for user `test@liferay.com` is **test** (see Figure 4-14). After introducing a password reminder, you should be redirected to the portal home page (see Figure 4-15). If you see this page, then your server is correctly configured and you can start deploying custom portlets.

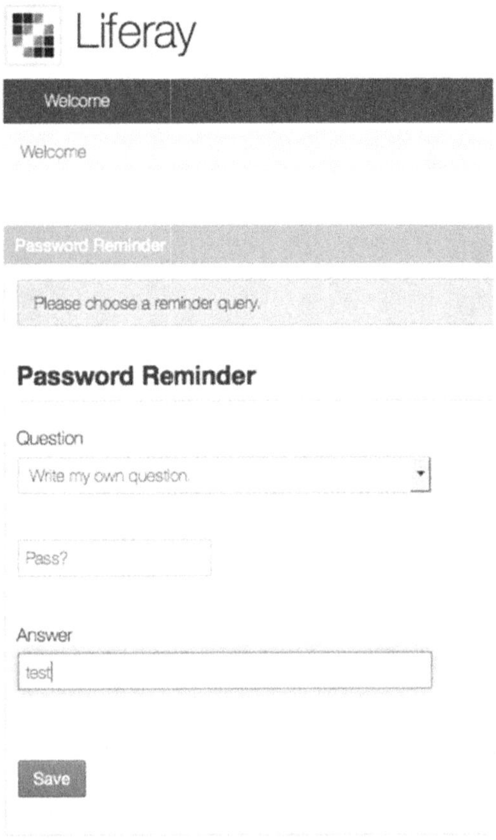

![Liferay Password Reminder page screenshot showing Welcome section, Password Reminder section with "Please choose a reminder query" text, Question dropdown "Write my own question", "Pass?" field, Answer field with "test", and Save button]

*Figure 4-14.* *Liferay Password Reminder page*

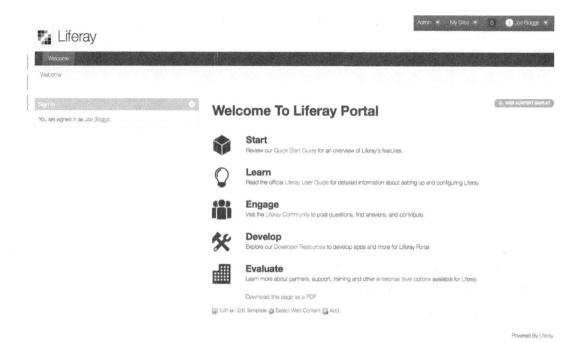

**Figure 4-15.** *Liferay Portal home page*

In Liferay, portlets have to be added manually to a **page** by selecting them from a list with available components. A page is usually part of a site. In Liferay, there are also **site templates**, which can be used to create multiple sites that inherit the configuration of a template. Of course, you could add the portlets directly to the home page you see after logging in, and then start testing them; but for the examples in this chapter, you will use Liferay the proper way.

The first step is to create a site template. To do this, expand the **Admin** menu and select **Control Panel**. Figure 4-16 shows where this option is found on the menu.

**Figure 4-16.** *Liferay Admin menu*

After selecting the Control Panel option, an admin page with all possibilities is displayed (see Figure 4-17).

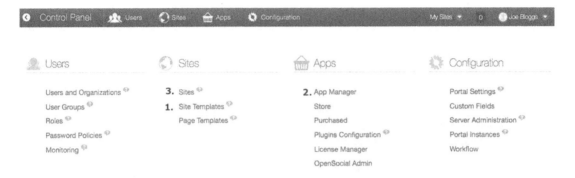

**Figure 4-17.** *Liferay admin page*

These options are numbered in Figure 4-17 to show you their order of usage when creating your site:

1. Link to the Site Templates administration page.

2. Link to the portlets (Applications) administration page.

3. Link to the Sites administration page.

This page takes care of administration for the portal application and all sites hosted by it. Sites can be secured or public. They can have users with different access roles and rights. They can have custom pages. Site templates can be created and user-provided portlets can be installed by using the App Manager. So let's create a public site and populate it with the provided portlet samples.

Click the **Site Templates** link to display the Site Template configuration page. Click the **+Add** button. The form for creating the site template is displayed (see Figure 4-18). Insert the name of the site template and a description, if you want (description is not mandatory, the site name is). Click the **Save** button.

***Figure 4-18.*** *Liferay create Site Template page*

The more extended site template configuration is next. Click the **Pages** option in the menu on the left. Next, click the **Site pages** option. In the center of the page, a set of options for all the pages in the site template are presented. One of these options is the theme for all pages. Select the **Dark** radio button under the **Color Schemes** section to use the dark scheme for the site template, because in the style sheet used in the example, the style is defined to be compatible with it (see Figure 4-5). Then click the **Save** button on the right. Figure 4-19 depicts the actual page and the order of operations.

1. Link to all site pages configurations.

2. Select the **Dark** theme option.

3. Link to the home page template configuration page.

4. Click the **Save** button.

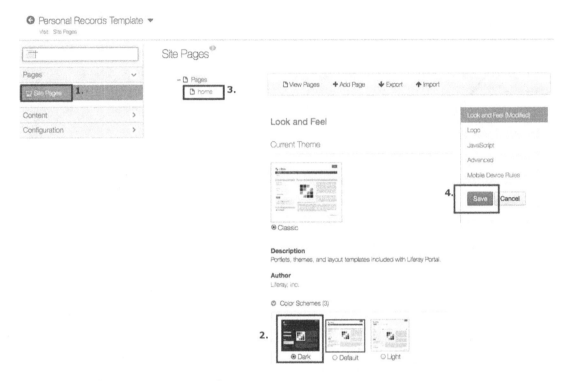

***Figure 4-19.*** *Liferay customize site template page*

Click the **home** link (3), to customize the home page. Change the name if you want; in this example, the first letter is in uppercase. Next, select a layout. The preferred layout is **2 Columns (50/50)**, so the portlets can be added side by side in the page. After doing this, click the **Save** button. A green message box should appear at the top of the page, letting you know that all went well (see Figure 4-20).

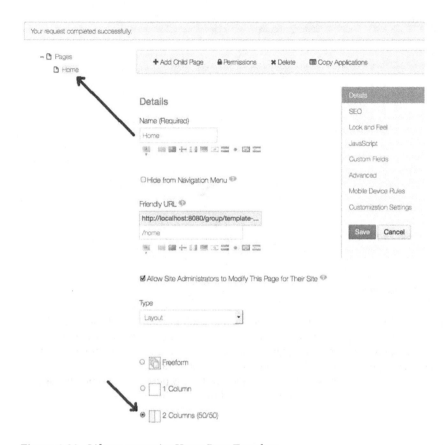

*Figure 4-20.* *Liferay customize Home Page Template*

So, now a site template has been created; it contains a single page named **Home**, which is the page the sample portlets implementations will be placed. To do that, you have to preview the site template, which is done by going back to the Site Templates Administration page and clicking the **Site Templates** button at the top of the page. A list with all the defined site templates is displayed. The last one on the list should be the recently created site template. Click the **Actions** button for the site and select the **View Pages** option (see Figure 4-21).

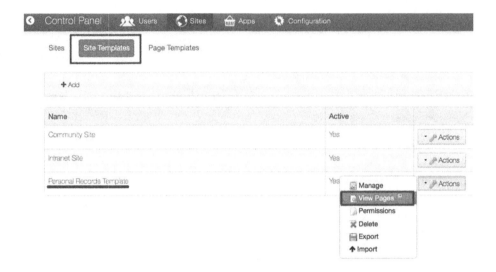

**Figure 4-21.** *Liferay Site Templates page*

In a new browser window or tab, your site template is opened for customizations. On the left, there is a light-blue button with a + sign on it. If you click it, a menu opens to allow you to modify the content of the home page. Since there is only one page, it is automatically selected. (When there are multiple pages to customize, you would just click a page header to select it, and then all customizations to be done on it.) Click the **Applications** menu item to see a list of the available out-of-the-box Liferay portlets to add on the page. They are grouped by category. The page in administration mode is shown in Figure 4-22.

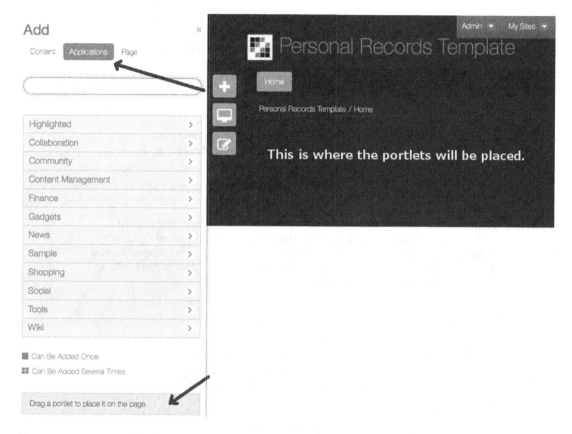

**Figure 4-22.** *Site Template home page in administration mode*

Now it is time to load the sample portlets.

Open the book-code project and run the **war** task under the 04-chapter-solution project. The execution of this task creates a *.war file under 04-chapter-solution\build\libs that needs to be deployed to the Liferay Portal. The module contains two portlets:

- **Hello World Portlet** is a simple portlet application with a controller created by implementing the o.s.web.portlet.mvc.Controller, as mentioned at the beginning of the chapter. The handleRenderRequest of this portlet sets an attribute to the model, which is displayed during the render phase.

```
import javax.portlet.ActionRequest;
import javax.portlet.ActionResponse;
import javax.portlet.RenderRequest;
import javax.portlet.RenderResponse;

import o.s.web.portlet.ModelAndView;
import o.s.web.portlet.mvc.Controller;

public class HelloWorldController implements Controller {
```

```
    public ModelAndView handleRenderRequest(RenderRequest request,
            RenderResponse response) throws Exception {
        Map<String, Object> model = new HashMap<String, Object>();
        model.put("helloWorldMessage",
                "Hello World from Spring WEB portlet example application!!");
        return new ModelAndView("helloWorld", model);
    }


    public void handleActionRequest(ActionRequest request,
                ActionResponse response) throws Exception {
            //we do not have action requests
    }
}
```

- **Hello World Portlet2** is a simple portlet application with a controller created and configured using a typical Spring configuration: annotations and XML. As a bonus, this portlet has a @ResourceMapping annotated method that is used to send a text directly to the browser. These types of methods can be used in AJAX calls, as mentioned at the beginning of this chapter.

```
import o.s.stereotype.Controller;
import o.s.ui.Model;
import o.s.web.bind.annotation.RequestMapping;
import o.s.web.portlet.bind.annotation.ActionMapping;
import o.s.web.portlet.bind.annotation.RenderMapping;
import o.s.web.portlet.bind.annotation.ResourceMapping;
@Controller("helloworld2")
@RequestMapping("VIEW")
public class HelloWorldController2 {

@RenderMapping
public String render(Model model){
    model.addAttribute("helloWorldMessage",
            "Hello World from Annotated Spring Portlet!!");
    return "helloWorld2";
}

//We do not need to do anything here.
//Empty method given as example of how action methods are defined.
@ActionMapping(value="doSomething")
public void action(ActionRequest request, ActionResponse response){
}

    //Example of resource request method
    @ResourceMapping(value = "getData")
    public void getData(ResourceRequest resourceRequest,
            ResourceResponse resourceResponse) throws IOException {
        resourceResponse.getWriter().write("Test data for Ajax call.");
    }
}
```

Please take the time to analyze the code and the configuration files, and then execute the task and build the *.war. If the task is executed correctly, you should see the result in 04-chapter-solution\build\libs. Compare Figure 4-23 with your own environment.

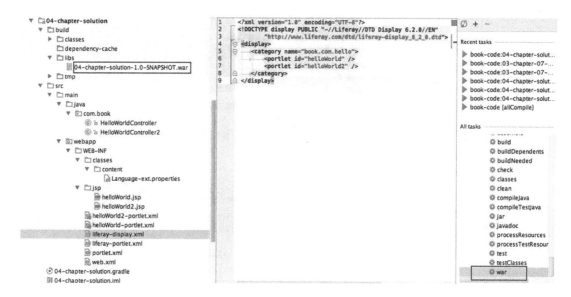

**Figure 4-23.** *The 04-chapter-solution portlet sample*

Now that you have the archive with the portlets, it is time to upload them to Liferay. For this you need to go the portal administration page (Control Panel) and click the **App Manager** link. A page with all available portlets is displayed.

The following actions must be performed:

1. Click the **Install** tab on the menu.

2. A page with an upload Form will be displayed, asking you to upload an **LPKG** or a **WAR** file. Click the **Browse** button. (On some systems, this button might be named **Choose File**.)

3. Select the 04-chapter-solution-1.0-SNAPSHOT.war file.

4. Click the **Install** button.

If the *.war file is installed correctly, a green message box appears on the top of the page with the message: *The plugin was uploaded successfully and is now being installed* (see Figure 4-24).

***Figure 4-24.*** *Using the App Manager to install custom portlets in Liferay*

---

! Community editions of Liferay may have minor bugs and throw exceptions, although everything is happening as it should. For example, the Liferay version used to test the portlet implementations, `liferay-portal-6.2-ce-ga4`, throws a *com.liferay.portal.kernel.messaging. MessageListenerException:java.lang. NullPointerException,* which is printed in the `catalina.out` log file, but the portlets are installed correctly.

---

To make sure that the portlets were installed correctly and are ready to use, click the **Manage** tab. The `04-chapter-solution-1.0-SNAPSHOT` application should be at top of the list because of its name, and if you expand the gray rectangle underneath, you should see something similar to what's shown in Figure 4-25.

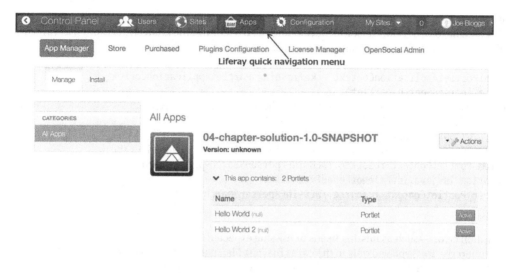

**Figure 4-25.** *Correctly installed portlet samples in Liferay*

Now is the time to go back to the site template and place these two portlets in the home page. Liferay has a quick navigation menu on top of the page, which can be used for faster navigation between administrative pages. (It is pinpointed to you in Figure 4-25). There is a **Sites** option on it. By clicking this, the Liferay site–related configurations page is displayed (see Figure 4-21). Now all you have to do is click the **Site Templates** button, and then preview the site template as shown earlier.

The page shown in Figure 4-22 should have an extra category now, the **Chapter 04 Sample**. Expand this, and then drag each portlet to the page and place it accordingly. The home page should look like what's shown in Figure 4-26; you can also see the new category group for the HelloWorld sample portlets.

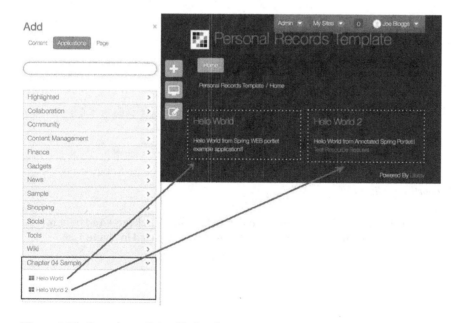

**Figure 4-26.** *Sample portlets added to the page*

Before creating a site using the template, the way to uninstall a war application should be presented, because things might go wrong during portlet development. For example, the following exception is thrown at Liferay deployment when the configuration of a portlet application is incorrect:

```
o.s.w.p.c.XmlPortletApplicationContext - Refreshing PortletApplicationContext
for namespace 'personSearch-portlet'...
o.s.b.f.x.XmlBeanDefinitionReader - Loading XML bean definitions from
PortletContext resource /WEB-INF/personSearch-portlet.xml
ERROR o.s.w.p.DispatcherPortlet - Context initialization failed
o.spring.beans.factory.BeanDefinitionStoreException: IOException parsing XML
document from PortletContext resource /WEB-INF/personSearch-portlet.xml;
nested exception is java.io.FileNotFoundException:
Could not open PortletContext resource /WEB-INF/personSearch-portlet.xml
...
```

Configuration errors—such as missing beans or missing expected configuration files (like in the preceding exception)—are displayed only in the catalina.out file. In the App Manager you can see the green message confirmation box as long as the file can be read. The difference is message under the portlet name in the Manage section: *There are no configurable plugins for this app.*

When this happens, click the **Manage** tab, and then click the **Actions** button attached to the application you want to uninstall. Select the **Uninstall** option. See Figure 4-27 for the message and uninstall option.

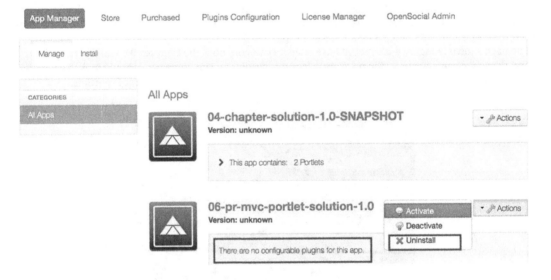

***Figure 4-27.*** *Uninstall a portlet application*

Now let's create a site. Select **Sites** from the top menu, and then select **Sites**. Click the **+Add** button. Next, select the **Personal Records Template**. The succession of these steps is depicted in Figure 4-28.

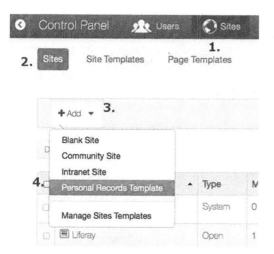

**Figure 4-28.** *The steps to create a site using a site template*

You will be directed to a new page, where a name and description can be inserted for the site. There are other options possible, but for now, just accept the default values and click the **Save** button. The page will look like the one shown in Figure 4-29.

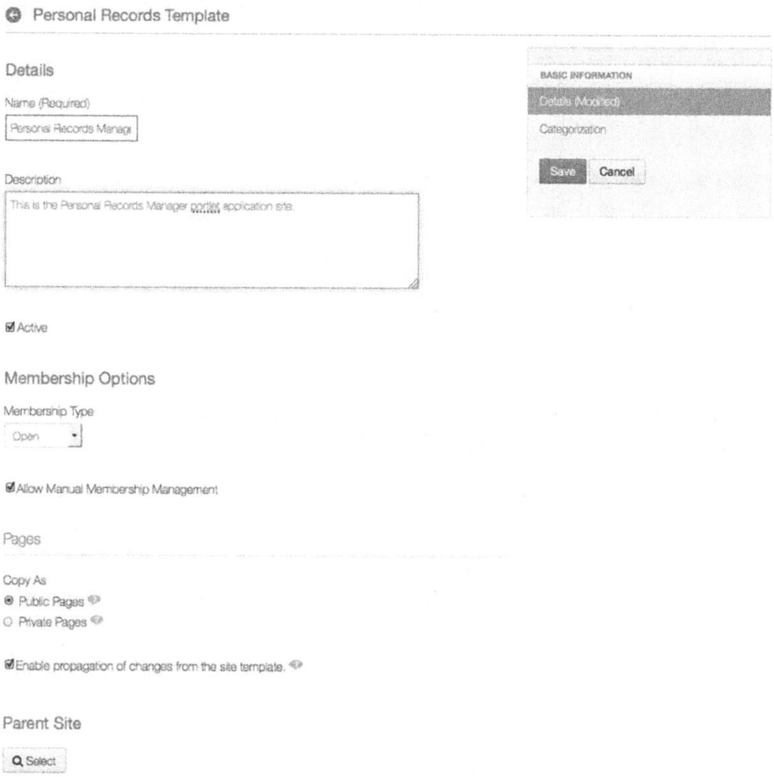

**Figure 4-29.** *Site configuration page*

After creating the site, more configuration options become available, and you can see them all in the page that is loaded after the save operation. A recommended practice is to customize the site URL, as Liferay will generate one from the site name (which might not be an acceptable URL). For example, for a site named *Personal Records Manager,* the site URL generated by Liferay is `personal-records-manager`. To modify a site URL, in the site configuration page, click the **Site URL** menu option on the right, and then change the generated site URL with the desired URL under the **Friendly URL** section, as depicted in Figure 4-30.

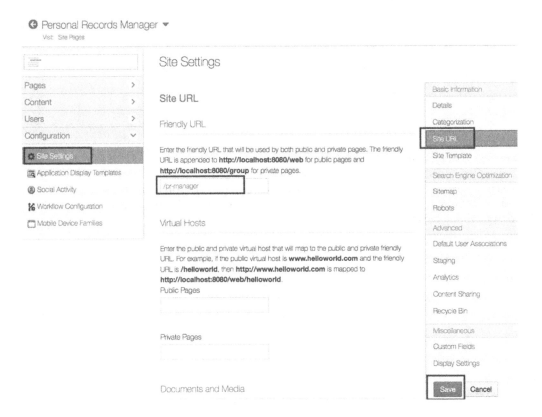

***Figure 4-30.*** *Site URL configuration*

Click the **Save** button, and then access the newly created site from the menu. Go to **My Sites**. The site name should appear in the menu. By clicking it, you should be redirected to the site home page (see Figure 4-31).

**Figure 4-31.** *Accessing a Liferay site*

After the two extra-simple HelloWorld portlets from the book-code project are added to the site, look in personal-records for the module named 06-pr-mvc-portlet-solution. This module contains two complex portlets: one for creating a Person instance and one for searching the Person database and deleting Person instances. These are complex portlets that access a database and perform actual data modification; they don't just display data. Most code samples mentioned in this chapter are from these portlets. These portlets have been developed in such a way that all Spring MVC has to offer is included: model attributes, Spring forms, automatic conversion and validation, and so on. The code for the Spring form and validation is the same as the one for forms used in a servlet environment, and you can find it all in Chapter 3. The reason for this is that servlet and portlet environments differ only by the type of requests being resolved and the way they are mapped to handlers. Once a request has been mapped to a handler, processing the data inside the body of a request is independent of the application type.

Please take a look at the project, and then deploy the portlets on Liferay and add them to the site template in the same manner presented so far. Your updated site should afterward look like what is shown in Figure 4-32, or a little different if you chose a different way to place your portlets in the page.

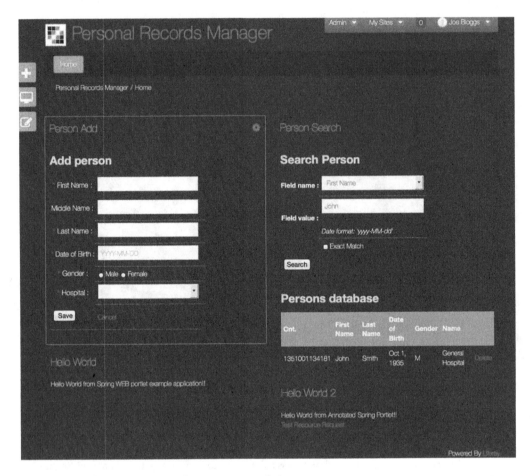

*Figure 4-32. The Personal Records Manager portal site*

# Summary

After reading this chapter, you should have a basic understanding of how to use the Spring MVC Portlet framework with the Liferay Portal application. Here is a list of things that you should remember in case you ever end up working on a portal project:

- Portlets are specialized web components that behave as stand-alone web applications and used to create composite pages in portal applications.

- The Spring MVC Portlet framework mirrors the Spring MVC framework. The role of the front controller is played by the DispatcherPortlet in portlet applications.

- A portlet works with two types of requests: render and action. The render requests do not involve business logic or data manipulation; they just request data from the portal to display it in the page. Actions do the actual data manipulation.

- Most Spring MVC infrastructure beans and features are available for use in portlet applications.

- Liferay is very compatible with Spring MVC Portlet; the configuration is totally decoupled.

# CHAPTER 5

■ ■ ■

# Spring RESTful Services

REST is an acronym for **RE**presentational **S**tate **T**ransfer. It was introduced and defined in 2000 by Roy Fielding in his doctoral dissertation. REST is a lightweight alternative to mechanisms like RPC (Remote Procedure Calls) and web services (SOAP, WSDL, etc.). REST is an *architecture style* for designing networked (distributed) applications. The idea is that, rather than using complex mechanisms such as CORBA, RPC, or SOAP to connect machines, simple HTTP is used to make calls between machines. RESTful applications use HTTP requests to post data (create and/or update), read data (e.g., make queries), and delete data. Thus, REST uses HTTP for all four CRUD (create/read/update/delete) operations.

## Core REST Concepts

The REST architectural style describes six constraints:

- **Uniform interface:** Defines the interface between client and server. Rest uses HTTP as an *application protocol*, as a platform, not just a transport protocol. The following HTTP specifications are used:

  - HTTP verbs are used as actions to execute on the resources (GET, PUT, PATCH, POST, DELETE, HEAD, and OPTIONS)[1]

  - URIs are used to identify resource names. The resources are conceptually separate from representations. Representations of the resources are returned from the server to the client, after a client request (typically JSON or XML). Representations contain metadata that can be used by the client to modify or delete the resource on the server, provided it has permission to do so.

  - HTTP response: Response codes, the body, and headers are used to deliver state to clients. Clients deliver state using body content, query-string parameters, request headers, and the URI.

---

[1]Although REST seems strongly connected to HTTP, REST principles can be followed using other protocols too, for example: POP, IMAP, and any protocol that uses URL-like paths and supports GET and POST methods.

- **Statelessness:** The server should contain no client state. Each request has enough context for the server to process the message. The URI uniquely identifies the resource, and the body contains the state (or state change) of that resource if the request is one that has a body (PUT, POST, PATCH). When working with a specific container, a session is used to preserve state across multiple HTTP requests. When using REST, there is no need for this, which increases the scalability because the server does not have to maintain, update, or communicate the session state.

- **Client-server:** A RESTful architecture is a client-server architecture, so the system is disconnected. The server might not be available all the time, so operations are asynchronous.

- **Cacheable:** Anything returned by the server can be cached explicitly (the server specifies conditions for caching), implicitly (the client uses its own caching conditions), or negotiated(the client and the server negotiate caching conditions)

- **Layered system:** The client cannot assume direct connection to the server. Sometimes a requested resource can be cached, and some other unknown software and hardware layers are interposed between the client and the server. Intermediary servers may improve system scalability and/or security by enabling load balancing, providing shared caches, and enforcing security policies.

- **Code on demand:** Executable code can be transferred as a representation to the client (usually JavaScript or compiled Java applications known as *applets*).

---

■ **Note** Processes running on different hosts communicate over a layered set of network protocols defined by the OSI model. The uppermost level is the **application layer** and protocols specific to it are called **application protocols**. This is the layer that is closest to the user, which means the user interacts directly with the software application. Between the application layer and the transport layer are two more layers.

The **transport layer** provides the functional and procedural means of transferring variable-length data sequences from a source to a destination host via one or more networks, while maintaining the quality of service functions. The protocols specific to it are called **transport protocols**.

When using REST, data is not just sent and received via HTTP (transport), but data is actively manipulated by the user in the context of an application. More information about network layers and protocols can be found on the Internet; if you are interested in finding out more, you can check out Wikipedia at `https://en.wikipedia.org/wiki/OSI_model`. Advanced networking is not the object of this book or the certification exam.

---

Complying with the first five constraints ensures that a RESTful application will be scalable, simple, easy to modify, portable, and reliable. The last constraint is optional; a REST application can be built without code being transferred to clients, if there is no need for such operations. The main REST HTTP methods are presented in Table 5-1.

***Table 5-1.*** *Message Converters*

| HTTP Method | Purpose | Observation |
| --- | --- | --- |
| GET | Read | Reads a resource; does not change it: therefore, it can be considered **safe**. Reading the same resource always returns the same result: therefore, it can be considered **idempotent.** |
| POST | Create | Used to create a new resource. **Neither safe nor idempotent**. Two identical POST requests will result in two identical resources being created or errors at application level. |
| PUT | Update | Most often used for update capabilities. **It is not safe**, because it modifies the state on the server, **but is idempotent** (unless subsequent calls of the same PUT request increments a counter within the resource, for example). |
| DELETE | Delete | Used to delete resources. **Not safe, but can be considered idempotent** because requests to delete a resource that no longer exists will always return a 404 (not found). |

To analyze contents of the REST requests and responses handled by the browser, the Firebug plugin in Firefox can be used. Simply install it directly from the official site (http://getfirebug.com/) and enable it by clicking the little bug on the right corner of the page (1). To see the contents of a request, just click on the Net tab (2), as depicted in Figure 5-1.

***Figure 5-1.*** *Using the Firebug plugin in Firefox to analyze REST requests and responses handled by the browser*

The following describes the GET example shown in Figure 5-2:

- It retrieves a representation of a resource.

- It might have length restrictions.[2]

- It is a safe operation; idempotent; repetitive execution that has no side effects.

- It is cacheable and ETags are used to keep tags on resource versions.[3]

- When a resource is not found, a **404 (Not Found)** status code is returned; otherwise **200 (OK)**

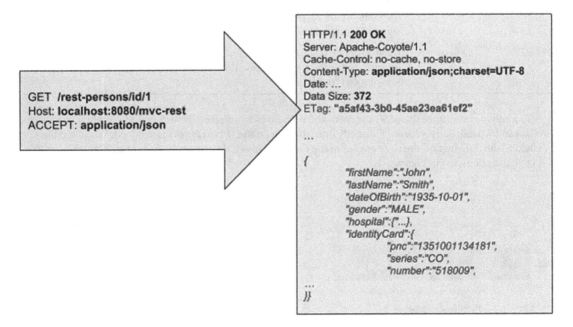

***Figure 5-2.*** *GET Request and Response example; snippets form the Firebug console*

The following describes the POST example shown in Figure 5-3:

- It creates a new resource.

- It is not idempotent; repetitive execution causes duplicate data and/or errors.

- The response has the created resource location URI in the response header.

- When the resource being created requires a parent that does not exist a **404 (Not Found)** status code is returned. When an identical resource already exists a **409 (Conflict)** status code is returned. When the resource was created correctly a **201 (Created)** status code is returned.

---

[2]Servers should be cautious about depending on URI lengths above 255 bytes, because some older client or proxy implementations may not properly support these lengths. When a browser does not support a certain request length, a **400 (Bad Request)** status code is returned.

[3]You can read more about ETags at http://en.wikipedia.org/wiki/HTTP_ETag.

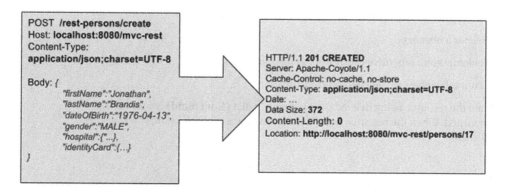

**Figure 5-3.** *POST Request and Response example*

The following describes the PUT example shown in Figure 5-4:

- It updates an existing resource or creates it with a known destination URI. The URI of a resource contains an identifier for that resource. If that identifier is not generated by the application, but can be created by the client a behavior such as this can be implemented: when a PUT request refers to an existing resource, the resource is updated, otherwise a new resource with the identifier from the URI and the contents in the request body is created.

- It is idempotent; repetitive execution has the same result.

- It is not safe; repetitive updates could corrupt data.

- When the resource being updated requires a parent that does not exist, or the resource requested to be updated does not exist, a **404 (Not Found)**, status code is returned. When the resource is updated correctly, a **200 (OK)** (or a **204 (No Content)** if not returning any content in the body) status code is returned.

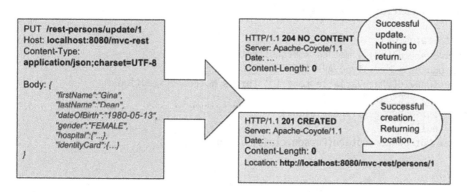

**Figure 5-4.** *PUT Request and Response example*

The following describes the DELETE example shown in Figure 5-5:

- It deletes a resource.

- It is idempotent; repetitive execution has the same result.

- It is not safe; repetitive deletes could corrupt data.

- When the resource being deleted does not exist, a **404 (Not Found)**, status code
  is returned. When the resource was deleted correctly, a **200 (OK)** status code is
  returned.

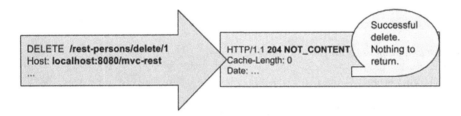

***Figure 5-5.*** *DELETE Request and Response example*

When it comes to REST, everything is about resource states and transferring them between a client
and a server, in different forms. The request specifies the representation type using the Accept HTTP
header for GET and the Content-Type HTTP header for PUT and POST, as you have seen in the preceding
images, because when the client is not a browser (remember Chapter 3), the Accept header is taken
into consideration. The URI extension can be used as a representation type identifier too. The response
reports the representation type returned using the Content-Type HTTP header. When using Spring, the
representation type is specified using an attribute of the @RequestMapping annotation and well-known
media types defined in the MediaType class:

```
@RestController
@RequestMapping(value = "/rest-persons")
public class PersonsRestController extends BaseController {
...
@ResponseStatus(HttpStatus.OK)
@RequestMapping(value = "id/{id}", method = RequestMethod.GET,
                produces = MediaType.APPLICATION_JSON_VALUE)
public Person getPersonById(@PathVariable Long id) throws NotFoundException {
    logger.info("-----> PERSON: " + id);
    Person person = personManager.findById(id);
    if (person == null) {
        throw new NotFoundException(Person.class, id.toString());
    }
    return person;
}
...
}
```

```
//Exception handler class for Rest errors.
@ControllerAdvice(basePackages = "com.pr.rest")
public class RestExceptionProcessor {
/

        Maps NotFoundException to a 404 Not Found HTTP status code.

    @ResponseStatus(value = HttpStatus.NOT_FOUND,
         reason = "This entity is not found in the system")
    @ExceptionHandler({NotFoundException.class})
    public void handleNotFound(NotFoundException nfe) {
        // just return empty 404
        logger.info("-----> Entity " + nfe.getObjType() +
         " with identifier" + nfe.getObjIdentifier() + "not found.");
    }
}
```

# HATEOAS

On his public blog,[4] Roy Fielding mentioned that most REST services are not really RESTful, because fully RESTful services should only return links. Basically, HATEOAS implies that when a client makes a REST request to a server, the server should return a response that informs the client of all possible REST operations using links. For example, a resource should contain links to related resources, including URIs for editing it and deleting it, and so forth. Following this idea, well-known author Leonard Richardson defined the **Richardson Maturity Model,**[5] which describes four levels of REST compliance:

- **Level 0**, also known as the *Swamp of POX*. Only HTTP is used as a transport method.

- **Level 1**, also known as the *Resource Level*. HTTP is used as a transport method and URIs are used to identify resources.

- **Level 2**, also known as the *HTTP Verb Level*. This is the level where HTTP headers, statuses, methods, distinct URIs and everything else HTTP has to offer to provide a REST service. At this level, HTTP is used the way it's meant to be.

- **Level 3**, also known as the *Hypermedia Controls Level*. This is the final level, where a fully complying REST service should be. **HATEOAS**, an abbreviation for **H**ypermedia **A**s **T**he **E**ngine **O**f **A**pplication **S**tate, is a constraint of the REST application architecture that distinguishes it from most other network application architectures. The principle is that a client interacts with a network application entirely through hypermedia provided dynamically by application servers.

The Spring team has developed a separate project to make it easy to implement RESTful services that comply with the third level. Spring HATEOAS[6] provides APIs to ease creating REST representations that follow the HATEOAS principle when working with Spring, and especially Spring MVC.

---

[4]This blog is at http://roy.gbiv.com.
[5]Martin Fowler has a great article on this at http://martinfowler.com/articles/richardsonMaturityModel.html.
[6]The project official page is at http://projects.spring.io/spring-hateoas/.

HATEOAS is a concept of application architecture, which defines the way clients interact with servers using hypermedia links they find inside representations returned by the server. To implement HATEOAS, resources representations must comply with a set of standards and contain hypermedia information. One of the most common standards used to hyperlink resources is HAL.[7] A resource in HAL is just a plain-old JSON or XML object with whatever properties needed, but that provides the possibility to hyperlink resources. The following is a code snippet showing what a resource representation that complies to the HAL standard looks like:

```
//GET Request: /persons/5 using JSON format
// Response representation returned below:
{
" links": {
    "self": { "href": "/persons/5" },
    "parents": [
      { "href": "/persons/2", "title": "mother" },
      { "href": "/persons/3", "title": "father }
    ]
},
    "firstName" : "John",
    "middleName" : "Constantine",
    "lastName" : "Smith",
    "dateOfBirth" : "1935-10-01",
    "gender" : "MALE",
    "hospital" : {
    "code" : "134181",
    "name" : "General Hospital",
    "address" : "Sample address",
    "location" : "Constance, Romania"
},
"identityCard" : {
    "pnc" : "1351001134181",
    "series" : "CO",
    "number" : "205727",
    "emittedAt" : "1949-10-01",
    "expiresAt" : "1985-10-01",
    "address" : "34eeb1d5-0ff4-4d4a-b811-4ff32aa15ada"
  }

}


//GET Request: /persons/5 analogous example using XML
<?xml version="1.0" encoding="utf-8"?>
<person rel="self" href="/person/5">
      <linkList>
          <link rel="parent" title="mother" href="/persons/2"/>
          <link rel="parent" title="father" href="/persons/3"/>
      </linkList>
```

---

[7]This is at http://stateless.co/hal_specification.html.

```
<firstName>John</firstName>
<lastName>Constantine</lastName>
<!-- other simple properties-->
...
<hospital>
        <code>134181</code>
        <!-- other simple properties-->
    ...
</hospital>
<identityCard>
        <pnc>1351001134181</pnc>
        <!-- other simple properties-->
    ...
</identityCard>

</person>
```

# Advantages of REST

The following list describes the advantages of REST.

- REST is simple.

- REST is widely supported.

- Resources can be represented in a wide variety of data formats (JSON, XML, Atom, etc.).

- You can make good use of HTTP cache and proxy servers to help you handle high loads and improve performance.

- It reduces client/server coupling.

- Browsers can interpret representations.

- JavaScript can use representations.

- A REST service can be consumed by applications written in different languages.

- It is easy for new clients to use a RESTful application, even if the application was not designed specifically for a client.

- Because of the statelessness of REST systems, multiple servers can be behind a load balancer and provide services transparently, which means increased scalability.

- Because of the uniform interface, documentation of the resources and basic API operations are unnecessary.

- The hypermedia constraint assures that application processing transitions are always navigable by clients, simply by following opaque server-provided links. Thus, the client does not need to understand anything more than the data format. (And when JSON is used, the data format is quite obvious.)

- Using REST does not imply specific libraries at the client level in order to communicate with the server. With REST, all that is needed is a network connection.

REST services can be secured, but as the interaction between the client and server is stateless, credentials have to be embedded in every request header. Basic authentication is the easiest to implement without additional libraries (HTTP Basic, HTTP Digest, XML-DSIG, or XML-Encryption), but it guarantees the lowest level of security. Basic authentication should never be used without TLS (formerly known as SSL) encryption because the credentials can be easily decoded otherwise. In Figure 5-6, you can see how basic authentication is used when a client communicates with a RESTful application that requires basic authentication.

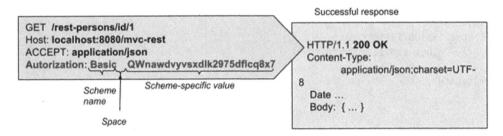

***Figure 5-6.*** *Basic authentication when using RESTful systems*

---

**!** When a collection is expected, it is enough use: /persons (plural) and /hospitals (plural). The /all link was used here because the original web controllers implemented in Chapter 3 were kept separate, so you can access the interface and verify the changes you are doing via REST in the browser. Basically, the REST and web functionalities are fully decoupled. And because the PersonsController was already mapped to /persons and the HospitalController was already mapped to /hospitals, there was no other way to do this but to map the REST controllers to different URLs.

**!** Snippets of code from the HospitalsRestController are not mentioned in the book, because the code is almost identical to the one for the REST methods in PersonsController; the only difference is the resource type. But the code is available for you to practice on in the book's code samples.

---

Other common protocols used with RESTful systems are OAuth 1.0a and OAuth 2.0. Custom security implementation should be used only if necessary, because the skill to understand cryptographic digital signatures is quite difficult to master.

There may be a lot more to say about REST in general, but the introduction to REST must end here, as this chapter is about Spring and how Spring can be used to develop RESTful applications. And you will notice that providing and consuming REST services with Spring is so easy that a deep understanding of REST is not actually needed.

# RESTful Applications Using Spring MVC

To learn how to implement and test RESTful services using MVC, module `09-pr-rest-practice` was created. This module contains the implementation of the operations depicted in Figure 5-7.

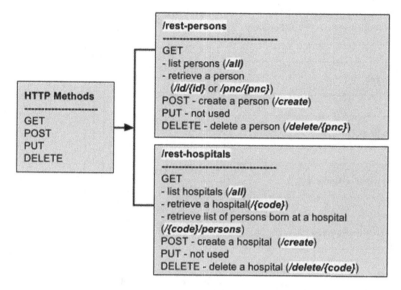

**Figure 5-7.** *RESTful architecture for the practice section*

## RESTful Clients with Spring

A RESTful application can be accessed by any type of client that can create the type of request supported by the application. To test a Spring RESTful application, Spring provides two classes: `RestTemplate` and `AsyncRestTemplate`.

The `RestTemplate` is Spring's central class for synchronous client-side HTTP access. This class provides a wide set of methods for each HTTP method, which can be used to access RESTful services and enforces REST principles.[8] Figure 5-8 depicts a correspondence between HTTP methods and `RestTemplate` methods that can be used to access REST services.

---

[8]Javadoc for this class can be found at `http://docs.spring.io/spring/docs/4.1.x/javadoc-api/org/springframework/web/client/RestTemplate.html`.

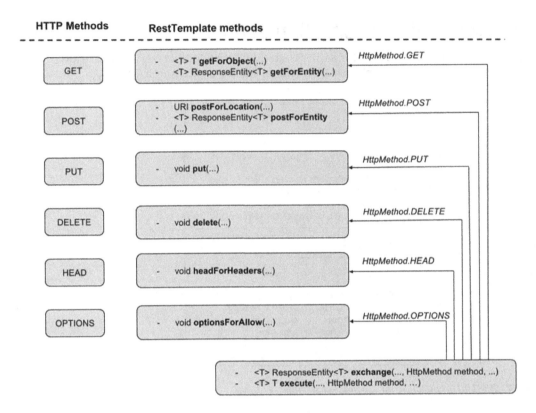

**Figure 5-8.** *RestTemplate api to HTTP methods correspondence*

As you can see, the execute and exchange methods can be used for any type of REST calls, as long as the HTTP method is given as a parameter for the methods. All methods are polymorphic,[9] and using one or another depends on the requirements and the developer's preferences. URI instances are returned to identify resources, and RestTemplate methods support URI templates. So, the following two calls are identical:

```
//using URI Template
String url = "http://localhost:8080/mvc-rest/rest-person/id/{id}";
Person person = restTemplate.getForObject(url, Person.class, "1");

// using URI
String url = "http://localhost:8080/mvc-rest/rest-personid/1";
Person person = restTemplate.getForObject(url, Person.class);
```

---

[9]Multiple methods with the same name, but different signatures are provided. Just check out the Spring API for RestTemplate at http://docs.spring.io/spring/docs/4.1.x/javadoc-api/org/springframework/web/client/RestTemplate.html.

200

The execute method can also be given a RequestCallback implementation as a parameter, which tells the RestTemplate what to do with the request before sending it to the server. Considering this, a GET request for a Person instance with id=1 could be written with the exchange method like this:

```
String url ="http://localhost:8080/mvc-rest/rest-person/id/{id}";
    Person person = restTemplate.execute(url, HttpMethod.GET,
    new RequestCallback() {
        @Override
        public void doWithRequest(ClientHttpRequest request)
            throws IOException {
            HttpHeaders headers = request.getHeaders();
            headers.add("Accept", MediaType.APPLICATION_JSON_VALUE);
            System.out.println("Request headers = " + headers);
        }
    }, new HttpMessageConverterExtractor<Person>(Person.class,
        restTemplate.getMessageConverters())
            , new HashMap<String, Object>() {{
        put("id", "1");
}});
```

Objects passed to and returned from the methods getForObject(), postForLocation(), and put() are converted to HTTP requests and from HTTP responses by HttpMessageConverters. Message converters are automatically detected and used by Spring in applications configured with <mvc:annotation-driven/> or @EnableWebMvc. In the code sample for this chapter, the representations are in JSON format, so MappingJackson2HttpMessageConverter is used. And because the message format is supported by default, the HttpMessageConverterExtractor<T> is not necessary in the previous example. Also, if no Accept header is specified, all formats supported by Spring are considered. So in this case, RequestCallback becomes unnecessary too, so you can stick to the simpler restTemplate.getForObject method that was mentioned in the previous code snippet.

Speaking of message converters, restTemplate deals only with objects, so it internally converts resources to representations, and vice-versa, using message converter implementations of the HttpMessageConverter<T> interface. Spring comes with a default long list of supported message converters, but if necessary, a developer can provide his own implementation of the HttpMessageConverter<T>. Table 5-2 provides a list of the most commonly used message converters and the datatype handled:

**Table 5-2.** *Message Converters*

| Message Converter | Data Type | Observation |
|---|---|---|
| StringHttpMessageConverter | text/plain | |
| MappingJackson2HttpMessageConverter | application/*+json | Only if Jackson 2 is present on the classpath |
| AtomFeedHttpMessageConverter | application/atom+xml | Only if Rome is present on the classpath |
| RssChannelHttpMessageConverter | application/rss+xml | Only if Rome is present on the classpath |
| MappingJackson2XmlHttpMessageConverter | application/*+xml | Only if Jackson 2 is present on the classpath |

To use a restTemplate, you can define and initialize it directly where you need it, or declare a bean and inject it. restTemplate handles HTTP connections internally, so the developer does not have to write extra code with opening and closing connections. A different HTTP client can also be used, and Apache provides an implementation that can be injected into a RestTemplate bean. This is highly recommended for production applications when authentication and HTTP connection pooling are usually needed.

To use the Apache Commons HttpClient, Spring provides a factory class named HttpComponentsClientHttpRequestFactory, which provides an HttpClient instance that uses a default org.apache.http.impl.conn.PoolingClientConnectionManager[10] that is able to service connection requests from multiple execution threads.

```
<bean id="restTemplate" class="o.s.web.client.RestTemplate">
    <property name="requestFactory">
        <bean class= "o.s.http.client.HttpComponentsClientHttpRequestFactory"/>
    </property>
</bean>
```

Configuring a RestTemplate bean using Java Configuration looks like this:

```
\\in the @Configuration and @EnableWebMvc annotated class
@Bean
  public RestTemplate restTemplate() {
      RestTemplate restTemplate = new RestTemplate();
      restTemplate.setRequestFactory(new HttpComponentsClientHttpRequestFactory());
      return restTemplate;
}
```

Other examples of restTemplate usage are in the following code snippet:

```
// GET request to retrieve all persons born at a hospital with a specific code
String url = "http://localhost:8080/mvc-rest/rest-hospitals/{code}/persons";

Person[] persons = restTemplate.getForObject(url, Person[].class, "134181");

// POST request to create a person
Person person = buildPerson();
final HttpHeaders headers = new HttpHeaders();
headers.setContentType(MediaType.APPLICATION_JSON);

final HttpEntity<Person> personRequest = new HttpEntity<>(person, headers);
String url = "http://localhost:8080/mvc-rest/rest-persons/create";
// this method returns the created resource
Person newPerson = this.restTemplate.postForObject(url, personRequest, Person.class);
//this method returns the URI of the created resource
URI uri = this.restTemplate.postForLocation(url, personRequest, Person.class);

//DELETE request to delete a person by id
String url = "http://localhost:8080/mvc-rest/rest-persons/delete/23";
restTemplate.delete(url);
```

---

[10]The class is part of the Apache http-client library. JavaDoc API can be accessed at http://hc.apache.org/httpcomponents-client-ga/httpclient/apidocs/org/apache/http/impl/ conn/PoolingClientConnection Manager.html.

REST services are used most commonly by AJAX components in a web application, and currently all HTTP methods are supported in AJAX. But most browsers do not support any other methods besides GET and POST in HTML forms. To use them in a form, Spring has introduced hidden methods. Basically, a hidden input is added to a form with a regular POST method. If the POST request is to be treated as a PUT request, the value of the field will be equal to this method name, as shown in the code sample below. A filter interceptor intercepts the request, searches for that parameter, and modifies the request accordingly before sending it to the appropriate handler.

For this to work, the Spring form has the method attribute value set to the desired HTTP method, and the resulting HTML form has a hidden field added:

```
<!-- Spring form -->
<sf:form method="put" action=".." modelAttribute="..">
    ...
</sf:form>

<!-- HTML form -->
<form method="post" action="...">
    <input type="hidden" name="method" value="put" />
    ...
</form>
```

The filter interceptor that takes care of intercepting requests and modifying the methods is the HiddenHttpMethodFilter, which can be configured in a web.xml file or in a class implementing WebApplicationInitializer.

```
<!-- in web.xml -->
  <!-- Enables use of HTTP methods PUT and DELETE -->
    <filter>
        <filter-name>httpMethodFilter</filter-name>
        <filter-class>o.s.web.filter.HiddenHttpMethodFilter</filter-class>
    </filter>

    <filter-mapping>
        <filter-name>httpMethodFilter</filter-name>
        <url-pattern>/*</url-pattern>
    </filter-mapping>

\\in class extending AbstractDispatcherServletInitializer
\\ or AbstractAnnotationConfigDispatcherServletInitializer
@Override
protected Filter[] getServletFilters() {
    return new Filter[] { new HiddenHttpMethodFilter()};
}
```

# Asynchronous REST Calls

At the beginning of this section, AsyncRestTemplate was mentioned. This class can be used to create Spring REST clients that make asynchronous calls to a REST service. The AsyncRestTemplate class is nothing other than a wrapper class for RestTemplate that provides the asynchronous behavior via a set of methods (analogous to the ones in RestTemplate) that return Future<T> wrappers (or ListenableFuture<F>

that *extends Future<T>* when a callback method is needed) instead of concrete data. An example of an asynchronous GET request can be found in the AsyncRestTemplateTest class, in the 07-pr-rest-solution. In the same class, you can also find an example with a callback.

```
private static final String PERSON_BASE_URL =
        "http://localhost:8080/mvc-rest/rest-persons/id/{id}";
AsyncRestTemplate asyncRestTemplate = new AsyncRestTemplate();
...


Future<ResponseEntity<Person>> futurePerson =
      asyncRestTemplate.exchange(url, HttpMethod.GET, entity, Person.class, "5");
  //waiting a little, to give time to the async call to complete
        Thread.sleep(1000L);

ResponseEntity<Person> result = futurePerson.get();
Person person = result.getBody();
assertNotNull(person);

//callback example
ListenableFuture<ResponseEntity<Person>> futurePerson =
      asyncRestTemplate.exchange(url, HttpMethod.GET, entity, Person.class, "5");
  futurePerson.addCallback(new ListenableFutureCallback<ResponseEntity<Person>>() {
                @Override
                public void onSuccess(ResponseEntity result) {
                 Person person = (Person) result.getBody();
                 assertNotNull(person);
                 }

                @Override
                public void onFailure(Throwable t) {
                    logger.error("------> Async call failure!", t);
                }
});
```

# Implementing REST with Spring MVC

There are multiple Java frameworks available for implementing RESTful applications: Spark, Restlet, JAX-RS(Java EE), and RESTEasy, but Spring MVC is the easiest to use. This section contains a lot of information and code snippets to convince you that this affirmation is true. REST support was added to Spring MVC in version 3.0, and although developing RESTful applications was always easy, in version 4.x things have become even more practical.

Among the aforementioned frameworks, JAX-RS is shipped with out-of-the-box Spring Integration. This framework encapsulates the Java API for RESTful web services (JAX-RS, defined in JSR 311). Jersey, the reference implementation of JAX-RS, implements support for the annotations defined in JSR 311, making it easy for developers to build RESTful web services by using the Java programming language. It is focused more on application-to-application communication, so the focus is not on browser clients. That's the amazing thing about Spring MVC—a Spring RESTful application does not care about its client type at all.

Spring MVC provides the following resources to build RESTful applications:

- The potential to declare status codes.

- URI templates.

- Content negotiation.

- Many message converters offer out-of-the-box support.

- RestTemplate and AsyncRestTemplate classes are used for easily creating client applications or for testing RESTful application services.

- Browsers are supported as clients, although HTTP method conversion is necessary for PUT and DELETE methods. When making REST requests from a web page, jQuery can be used (this is covered in Chapter 6).

A few of these have already been mentioned in the previous section, as they were involved in creating REST clients; the others are covered in this section.

To develop a RESTful service class with Spring MVC, you have to do the most obvious thing: create a controller that contains handler methods that return resources representations instead of views, which are the actual response body. In Spring 3.0, we had to do the following:

```
@Controller
@RequestMapping(value = "/rest-persons")
public class PersonsRestController {

@Autowired
PersonManager personManager;

    @ResponseStatus(HttpStatus.OK)
    @RequestMapping(value = "/id/{id}", method = RequestMethod.GET)
     public @ResponseBody Person getPersonById(@PathVariable Long id)
          throws NotFoundException {
        Person person = personManager.findById(id);
        if (person == null) {
            throw new NotFoundException(Person.class, id.toString());
        }
        return person;
    }
}
```

Looks like any MVC controller, right? The only difference is the @ResponseBody that indicates a method return value should be bound to the web response body. The advantage here is that, in the same controller you can also have methods that are not used to provide REST representations, having all the people management data in one place. But, because it is a good practice to decouple code with different scopes, in Spring MVC 4.0 the @RestController was introduced. This annotation is conveniently annotated with

@Controller and @ResponseBody, which practically means that if you annotate a class with it, all handler methods are transparently annotated with @ResponseBody. Also, the purpose of this controller becomes quite obvious—it handles only REST requests. Thus, the preceding code becomes the following:

```
@RestController
@RequestMapping(value = "/rest-persons")
public class PersonsRestController extends BaseController {

    @ResponseStatus(HttpStatus.OK)
    @RequestMapping(value = "/id/{id}", method = RequestMethod.GET)
     public Person getPersonById(@PathVariable Long id) throws NotFoundException {
     ... // identical content as above
     }
}
```

And this is all. All methods defined inside this class can then be called from REST clients, and they will receive the requested representations. What happens in the background—the way that the DispatcherServlet is involved—is depicted in Figure 5-9.

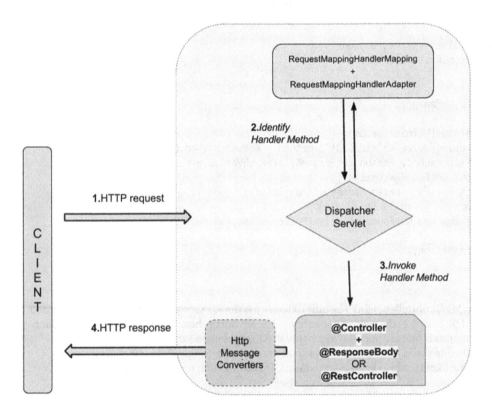

*Figure 5-9. Spring MVC RESTFul Container*

So basically, the controller methods return data directly to the client—data that no longer needs to be processed in order to render a view. Every time a request is mapped to a handler method that has parameters annotated with @RequestBody, or the method is annotated with @ResponseBody, Spring loops over all HttpMessageConverters; it is seeking the first that fits the given MIME type and class, and then uses it for the actual conversion.

Mapping requests to methods is the same as with web controllers. All annotations applicable in web handler methods are applicable in REST handler methods too: @PathVariable, @Valid, and so forth. @RequestParam can be used too, but this would break the REST constraints mentioned at the beginning of the chapter.

## HTTP Status Codes

When a web application returns a response, that response has a status code that describes a certain state of the returned resource or the result of the operation that the request triggered on the server. The most familiar is probably the 404 Not Found status code that is returned when a requested resource cannot be found. A full list of HTTP status codes can be found on Wikipedia, which you should look at if you are curious about and unfamiliar with HTTP status codes.[11]

RESTful applications use HTTP status codes to communicate with their clients. With Spring MVC, the status code of a response can be set easily using the @ResponseStatus annotation. This annotation can receive as a value any of the constants defined in Spring class HttpStatus. Table 5-3 contains the most common response statuses used in RESTful applications.

Here are some examples of @ResponseStatus annotated REST handlers that you will work with in the practice project for this chapter:

```
@ResponseStatus(HttpStatus.NO_CONTENT)
@RequestMapping(value = "/delete/{pnc}", method = RequestMethod.DELETE)
public void deletePerson(@PathVariable String pnc) throws NotFoundException {
    ...
}


@ResponseStatus(HttpStatus.CREATED)
@RequestMapping(value = "/create", method = RequestMethod.POST,
            produces = MediaType.APPLICATION_JSON_VALUE,
            consumes = MediaType.APPLICATION_JSON_VALUE)
public Person createPerson(@RequestBody @Valid Person newPerson) {
    ...
}


@ResponseStatus(HttpStatus.OK)
    @RequestMapping(value = "/all", method = RequestMethod.GET,
    produces = MediaType.APPLICATION_JSON_VALUE)
public List<Person> getAll() {
...
}
```

---

[11]See http://en.wikipedia.org/wiki/List_of_HTTP_status_codes.

*Table 5-3.* *HTTP Status Codes*

| HTTP Status | HttpStatus Constant | Observation |
|---|---|---|
| 200 | OK | Successful GET with returned content. |
| 201 | CREATED | Successful PUT or POST; location header should contain URI or new resource. |
| 204 | NO_CONTENT | Empty response; after successful PUT or DELETE. |
| 404 | NOT_FOUND | Resource was not found. |
| 403 | FORBIDDEN | Server is refusing to respond to the request, because the response is not authorized. |
| 405 | METHOD_NOT_ALLOWED | HTTP method is not supported for the resource identified by the Request-URI. |
| 409 | CONFLICT | Problems when making changes, when PUT or POST try to save data that already exists and is marked as unique |
| 415 | UNSUPPORTED_MEDIA_TYPE | The server is refusing to service the request because the entity of the request is in a format not supported by the requested resource for the requested method. |

! The "`produces`" and "`consumes`" properties are covered later in the chapter.

! Normally, void or null returning methods result in a default view name determined by the request's path information (from `@RequestMapping` annotations on the class and method, as explained in Chapter 3).The `@ResponseStatus` overrides the default behavior, causing a null `ModelAndView` to be used, which indicates that the response has been handled by the controller method already. So, obviously the `@ResponseStatus` is mandatory for a RESTful handler method returning void or null.

## Exception Handling

The status codes can be used for exception handlers too. Yes, RESTful handlers can also throw exceptions, and they have to be properly handled. Similar to Spring MVC web specific controllers, exception handlers can be defined either in the body of the REST controller, or they can be defined in class annotated with `@ControllerAdvice`. And the same `ExceptionHandler` annotation is used to annotate the exception handler methods. In the next code snippet, such a class was defined with two exception handlers for different types of exceptions, and the handlers were limited to the `com.pr.rest` package, using the `basePackages` attribute, in order to handle exceptions thrown only by controllers in that package.

```
  @ControllerAdvice(basePackages = "com.pr.rest")
public class RestExceptionProcessor {
    private Logger logger = LoggerFactory.getLogger(RestExceptionProcessor.class);

    //Maps IllegalArgumentExceptions to a 404 Not Found HTTP status code
    @ResponseStatus(value = HttpStatus.NOT_FOUND,
          reason = "This entity is not found in the system")
    @ExceptionHandler({NotFoundException.class})
    public void handleNotFound(NotFoundException nfe) {

      // just return empty 404
      logger.info("-----> Entity " + nfe.getObjType() + " with identifier"
          + nfe.getObjIdentifier() + "not found.");
}

      // Maps DataIntegrityViolationException to a 409 Conflict HTTP status code.
      @ResponseStatus(value = HttpStatus.CONFLICT,
            reason = "Another entity with the same identity exists")
      @ExceptionHandler({DataIntegrityViolationException.class})
      public void handleAlreadyExists() {
            // just return empty 409
            logger.info("-----> Entity save operation failure");
      }
}
```

Content can be returned using an exception handler, but in this case, the client must be implemented to handle the response.

```
@ExceptionHandler(NotFoundException.class)
    @ResponseStatus(value= HttpStatus.NOT_FOUND)
    @ResponseBody
    public JsonError personNotFound(HttpServletRequest req, NotFoundException ex) {
        Locale locale = LocaleContextHolder.getLocale();
        String errorMessage = messageSource.
                         getMessage("error.no.person.id", null, locale);

        errorMessage += ex.getObjIdentifier();
        String errorURL = req.getRequestURL().toString();

        return new JsonError(errorURL, errorMessage);
}

    ...
public class JsonError {
    private String url;
    private String message;

    public JsonError(String url, String message) {
       this.url = url;
       this.message = message;
    }

    // getters and setters
}
```

## The "produces" and "consumes" Properties

In the previous examples, the consumes and produces annotation properties of the @RequestMapping were used. These two attributes are used to narrow the primary mapping for a request. The consumes attribute defines the consumable media types of the mapped request (defined on the server) and the value of the Content-Type header (defined on the client side) must match at least one of the values of this property in order for a method to handle a specific REST request. Let's say, for example, that in the REST client, the following headers were set:

```
final HttpHeaders headers = new HttpHeaders();
final String url = "http://localhost:8080/mvc-rest/rest-persons/create";
\\"application/json"
headers.setContentType(MediaType.APPLICATION_JSON);
final HttpEntity<Person> personRequest = new HttpEntity<>(person, headers);
        Person newPerson =
                restTemplate.postForObject(url, personRequest, Person.class);
```

On the server, the following REST handler would be mapped to process this request:

```
@ResponseStatus(HttpStatus.CREATED)
@RequestMapping(value = "/create", method = RequestMethod.POST,
  produces = MediaType.APPLICATION_JSON_VALUE,
  consumes = {MediaType.APPLICATION_JSON_VALUE,
  //Public constant media type for {@code application/octet-stream}.
    MediaType.APPLICATION_OCTET_STREAM})
public Person createPerson(@RequestBody @Valid Person newPerson) {
...
}
```

The produces attribute defines the producible media types of the mapped request, narrowing the primary mapping. The value of the Accept header (on the client side) must match at least one of the values of this property in order for a method to handle a specific REST request. Let's say, for example, that in the REST client there is the following request:

```
final  String  url  =  "http://localhost:8080/mvc-rest/rest-persons/id/{id}";
Person  person  =  restTemplate.execute(url,  HttpMethod.GET,  request  -> {
            HttpHeaders headers = request.getHeaders();
            headers.add("Accept", MediaType.APPLICATION_JSON_VALUE);
        }, new HttpMessageConverterExtractor<>(Person.class,
            restTemplate.getMessageConverters())
                , new HashMap<String, Object>() {{
          put("id", "1");
        }});
```

---

! As mentioned, the code for making a REST request for a person can be far simpler than what was depicted earlier. The execute method was used here to show how this method can be used.

---

On the server, the following REST handler would be mapped to process this request:

```
@ResponseStatus(HttpStatus.OK)
@RequestMapping(value = "/id/{id}", method = RequestMethod.GET,
    produces = MediaType.APPLICATION_JSON_VALUE)
public Person getPersonById(@PathVariable Long id) throws NotFoundException {
        return personManager.findById(id)
}
```

## Accessing Servlet Environment and Request Data

Because RESTful controllers are run in a servlet environment, and the interface is the DispatcherServlet, the servlet environment properties can be injected and accessed in the same manner presented in Chapter 3. The RESTful handler methods can have flexible signatures. HttpServletRequest or HttpServletResponse can be used as parameters, and Spring will take care of populating them for you. The @PathVariable and @RequestParam annotations can be used to tell Spring to inject request data automatically. @Valid can be used to validate resources submitted with POST or PUT. And so on. Even SpEL expressions are supported. The next example depicts a REST handler for a POST method, which creates a person and adds the URI of the new resource; this is built from the original request URL that is populated by Spring as a value for the Location header:

```
@ResponseStatus(HttpStatus.CREATED)
@RequestMapping(value = "/create2", method = RequestMethod.POST)
    public void createPerson2(@RequestBody @Valid Person newPerson,
            @Value("#{request.requestURL}")StringBuffer originalUrl,
            HttpServletResponse response) {

            Person person = personManager.save(newPerson);
            logger.info("-----> PERSON: " + person);
            response.setHeader("Location",
                    getLocationForPersonResource(originalUrl, person.getId()));
}

//Determines URL of person resource based on the full URL of the given request,
//appending the path info with the given childIdentifier using a UriTemplate.
protected static String getLocationForPersonResource
    (StringBuffer url, Object childIdentifier) {
    String newURL = url.toString();
    newURL = newURL.replace("create2", "id/{id}");
    UriTemplate template = new UriTemplate(newURL);
    return template.expand(childIdentifier).toASCIIString();
}
```

Another method for accessing request and response is the HttpEntity<T> class and its subclasses: RequestEntity<T> and ResponseEntity<T>. By using these classes, you can get access to the request and response body. RequestEntity<T> and ResponseEntity<T> can be used as follows:

- In the REST client to encapsulate every detail about a REST request that is made by calling restTemplate.exchange.

```
final String url = "http://localhost:8080/mvc-rest/rest-persons/id/{id}";

final RequestEntity<Person> entity = RequestEntity.post(new URI(url))
            .accept(MediaType.APPLICATION_JSON)
            .contentType(MediaType.APPLICATION_JSON)
//setting a custom header that will be accessed in the handler method
            .header("custom", "true")
            .body(person);

    ResponseEntity<Person> response = restTemplate.exchange(entity,
                                        Person.class);
    Person newPerson = response.getBody();

    //get URI location for the Person created
    HttpHeaders headers = response.getHeaders();
    URI uri = headers.getLocation();
```

- In the RESTful handler method to access request headers, read the body of a request, and write headers to the response stream.

```
@ResponseStatus(HttpStatus.CREATED)
@RequestMapping(value = "/create3", method = RequestMethod.POST)
public ResponseEntity<Person> handle(HttpEntity<Person> requestEntity,
            @Value("#{request.requestURL}") StringBuffer originalUrl)
                throws UnsupportedEncodingException {
    // will return "true"
     String requestHeader = requestEntity.getHeaders().getFirst("custom");
    //we are just making sure the header is the one sent from the client
    assertTrue(Boolean.parseBoolean(requestHeader));

    Person person = requestEntity.getBody();
    Hospital hospital = hospitalManager.
        findByCode(person.getHospital().getCode());
    person.setHospital(hospital);
    Person newPerson = personManager.save(person);

    HttpHeaders responseHeaders = new HttpHeaders();
    responseHeaders.set("Location",
            getLocationForPersonResource(originalUrl, person.getId()));
    return new ResponseEntity<>(newPerson, responseHeaders,
        HttpStatus.CREATED);
}
```

! As with @RequestBody and @ResponseBody, Spring uses HttpMessageConverter<T> to convert to and from the request and response streams. The HttpMessageConverter<T> and supported implementations were covered in the "RESTful Applications Using Spring MVC" section.

## Asynchronous REST Services Using @Async Annotated Methods

The "Asynchronous REST Calls" section showed how to make an asynchronous REST call using the AsyncRestTemplate class. In that case, the client did the rest call and could then focus on other operations until the Future object returned the concrete data.

But asynchronous calls can be made in a different way using @Async annotated methods. This annotation marks a method as a candidate for asynchronous execution. It can also be used at type level; in this case, all methods in the class are considered asynchronous. Asynchronous methods can have any signature and any parameter types. There are absolutely no restrictions about this. However, the return type is restricted to void and Future (and implementations of this interface). Immediately after a client calls an asynchronous method, the invocation returns and the execution of the method is submitted to a Spring TaskExecutor[12]. Asynchronous methods that return void are used when the client does not expect a reply.

By default, to execute a method annotated with @Async, the executor that is used is the one supplied to the <task:annotation-driven/> element. (The Spring Task namespace was introduced in Spring 3.0 to help configure TaskExecutor and TaskScheduler instances.)

```
<task:annotation-driven executor="prExecutor"/>
<task:executor id="prExecutor" pool-size="100"/>
```

In Java Configuration, support for @Async can be enabled using @EnableAsync in one of the configuration classes of the application—those annotated with @Configuration. To provide a different executor, like in the preceding XML example, the class must implement org.springframework.scheduling. annotation.AsyncConfigurer and provide a concrete implementation for the getAsyncExecutor method.

```
@Configuration
@EnableAsync
 public class AppConfig implements AsyncConfigurer {

    @Override
    public Executor getAsyncExecutor() {
        ThreadPoolTaskExecutor executor = new ThreadPoolTaskExecutor();
        executor.setCorePoolSize(100);
        executor.initialize();
        return executor;
    }
    ...
}
```

---

[12]Spring's TaskExecutor interface is equivalent to the java.util.concurrent.Executor interface and extends it without modifying the API in order for clients to declare a dependency on an executor and receive any TaskExecutor implementation. It was created to remove the need for Java libraries when using thread pools.

Also the @Async annotation has a value attribute to indicate that an executor other than the default should be used when the executor[13] is defined as a bean:

```
@Async("otherExecutor")
public Future<Person> findPerson(Long id) throws InterruptedException {
    String url = "http://localhost:8080/mvc-rest/rest-persons/id/{id}";
    Person person = restTemplate.getForObject(url, Person.class, "1");
    Thread.sleep(1000L);
    return new AsyncResult<>(person);
}


<!-- in a spring configuration file we define an Executor bean -->
  <bean id="otherExecutor"
        class="o.s.scheduling.concurrent.ThreadPoolTaskExecutor"
        init-method="initialize" destroy-method="shutdown">
        <property name="corePoolSize" value="100"/>
  </bean>

// in a class annotated with @Configuration
@Bean(name="otherExecutor", destroyMethod = "shutdown",
     initMethod = "initialize")
    ThreadPoolTaskExecutor getExecutor() {
        ThreadPoolTaskExecutor executor = new ThreadPoolTaskExecutor();
        executor.setCorePoolSize(100);
        return executor;
    }
```

! An example of an @Async annotated method and usage can be found in 07-pr-rest-solution. The example is covered in the "Practical Exercise" section.

## Intercepting REST Calls

There is a section in Chapter 3 about handler interceptors for controller methods, which mentions that REST requests can be intercepted too, but the REST interceptors have to implement the ResponseBodyAdvice<T> or extend one of its subclasses and provide the proper implementation for the beforeBodyWrite and supports.

When extending JsonViewResponseBodyAdvice or AbstractMappingJacksonResponseBodyAdvice, the beforeBodyWriteInternal method must be implemented, because the AbstractMappingJacksonResponseBodyAdvice class provides a concrete implementation for beforeBodyWrite, which calls beforeBodyWriteInternal after creating a proper JSON body container. ResponseBodyAdvice<T> implementation allows you to customize the response after the execution of a @ResponseBody or a ResponseEntity<T> method, but before being passed for conversion to an HTTP message converter. These interceptors are annotated with @ControllerAdvice and are automatically picked up and used by Spring.

---

[13]You can see all methods available for a ThreadPoolTaskExecutor at http://docs.spring.io/spring/docs/4.1.x/javadoc-api/org/springframework/scheduling/concurrent/ThreadPoolTaskExecutor.html.

In the 07-pr-rest-solution module, such an interceptor is implemented for you:

```
@ControllerAdvice(basePackages = "com.pr.rest")
//this interceptor is retricted to the classes in package "com.pr.rest"
public class AuditRestInterceptor
    extends JsonViewResponseBodyAdvice {
    private Logger logger = LoggerFactory.getLogger(AuditRestInterceptor.class);

    @Override
    public boolean supports(MethodParameter returnType, Class converterType) {
        logger.info("-----> Audit REST interceptor supports(Person.class) ? "
                + Person.class.isAssignableFrom(returnType.getParameterType()));
        return (super.supports(returnType, converterType)
                && returnType.getMethodAnnotation(JsonView.class) != null);

    }

....
}
```

The supports method tests if the AuditRestInterceptor supports the given controller method return type and the selected HttpMessageConverter<T> type.

The value logged in the preceding supports method implementation is true if the controller method return type is assignable to a reference of type Person.

```
  @ControllerAdvice(basePackages = "com.pr.rest")
//this interceptor is retricted to the classes in package "com.pr.rest"
public class AuditRestInterceptor
    extends JsonViewResponseBodyAdvice {
    private Logger logger = LoggerFactory.getLogger(AuditRestInterceptor.class);
    ...

    @Override
    protected void beforeBodyWriteInternal(MappingJacksonValue bodyContainer,
            MediaType contentType, MethodParameter returnType,
            ServerHttpRequest request, ServerHttpResponse response) {
        logger.info("-----> Audit REST interceptor beforeBodyWrite");
        response.getHeaders().add(HttpHeaders.CONTENT_ENCODING, "UTF-8");
        super.beforeBodyWriteInternal(bodyContainer, contentType, returnType,
            request, response);
    }
}
```

In the beforeBodyWriteInternal, the CONTENT_ENCODING header is added to the response, so the presence of this header can be tested in the client and you can make sure that the interceptor did its job. After that, the super.beforeBodyWriteInternal() is called to keep the original behavior of the extended class, which is to modify the response body before being converted and sent back to the client.

215

You see this interceptor in action when testing your REST services, because the log messages are printed in the log console.

```
INFO c.p.r.AuditRestInterceptor - -->
      Audit REST interceptor supportsPerson.class ? true
INFO c.p.r.AuditRestInterceptor - --> Audit REST interceptor beforeBodyWrite
```

# Using Spring HATEOAS

HATEOAS and Spring HATEOAS project were mentioned at the beginning of the chapter. When the Hypermedia REST constrains are respected by a REST service, it is said that the service is a **Hypermedia Driven REST web service**. Hypermedia is quite important for REST, because it allows you to build services that are almost fully decoupled from their clients. The representations returned by the REST services contain links that indicate further locations of resources that the client needs access to.

To build a Hypermedia Driven REST web service with Spring, the `spring-hateoas` dependency must be added to the project. The current version of spring-hateoas is 0.17.0.RELEASE. This library (it is only one jar currently, but it will probably grow into a framework) provides a set of classes used to generate resource URIs. It also provides classes to decorate representations with links to return to the HATEOAS complying client.

In this chapter's examples, the `Person` class is wrapped inside a `PersonHateoas` class that extends the core class of spring-hateoas: `ResourceSupport`. This class provides methods useful to add links to representations and to access representations links. The `PersonHateoas` looks like this:

```
...
import com.fasterxml.jackson.annotation.JsonCreator;
import com.fasterxml.jackson.annotation.JsonProperty;
import org.springframework.hateoas.ResourceSupport;

public class PersonHateoas extends ResourceSupport {

    private Person person;

    @JsonCreator
    public PersonHateoas(@JsonProperty("person") Person person) {
        this.person = person;
    }

    public Person getPerson() {
    return person;
    }
}
```

The `PersonHateoas` class has a field of type `Person`. By extending class `ResourceSupport`, methods to generate HATEOAS links and references are inherited. When requesting a `Person` resource from a HATEOAS REST service, a `PersonHateoas` is serialized and sent to the client. When the serialization is done in JSON format, some specific JSON annotations are needed when declaring the `PersonHateoas` class. The `@JsonProperty` specifies that at serialization time, the resulted object will contain a property named `person` that will be mapped to a serialized version of the `Person` instance. Looks like a simple POJO, right? Well, that's what it is.

A controller that returns an instance of PersonHateoas must define handler methods that populate the PersonHateoas instances with HAREOAS-specific links. In order to do, Spring offers utility methods that allow you to create links by pointing to controller classes, which are grouped under the ControllerLinkBuilder. The controller and the method do nothing special, except that before returning the response, the personHateoas object is populated with its own URI, using utility methods from the ControllerLinkBuilder class that link together in a very readable way. For example, the underlined code snippet in the previous example can be read like this: *Add link to which the handler method* getPersonHateoasById *from the* PersonHateoasController *class is mapped, with PathVariable id equal to* person.getId() *to the* personHateoas ph *instance*. The sources for spring-hateoas are available on GitHub at https://github.com/spring-projects/spring-hateoas.

In the following code snippet, the linkTo and methodOn methods from ControllerLinkBuilder are statically imported and used to generate the resource link for the Person instance with id=1.

```
...
import static org.springframework.hateoas.mvc.ControllerLinkBuilder.linkTo;
import static org.springframework.hateoas.mvc.ControllerLinkBuilder.methodOn;

@RestController
@RequestMapping(value = "/hateoas")
public class PersonHateoasController {

private Logger logger = LoggerFactory.getLogger(PersonHateoasController.class);

@ResponseStatus(HttpStatus.OK)
@RequestMapping(value = "/{id}", method = RequestMethod.GET,
      produces = MediaType.APPLICATION_JSON_VALUE)
public HttpEntity<PersonHateoas> getPersonHateoasById(
      @PathVariable Long id) throws NotFoundException {
    logger.info("-----> PERSON: " + id);
    Person person = personManager.findById(id);
    if (person == null) {
        throw new NotFoundException(Person.class, id.toString());
    }
    PersonHateoas ph = new PersonHateoas(person);
    ph.add(
        linkTo(
            methodOn(PersonHateoasController.class)
                .getPersonHateoasById(person.getId())
        ).withSelfRel()
    );
    return new ResponseEntity<>(ph, HttpStatus.OK);
    }
}
```

In the previous example, the controller class is the one that takes care of setting the links by inspecting the mappings. But Spring provides another way—by using EntityLinks implementations. To use them, the controller class must be annotated with @ExposesResourcesFor, which makes EntityLinks available by dependency injection. Also, the configuration class must be annotated with @EnableEntityLinks. The EntityLinks interface API exposes methods to access links pointing to controllers backing an entity type. So the controller becomes this:

```
...
import org.springframework.hateoas.EntityLinks;
import org.springframework.hateoas.ExposesResourceFor;
@Controller
@ExposesResourceFor(Person.class)
@RequestMapping("/hateoas")
public class PersonHateoasController extends BaseController {
    private Logger logger = LoggerFactory.getLogger(PersonHateoasController.class);

    @Autowired
    private EntityLinks entityLinks;

    @RequestMapping(value = "/{id}", method = RequestMethod.GET,
            produces = "application/hal+json")
    public HttpEntity<PersonHateoas> getPersonHateoasById
       (@PathVariable Long id) throws NotFoundException {
       logger.info("-----> PERSON: " + id);
       Person person = personManager.findById(id);
       if (person == null) {
           throw new NotFoundException(Person.class, id.toString());
       }
       PersonHateoas ph = new PersonHateoas(person);

       ph.add(entityLinks.linkForSingleResource(Person.class, id).withSelfRel());
       return new ResponseEntity<>(ph, HttpStatus.OK);
    }
}
```

And the @EnableEntityLinks annotation is added to the configuration class. Also, to enable HAL support, the EnableHypermediaSupport should be added to the configuration class too.

```
import org.springframework.hateoas.config.EnableEntityLinks;
import org.springframework.hateoas.config.EnableHypermediaSupport;
import org.springframework.hateoas.config.EnableHypermediaSupport.HypermediaType;
...
@EnableEntityLinks
@EnableHypermediaSupport(type= {HypermediaType.HAL})
@Configuration
@EnableWebMvc
@ComponentScan(basePackages = {"com.pr, com.pr.web, com.pr.rest, com.pr.hateoas"})
@ImportResource({"classpath:spring/app-service-config.xml",
  "classpath:spring/db-config.xml"})
public class WebConfig extends WebMvcConfigurerAdapter {
....
}
```

The full documentation for spring-hateoas can be found at http://docs.spring.io/spring-hateoas/docs/current/reference/html/.

The **Hypermedia Driven REST web service** that was just created can be tested with restTemplate, just like any REST service. But to deserialize the HATEOAS links correctly, a custom MappingJackson2HttpMessageConverter must be set for the restTemplate. The ObjectMapper must also be customized to register the Jackson2HalModule implementation provided by Spring HATEOAS.

```
import org.springframework.core.ParameterizedTypeReference;
import org.springframework.hateoas.Resource;
import org.springframework.hateoas.hal.Jackson2HalModule;
...
public class PersonHateoasControllerTest {

    @Test
    public void getHateoasPerson() throws Exception {
        ObjectMapper mapper = new ObjectMapper();
        mapper.configure
                (DeserializationFeature.FAIL_ON_UNKNOWN_PROPERTIES, false);
        mapper.registerModule(new Jackson2HalModule());

        MappingJackson2HttpMessageConverter
            converter = new MappingJackson2HttpMessageConverter();
        converter.setSupportedMediaTypes(
                MediaType.parseMediaTypes("application/hal+json"));
        converter.setObjectMapper(mapper);

        RestTemplate restTemplate = new RestTemplate(
                Collections.<HttpMessageConverter<?>> singletonList(converter));

        String url = "http://localhost:8080/mvc-rest/hateoas/{id}";

        ResponseEntity<PersonHateoas> responseEntity =
                restTemplate.getForEntity(url, PersonHateoas.class, "1");
        PersonHateoas personHateoas = responseEntity.getBody();

        assertNotNull(personHateoas);
        assertTrue(personHateoas.hasLinks());
        assertEquals("http://localhost:8080/mvc-rest/hateoas/1",
                    ppersonHateoas.getLink("self").getHref());
        assertEquals("John", personHateoas.getPerson().getFirstName());
        assertEquals("Smith", personHateoas.getPerson().getLastName());
    }
}
```

And the response sent to the client will look like this:

```
{"person":
    {"firstName":"John",
     "middleName":null,
     "lastName":"Smith",
     "dateOfBirth":"1935-10-01",
     "gender":"MALE","
     "hospital":{...},
     "identityCard":{...},
     " links":{"self":{"href":"http://localhost:8080/mvc-rest/hateoas/1"}}
  }
```

---

! The `hospital` and `identityCard` objects are not displayed in the previous example, as their contents are not relevant for it. The content of those properties represents the JSON serialization of the `hospital` and `identityCard` fields specific to the `Person` instance. Their contents are displayed in Figure 5-15.

---

The response body contains two properties: `"person"` and `"links"`. The `"person"` property value is the JSON representation of the `Person` instance with id=1. The `"links"` property contains a link and its meaning. The `"rel":"self"` tells the client that the link points to the current resource. In this chapter, the fundamentals of creating and consuming RESTful services with Spring MVC were covered, which is enough for the certification exam.

# Summary

After reading this chapter, you should have a proper understanding of how Spring can be used to provide and consume REST services. Here is a simple list of topics that you should keep handy when reviewing your acquired knowledge:

- What is REST?
- What type of clients can access a web application?
- How are resources exposed to the client?
- How many types of representations are supported?
- What is the difference between `@Controller` and `@RestController`?
- Make sure that you can describe Spring MVC support for RESTful applications.
- Understand how to access request/response data.
- Use message converters.
- How is asynchronous REST supported?
- What is HATEOAS?
- How do you build a HATEOAS complying service with Spring HATEOAS and MVC?

# Quick Quiz

**Question 1:** What is REST?

    A.    a software design pattern

    B.    a framework

    C.    an architecture style

**Question 2:** Which of the following methods are HTTP methods?

    A.    PUT

    B.    GET

    C.    SUBMIT

    D.    OPTIONS

**Question 3:** What Spring class can be used to access and test REST services?

    A.    RestTemplate

    B.    AsyncRestTemplate

    C.    Both

    D.    None

**Question 4:** What does the RestTemplate handle?

    A.    Resources

    B.    Representations

    C.    Both

**Question 5:** What can be said about the @RestController annotation?

    A.    It is used to declare a controller providing REST services.

    B.    Is annotated with @Controller and @ResponseBody.

    C.    Controller methods annotated with @RequestMapping assume @ResponseStatus semantics by default when the controller is annotated with @RestController.

**Question 6:** What is the effect of annotating a method with @ResponseStatus?

    A.    The default behavior for resolving to a view for methods returning void or null is overridden.

    B.    The HTTP status code matching the @ResponseStatus is added to the response body.

    C.    It forces usage of HTTP message converters.

**Question 7:** Which of the following HTTP message converters are supported by Spring MVC?

    A.    StringHttpMessageConverter

    B.    MappingJackson2HttpMessageConverter, but Jackson2 must be in the classpath

    C.    YamlMessageConverter

**Question 8:** Which of the following RestTemplates can be used to make a GET REST call to a URL?

    A.   `restTemplate.getForObject(...)`

    B.   `optionsForAllow(...)`

    C.   `getForEntity(...)`

    D.   `exchange(..., HttpMethod.GET,...)`

**Question 9:** Does the following REST handler method comply with the HATEOAS constraint?

```
@ResponseStatus(HttpStatus.CREATED)
@RequestMapping(value = "/create", method = RequestMethod.POST,
    produces = MediaType.APPLICATION_JSON_VALUE,
    consumes = MediaType.APPLICATION_JSON_VALUE)
    public Person createPerson(@RequestBody @Valid Person newPerson) {
    logger.info("-----> CREATE");
    Hospital hospital = hospitalManager.findByCode(
        newPerson.getHospital().getCode());
    newPerson.setHospital(hospital);
    Person person = personManager.save(newPerson);
    logger.info("-----> PERSON: " + person);
    return person;
}
```

    A.   Yes, because it returns a representation of the object that was created.

    B.   No, because it does not set the location header to the URI of the created resource.

    C.   This is not a REST handler method.

    D.   No, because a `Link` object is not added to the returned resource.

# Practical Exercise

The practical exercises for this chapter require you to develop some REST client test methods to check your understanding of implementing RESTful application with Spring MVC. The project module is named **07-pr-rest-practice**. An analogous module with proposed solutions exists, which is named **07-pr-rest-solution**. The projects and their TODOs are shown in Figure 5-10.

**Figure 5-10.** *Projects associated with this chapter*

The project is split into packages that contain classes grouped by purpose:

- com.pr.config contains the Java Configuration class used to configure the application.

- com.pr.hateoas contains classes that describe a hypermedia-driven REST web service

- com.pr.problem contains classes that handle the exceptions thrown in the application.

  - GlobalExceptionHandler handles exceptions thrown by methods in the controllers under the com.pr.web package. The restriction is done using @ControllerAdvice(basePackages = "com.pr.web").

  - NotFoundException is a type of exception thrown when a resource cannot be found.

  - RestExceptionProcessor handles exceptions thrown by methods in the REST controllers under the com.pr.rest package.

- com.pr.rest contains classes that implement REST services and interceptors.

  - AuditRestInterceptor is an interceptor for REST services that prints simple messages and adds a header to the response before it is written.

  - HospitalsRestController is a REST controller for managing Hospital resources.

  - PersonsRestController is a REST controller for managing Person resources.

- com.pr.web contains the web controllers that receive requests from a browser and return views. The structure of the project is depicted in Figure 5-11.

***Figure 5-11.*** *Package organization of the 07-pr-rest-practice project module*

The tests for the rest controllers are located under the same packages as the controllers being tested. The only exception is the com.pr.async that contains a configuration class, a service class, and a test class used to test an asynchronous REST method annotated with @Async. You have no TODO tasks in this package; the example is simply provided for you to run it and see how an REST asynchronous is made.

All the TODO tasks are in the RestPersonControllerTest class. They cover GET, POST, and DELETE operations.

The practical exercise for this chapter requires Gradle tasks to be run in parallel, because the REST tests require the web application to be started. To do this, you have to create an Intellij IDEA Gradle launcher to start the application, and another to stop it. The test cases are run by right-clicking the method you want to execute, and then selecting **Run** from the menu that appears.

To create a Gradle launcher, you have to do the following:

1. In the Gradle Task view, right-click the **appStart** task. A menu is displayed. Select **Create personal-records:07-pr-rest-practice**.

2. In the popup check the **Single instance only** check box. Modify the name to something more relevant, like **mvc-rest-start**.

3. Click **Apply**, and then **OK**. Your launcher should be available in the Intellij IDEA launcher menu.

The flow for creating a Gradle launcher is depicted in Figure 5-12. Do the same to create a launcher for the appStop task.

***Figure 5-12.*** *Creating a Gradle launcher*

Then from the launcher menu, select the **mvc-rest-start** launcher and start the application. If the application starts correctly, you should see in the console the following log:

```
INFO    Jetty 9.2.10.v20150310 started and listening on port 8080
INFO    mvc-rest runs at:
INFO     http://localhost:8080/mvc-rest
Run 'gradle appStop' to stop the server.
```

Open the link in a browser. You should see the page shown in Figure 5-13.

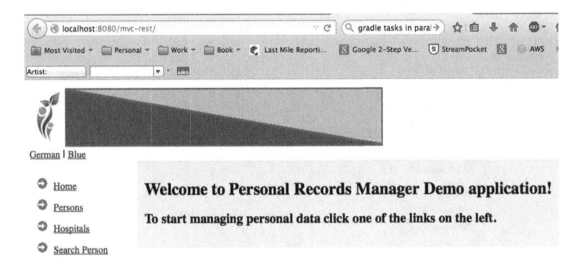

***Figure 5-13.*** *The mvc-rest web application*

The web application will help you verify that your REST requests have executed correctly.

Once you have the web application up, you can go ahead and try to solve the TODO tasks. There are eight TODOs, numbered from 15 to 22, that require you to perform certain types of REST requests.

---

! GET requests can be done directly in the browser, so if you want to get creative with GET REST handler methods, you can test them in a browser. For example, try to access `http://localhost:8080/mvc-rest/rest-persons/id/1`. You should see a JSON reply like the one depicted in the Figure 5-14.

---

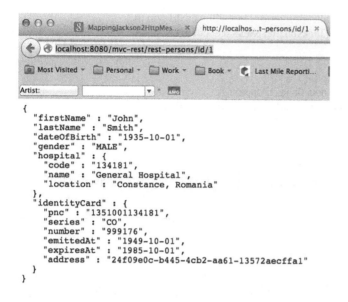

```json
{
  "firstName" : "John",
  "lastName" : "Smith",
  "dateOfBirth" : "1935-10-01",
  "gender" : "MALE",
  "hospital" : {
    "code" : "134181",
    "name" : "General Hospital",
    "location" : "Constance, Romania"
  },
  "identityCard" : {
    "pnc" : "1351001134181",
    "series" : "CO",
    "number" : "999176",
    "emittedAt" : "1949-10-01",
    "expiresAt" : "1985-10-01",
    "address" : "24f09e0c-b445-4cb2-aa61-13572aecffa1"
  }
}
```

***Figure 5-14.*** *JSON response for a GET REST request*

To format JSON representations properly for display, a @MappingJackson2HttpMessageConverter bean has to be defined and configured accordingly. There are two ways of doing this:

- Call setPrettyPrint on the @MappingJackson2HttpMessageConverter

```java
@Bean
public MappingJackson2HttpMessageConverter
            mappingJackson2HttpMessageConverter() {
    MappingJackson2HttpMessageConverter converter
                    = new MappingJackson2HttpMessageConverter();
    converter.setObjectMapper(objectMapper());
    converter.setPrettyPrint(true);
    return converter;
}

@Bean
public ObjectMapper objectMapper() {
    return new ObjectMapper();
}
```

- Enable the indentation of the serialization output by calling enable on the objectMapper set for the @MappingJackson2HttpMessageConverter bean

```
@Bean
public ObjectMapper objectMapper() {
    ObjectMapper objMapper = new ObjectMapper();
    objMapper.enable(SerializationFeature.INDENT_OUTPUT);
    return objMapper;
}
```

! POST and DELETE requests can be tested using a Firefox plugin called Poster.[14] Figure 5-15 shows a REST POST request and response done with Poster.

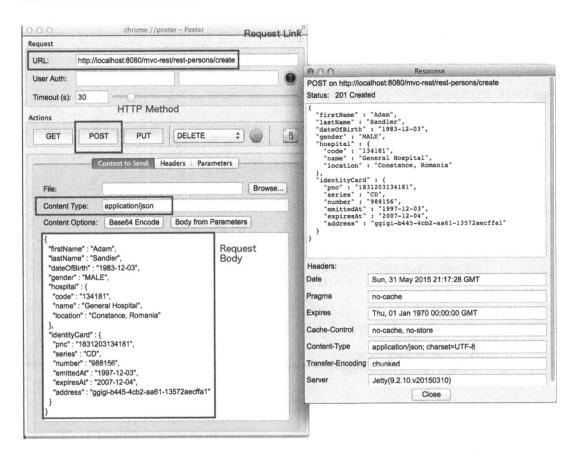

**Figure 5-15.** *POST REST request and response done with Poster. You have to copy and paste the RequestBody into the Poster content text area*

---

[14]The plugin can be found at https://addons.mozilla.org/en-US/firefox/addon/poster/.

■ ■ ■

# CHAPTER 6

# Spring Web with AJAX

The topic of this chapter is not a subject in the certification exam, but it is useful to know all the tools that can be used to develop a web application in the most efficient way. A properly designed user interface should ensure that a request is sent to the server only when the content of the request is complete and valid so that it can be used by a server operation. Using requests between the client and the server application is not a good practice. It is time-consuming and can go wrong when the network connection is unstable.

## What Is AJAX?

AJAX is an acronym for **a**synchronous **J**avaScript **and** **X**ML, but over the years, this term has grown and means so much more than the technologies that make the acronym. AJAX describes the way that various web technologies can make web applications highly responsive and provide the user with an almost desktop-like interaction. Basically, web applications developed with AJAX can provide rich interaction, just-in-time information, and dynamic information without a page refresh. Of course, this comes with programming complexity; some of the logic that happens on the server must be moved on the client side, where the logic must be implemented in JavaScript. The most obvious example is the validation of user input. There's no point in sending invalid data to the server, right?[1]

Before AJAX, a web application functioned like this:

1.   The user requested a page using a browser.

2.   The server where the web application was installed created and sent a response to be rendered in the browser.

3.   The user sent some data to the server.

4.   The server received the data and validated it. If the validation failed, the data and validation errors were put into a response that was sent back to the browser.

5.   The response was received by the browser, which displayed the new page.

---

[1]There are JavaScript libraries that can validate form user input before submission; for example, the jQuery validation plugin (http://jqueryvalidation.org).

This happens for any user request; the whole page is rebuilt and displayed every time a response is received from the server. It is quite a time-consuming process, depending on the health of the network, and the user may see an annoying flickering as the web pages are displayed. Figure 6-1 depicts the traditional pre-AJAX web application communication flow with the client.

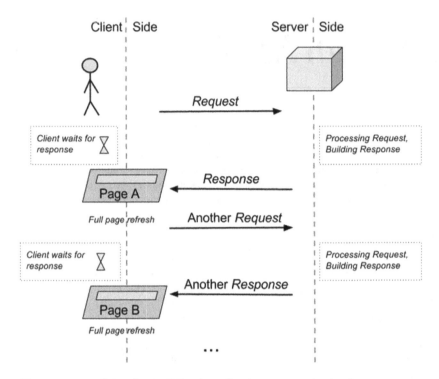

**Figure 6-1.** *Traditional pre-AJAX web application communication flow*

The validation case was chosen because an example of an editing form with validation was presented in Chapter 3 (the 05-pr-mvc-form module). The validation was implemented on the server side using the @Valid annotation. This can be easily seen by installing the Firebug plugin in Firefox (see the Net tab). All the steps mentioned next are depicted in Figure 6-2.

1.  Start **05-pr-mvc-form-solution**.

2.  Open the Firebug console (1), click the **Net** tab (2), and then click (3) **Enable**.

3.  Click the **Persons** menu item (4). Select a user (5), click the link to see the details, and then click the **Edit** link (6).

4.  Click the **Clear** option (7) in the Firebug console to make sure that you do not have previous requests polluting the console.

5.  Delete the first name (8) and last name (9). Click **Save** (10) and then analyze what is shown in the **Net** console.

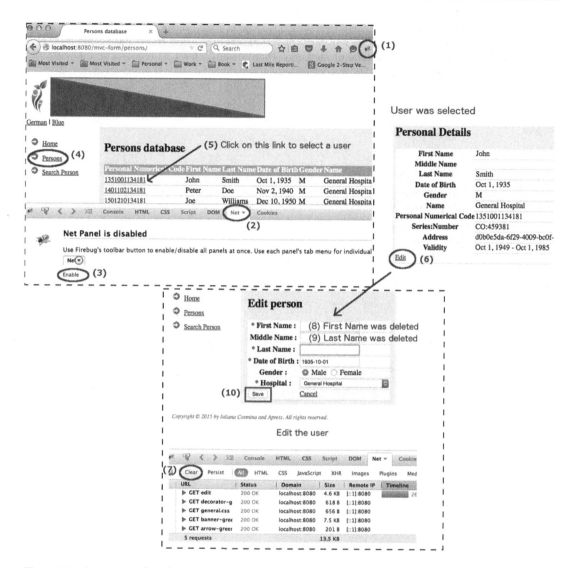

*Figure 6-2. Steps to analyze the communication between client and server*

After performing the last step, you should see the POST request in the console. If you expand it, you see the response sent by the server (returned by the DispatcherServlet), a new HTML page containing the HTML code of the page, plus the validation elements. There are also a few GET requests for the static contents of the page, which are handled by the default servlet container for static resources. Figure 6-3 depicts the last communication with the server.

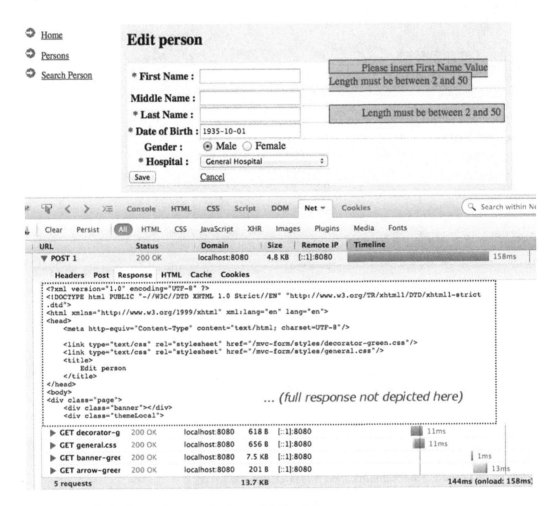

***Figure 6-3.*** *The final step of communication, validation failure response*

In the preceding example, a POST request was sent to the server. The validation was executed on the server and failed, so no data was saved. Basically, this was a useless request, and the full page was rebuilt and redisplayed just to show the user what was wrong with the data. The GET requests to retrieve the header and footer information, and the styling *.css files, are also useless, because they are used to retrieve information already present in the page. These useless requests can be avoided either by using caching or by making sure only the form part of the page is dynamic. AJAX can help with this. A request can be sent to the server with the form data by using an AJAX request; the data retrieved from the server can be used to rebuild only a part of the page by using an AJAX callback. Or even better, validation can be performed on the client side by using JavaScript (pure or competent JavaScript libraries like the jQuery validation plugin). And an AJAX request sends data to the server, which is processed successfully. This is just an example. AJAX can also be used when searching data. An autocomplete behavior can be implemented for the search field by using an AJAX call to build a list (server side) and afterward to display the list using JavaScript (usually below the autocomplete input).[2]

One of the most popular JavaScript frameworks is jQuery[3] because it is small and provides a wide range of functionalities—document traversal and manipulation, event handling, and animations—in a very practical way. Most popular JavaScript frameworks are actually developed using jQuery.[4]

A new way of developing web applications nowadays is to totally decouple the Web from server functionality, keeping all web logic on the client and all back-end logic on the server, reducing communication between the client and the server as much as possible, and handling requests in a manner similar to REST. AJAX remoting was not supported until Spring 3. JSON also became very popular once jQuery took off and it is now the most common format for performing data exchange between a client and a server.

---

**!** A sample of this behavior is implemented in the `RestSearchController` that you can find in the `08-pr-ajax-solution`. It is presented in detail later in the chapter.

---

# Making AJAX Requests

AJAX requests can be made using a JavaScript object of type `XMLHttpRequest`, which was designed by Microsoft and adopted by Mozilla, Apple, and Google, and standardized in W3C[5]. All modern browsers support it. To create an instance of `XMLHttpRequest`, you just instantiate it:

```
var xhr = new XMLHttpRequest();
```

---

[2]jQuery UI provides a plugin that to implement the behavior with little effort (`https://jqueryui.com/autocomplete/`).
[3]The official jQuery site (`https://jquery.com`).
[4]Examples include jQuery UI (`https://jqueryui.com`), Bootstrap (`http://getbootstrap.com`), AngularJS (`https://angularjs.org`).
[5]See `http://www.w3.org/TR/XMLHttpRequest/`.

The xhr object can make requests to a server and update only a portion of the page. Figure 6-4 depicts XMLHttpRequest. When the client sends a request using this type of object, the server responds by populating the xhr.responseText property.

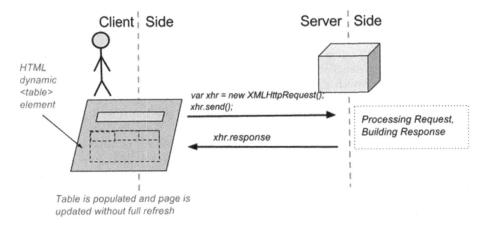

**Figure 6-4.** *AJAX request diagram*

A search request for a person with a first name that contains the letter *a* can be send to the server using a function similar to the following. Everything after ? are request parameters.

```
<script type="text/javascript">
var url="${personsUrl}/ajax?fieldName=firstName"
        "&fieldValue=a"
        "&exactMatch=false";
var xhr = new XMLHttpRequest();
xhr.open("GET", url);
xhr.send();
xhr.onreadystatechange =
    function () {
        if (xhr.readyState == 4 && xhr.status == 200) {
            displayResults(xhr.response);
        }
    }
};
</script>
```

The xhr.send() method has multiple forms. It sends the request body to the URL that a connection was previously open to by calling xhr.open("GET", url). In the previous example, there was no request body to send, because all the request parameters were in the URL.

The readyState can have different values, but the one in the fourth example tests if the request has finished and the response is ready. The status property is the HttpStatus value that was mentioned in Chapter 3; it is result code from the server. If you want to know more about the XMLHttpRequest type, you can take a look at the full specifications at https://xhr.spec.whatwg.org/. But since jQuery was introduced, there's been no need to use it explicitly because there are better and more practical ways to make AJAX requests.

**!** An example for making a request using an object of type XMLHttpRequest can be found in the 08-pr-ajax-solution. Just look for the legacySearch JavaScript function in the search.jsp file. To test that function, just comment the $.getJSON call in line 112 and uncomment the legacySearch call in line 113. Restart the application and try it. But you might want to do this after finishing reading this chapter, when your understanding of jQuery, JavaScript, and the logic of the application will make things easier for you.

As you can see, using objects of type XMLHttpRequest to perform AJAX calls is quite cumbersome. A lot of problems might appear when the response type is something more complex than text; like JSON, for example, because a lot of extra code has to be written to perform conversions that get the response body in a proper format.

The methods and properties of the XMLHttpRequest class used in the previous example are explained in Table 6-1.

**Table 6-1.** *XMLHttpRequest Methods and Properties*

| Method | Description |
| --- | --- |
| open(*http method, URL,* [asynch-Flag, username, password]) | Initializes a request. This method is to be used from JavaScript code. |
| send(*content in various formats*) | This method sends a request. The content can be null. If the request is asynchronous (which is the default), this method returns as soon as the request is sent. |
| onreadystatechange | This property returns an EventHandler every time the readyState attribute changes. |
| readystate | Returns an unsigned short, the state of the request, and the API. (http://www.w3.org/TR/XMLHttpRequest/#xmlhttprequest) defined values are: 0 -> UNSENT : open() was not called yet 1 -> OPENED : send() was called 2 -> HEADERS_RECEIVED : send() was called and headers and status are available 3 -> LOADING : downloading; responseText holds partial data 4 -> DONE : the request was completed |
| status | This property is of type unsigned short and contains the HTTP result code. Most common values are 200 -> ok 201 -> Created 400 -> bad request 404 -> not found 403 -> forbidden 500 -> internal server error |
| responseText | This property contains the response to the request as text, or null if the request was unsuccessful or has not yet been sent. |

# Introducing jQuery

In the practice exercise, you will perform a search request that updates only the content of a `<div>` element. The JSP page is /webapp/WEB-INF/persons/search.jsp. The contents are as follows:

```jsp
<%@ taglib prefix="c" uri="http://java.sun.com/jsp/jstl/core" %>
<%@ taglib prefix="fn" uri="http://java.sun.com/jsp/jstl/functions" %>
<%@ taglib prefix="spring" uri="http://www.springframework.org/tags" %>
<%@ taglib prefix="sf" uri="http://www.springframework.org/tags/form" %>

<h2>
  <spring:message code="persons.search.title"/>
</h2>

<div class="form">
   <spring:url value="/persons" var="personsUrl"/>
   <sf:form modelAttribute="criteriaDto" method="get">
     <table>
      <tr>
        <th>
          <label for="fieldName">
            <spring:message code="label.Criteria.fieldname"/> :
          </label>
        </th>

        <td>
          <sf:select path="fieldName" id="fieldName">
            <sf:option value="firstName">
                <spring:message code="label.Person.firstname"/>
            </sf:option>
            <sf:option value="lastName">
                <spring:message code="label.Person.lastname"/>
            </sf:option>
            <sf:option value="dob">
                <spring:message code="label.Person.dob"/>
            </sf:option>
            <sf:option value="pnc">
                <spring:message code="label.ic.pnc"/>
            </sf:option>
            <sf:option value="hospital">
                <spring:message code="label.Hospital.name"/>
            </sf:option>
          </sf:select>
        </td>
        <td></td>
      </tr>
      <tr>
        <th>
          <label for="fieldValue">
            <span class="man">*</span>
            <spring:message code="label.Criteria.fieldvalue"/> :
          </label>
```

```
        </th>
        <td><sf:input path="fieldValue" id="fieldValue"/>
         <em>
             <br><spring:message code="label.dateFormat.accepted"/>
         </em>
        </td>
        <td><label class="error" id="fieldValueError"/>
        </td>
      </tr>
      <tr>
        <td></td>
        <td colpan="2">
          <sf:checkbox path="exactMatch" id="exactMatch"/>
          <spring:message code="label.Criteria.exactmatch"/>
        </td>
      </tr>
      <tr>
        <td>
          <input id="searchButton" type="submit"
           value="<spring:message code='command.search'/>"/>
        </td>
        <td>
          <input id="cancelButton" type="submit"
           value="<spring:message code='command.cancel'/>"/>
        </td>
      </tr>
      <tr>
        <td colspan="3">
        <!-- HTML element that will be dynamically populated -->
            <label class="error" id="noResults"/>
        </td>
      </tr>
    </table>
  </sf:form>
</div>

<!-- The div with results, that will be loaded dynamically -->
<div id="resultDiv">
  <table>
    <thead>
    <tr>
      <td>
        <spring:message code="label.ic.pnc"/>
      </td>
      <td>
        <spring:message code="label.Person.firstname"/>
      </td>
      <td>
        <spring:message code="label.Person.lastname"/>
      </td>
    </tr>
    </thead>
```

```
    <tbody id="resultTable">
    </tbody>
  </table>
</div>

<script type="text/javascript">
$(document).ready(function () {
    // JavaScript content to make the page dynamic
}
</script>
```

A few Spring form elements have been replaced with HTML elements that will be displayed and populated by JavaScript methods. HTML elements from a page can be populated or emptied, hidden or displayed using JavaScript. If you click the **Search** button, a request (only one) is made to retrieve results, and the resultTable is populated and the resultDiv is displayed. Figure 6-5 depicts an AJAX request to search for people. The result table is populated and displayed with the response returned. As you can see, no other requests are necessary. This is the power of AJAX: a practical way of retrieving from server only the information that is really needed.

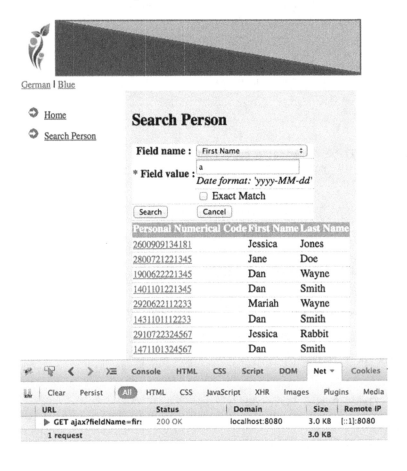

***Figure 6-5.*** *AJAX request*

The JavaScript code that is missing from the earlier code snippet is written using jQuery. By providing functions that are more practical and easier to use, this framework helps the developer to focus on the key aspects of making a request: which resource is requested from the server (the URI), which parameters are to be used for the request, and which callback method is to be executed when the response is received.[6] That is what jQuery is—a library or a collection of JavaScript functions that a developer can use to avoid writing complicated JavaScript logic. jQuery provides the following features:

- DOM element selection

- DOM element manipulation

- CSS manipulation

- Events and event-related functions

- JavaScript effects and animations

- Strong cross-browser support

- Small footprint and speed

- Functions for JSON parsing

To use jQuery, the jquery.js file containing JavaScript functions has to be referred in the page. When using Spring and Tiles, the jquery.js file is referred in the template file that builds every page of the site. The jquery.js file can be added to the project or it can be referred directly from the Web if access to the Internet is assumed to always be possible. The 08-pr-ajax-practice is the project for this chapter and its structure is depicted in Figure 6-6.

***Figure 6-6.*** *Practice project to exercise Spring with AJAX*

---

[6]Some jQuery AJAX methods allow definition of two callback methods: one for successful requests and one for failed ones.

The jQuery.js file is part of the project; it is stored under \webapp\js. Its name is postfixed with the version of jQuery—in this case, 2.1.4; it is referred in \webapp\WEB-INF\templates\layout.jsp like this:

```
<head>
  <script type="text/javascript" src="<c:url value='/js/jquery-2.1.4.js' /> ">
  </script>
</head>
```

When Internet access is always assumed, the file does not have to be part of the project; it can be referred directly using the link from the official site:

```
<head>
  <script type="text/javascript" src="http://code.jquery.com/jquery-2.1.4.min.js">
  </script>
</head>
```

On the official site, two versions are available. The development version, which was copied in the project, is uncompressed and has proper formatting that is readable; it should be used during development. The minified (obfuscated) version is compressed, not readable, reduced in size, and appropriate for production use.[7]

# jQuery HTML DOM Manipulation

The principle of jQuery is to select an element(s) and perform some action(s) on it (them):

```
$(selector).action();
```

The $ is actually a variable of type jQuery that is added to the current page when the jquery.js file is referred. Every function defined in the jQuery type can thus be used. You can check this for yourself by inspecting the code in the jquery.js. You find the following:

```
jQuery = function( selector, context ) { ...}
window.jQuery = window.$ = jQuery;
```

The selector can be anything: an HTML id, a CSS class, an HTML element type, or a combination of any of these. jQuery is flexible like that. The identification of the element is done by a selector engine. Examples are depicted in the following code snippet:

```
<!-- Selecting elements by type -->
$("p")   // selects all <p> elements in the page
$("p a") // selects all anchor tags inside a paragraph tag

<!-- Selecting element having id=resultDiv-->
$("#resultDiv")

<!-- Selecting all elements with class=error -->
$(".error")
```

---

[7]Smaller resources load faster on browsers; that's why production minified files are recommended.

The *action* can be any function available for that HTML element. For example, the val and text functions get and set values for a field:

```
<!-- Getting the value form a text field -->
var fieldName = $("#fieldName").val();
<!-- Setting the "John" value of text field -->
$("#fieldValue").val("John");
<!-- Setting the value of a label element -->
$("#fieldValueError").text(err);
```

And there are special functions to manipulate HTML, such as adding, removing, replacing, displaying, or showing extra elements :

```
<!-- The contents of the element with id "resultTable" are deleted-->
$("#resultTable").empty();
<!-- Adding HTML elements to the element with "resultTable" id -->
$("#resultTable").append("<tr><td>123456</td></tr>")
<!-- Replacing HTML content of the element with "resultTable" id-->
$("#resultTable").html("<tr><td>123456</td></tr>");
<!-- Hide all elements with class "error" -->
$(".error").hide();
<!-- Fading out element with certain speed: slow/fast/normal -->
$("#resultDiv").fadeOut("fast");
<!-- Fading in element with certain speed: slow/fast/normal -->
$("#resultDiv").fadeIn("fast");
```

Specific behavior can be attached to elements using JavaScript HTML DOM events.[8]

```
<!-- Attach 'onClick' event handler to the search button using HTML.
Static - the event handler is always bound to the button-->
<input id="searchButton"
        type="submit"
        value="<spring:message  code='command.search'/>"
        onclick="submitSearch"/>

// Attach 'onClick' event handler to the search button using javascript
// Dynamic - developer can decide when/if the event handler
// is bound to the search button.The following function is called when the DOM

// is ready
$(function() {
    $("#searchButton").onclick = submitSearch;
});
```

An HTML event called DOMContentLoaded triggers on an HTML document when the page is ready. It waits for the full HTML and scripts, and then triggers. The ${function){} is equivalent to $(document). ready(function () {} and handles the ready event. This ensures that the JavaScript code in the body is executed after all the HTML elements were rendered.

---

[8]The complete list of HTML DOM events can be found at http://www.w3schools.com/jsref/dom_obj_event.asp.

After the submitSearch method is bound to the searchButton, the method is called when the button is clicked. The body of the method contains jQuery HTML element manipulation statements.

```
function submitSearch(event) {
   //prevent submission of the form so this function can send the request
   event.preventDefault();

   // extract values form HTML elements
    var fieldName = $("#fieldName").val();
    var fieldValue = $("#fieldValue").val();
    var exactMatch = $("#exactMatch").is(":checked");

   //validate parameters before sending the request
   if (isValid(fieldName, fieldValue)) {
   //definition of the isValid method is not relevant in this context
   // and will be covered later

    var params = {
       fieldName: fieldName,
       fieldValue: fieldValue,
       exactMatch: exactMatch
   };
   //clear errors from previous attempts if any
   $(".error").hide();

   //sending request to http://localhost:8080/mvc-ajax/ajax
   $.getJSON("${personsUrl}/ajax", params, displayResults);
   //definition of the displayResults method is not relevant in this context
   // and will be covered later
   }
   return false;
}
```

In earlier versions of jQuery, the .bind() method was used for attaching an event handler directly to elements.

```
$(function() {
   $("#searchButton").bind("click", submitSearch);
  }
```

The same can be done using the jQuery click() function to directly bind a function to the button:

```
$(function() {
   $("#searchButton").click(
   function (event) {
           //content of submitSearch method mentioned earlier
   });
});
```

# jQuery AJAX Calls

jQuery provides methods to make AJAX calls using the `ajax` method. Because the syntax of this method is complicated, wrappers for performing GET and POST requests are provided.[9]

`$.get(URL, parameters, callback, dataType)`

- URL: The URL of the server resource being requested via GET

- `parameters`: Any data that should be sent to the server using a GET request (string, Object, Array)

- `callback`: A function to be executed after the request is completed

- `dataType`: The type of data representing the response body (text, XML, JSON, etc.)

This method can be used like this:

```
$(function() {
  $("#searchButton").bind("click", submitSearch);
});

function submitSearch(event) {
 ...
 // code to extract parameters is the same as previous example

 //sending request to http://localhost:8080/mvc-ajax/ajax
    $.getJSON("${personsUrl}/ajax", params, displayResults);
   }
}
```

The `displayResults` method should receive a JSON array as an argument that transforms into `<tr/>` elements that will be added to the `resultTable`. Each line contains a link (which is the person's personal numeric code) to the details page in the first column, the first name in the second column, and the last name in the third column. The HTML code should be similar to the following:

```
<tr>
 <td>
   <a href="#" onclick="getPersonDetails('2600909134181')">
      2600909134181
   </a>
 </td>
 <td>Jessica</td>
 <td>Jones</td>
</tr>
```

---

[9]The full API for jQuery in a very readable format can be accessed at `http://jqapi.com/`.

The link is a function call that displays a pop-up with that person's information. The personal numeric code is used as an argument, because the person id is not serialized and it is not used in the JavaScript functions for security reasons.

```
function displayResults(results) {
  if (results.length == 0) {
    $("#noResults").fadeIn("fast");
    $("#noResults").text("No results for search");
  } else {
    $("#resultTable").empty();
    results.forEach(function(person){
        $("#resultTable").append(
          "<tr>"
          + "<td>"
          +'<a href="#"' + 'onclick="getPersonDetails('
          + "'"+ person.identityCard.pnc +"'" + ')">'
          + person.identityCard.pnc +'</a>'
          + "</td>"
          + "<td>" + person.firstName + "</td>"
          + "<td>"+ person.lastName + '</td>'
          +"</tr>");
    });
    $("#resultDiv").fadeIn("fast");
  }
}
```

- $.getJSON(URL, parameters, callback): Load JSON-encoded data from the server using a GET HTTP request. Basically, equivalent to $.get (URL, parameters, callback, "json"). The parameters argument is an object containing the request parameters and their values. Before making the request, that object is parsed and the parameter names and values are extracted and added to the request URL.

- $.post(URL, parameters, callback, dataType): A method to make a POST request. Parameters have the same meaning, as mentioned previously for $.get.

---

! In JavaScript and HTML, the single quote(') and double quote(") have the same meaning and can be used together in complicated text constructions to avoid escaping them. This was done in the previous code snippet to create the contents of the "resultTable" element.

! The JavaScript code in this chapter's example might not be optimal, but it was written in such a way to use all the examples given in the book.

---

# Spring MVC, AJAX, and jQuery

The main advantage of AJAX is that you can have one JSP page that handles the request and the result, so no need to redirect to another page (view) to display the result. When using Spring, a controller handles the AJAX request. The controller method to handle AJAX requests has the following typical syntax:

```
@RequestMapping(value = "/ajax", method = RequestMethod.GET)
public @ResponseBody
  List<Person> getPersons(CriteriaDto criteria) {
    try {
      List<Person> persons = personManager.getByCriteriaDto(criteria);
      return persons;
    } catch (InvalidCriteriaException ice) {
      ice.printStackTrace();
    }
    return new ArrayList<>();
}
```

Of course, a view cannot represent the response, so the controller methods must be annotated with @ResponseBody. The response will be serialized to JSON because the client (the $.getJSON in this case) accepts this content type. And because the jackson library is in the classpath of the project, Spring does its thing, and serializes the response properly, without the need for any other configuration.

If the client does not specify the type of the format for the response, then produces = MediaType. APPLICATION_JSON_VALUE should be added to the @RequestMapping annotation. But using this attribute when the client requests the default format would just be redundant.

getByCriteriaDto is a service method to search a person using the criteria provided by the user. It was covered in Chapter 3.

The client jQuery method is depicted in the following code snippet:

```
$("#searchButton").click(
  function (event) {
    event.preventDefault();
    var fieldName = $("#fieldName").val();
    var fieldValue = $("#fieldValue").val();
    var exactMatch = $("#exactMatch").is(":checked");
    //console.log('Criteria:' + fieldName + ", " + fieldValue
      + ", " + exactMatch);

    if (isValid(fieldName, fieldValue)) {
      var params = {
      fieldName: fieldName,
      fieldValue: fieldValue,
      exactMatch: exactMatch
    }
    $(".error").hide();
    $.getJSON("${personsUrl}/ajax", params, displayResults);
    }
    return false;
});
```

```
    //global variables representing internationalized error messages
    // they are set by the controller
    var fieldValueErrMessage = "${fieldValueErrMessage}";
    var fieldDateErrMessage = "${fieldDateErrMessage}";

function isValid(fieldName, fieldValue){
    var err='';
     if(fieldValue.length == 0) {
         err = fieldValueErrMessage;
       } else if(fieldName == 'dob' && !isValidDate(fieldValue)) {
         err = fieldDateErrMessage;
    }

if(err.length > 0) {
   $("#fieldValue").focus();
   $("#fieldValueError").text(err);
   $("#fieldValueError").fadeIn('fast');
     return false;
   }
   return true;
}
```

As mentioned, the params object is constructed to group the parameter names and values for the GET request. Even if it looks like a JSON object, it is not, and it does not need to be because it is not used as such. The params object is not placed in the body of the request to be deserialized in the controller; instead, its content is extracted and added as request parameters to the request URL before making the request. Spring MVC takes these parameters and uses them to create an argument of type CriteriaDto, which is then passed as arguments of the search method in the controller.

The isValid method validates the request parameters and displays an error message if the parameters are invalid. If the request parameters are valid, the request is sent to the server and the response is processed using the displayResults method. The isValidDate is a utility method that matches a string to a date format.

## Using REST-Style Remoting with JSON

If the request body and the response body are both in JSON format, considering that an AJAX request is all about data exchange, REST could be used to make AJAX calls. So instead of using @Controller, @RestController could handle AJAX calls. The JavaScript must change too. To demonstrate how this can be done, a new menu option was created in 08-pr-ajax-solution. A new form was also added. They are depicted in Figure 6-7.

***Figure 6-7.*** *Menu item and form for using a RestController to perform a search*

The form is a simplified version of the one previously used, because the field name in the search criteria is not selectable anymore. This was done to reduce the complexity of the JavaScript and to focus on the AJAX request. The only restriction now is for the user-inserted string to not be empty. Also, the page technically does not even need a Spring form anymore. A POST request can be done without having a form by using the jQuery $.ajax method to perform the AJAX call. So no model attribute is needed to populate the form; you have a simpler web interface, as another Spring component was removed. The following code can be found in /webapp/WEB-INF/persons/rest-search.jsp:

```
<div class="person">
    <spring:url value="/rest-search/perform" var="searchUrl"/>
        <table>
            <tr>
                <th>
                    <spring:message code="label.Criteria.fieldname"/> :
                </th>

                <td>
                    <label>
                        <spring:message code="label.Person.firstname"/>
                    </label>
                </td>
                <td></td>
            </tr>
            <tr>
                <th>
                    <span class="man">*</span>
                     <spring:message code="label.Criteria.fieldvalue"/> :
                </th>
                <td><input name="fieldValue" id="fieldValue"/>
                </td>
```

```
                        <td>
                        </td>
                    </tr>
                    <tr>
                        <td></td>
                        <td colpan="2">
                            <input type="checkbox" id="exactMatch" />
                            <spring:message code="label.Criteria.exactmatch"/>
                        </td>
                    </tr>
                    <tr>
                        <td>
                            <input id="searchButton" type="submit"
                                value="<spring:message code='command.search'/>"/>
                        </td>
                        <td>
                            <input id="cancelButton" type="submit"
                                value="<spring:message code='command.cancel'/>"/>
                        </td>
                    </tr>
                    <tr>
                        <td colspan="3"><label class="error" id="noResults"/></td>
                    </tr>
                </table>
        </div>

        <div id="resultDiv">
        <!-- this div does not change-->
        </div>
```

To display the form, a different controller than the one handling the AJAX request has to be used, because a REST controller does not use views.

```
@Controller
@RequestMapping(value = "/rest-search")
public class RestFormController {

    // Displays the REST customized person search form to the user
    @RequestMapping(method = RequestMethod.GET)
    public String search() {
        return "persons/rest-search";
    }
}
```

The controller to handle the AJAX requests is a typical REST controller, annotated with @RestController, which was introduced in Chapter 5. The method handling the AJAX request expects the criteria to be submitted in JSON format (the consumes attribute) and provides a response that will be serialized to the JSON format (the produces attribute).

```java
@RestController
@RequestMapping(value = "/rest-search/perform")
public class RestSearchController {

    @Autowired
    protected PersonManager personManager;

    @ResponseStatus(HttpStatus.OK)
    @RequestMapping(method = RequestMethod.POST,
            produces = MediaType.APPLICATION_JSON_VALUE,
            consumes = MediaType.APPLICATION_JSON_VALUE)
    public List<Person> getAll(@RequestBody CriteriaDto criteria)
        throws InvalidCriteriaException {
        if (criteria.getFieldValue() == null || criteria.getFieldValue().isEmpty()) {
            return personManager.getByCriteriaDto(criteria);
        }
        return new ArrayList<>();
    }
}
```

To make things more interesting, two callbacks will be used: one for the case when the request is resolved correctly and one for the case when the request fails.

```html
<script type="text/javascript">
$(function () {

  $("#searchButton").click(
      function (event) {
      event.preventDefault();
       sendAjaxReq();
  });

});
function sendAjaxReq(){
      var fieldValue = $("#fieldValue").val();
      var exactMatch = $("#exactMatch").is(":checked");

      if (fieldValue != '') {
          $.postJSON("${searchUrl}",
          JSON.stringify({
              "fieldName": "firstName",
              "fieldValue": fieldValue,
              "exactMatch": exactMatch}),displayResults);
    // the displayResults method was not changed
      }
  }
```

```
//function is added to the jQuery object
// so it can be called with $.postJSON
$.postJSON = function(url, data, callback) {
        return $.ajax({
            "type": "POST",
            "url": url,
            "contentType": "application/json",
            "data": data,
            "dataType": "json"
        }).done(function(results) {
            displayResults(results);
        }).fail(function (){
            alert("ERROR!");
        });
};
```

The first new function that requires attention is JSON.stringify, which converts a JavaScript value to a JSON string. This is needed because the $.ajax method performs a POST into a CriteriaDto object at the controller level. The response is already in JSON format, so its sister method, JSON.parse, which transforms a string into a JSON object, is not needed.[10]

The done and the fail callback methods can be chained with the $.ajax call. They are called on the request object that is returned by the $.ajax method.

Depending on the requirements of the application, the implementation with Spring MVC or Spring REST can be used. The last one is usually recommended for applications that also have clients that do not use a web interface, like REST web services, mobile applications, and so forth.

# Custom Tags

Web applications are deployed on application servers when they are used in production. When the applications are small, multiple applications can be deployed on the same server, and each of them should have a contextPath defined for requests to be filtered and received by the appropriate application. The application does not know on which server it will be deployed, on which port the server was configured to work on, and under which name the application will be available, because that's what a context is, sort of. Other applications can be deployed on that server, and without a context for each of them, the server would not be able to forward requests to the specific application. That is why all links in an application must be relative to the context of the application.

In the sample applications used with this book, a context path is defined by configuring the Gretty plugin:

```
gretty {
    port = 8080
    contextPath = '/mvc-ajax'
}
```

---

[10]The API for these two functions can be found at https://msdn.microsoft.com/library/cc836459%28v=vs.94%29.aspx .

Each request to any resource of this application contains `mvc-ajax` because of that setting. All the links in the application are relative to this context, so in case the context changes, the links still point to the correct resources. When the application is started locally, it can be accessed at the following link: `http://localhost:8080/mvc-ajax`. This link can be considered an entry point in the application. If `contextPath ='/mvc-ajax'` changes to `contextPath = '/myproject'`, the entry point link changes to `http://localhost:8080/myproject` and all the other links in the application are relative to the new context as well.

To generate a link relative to an application context in a JSP page, development Java scriptlets were used at the beginning of Java Web applications:

```
<a href="<%=request.getContextPath()%>Display Persons</a>
```

But scriptlets make the JSP code quite difficult to read, and they could not be inherited or reused. They became obsolete in JSP 2.0. The smarter features that replaced them are called *JSP tags*. These are custom JSP elements that can be used inside a JSP page to add extra functionality or wrap up repetitive JSP code. To create a URL relative to the context of an application, the `c:url` can be used like this:

```
<%@ taglib prefix="c" uri="http://java.sun.com/jsp/jstl/core"%>
<c:url value="/persons" var="url"/>
<a href="${url}">Display Persons</a>
```

With the `spring:url` tag, a link relative to the context can be defined in a JSP page in a similar way as using `c:url`:

```
<%@ taglib prefix="spring" uri="http://www.springframework.org/tags"%>
<spring:url value="/persons" var="url"/>
<a href="${url}">Display Persons</a>
```

JSP tags make the JSP pages more readable. The most popular JSP tag collection is JSTL (**JSP S**tandard **T**ag **L**ibrary).[11] The `c:url` tag is one of the core tags in this library. If you want to take a look at the contents of the JSTL library, go to Intellij IDEA and look in the Project view. There is a node named **External Libraries**. Expanding that node makes all the dependencies of the project become visible. Look for `Maven:javax.servlet:jstl:1.2` and expand that node; you should see something similar to what's shown in Figure 6-8.

---

[11]JSTL is part of the JEE web development platform and extends the JSP specification by adding a set of JSP tags that can be used for the most common tasks, like XML and text processing, conditional execution, loops, and so forth. More details about tag libraries can be found on the official page `https://jstl.java.net/`.

**Figure 6-8.** *Contents of the jstl.jar library*

A developer can create his own custom JSP tags to define a custom task and use it in a JSP page. To create a custom tag, a dedicated file containing JSP code needs to be created for that tag (in Figure 6-8, the dedicated files are the ones with .tld extension). A class and a *.tld file (tag library descriptors) are needed if the tag is complex (the tld file and the class are more verbose and won't be covered in this book).

In the following code snippet, you can see the definition of a custom tag that allows context relative URL to be generated in a simple manner (and tests it too):

```
<!-- WEB-INF/tags/smart.tag -->
<%@ taglib prefix="c" uri="http://java.sun.com/jsp/jstl/core"%>
<%@ attribute name="inputURL" required="true" rtexprvalue="true"%>
<%@ attribute name="text" required="true" rtexprvalue="true"%>
<c:url value="${inputURL}" var="url"/>
<a href="${url}">${text}</a>

<!-- usage in a JSP file -->
<%@ taglib prefix="url" tagdir="/WEB-INF/tags"%>
...
<url:smart inputURL="/persons/search/" text="Search Persons"/>
```

The `inputURL` and `text` are tag attributes that are populated when the tag is used. The following is the HTML code that results from the `<url:smart />` line:

```
<a href="/mvc-ajax/persons/search/">Search Persons</a>
```

If you are interested in learning more about custom tag creation, Oracle has a very good public tutorial.[12]

# Summary

After reading this chapter, you should have a proper understanding of how Spring can be combined with AJAX technologies to create efficient web applications with responsive pages. Here is a small list of questions that you might want to keep handy when reviewing your acquired knowledge:

- What is AJAX?

- What is an instance of `XMLHttpRequest` used for?

- What is jQuery and how can it be used to access Spring applications?

- What is a custom JSP tag is and how do you create one?

# Quick Quiz

**Question 1:** What is AJAX?

- A. a framework to create responsive web pages

- B. a set of standards on how to create responsive web pages

- C. an acronym for *Asynchronous JavaScript and XML*

- D. a set of technologies that can be used to create highly responsive web applications

**Question 2:** What can be said about jQuery?

- A. It is a tag library.

- B. It is a set of technologies to create responsive web pages.

- C. It is the most popular JavaScript library.

**Question 3:** What jQuery method can be used to make a GET request?

- A. `$.get`

- B. `$.getJSON`

- C. `$.ajax`

- D. `$.post`

---

[12]Oracle custom tags creation; see `https://docs.oracle.com/javaee/7/tutorial/`.

**Question 4:** What is a custom JSP tag?

    A.    a custom tag is a user-defined JSP language element

    B.    a special class that handles JSP tasks execution

# Practical Exercise

The practical exercises for this chapter require you to develop a REST handler method to search and return a list of people matching the criteria sent from the browser, as well as a few JavaScript functions using jQuery to display results and errors. You'll use the `08-pr-ajax-practice` project module. `08-pr-ajax-solution` is analogous module with a proposed solution. This module also contains extra implementations that were mentioned earlier in the chapter.

The TODO tasks for this chapter are shown in Figure 6-9.

***Figure 6-9.*** *TODO tasks for Spring with AJAX practice module*

The PersonsSearchController is the controller used to handle requests that come from the search.jsp page. The PersonsController contains a single method that is used to retrieve a person's information and return it to the client in JSON format. The rest of the project setup (configuration and tiles) are the same as in previous modules. No extra settings are needed to handle AJAX requests.

The application is configured via Jetty to run at http://localhost:8080/mvc-ajax. Just run the application using 'gradle appStart' and stop it using 'gradle appStop'.

After you complete the proposed TODOs, as a bonus exercise, you can try creating the start custom tag described in the last section of this chapter.

# CHAPTER 7

■ ■ ■

# Spring Web Flow

As time went by, and more and more services could remotely use web applications, the web applications became more complex—and designing and implementing them became a cumbersome process. Most applications imply creating objects and passing them through several states, or creating objects depending on each other. Spring Web Flow (SWF) is a component of the Spring Framework's web stack that was created to help develop complex applications by reducing the difficulty in development.

The Spring Web Flow complements the @Controller model and provides the infrastructure needed to build complex web applications that support controlled page navigation and state transition; all of this adds up to a rigorously defined conversation between the end user and the application. It is possible to write such applications with any other web technology, but the definition of a flow is interconnected with the rest of the web components; it is scattered all over the implementation, which makes refactoring and maintenance a real pain. What Spring Web Flow brings to the table is the possibility to define flows as separate components detached from the rest of the implementation—web-specific classes and views. The flow components can be defined and used similar to the way beans are used in Spring. Flow definitions can be inherited, thus implementing flow hierarchies. Flows can be reused and customized as needed.

As this book being is written, the current version of Spring Web Flow is the 2.4.2.RELEASE,[1] so this is the version added as a dependency for the Web Flow chapter sources. This version includes the ability to configure flows using Java Configuration and many other features.

The main library is called `spring-webflow`. When building the project for the first time, the `spring-js` and `spring-binding` transitive dependencies should be downloaded too.

## What Is a Flow?

A flow models the sequence of steps necessary to perform a task. The most common and simple flow example is ordering items on the Internet. This operation requires the following steps in which the user is guided through: choose item, proceed to checkout, create an account or log in to your account, insert shipping detail, insert payment details, and approve payment to complete the process. Each failure to provide the correct information stops the user from advancing to the next step. If the user wants to go back and review a previous screen, he can do so, unless configured otherwise. But there are web operations that depend on the data received from the user to direct them from one flow to another.

---

[1]The official site of the project (`http://projects.spring.io/spring-webflow/`) is usually updated late, so it might show an earlier version; the most recent release can be found on the Maven public repositpry site at `http://mvnrepository.com`.

By using the Personal Records Manager at the completion of this chapter, you will be able to create an account and personal data for a person. This operation requires you to design a flow that executes the following steps:

1. Insert personal data.

2. If the hospital where the user was born is in the system, select it.

3. Otherwise, the user is directed to the page where he can create a Hospital instance.

4. Return to the previous step and complete creating the Person instance.

5. Insert IdentityCard data.

6. Review data.

7. If the person is an adult (age > 18), add an account.

These steps are depicted in Figure 7-1.

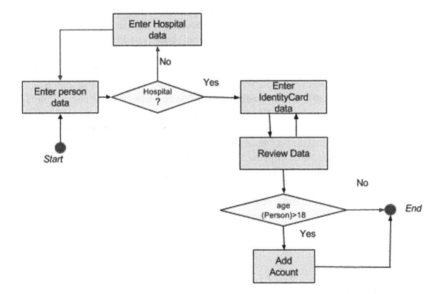

***Figure 7-1.*** *Personal Records Manager web flow*

In Spring Web Flow, a flow consists of a series of steps called **states**. A flow will always have only one start point and one or more end points. Leaving one state and passing into another can be restricted by the result of a conditional expression. Entering a new state usually results in a view being displayed to the user. The user works with the view, causing user events to occur. The user events trigger transitions between states, which in turn cause navigation to another view.

Aside from making development easier and clearer, Spring Web Flow was created to solve the following problems related to complex web navigation:

- Duplicate submissions.

- Pop-up window support within a flow.

- State synchronization problems between the server and the client caused by using the browser's back and refresh buttons.

- State collisions between windows.

- Stale session state. (A session can end up containing inactive data, when a timeout is set. The inactive items must be precisely identified and purged.)

- Short-circuiting navigation rules. (Possibility to jump over steps in the navigation, depending on navigation conditions.)

# Web Flow Architecture

In Spring Web Flow, flows are defined using an XML-based flow definition language. The backing classes follow the model already established by Spring MVC. Spring Web Flow provides its own classes to identify handler methods matching flow execution requests and resolving views. The DispatcherServlet is still the front controller when the application is servlet based. For implementation with portlets, there is an analogous implementation provided with DispatcherPortlet(s) as entry points. The similarities with the Spring MVC model can be observed in Figure 7-2.

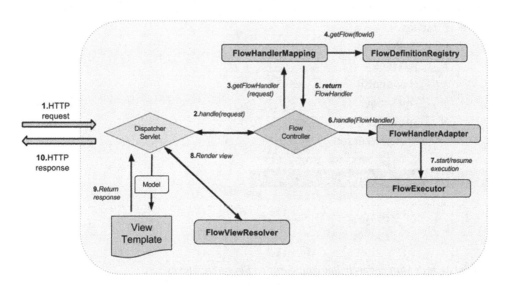

***Figure 7-2.*** *The Spring Web Flow backing classes*

The FlowController class is the adapter between the Spring MVC Controller layer and the Spring Web Flow engine. Its responsibility is to provide implementation so that Spring Web Flow can run embedded as a controller within a DispatcherServlet. So basically, the FlowController is itself a front controller for Spring Web Flow.

The FlowHandlerMapping maps all flow requests to the appropriate handlers using FlowDefinitionRegistry. The FlowHandlerAdapter takes care of executing the flow handler methods in a servlet environment using the FlowExecutor implementation.

After they do their jobs, the DispatcherServlet uses the FlowViewResolver interface to resolve a view from the state of an executing flow.

When working with flows, each flow definition is declared in a specific configuration file and is registered in the system by the FlowDefinitionRegistry. For each flow in the system, a configuration file is created and placed in the same directory with all resources implied in the flow execution: views templates, property files, and others. In Figure 7-3, you can see how the files are organized in the practice project for this chapter.

*Figure 7-3. Personal Records Manager web flow configuration file and resources*

The newPerson-flow.xml configuration file contains the states that the users are directed through to create a new person. For now, the empty file is presented containing only the Spring Web Flow namespace used to define flow elements:

```xml
<?xml version="1.0" encoding="UTF-8"?>
<flow xmlns="http://www.springframework.org/schema/webflow"
    xmlns:xsi="http://www.w3.org/2001/XMLSchema-instance"
    xsi:schemaLocation="http://www.springframework.org/schema/webflow
      http://www.springframework.org/schema/webflow/spring-webflow.xsd">

  <!-- states and actions will be placed here later -->
</flow>
```

The flows are exposed to the client as web resources. The client starts flows by accessing these resources. For example, accessing http://localhost:8080/webflow-basic/persons/newPerson starts the newPerson flow. (The reason the URL has that particular structure is explained later.) Starting a flow actually means *starting a new flow execution*, meaning an execution context for the task currently *in progress* is created. The execution context is *user session-scoped*, meaning all the variables and data needed for the execution of the task is kept in the user session, unless an execution step requires otherwise. (Sometimes data can be saved to the database and removed from the session.)

# Web Flow Internal Logic

When the flow starts executing, you can use the URL changing to

```
http://localhost:8080/webflow-basic/persons/newPerson?execution=e1s1
```

The parameter execution is the session-scoped execution key. Its value contains the flow execution identifier (e1) and the identifier of the execution step that is currently in progress (s1). Every time the flow progresses a step, the step identifier is incremented. Every time a new flow execution is started, the execution identifier is incremented.

A user resumes flow executions by clicking buttons in the interface—buttons (or links) that have events associated with them using the name property. For example:

```html
<button id="newPersonButton" name=" eventId proceed" type="submit">
    <spring:message code="command.proceed" />
</button>
```

So when the button with the newPersonButton id is clicked, a request is sent to the URL.

```
.../persons/newPerson?execution=e1s1&_event_id=proceed
```

The data provided by the user is bound to the flow context. The flow handles the event, processes the data as defined, and decides what to do next based on the definition of the flow: display a new view to the user, display the same view, and remain in the same step of execution if validation failed or ends the flow. When a flow execution has ended, the execution cannot be resumed; this implies that the transaction cannot be completed multiple times. After a flow execution ends, the flow state is automatically cleaned.

The interaction between a client and a flow always consists of two separate steps: the client will request a resource or activate (trigger) an event and the flow will redirect to the appropriate state. This means that each web flow interaction involves *two* requests: the client request and the flow redirect request. This has another implication: the data submitted by the initial request will not be available after the redirecting is done and the next view has already been rendered. But there are ways of persisting the data across requests when using web flows; this is covered later in the chapter. In Figure 7-4, the interaction between the client and a flow is displayed.

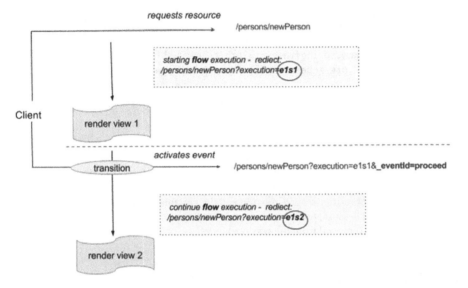

**Figure 7-4.** *Schema of an interaction between the client and a flow*

# Configuration and Infrastructure Beans

Spring provides two ways of configuring the environment in which the web flow components can be used: using an the XML namespace and defining the infrastructure beans in an `webflow-config.xml` file, or using Java Configuration annotations by defining a configuration class that extends a specific Spring class.

---

■ !   The configuration file can be named in whatever way the developer desires, as long as it is relevant in the context of the developed application. The beans can be defined in any other Spring configuration file already existing in the application; but the recommended approach and best practice is to keep infrastructure beans definitions grouped by their purpose. In the application used for practice with this book, the beans are grouped as follows:

- MVC infrastructure beans in `mvc-config.xml`
- Application custom beans in `app-config.xml`
- Web Flow infrastructure beans in `webflow-config.xml`
- Security infrastructure beans in `security-config.xml`

---

When configuring an application that uses Web Flow, there are roughly three steps that have to be covered:

1. A **flow executor** and a **flow registry** bean have to be defined and configured to match the structure of the application so that the flows can be executed correctly by Spring Web Flow.

2. A **flow adapter** and a **flow mapping** bean have to be defined and added to the list of existing handler mapping and handler adapter beans for the Spring MVC configuration to enable flow handling by Spring MVC.

3. An **MvcViewFactoryCreator** bean has to be created and configured to use the bean view resolvers already defined in the application.

The following two sections cover how this is done when using XML and Java Configuration.

# Configuration Using XML

As mentioned in previous chapters, the Spring MVC configuration infrastructure beans are defined in the examples of this book into a file named mvc-config.xml. In this file, FlowHandlerMapping and FlowHandlerAdapter bean definitions have to be added:

```xml
<?xml version="1.0" encoding="UTF-8"?>
<beans xmlns="http://www.springframework.org/schema/beans"
       xmlns:xsi="http://www.w3.org/2001/XMLSchema-instance"
       xmlns:mvc="http://www.springframework.org/schema/mvc"
       xmlns:p="http://www.springframework.org/schema/p"
       xsi:schemaLocation="http://www.springframework.org/schema/mvc
       http://www.springframework.org/schema/mvc/spring-mvc.xsd
               http://www.springframework.org/schema/beans
               http://www.springframework.org/schema/beans/spring-beans.xsd">

  <mvc:annotation-driven
   conversion-service="typeConversionService"
   validator="validator"/>

  <bean id="validator"
   class="org.springframework.validation.beanvalidation.LocalValidatorFactoryBean"/>

<!-- Define a custom ConversionService -->
  <bean id="typeConversionService"
    class="o.s.format.support.FormattingConversionServiceFactoryBean">
    ...
  </bean>
```

```xml
<!-- other Spring MVC specific beans, look in Chapter 3 for reference -->
...
 <!-- Maps requests to flows in the flowRegistry; e.g. a path of
    /persons/newPerson looks for a flow with id "persons/newPerson" -->
    <bean id="flowMappings"
      class="org.springframework.webflow.mvc.servlet.FlowHandlerMapping"
          p:order="-1"
          p:flowRegistry-ref="flowRegistry"/>

    <!-- Dispatches requests mapped to flows to FlowHandler implementations -->
    <bean class="org.springframework.webflow.mvc.servlet.FlowHandlerAdapter"
        p:flowExecutor-ref="flowExecutor"/>

</beans>
```

In the previous example, because `<mvc:annotation-driven/>` is used, the annotation-driven
Spring MVC Controller programming model is automatically enabled, and no other HandlerMapping
implementation needs to be defined. However, the `FlowHandlerMapping` must be the first HandlerMapping
implementation used to try to retrieve a mapping to make sure that the flow is identified correctly; that's why
`order="-1"` is used to set the highest priority in the handler mappings list. This class returns `null` in the case
of no flow id match, allowing the next handler mapping in the chain to execute.

In the `webflow-config.xml` file, the Spring Web Flow–specific beans are defined and the specific
namespace are used:

```xml
<?xml version="1.0" encoding="UTF-8"?>
<beans xmlns="http://www.springframework.org/schema/beans"
    xmlns:xsi="http://www.w3.org/2001/XMLSchema-instance"
    xmlns:webflow="http://www.springframework.org/schema/webflow-config"
    xsi:schemaLocation="
      http://www.springframework.org/schema/beans
      http://www.springframework.org/schema/beans/spring-beans.xsd
      http://www.springframework.org/schema/webflow-config
    http://www.springframework.org/schema/webflow-config/spring-webflow-config.xsd">

    <!-- Executes web flows -->
    <webflow:flow-executor id="flowExecutor" flow-registry="flowRegistry" />
    <!-- Contains the flows defined by this application -->
    <webflow:flow-registry id="flowRegistry" base-path="/WEB-INF"
        flow-builder-services="flowBuilderServices">
        <webflow:flow-location-pattern value="**/*-flow.xml" />
    </webflow:flow-registry>

    <!-- Configures services needed to build flow definitions -->
    <webflow:flow-builder-services id="flowBuilderServices"
        view-factory-creator="mvcViewFactoryCreator"
          conversion-service="conversionService"
          development="true" />
```

```
<!-- Configures Web Flow to render Tiles views resolved by Spring MVC -->
<bean id="mvcViewFactoryCreator"
    class="org.springframework.webflow.mvc.builder.MvcViewFactoryCreator">
    <property name="viewResolvers" ref="tilesViewResolver" />
    <property name="useSpringBeanBinding" value="true"/>
</bean>

<!-- Configures Web Flow to automatically convert custom types
     (using the same converter as for Spring MVC) -->
<bean id="conversionService"
    class="org.springframework.binding.convert.service.DefaultConversionService">
    <constructor-arg ref="typeConversionService" />
</bean>
```

`</beans>`

The Spring webflow-config namespace provides XML elements that make defining Spring Web Flow components more practical and more readable for the user, but a more detailed explanation is needed for the preceding configuration.

- flowExecutor: This bean created is of type FlowExecutorImpl and it uses the flowRegistry bean to identify all flows eligible for execution. This bean is the entry point into the Web Flow system, as it manages starting and resuming flow executions. When an executor bean is created, Spring automatically looks for a flow registry bean named flowRegistry, so the preceding definition can be simplified to

  ```
  <webflow:flow-executor id="flowExecutor"/>
  ```

  Also, because this is the central bean of the Spring Web Flow engine, listeners can be registered for it to verify rights to perform specific execution steps or audit the execution steps for debugging purposes.

  ```
  <webflow:flow-executor id="flowExecutor">
      <webflow:flow-execution-listeners>
          <webflow:listener ref="secureFlowExecutionListener" />
          <webflow:listener ref="auditFlowExecutionListener" />
      <webflow:flow-execution-listeners>
  </webflow:flow-executor>
      ...
  <bean id="secureFlowExecutionListener"
    class="org.springframework.webflow.security.SecurityFlowExecutionListener"/>
  <bean id="auditFlowExecutionListener"
      class="com.pr.audit.AuditFlowExecutionListener"/>
  ```

---

■ !  The flow execution listeners can be configured to be applied only on certain flows; for example:

```
<webflow:listener ref="secureFlowExecutionListener"
  criteria="administrativeFlow1, administrativeFlow2"/>
```

---

The `flowExecutor` can be configured to tune flow execution persistence settings by adding a customized definition for `flow-execution-repository`.

```
<webflow:flow-executor id="flowExecutor" flow-registry="flowRegistry">
<webflow:flow-execution-repository max-executions="5"
  max-execution-snapshots="30" />
</webflow:flow-executor>
```

The `max-executions` property is used to configure the maximum number of persistent flow executions allowed per user session. When the maximum number of executions is exceeded, the oldest execution is removed.

The `max-execution-snapshots` property is used to configure the maximum number of history snapshots allowed per flow execution. History snapshots enable browser Back button support. When snapshotting is disabled, pressing the browser Back button will not work. It will result in using an execution key that points to a snapshot that has not been recorded.

- `flowRegistry`: Each flow definition registered in this registry bean is assigned a unique identifier. The base-path property is used specify the root directory, under which all the flow definition files are found; usually this is the WEB-INF directory. The flow-location-pattern further narrows the search for the flow definitions, providing a wildcard template file name for the flow definition files. But flow definitions can be also registered one at a time using flow-location elements. For example:

  ```
  <webflow:flow-registry id="flowRegistry" base-path="/WEB-INF"
      flow-builder-services="flowBuilderServices">
      <webflow:flow-location path="persons/newPerson/newPerson-flow.xml"/>
  </webflow:flow-registry>
  ```

- `flowBuilderServices`: This bean registers custom implementations of services needed to build flow definitions: view resolvers, data convertors, formatters, validators, and others. In version 2.4.0.RELEASE, the validation-hints were added, so flow definition can apply partial validation on the model through the validation-hints attribute supported on view state and transition elements. This bean was modified to add a property named validation-hint-resolver that can be used to set a custom validation hints resolver. (An example is presented later in the book.)

---

■ ! The `development="true"` is quite important, because as you will solve the practice exercises, you might not want to restart the application every time you make a change to a flow definition. Setting the development property to "true" ensures that changes to a flow definition is autodetected and results in a flow refresh.

---

- mvcViewFactoryCreator: This bean is used by a FlowBuilder to configure a flow's view states with Spring MVC-based view factories. In this case, the tiles view resolver is injected into it, so it can be used to resolve view states using it. The useSpringBeanBinding property is set to "true" to enable the same binding system used by the Spring MVC in a Web Flow environment.

- conversionService: This bean is a wrapper for the conversion service bean used by Spring MVC, which is provided to the flowBuilderServices bean to be used during a flow execution.

## Configuration Using Annotations

For the 09-pr-webflow-basic-practice, a full Java Configuration is used; no web.xml. Three classes were defined for such proposes under the com.pr.config package. Figure 7-5 depicts all three classes, their parents, and the relationship between them.

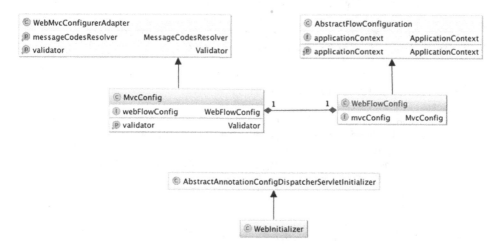

***Figure 7-5.*** *Configuration classes for Personal Records Manager project when Spring Web Flow is used*

■ ? Can you tell which class takes care of a certain part of the infrastructure just by looking at the diagram in Figure 7-5?

Each class covers a part of the infrastructure setup needed to run a Spring web application without a web.xml file that uses Spring Web Flow.

- The MvcConfig class encapsulates the Spring MVC infrastructure bean definitions that were covered in Chapter 3. To plug in the Web Flow beans, some modifications were done. The webFlowConfig was injected so the handler mapping and handler adapter specific to flows could be configured.

```
...
import org.springframework.webflow.mvc.servlet.FlowHandlerAdapter;
import org.springframework.webflow.mvc.servlet.FlowHandlerMapping;

@Configuration
@EnableWebMvc
public class MvcConfig extends WebMvcConfigurerAdapter {
    @Autowired
    private WebFlowConfig webFlowConfig;

    //other Spring MVC infrastructure beans: formatters, interceptors,
    // resolvers, etc. Review Chapter 3 for reference.
    ...

    //Web Flow specific infrastructure beans
      @Bean
    public FlowHandlerMapping flowHandlerMapping() {
        FlowHandlerMapping handlerMapping = new FlowHandlerMapping();
        handlerMapping.setOrder(-1);
        handlerMapping.setFlowRegistry(this.webFlowConfig.flowRegistry());
        return handlerMapping;
    }

    @Bean
    public FlowHandlerAdapter flowHandlerAdapter() {
        FlowHandlerAdapter handlerAdapter = new FlowHandlerAdapter();
        handlerAdapter.setFlowExecutor(this.webFlowConfig.flowExecutor());
        handlerAdapter.setSaveOutputToFlashScopeOnRedirect(true);
        return handlerAdapter;
    }
}
```

The WebFlowConfig class encapsulates the Spring Web Flow infrastructure bean definitions. To align these beans with Spring MVC, the mvcConfig bean was injected, so formatter, validators, and view resolvers could be accessed and set to use during flow executions. This class extends the Spring specialized AbstractFlowConfiguration class, which does not provide any configuration itself but provides access via protected methods to builders for flow executor (getFlowExecutorBuilder()), flow registry (getFlowDefinitionRegistryBuilder()), and flow builder services (getFlowBuilderServicesBuilder()).

```
...
import org.springframework.webflow.config.AbstractFlowConfiguration;
import org.springframework.webflow.definition.registry.FlowDefinitionRegistry;
import org.springframework.webflow.engine.builder.support.FlowBuilderServices;
import org.springframework.webflow.executor.FlowExecutor;
import org.springframework.webflow.mvc.builder.MvcViewFactoryCreator;

@Configuration
public class WebFlowConfig extends AbstractFlowConfiguration {

    @Autowired
    private MvcConfig mvcConfig;

    @Bean
    public FlowExecutor flowExecutor() {
        return getFlowExecutorBuilder(flowRegistry())
        // apply the listener for all flow definitions
          .addFlowExecutionListener(new AuditFlowExecutorListener(), "*")
          .build();
    }

    @Bean
    public FlowDefinitionRegistry flowRegistry() {
        return getFlowDefinitionRegistryBuilder(flowBuilderServices())
                .setBasePath("/WEB-INF")
                .addFlowLocationPattern("/**/*-flow.xml")
                .build();
    }

    @Bean
    public FlowBuilderServices flowBuilderServices() {
        return getFlowBuilderServicesBuilder()
                .setViewFactoryCreator(mvcViewFactoryCreator())
                .setValidator(this.mvcConfig.validator())
                .setConversionService(conversionService())
                .setDevelopmentMode(true)
                .build();
    }

    @Bean
    public MvcViewFactoryCreator mvcViewFactoryCreator() {
        MvcViewFactoryCreator factoryCreator = new MvcViewFactoryCreator();
        factoryCreator.setViewResolvers(Arrays.<ViewResolver>asList(
                this.mvcConfig.tilesViewResolver()));
        factoryCreator.setUseSpringBeanBinding(true);
        return factoryCreator;
    }
```

```
        @Bean
        DefaultConversionService conversionService() {
            return new DefaultConversionService(
                conversionServiceFactoryBean().getObject());
        }

        @Bean
        FormattingConversionServiceFactoryBean conversionServiceFactoryBean() {
            FormattingConversionServiceFactoryBean
                fcs = new FormattingConversionServiceFactoryBean();
            Set<Formatter> fmts = new HashSet<>();
            fmts.add(this.mvcConfig.dateFormatter());
            fmts.add(this.mvcConfig.hospitalFormatter());
            fcs.setFormatters(fmts);
            return fcs;
        }
    }
```

■ !   To tune the flow execution persistence settings in Java, the following configuration has to be present in the WebFlowConfig class:

```
@Bean
public FlowExecutor flowExecutor() {
 return getFlowExecutorBuilder(flowRegistry())
 .addFlowExecutionListener(new AuditFlowExecutorListener(), "*")
   .setMaxFlowExecutions(5)
   .setMaxFlowExecutionSnapshots(30)
   .build();
}
```

- The WebInitializer class provides the Servlet 3.0 configuration that replaces the web.xml file. The configuration classes are added to the array of configuration classes used to create the application context by providing the proper implementation for the getRootConfigClasses.

```
public class WebInitializer extends
    AbstractAnnotationConfigDispatcherServletInitializer {

    @Override
    protected Class<?> getRootConfigClasses() {
        return null;
    }

    @Override
    protected Class<?> getServletConfigClasses() {
        return new Class<?>{
                MvcConfig.class,
                WebFlowConfig.class
        };
    }
```

```
    @Override
    protected String getServletMappings() {
        return new String{"/"};
    }

    @Override
    protected Filter getServletFilters() {
        CharacterEncodingFilter cef = new CharacterEncodingFilter();
        cef.setEncoding("UTF-8");
        cef.setForceEncoding(true);
        return new Filter{new HiddenHttpMethodFilter(), cef};
    }
}
```

At this time, you might be wondering about the `FlowController` that you saw in Figure 7-2 and why it wasn't mentioned anywhere in the configuration section. This class is the bridge between the Spring MVC Controller layer and the Spring Web Flow engine; it allows Spring Web Flow to run embedded as a Controller within a DispatcherServlet and it is used internally. This class uses the handlers and executor defined in the configuration to execute flows; it does this transparently.[2]

---

■ ! Before continuing to the next section, look at the `09-pr-webflow-basic-practice` module under the `person-manger` project. Start the application using the `appStart` Gretty task for this module. In the browser, you will notice that a new link has appeared, named `New Person`. The application is depicted in Figure 7-6.

If you click the link, you will notice it fails with a 404 error. This is because no handler has been registered for this resource URL. A few configurations have been set up, but some beans and configurations are missing so that this application can use the Spring Web Flow engine. This is left for you to do. The TODO tasks contain comments that direct you where you could implement the required changes. This module will help you test your understanding of the Spring Web Flow Java Configuration. The configuration files have been created, but it is your responsibility to fill them correctly. The flow itself is empty, and no execution step is defined.

After clicking **New Person** link, you see the form in Figure 7-6. This means your configuration is correct and you can continue with the chapter. If you have difficulties in completing the configuration, you can look at the `09-pr-webflow-basic-solution` module, which contains the proposed solution for the given tasks.

---

[2]The code for the class is publicly available on GitHub at `https://github.com/spring-projects/spring-webflow/blob/master/spring-webflow/src/main/java/org/springframework/webflow/mvc/servlet/FlowController.java`.

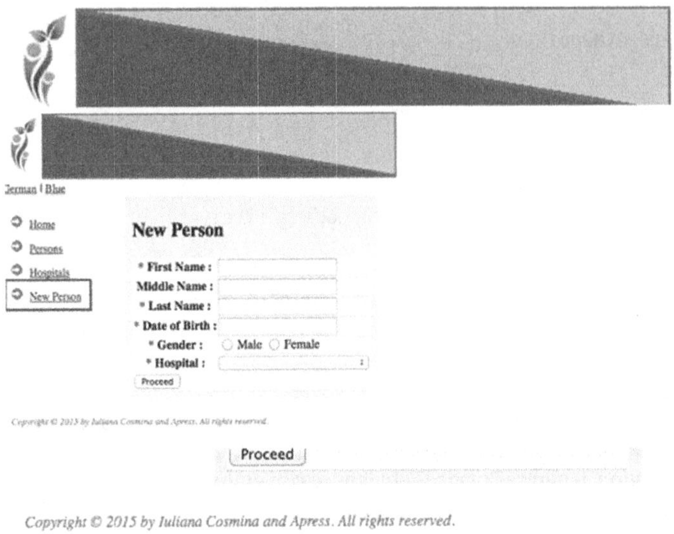

**New Person**

* First Name :
Middle Name :
* Last Name :
* Date of Birth :
* Gender :    ○ Male  ○ Female
* Hospital :

*Figure 7-6.* *Link to the New Person flow*

# Create a Flow

A flow describes a sequence of steps that is executed in the order established by the flow definition. A web flow is made of tree types of elements: states, transitions, and data. In a flow definition, the following types of states can be used:

- **View state**: In this type of state, the execution of a flow is paused to render a view to the user and wait for input data. It is defined using the `<view-state ../>` XML element.

- **Action state**: In this type of state, Java code is executed, and sometimes the next state to transition to depends on the outcome of this code. It is defined using the `<action-state ../>` XML element.

- **Decision state**: In this type of state, some branch logic is implemented using the XML flow definition language. It is defined using the `<decision-state ../>` XML element.

- **Subflow state**: The execution is transferred to another flow. When the subflow execution is completed, the execution will return to this state. It is defined using the `<decision-state ../>` XML element.

- **End state**: The final state of the flow execution. It is not mandatory for this state to render a view, but usually a confirmation view is rendered to the user. It is defined using the `<end-state ../>` XML element.

The states will be referred to using the XML element names in order to faciltate association between the state type and the element used to configure it.

The switch from one state to the other is called a **transition** and it is triggered by events. Some data can be shared among states, depending on the **scope** of that data. The simple schema of a flow definition and composing elements is depicted in Figure 7-7. The data is the information that is carried from one state to the other; it has a life span that depends on the scope on which it was declared.

272

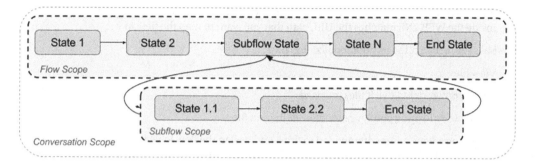

**Figure 7-7.** *The general schema of a flow definition and composing elements*

## Flow Definition

A flow is defined in a single XML file, and all the states composing it are defined as child elements of the flow element. The content of the flow element is actually a task algorithm. All resources used by a flow (views, internationalization files) when being executed must be placed in the same directory as the flow definition file. Basically, each flow defined in an application has its own directory that contains all flow definition resources. This was mentioned in the "Spring Web Flow Architecture" section. In this section, all the necessary steps in defining a flow are covered in detail. For example, to develop the /persons/newPerson flow, the following has to be created (use Figure 7-8 or reference ).

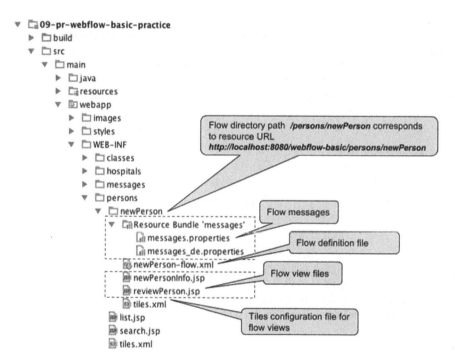

**Figure 7-8.** *The components of a flow definition*

- A directory with the same name as the flow you are trying to create, so as the path inside the WEB-INF matches the URL path that you want to map the flow to

- `message.properties` internationalization files

- View files

- A tiles configuration file, if tiles are used

- A `*-flow.xml` spring configuration flow definition file

When developing a flow, it is recommended to think and design the flow logic first—define the states and transitions, review the flow with business analysts, use mock views (plain HTML files that replace the view in testing scenarios)—to depict the steps and then add the behavior. To define the states of a flow, the `*-flow.xml` file must be populated. Usually, the first step is a view-state that displays a view to the user to provide data to the flow.

```
<!-- newPerson-flow.xml -->
<?xml version="1.0" encoding="UTF-8"?>
<flow xmlns="http://www.springframework.org/schema/webflow"
    xmlns:xsi="http://www.w3.org/2001/XMLSchema-instance"
    xsi:schemaLocation="http://www.springframework.org/schema/webflow
        http://www.springframework.org/schema/webflow/spring-webflow.xsd">

    <view-state id="enterPersonInfo"/>
</flow>
```

The `view-state` id resolves to a view template; by default, a `*.jsp` file is searched for in the current directory. View resolution is pluggable, depending on the view technology used. In the examples given in this book, Apache Tiles are used to define and resolve views; so the view to display when entering the `enterPersonInfo` state is defined in the `tiles.xml` under the `flow` directory. The views used for the workflows extend the same tiles template, `webapp/WEB-INF/standard/layout.jsp`, defined for views in Chapter 3.

```
<!-- tiles.xml -->
<?xml version="1.0" encoding="UTF-8"?>
<!DOCTYPE tiles-definitions PUBLIC
        "-//Apache Software Foundation//DTD Tiles Configuration 3.0//EN"
        "http://tiles.apache.org/dtds/tiles-config_3_0.dtd">

<tiles-definitions>

    <definition name="enterPersonInfo" extends="layout">
        <put-attribute name="pageTitle" value="persons.new.title" />
        <put-attribute name="content"
                value="/WEB-INF/persons/newPerson/newPersonInfo.jsp" />
        <put-attribute name="menuTab" value="newPerson" />
    </definition>
</tiles-definitions>
```

In the newPersonInfo.jsp view file template, the user event is linked to a button using the name attribute.

```
<!-- newPersonInfo.jsp -->
<h2>
    <spring:message code="persons.new.title"/>
</h2>

<div class="person">
    <sf:form id="newPersonForm" method="POST" modelAttribute="person">
        <table>
            <tr>
                <th>
                    <label for="firstName">
                        <span class="man">*</span>
                            <spring:message code="label.Person.firstname"/> :
                    </label>
                </th>
                <td><sf:input path="firstName"/></td>
                <td><sf:errors cssClass="error" path="firstName"/></td>
            </tr>
            <!-- other form elements -->
            ...
            <tr>
                <td colspan="2">
                    <button id="newPersonButton" name="_eventId_proceed"
                        type="submit">
                        <spring:message code="command.proceed" />
                    </button>
                </td>
            </tr>
        </table>
    </sf:form>
</div>
```

Next, a transition must be defined by adding the <transition> element as a child to the state you are transitioning from when a user event is activated. If no navigation is performed (for example, when validation fails), the initial view is refreshed.

```
<!-- newPerson-flow.xml -->
<flow ...>
<view-state id="enterPersonInfo">
        <transition on="proceed" to="reviewPerson" />
</view-state>

<view-state id="reviewPerson">
        <transition on="confirm" to="enterIdentityCard"/>
</view-state>
...
</flow>
```

When performing typical web navigations, there is always a Cancel button that allows the user to cancel the whole process. When using Spring Web Flow, this can be done by declaring a `<global-transition>` element, but using global transition elements sort of breaks the flow. It's similar to using a goto statement. It also makes the flow definition less readable.[3]

```
<flow ...>
    <global-transition on="cancel" to="cancelled" />
    ...
</flow>
```

A flow can have one or multiple end-states defined (`<end-state>` elements are used to define them) and a flow execution can end in any of them, based on the events the user triggers. After a flow execution reaches an end state, the flow terminates and the outcome is returned, unless the end state sends a final response or redirects the user to another resource, typically a confirmation page.

```
<flow ...>
    <end-state id="end" />
</flow>
```

Redirecting to a confirmation page after a flow has finished the execution is tricky, as the flow data is gone. The solution is to use a redirect to a stateless confirmation page and to use a parameter that has a value that can be used to display confirmation data. The `<end-state>` element has a view attribute that can be used to specify the URL to redirect to.

```
<flow ...>
<end-state id="finish"
            view="externalRedirect:contextRelative:/person/1" />
</flow>
```

---

■ **!**   The value is hard-coded id value ("1") in the previous example only because the concept that could be used to make that link dynamic— **flow variable**—has not been covered yet.

---

The `contextRelative` prefix is one of the explicit redirects supported in the context of a flow execution. Without these prefixes, the returned resource location is relative to the current servlet mapping. The flow redirect prefixes help you have more control over where the user is redirected. The following is the complete list of flow redirection prefixes:

- `servletRelative`: Redirects to a resource relative to the current server

- `contextRelative`: Redirects to a resource relative to the current web application context path

- `serverRelative`: Redirects to a resource relative to the server root

- `http://` or `https://` Redirects to a fully qualified resource URI

---

[3]The GOTO statement (see `https://en.wikipedia.org/wiki/Goto`).

These redirect prefixes are supported in a flow definition together with the externalRedirect: directive in view-state or end-state elements. The view-state element has a view property that can be used to specify a different view than the one with the same state id, and this view can be outside the newPerson flow directory:

```
<flow ...>
    <view-state id="reviewPerson"
        view="externalRedirect:contextRelative:/verifyPerson">
            <transition on="confirm" to="enterIdentityCard"/>
    </view-state>
</flow>
```

A flow can also redirect to a different flow by using the flowRedirect: directive in its end state; this basically means the current flow ends and a new one is started.

In conclusion, when creating a web flow, it is recommended that the following steps be followed in this order:

1.  Define view states and end states.

2.  Define transition between states.

3.  Create mock views to test the connection of the states.

4.  Add the intended behavior.

To create a web flow like the one shown in Figure 7-1, the following must be done:

- When **defining view states and end states**, the focus is on the steps that the user is guided through. The why (conditions and events) and how (business logic) is left for later.

```
<flow ...>
<!-- newPerson-flow.xml -->
<view-state id="enterPersonInfo" />
<view-state id="enterHospitalInfo" />
<view-state id="enterIdentityCard" />
<view-state id="reviewPersonData" />
<view-state id="enterAccountInfo" />
<view-state id="reviewAccountData" />
<end-state id="end" />
</flow>
```

- Then transitions should be defined as follows:

```
<!-- newPerson-flow.xml -->
<flow ...>
<view-state id="enterPersonInfo" >
        <transition on="addHospital" to="enterHospitalInfo" />
        <transition on="proceed" to="enterIdentityCard" />
</view-state>

 <view-state id="enterHospitalInfo" >
        <transition on="save" to="enterPersonInfo" />
</view-state>
```

```
<view-state id="enterIdentityCard" >
      <transition on="review" to="reviewPersonData" />
</view-state>

<view-state id="reviewPersonData" >
      <transition on="addAcount" to="enterAccountInfo" />
</view-state>

<view-state id="enterAccountInfo" >
      <transition on="review" to="reviewAccountData" />
</view-state>

<view-state id="reviewAccountData" >
      <transition on="save" to="end" />
<view-state>

<end-state id="end" />
</flow>
```

- To test the connections between the states, mock views should be created. This is
  an approach that helps users interact with the flow process to test the transitions
  between the states. Mock views contain static data; no extra data needs to be
  inserted by the user and no validation is performed. The dynamic behavior is added
  later, when the back end of the application is developed.

```
<!-- newPersonInfo.jsp -->
<h2> Mock New Person </h2>
<div class="person">
    <form id="newPersonForm" method="POST" >
        <table>
            <tr>
                <th>
                    First Name
                </th>
                <td><input path="firstName"/></td>
            </tr>
            <!-- other form elements -->
            ...
            <tr>
                <td colspan="2">
                    <button id="newPersonButton" name=" eventId proceed"
                            type="submit">
                        Proceed
                    </button>
                </td>
            </tr>
        </table>
    </form>
</div>
```

```
<!-- enterIdentityCard.jsp -->
<h2> Mock New Account </h2>
<div class="identityCard">
    <form id="newIdentityCardForm" method="POST" >
        <table>
            <tr>
                <th>
                    Account Number
                </th>
                <td><input path="accountNumber"/></td>
            </tr>
            <!-- other form elements -->
            ...
            <tr>
                <td colspan="2">
                    <button id="newAccountButton" name="_eventId_review"
                            type="submit">
                        Review
                    </button>
                </td>
            </tr>
        </table>
    </form>
</div>

<!-- other mock views look similar so their content will not be listed here -->
```

---

■ **!**   As you probably noticed in the previous example, only view and end states were used. This is because these are the simplest states that can be used to create a flow; also, defining them is very easy and intuitive. The other types of states (action, decision, and subflow) are covered later and added, one by one, to the flow you have become familiar with to allow you to gradually increase your understanding of Spring Web Flow.

---

# Testing Web Flows

Every flow in an application should have a unit test to verify that the flow logic works as expected. The Spring Web Flow provides a test class at org.springframework.webflow.test.execution. AbstractXmlFlowExecutionTests that has to be extended to use unit tests to test flows. This class provides the test infrastructure needed to test that a flow definition executes as expected; no Spring or JUnit annotations are needed. All that is needed is for the getResource(FlowDefinitionResourceFactory resourceFactory) method to be implemented correctly is to provide the test a flow definition file.

```java
import org.springframework.webflow.config.FlowDefinitionResource;
import org.springframework.webflow.config.FlowDefinitionResourceFactory;
import org.springframework.webflow.test.MockExternalContext;
import org.springframework.webflow.test.execution.AbstractXmlFlowExecutionTests;

public class NewPersonFlowTest extends AbstractXmlFlowExecutionTests {
    private static final String ENTER_PERSON_INFO = "enterPersonInfo";
    private static final String ENTER_IDENTITY_CARD = "enterIdentityCard";
    private static final String REVIEW_ACCOUNT_DATA = "reviewAccountData";
    private static final String END = "end";

    @Override
    protected FlowDefinitionResource getResource
            (FlowDefinitionResourceFactory resourceFactory) {
        return resourceFactory.createFileResource(
            "src/main/webapp/WEB-INF/persons/newPerson/newPerson-flow.xml");
    }

    public void testStart() throws Exception {
        startFlow(new MockExternalContext());
        assertCurrentStateEquals(ENTER_PERSON_INFO);
    }

    public void testEnterPersonInfoProceed() throws Exception {
        setCurrentState(ENTER_PERSON_INFO);
        MockExternalContext externalContext = new MockExternalContext();
        externalContext.setEventId("proceed");
        resumeFlow(externalContext);
        assertCurrentStateEquals(ENTER_IDENTITY_CARD);
    }

// other similar transition tests
..

    public void testReviewPersonConfirm() throws Exception {
        setCurrentState(REVIEW_ACCOUNT_DATA);
        MockExternalContext externalContext = new MockExternalContext();
        externalContext.setEventId("save");
        resumeFlow(externalContext);
        assertFlowExecutionEnded();
        assertFlowExecutionOutcomeEquals(END);
        assertTrue(externalContext.getExternalRedirectRequested());
        assertEquals("contextRelative:/persons/1",
                externalContext.getExternalRedirectUrl());
    }
}
```

The testStart method starts the flow by calling startFlow and tests that the flow has entered the start state by calling assertCurrentStateEquals.

The testEnterPersonInfoProceed tests that starting from an exact state when an event is triggered, the transition is done to the expected state. Triggering the event is done by using a mock context and calling setEventId on it.

---

■ !  Before continuing to the next section, take a look at the 10-pr-webflow-fundamentals-practice module under the person-manger project. All the files necessary for creating a very simple flow have been provided for you. Figure 7-9 depicts the simplified version of the newPerson flow that is required to complete the practice example. It uses mock views and only **view states**; no business logic is required to complete this practice exercise. The purpose of this module is to help you test your understanding of defining states and transitions, and using mock flows and testing the simple flow you have created.

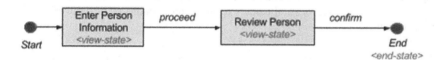

**Figure 7-9.** *Link to the simplified New Person flow*

This flow guides the user through the process of creating a person using the minimum amount of information. The first step of this flow should display a form to the user. After submitting the form, the user should be taken to a screen where he can review the information before being confirmed. After confirming, the user should be taken to the screen displaying the details of the completed transaction.

The practice module has ten TODO tasks to be resolved, numbered from 40 to 49. Each task has a short description instructing you on what you have to do. The web application can be started by executing the appStart Gradle task. The newPerson flow definition has been completed and the execution works completely if the user can be guided through all the expected steps. The test has been implemented correctly if all the methods pass.

When executing the flow, and the current state is the reviewPersonData. Try clicking the Back button of the browser to see what happens. You should be able to go back and resubmit. No browser warnings should occur, and the Request URL should depict that you are back to the previous step of the same flow execution.

If the current URL were http://localhost:8080/persons/newPerson?execution=e1s2, clicking the Back button should redirect the user to http://localhost:8080/persons/newPerson?execution=e1s1.

Try the same after the flow has finished its execution and note the parameters in the request URL. The flow execution should be restarted and the execution URL parameter should have the expected value.

---

---

■ ?  Can you remember how the execution parameter value should change when a new flow execution is started?

---

## Actions and Scopes

During the execution of a web flow, it is expected for business services to be called for the flow to accomplish its task. Using view states only rendering a view and establishing the next view state in the navigation is possible. Thus, more elements are needed to define which business services are called and what to do with the results in the context of a flow. These elements are called **actions**; they can be called within a flow on several execution points.

Actions are defined in Spring Web Flow using the Spring Expression Language. Most of the time, their result has to be stored in a flow variable that has a life span defined by the scope that they are declared for. Explaining the type of actions that can be defined for a web flow, and when and how they should be used, cannot be done properly without first mentioning **web flow scopes**.

In Figure 7-7, in the bottom-left corner of each rectangle grouping state, you see a scope specific to that group of states, written in italics. Within a flow, you can define instance variables. For example, when creating a new person using a flow, the Person instance can be stored in a flow variable and be made available during the flow execution; and so at the end of the flow execution, redirection can be done to a page to render the instance just created:

```
<flow ...>
    <var name="person" class="com.pr.ents.Person"/>
    ...
    <end-state id="finish"
            view="externalRedirect:contextRelative:/person/#{person.id}" />
</flow>
```

Flow variables and other data objects exist in a **scope**, and when using web flows, multiple types of scopes are available to implement the desired functionality. Each flow provides a *context* where objects are stored. The *data scopes* are provided by this context and its state is managed by the Spring Web Flow. During flow execution, objects are added to different scopes, depending on the flow definition. They are cleaned when they go out of scope.

The previous example depicted the explicit creation of a flow variable; the <var /> element was used for that. But variables can be assigned dynamically by using actions. The advantage of using actions to assign variables is that the variables can be assigned to any scope possible. Explicit variables, declared with <var/>, can be assigned only a *flow* scope and a *view* scope. There are five web flow scopes that are supported by the context of a flow:

- **Flow scope**: This is the scope that lasts until the flow ends.

- **View scope**: This is the scope associated with each view-state.

- **Request scope**: This is the scope matching a single request

- **Flash scope**: This the scope allocated when a flow starts; it is cleaned automatically after each view is rendered and destroyed when the flow ends.

- **Conversation scope**: This is a global execution scope; all subflows share this scope. It gets allocated when a top-level flow starts and it is destroyed when the top-level flow ends.

---

■ !   The conversation-scoped objects are stored in the HTTP session and should generally be serializable to account for typical session replication.

---

## Flow Variables

The scope of a variable can be determined contextually. For example, when the explicit definition of a variable is directly under the `<flow/>` element, the scope for that variable is the **flow scope**. When the explicit definition of a variable is under the `<view-state/>` element, the scope of that variable is **view scope**. But when using EL expressions and Java code, the scope needs to be specified explicitly.

When using `<var/>` to define variables, you have to keep in mind that if the objects are complex and require other properties to be injected, they must either have a constructor, setters annotated with @Autowired, or both depending on the chosen configuration.

```
<!-- newPerson-flow.xml -->
<flow ...>
    <var name="identityCardProcessor" class="com.pr.webflow.IdentityCardProcessor"/>
    ...
</flow>

// com.pr.webflow.IdentityCardProcessor.java
public class IdentityCardProcessor implements Serializable {
    private IdentityCardManager identityCardManager;

    @Autowired
     public IdentityCardProcessor(
            IdentityCardManager identityCardManager){...}
}
// or
public class IdentityCardProcessor implements Serializable {
    private IdentityCardManager identityCardManager

    @Autowired
    public void setIdentityCardManager(
            IdentityCardManager identityCardManager){...}
}
```

Explicit variables are most often used as data models for views. They are used to pass as arguments to business services invoked by the flow; such an implementation is depicted in Figure 7-10.

```
<!-- newPerson-flow.xml -->

<flow ...>
    <!-- variable declaration-->
    <var name="person" class="com.pr.ents.Person"/>

    <!-- using the variable as data model for view-->
    <view-state id="enterPersonInfo" model="person">

        <transition on="proceed" to="reviewPerson">
            <!-- using the variable as argument to service invocation  -->
            <evaluate expression="validationService.checkNonDuplicate(person)"/>
        </transition>
    </view-state>
</flow>
```

***Figure 7-10.*** *Explicit flow variable usages example*

---

■ **?** From what has been covered so far, can you tell to which scope the person variable in the previous code sample belongs?

---

Explicit variables can be defined as view-scoped objects too. In this case, the variable is created when the view-state is entered and is destroyed when the transition to the next view-state occurs. They can be used as data models for a single view. They are often updated using AJAX requests before being used for the expression conditioning the transition to the next state; such an implementation is depicted in Figure 7-11.

```xml
<!-- newPerson-flow.xml -->

<flow ...>
    <!-- using the variable as data model for view-->
    <view-state id="enterPersonInfo" model="person">

        <!-- variable declaration-->
        <var name="person" class="com.pr.ents.Person"/>

        <transition on="proceed" to="reviewPerson">
            <!-- using the variable as argument to service invocation  -->
            <evaluate expression="validationService.checkNonDuplicate(person)"/>
        </transition>
    </view-state>
</flow>
```

***Figure 7-11.*** *Explicit flow variable in view scope usages example*

In the previous examples, you can see that performing the transition depends on the result of the evaluation of the expression in the <evaluate /> element. The expression in that element is a **standard EL expression** that can be evaluated directly by the EL; it does not need to be enclosed in delimiters such as #{ }. The delimiters are not needed when the expression is a string that represents a method call or property access, and using them will throw an IllegalArgumentException.

The delimiters are only needed when the argument string is a **template EL expression** that implies mixing literal text with one or more standard expressions, as in the redirect link for the end state in previous examples.

```xml
<flow ...>
    <end-state id="finish"
            view="externalRedirect:contextRelative:/person/#{person.id}" />
</flow>
```

## Conversation Variables

The conversation scope is the widest web flow scope. Variables defined within this scope are available to subflows too. The conversation variables are similar to global variables and have the same disadvantages. Conversation variables introduce a dependency between top-level flows and their subflows; that's why the recommendation is to not use them if a different option exists. When working with subflows, input/output parameters can be used to avoid conversation variables. A variable can be assigned to the conversation scope using the <evaluate /> element.

In the following example, a `Person` instance retrieved using a `PersonManager` service is being assigned to the conversation scope:

```
<flow ...>
<!-- The result of this expression is stored into the person variable -->
    <evaluate result="conversationScope.person"
            expression="personManager.findById(personId)"/>
</flow>
```

## Request and Flash Scopes

Attributes placed in **flash scope** exist through the life of the current request and until the next view rendering. After the view renders, the flash scope is cleared. Flash scope is typically used to store messages that should be preserved until after the next view renders. This scope is useful to pass data from one request to another as one flow state involves two requests, as depicted in Figure 7-4.

- The first request lasts between the transition from the current state until entering the next state.

- The second lasts from the moment before the view is rendered to the end of rendering the same state.

You can consider the flash scope as an extension of the request scope in the Web Flow context, because the request scope is not quite useful when using web flow, as is explained later in this section.

Attributes placed in **request scope** exist for the life of the current request into the flow execution. When the request ends, any attributes in request scope goes out of scope. Variables should be assigned the request scope when their values are refetched every time a state is redisplayed. If the data can be cached, the view scope would be more appropriate for the variable.

---

▣ ! The request scope can be useful when creating a sports betting site. The application should have a web flow defined, through which the user can place a bet. A request variable should be used to extract the most recent results of games being played, so the user can be informed in real time of his winning chances.

---

Also, data with request scope can be used in cases where it is needed only to initialize the next view; but it should not be displayed by it.

---

▣ ! Consider the example of a betting site: only the list of games currently being played should be displayed, so a specific time interval value can be stored in a variable and used as criteria for selection.

---

To implement the previously mentioned cases, the flow scope can be used, and the games the user can bet on can be retrieved using AJAX calls. Request scope is pretty useless, considering that usually a developer is interested in sharing the data between the two requests implied by a web flow state.

Figure 7-12 is a simple diagram with the duration of the flash scope and the request scope depicted to make their differences in the context of a flow execution more obvious.

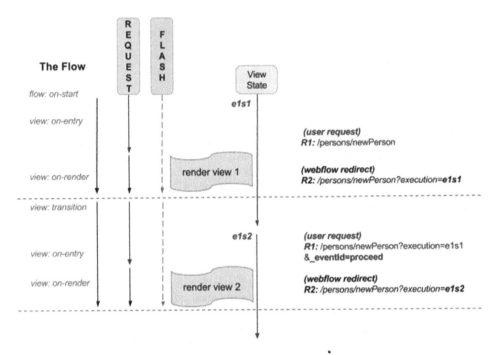

**Figure 7-12.** *Comparison between request and flash scope*

In Figure 7-12, you can clearly see the two requests implied by a flow state. One of them is the user request to start the flow with URL /person/newPerson. Accessing this URL makes the web flow engine send a request to /persons/newPerson?execution=e1s1. The request to this web flow resource is the second request. The two arrows under the REQUEST bubble show exactly how long the attributes in the request scope is available. And under the FLASH bubble, you can see the longer arrow, which depicts how long the attributes in the flash scope are available. The execution points— :on-entry, on-render, and so forth—are covered in the next section.

## Actions

Now that web flow scopes have been covered, it is time to introduce **actions**. Actions execute behavior at specific points within the flow. There are several points where you can execute actions:

- **on flow start**: The <evaluate /> element is declared as a child of the <on-start /> element that marks the start of a flow execution. This action is executed only once, when the flow execution starts.

```
<flow ...>
  <on-start>
    <evaluate expression="..."/>
  </on-start>
</flow>
```

- **on state entry**: The <evaluate /> element is declared as a child of the <on-entry /> element that marks the entry in a state. (A view state in the following example). This action is executed only once, when entering the state.

```
<flow ...>
    <view-state ...>
        <on-entry>
            <evaluate expression="..."/>
        </on-entry>
    </view-state>
</flow>
```

- **on view render**: The <evaluate /> element is declared as a child of the <on-render /> element that marks the moment immediately before a view is rendered. The action is executed on every browser refresh.

```
<flow ...>
    <view-state ...>
        <on-render>
            <evaluate expression="..."/>
        </on-render>
    </view-state>
</flow>
```

- **on transition execution**: The <evaluate /> element is declared as a child of the <transition /> element. Actions imply evaluating expressions and the results are assigned to variables that have a specific scope assigned. The <evaluate /> action element used in the following example can be used to evaluate an expression and assign the result a specific scope. It can **prevent** a transition if an exception is thrown or false is returned as a result when the expression is evaluated. How exceptions are handled in the web flow context is covered later in the chapter. Only one <evaluate /> expression is allowed.

```
<flow ...>
    <view-state ...>
        <transition on="confirm" to="nextStep">
            <evaluate expression="..."/>
        </transition>
    </view-state>
</flow>
```

- **on state exit**: The <evaluate /> element is declared as a child of the <on-exit/> element that marks the exit of a state. (A view state in the following example). This action is executed only once, when exiting the state.

```
<flow ...>
    <view-state ...>
        <on-exit>
            <evaluate expression="..."/>
        </on-exit>
    </view-state>
</flow>
```

- **on flow end**: The `<evaluate />` element is declared as a child of the `<on-end />` element that marks the end of a flow execution. This action is executed only once, when the flow execution ends.

```
<flow ...>
...
    <on-end>
        <evaluate expression="..."/>
    </on-end>
</flow>
```

The examples presented so far were simplified to set the focus on the syntax when defining your actions. The following example is a concrete one that you will use in the practice exercises:

```
<flow ...>
<!-- newPerson-flow.xml -->
  <view-state id="enterPersonInfo">
      <on-render>
          <evaluate expression="hospitalManager.findAll()"
              result="flowScope.hospitalList" />
      </on-render>
      <transition on="proceed" to="reviewPerson" />
  </view-state>
</flow>
```

The `<evaluate />` element can also be used to resolve properties on beans and even perform conversions. The actions are usually expressed in Spring EL,[4] but Unified EL Standard and OGNL are supported too. Using this type of syntax makes the actions more concise for executing behavior and easier to read from a development point of view.

A Spring EL expression has the following template:

```
<variable_name>.property_or_method
```

The variable_name is resolved against the current flow context. Variables referring to data scopes (flowScope, viewScope, requestScope, etc.) should only be used when assigning a new variable to one of the scopes. To resolve a flow variable, reserved variables are searched first, then the variable is searched within each flow scope, starting with request and expanding the scope gradually: flash, view, flow, conversation. If the variable is not found, the flow application context is searched for a bean matching the variable name. Let's look at a few examples to make usage of Spring EL expressions with web flows easier to understand:

- flowScope.person: The person variable is resolved in flow scope

- person: The person variable is searched in all scopes

- hospitalManager.findAll(): The findAll method is called on the hospitalManager variable (in this book's examples, hospitalManager is actually a bean).

- hospitalManager.findByCode(hospitalCode): Calling a bean method and using the hospitalCode variable as an argument.

---

[4]See http://docs.spring.io/spring/docs/current/spring-framework-reference/html/expressions. html#expressions-language-ref.

When using Spring EL to write expressions, a few reserved variables can be used without any prior manual initialization (Spring takes care of initializing them).

- **scope-specific variables**: requestScope, flashScope, viewScope, flowScope, conversationScope

- **environment-specific variables**: flowExecutionUrl, flowRequestContext, requestParameters, externalContext, messageContext, resourceBundle, currentEvent, currentUser

- externalContext.sessionMap is used to access HTTP session contents. (No sessionScope variable exists in the context of a flow definition.)

Some of these variables can be used in view template files also; in JSP, all scope variables are accessible, flowExecutionUrl is the URL of the current page, flowRequestContext is the RequestContext. Additional variables are available: pageScope, requestParameters, sessionScope, and so forth.

So far, only the <evaluate /> element has been used, but there are alternatives more suitable in particular cases. The <set /> action element is used to set the value of a variable, but it does not prevent a transition and can be used multiple times within a transition element. For example, if you just want to view the details on a person after it was selected from a list; there is nothing to evaluate, you just want view some data. The <set /> element is more suitable for this case:

```
<flow ...>
<!-- reviewPerson-flow.xml -->
  <view-state id="reviewPersonInfo">
    <on-render>
      <evaluate expression="personManager.getByDateOfBirth(dob)"
            result="viewScope.persons" result-type="dataModel" />
    </on-render>
    <transition on="select" to="viewPerson">
      <set name="flowScope.person" value="persons.selectedRow" />
    </transition>
  </view-state>
</flow>
```

When using <set />, a scope must be specified when creating a *new* variable, as there is no default. In the following example, the firstName variable is assigned to the flowScope scope.

```
<set name="flowScope.firstName"
        value="requestParameters.firstName"/>
```

When updating an existing variable, or one of its properties, the scope is no longer required and the algorithm presented previously is used to perform scope resolution.

```
<set name="person.firstName"
        value="requestParameters.firstName"/>
```

## Request Parameters

In the previous code sample, the requestParameters system variable was used. This variable contains all the URL parameters for the current request. These parameters are not in the requestScope, and if they are needed further in the execution flow, they need to be assigned to a proper scope; otherwise, they will be lost when the current request ends.

```
<view-state id="reviewPersonInfo">
  <transition on="cancel" to="cancelled">
    <evaluate expression=
        "personManager.delete(requestParameters.personId)">
    </transition>
</view-state>
```

■ **?** To test your understanding, look at the following code snippet:

```
<view-state id="practiceInfo">
 <on-entry>
 <set name="flashScope.var1" value="var1" >
 <set name="requestScope.var2" value="var2" >
 <on-entry>
 <on-render>
 <set name="requestScope.var3" value="var3" >
 <set name="flashScope.var4" value="var4" >
 <set name="requestScope.var5" value="var5" >
 </on-render>
</view-state>
```

Try to determine which of the following affirmations is true and which is not, and why.[5]

1.  var2 is available after the view is rendered.

2.  var2 can be used to initialize the view, but is lost when the view is rendered.

3.  var1, var3, var4, and var5 are available after the view is rendered.

4.  var1 is lost if the view is refreshed.

---

[5]1. False. This variable is defined in the first requestScope and a state has two requests. Rendering the view is done in the second request. 2. True. As explained earlier. 3. True. var1 and var4 are defined in flashScope; var3 and var5 are defined in the scope of the rendering requestScope. 4. True. var1 is lost because it is defined when entering the state, and if the page is reloaded, entering the page is done only once. So when the page is reloaded, the flash scope is cleaned and var1 is lost.

Actions are really useful components of a flow, but a flow definition must stay clear and readable. The recommended practice is to keep your flow definition as simple as possible, use actions only to prevent transactions or to decide to which state to transition next. The heavy-lifting actions should be performed in Java.

As you probably figured out by now, a web flow definition is a bridge between the service and the web layer that can be used to control the navigation.

## Model Objects

In Chapter 3, you learned about controllers, models, and views. A model object handles data used in a view. The views used in web flows view states also need model objects to render data. In web flow definitions, model objects can be assigned different scopes and are associated to a view state using the model attribute.

```
<flow ...>
    <view-state id="enterPersonInfo" model="person">
        ...
    </view-state>
</flow>
```

The model object is accessible from the view template files and can be set as a model attribute for forms. The Spring forms used in web flow views are identical to the ones used when working with Spring MVC; the only difference is represented by the Submit button, which is used to trigger a user event when using web flows. This is what a Spring MVC view used to save a Person instance looks like:

```
<!-- addPerson.jsp -->
<%@ taglib prefix="spring" uri="http://www.springframework.org/tags" %>
<%@ taglib prefix="sf" uri="http://www.springframework.org/tags/form" %>
    <spring:url value="/persons/{id}" var="editUrl">
        <spring:param name="id" value="${person.id}"/>
    </spring:url>
    <sf:form modelAttribute="person" action="${editUrl}" method="POST">
        <table>
            <tr>
                <th>
                    <label for="firstName">
                        <span class="man">*</span>
                        <spring:message code="label.Person.firstname"/> :
                    </label>
                </th>
                <td><sf:input path="firstName"/></td>
                <td><sf:errors cssClass="error" path="firstName"/></td>
            </tr>
            <!-- other form fields-->
            ...
            <tr>
                <td>
                    <button id="saveButton" type="submit">
                        <spring:message code="command.save"/>
                    </button>
                </td>
                <td>
```

```
                    <a href="${editUrl}">
                        <spring:message code="command.cancel"/>
                    </a>
                </td>
            </tr>
        </table>
</sf:form>
```

This is what a Spring Web Flow view used to save a Person instance looks like:

```
<!-- newPersonInfo.jsp -->
<%@ taglib prefix="spring" uri="http://www.springframework.org/tags" %>
<%@ taglib prefix="sf" uri="http://www.springframework.org/tags/form" %>
<sf:form modelAttribute="person" method="POST" id="newPersonForm">
 <table>
        <tr>
            <th>
                <label for="firstName">
                    <span class="man">*</span>
                    <spring:message code="label.Person.firstname"/> :
                </label>
            </th>
            <td><sf:input path="firstName"/></td>
            <td><sf:errors cssClass="error" path="firstName"/></td>
        </tr>
        <!-- other form fields-->
        ...
        <tr>
            <td>
                <button id="newPersonButton" name="_eventId_proceed"
                        type="submit">
                    <spring:message code="command.proceed" />
                </button>
            </td>
            <td>
                <button id="cancelOpButton" name="_eventId_cancel"
                        type="submit">
                    <spring:message code="command.cancel" />
                </button>
            </td>
        </tr>
    </table>
</sf:form>
```

The cancel user event is handled by a global transition, a concept that is covered later.

The model is populated with the request parameter process, also known as **data binding**. Validation and conversion are supported for all properties, but can be suppressed if needed (usually during development) using the bind and validation attributes on the <transition /> element, by setting them to "false".

```
<view-state id="enterPersonInfo"
```

```
        model="person">
  <transition on="submit" to="reviewPersonInfo" />
  <transition on="cancel" to="end"
                bind="false" validate="false"/>
</view-state>
```

When using Spring MVC, the @InitBinder annotation was used to customize the properties of a model object that should be binded to a view. Spring Web Flow has an equivalent for this too, because there is no point in binding properties that the user does not modify or is not meant to use for security reasons. For example, after personal data is introduced and the validation has passed, the enterIdentityCardInfo data used to generate the unique personal numerical code should no longer be editable by the user; otherwise, the personal numerical code is no longer valid. The <binder /> element can be used to white-list elements eligible for binding, like in the following example:

```
<!-- enterIdentityCardInfo-floq.xml -->
<view-state id="enterIdentityCardInfo"
        model="identityCard">
  <binder>
        <binding property="series" required="true"/>
        <binding property="number" required="true"/>
        <!--current date will be used-->
        <binding property="emittedAt" required="false"/>
        <!-- current date 10 years will be used-->
        <binding property="expiresAt" required="false"/>
        <binding property="address" required="true"/>
  </binder>
</view-state>
```

When the form is really big, the model object has a lot of fields and the web flow definition might become too verbose. A more appropriate solution in cases like this is to create a validator bean or method for the model objects, as covered in Chapter 3.

## Validation, Formatting, and Conversion

Formatters and converters used with web flows are the same as in Spring MVC: default ones are present out of the box, and custom formatters and converters have to be declared and associated with the web flow engine using the flow builder services, as shown in the "Configuration and Infrastructure Beans" section. The same goes for validators: they have to be set on the flow builder services to be used.

---

■ !   A Spring **convertor** is a general-purpose class used for conversion between two types that implement org.springframework.core.convert.converter.GenericConverter or one of its subinterfaces, or implement org.springframework.core.convert.converter.Converter<S,T> or subinterfaces.

A Spring **formatter** is a class specializing in transforming objects into strings or vice-versa, because when Spring MVC or Spring Web Flow is used, this is the focus of model objects. The classes must implement the `org.springframework.format.Formatter<T>` interface or one of its subinterfaces. The `Formatter<T>` interface is favored by developers because it is more suitable for web applications.

---

Although the registered converters are applied to any model objects, if needed, a different converter can be set for a property using the converter attribute of the `<binding />` element. A converter cannot be specified in the web flow definition on a property that is not required; otherwise, when no value is provided, validation errors are generated and rendered in the view.

```xml
<!-- enterIdentityCardInfo-floq.xml -->
<view-state id="enterIdentityCardInfo"
        model="identityCard">
  <binder>
        <binding property="series" required="true"/>
        <binding property="number" required="true"/>
        <binding property="emittedAt" required="true" converter="simpleDate"/>
        <binding property="expiresAt" required="true" converter="simpleDate"/>
        <binding property="address" required="true"/>
  </binder>
</view-state>
```

**JSR 349 bean validation** is supported and annotations on the form object properties are used to set up the validation; but to enable it, a bean of type `LocalValidatorFactoryBean` has to be defined and set on the on the `flowBuilderServices` bean. A validator set on the `FlowBuilderServices` bean is applied to all model objects in the application. For customizations, custom validators can also be used, just like in Spring MVC.

---

■ ! Remember the annotation validations?

```java
@Entity
@SequenceGenerator(name = "seqGen", allocationSize = 1)
public class Person implements Serializable {
 @Column(nullable = false)
 @Size(min=2, max=50)
 @NotEmpty
 public String firstName;
 @Enumerated(EnumType.STRING)
 @NotNull
 private Gender gender;

 ...

}
```

---

When it comes to validation, there is one major difference between Spring MVC and Spring Web Flow—the template of the internationalized validation message keys. In Spring Web Flow, the message key must match the following template to be picked up automatically. In Spring MVC, the message name is placed at the beginning; in Spring Web Flow is placed at the end.

```
#MVC
messageName.modelObject.property
 #Web Flow
modelObject.property.messageName
```

But this difference can be eliminated by using a bean of type DefaultMessageCodesResolver that is set on the MvcViewFactoryCreator. Here is the XML configuration needed to make this happen:

```
<!-- webflow-config.xml -->
  <!-- Configures Web Flow to render Tiles views resolved by Spring MVC -->
  <bean id="mvcViewFactoryCreator"
      class="org.springframework.webflow.mvc.builder.MvcViewFactoryCreator">
      <property name="viewResolvers" ref="tilesViewResolver" />
      <property name="useSpringBeanBinding" value="true"/>
      <property name="messageCodesResolver" ref="mcr" />
  </bean>

      <bean id="mcr"
          class="org.springframework.validation.DefaultMessageCodesResolver"/>
```

And here is the Java Configuration:

```
\\ WebFlowConfig.java
@Bean
  public MvcViewFactoryCreator mvcViewFactoryCreator() {
      MvcViewFactoryCreator factoryCreator = new MvcViewFactoryCreator();
      factoryCreator.setViewResolvers(Arrays.<ViewResolver>asList(
          this.mvcConfig.tilesViewResolver()));
      factoryCreator.setUseSpringBeanBinding(true);
      factoryCreator
          .setMessageCodesResolver(messageCodesResolver());
      return factoryCreator;
  }

@Bean
public DefaultMessageCodesResolver messageCodesResolver(){
    return new DefaultMessageCodesResolver();
}
```

Another way to validate a model object is to use **programmatic validation**. You can define a validation method in the model object class specific to the view state. The method must have a specific name to be discovered and the convention naming is

```
"validate" + {view-state-id(first letter is up-cased)}
```

So if instead of using a Person instance as model object, a specific form object implementation would be used. That implementation can also be defined with a view-state specific validation method:

```
<!-- Flow definition file-->
<view-state id="enterPersonInfo" model="personModelObject" >
    ...
</view-state>

<!-- PersonModelObject.java -->
public class PersonModelObject implements Serializable {
        public void validateEnterPersonInfo(
                ValidationContext validationContext) {
                ...
        }
}
```

Keep in mind that model objects are being serialized and deserialized by Spring to populate the form with values, or retrieve field values from the form, so the model object class must implement the java. io.Serializable interface.

If the model object cannot be modified, a validator bean can be used. The bean name must match a specific convention:

```
{model object name} + "Validator"
```

To be automatically detected, the validation method must match the preceding conventions, but the signature has an extra parameter—the model object that is automatically passed as an argument.

```
<!-- Flow definition file-->
<view-state id="enterPersonInfo" model="person" > ...</view-state>

<!-- PersonValidator.java -->
@Component
public class PersonValidator {
        public void validateEnterPersonInfo(
                Person person,
                ValidationContext validationContext) {
                ...
        }
}
```

■ !   When writing a validator class and using annotations to define the bean, make sure to specify a name corresponding to the convention mentioned earlier, or make sure that you name the class appropriately.

Another way of defining validation with web flows is using the <evaluate /> element to call validation methods and prevent transitions if the validation fails. But doing this is not recommended because it will overcrowd the flow definition. Still, in some cases, this kind of approach could be necessary, so that's why it is covered.

```
<!-- Flow definition file-->
<view-state id="enterPersonInfo" model="person" >

    <transition on="submit" to="enterIdentityCardInfo">
      <evaluate expression="personValidator.check(person, messageContext)"/>
    </transition>
</view-state>

<!-- PersonValidator.java -->
@Component("personValidator")
public class PersonValidator{
        public boolean check(
                Person person,
                MessageContext messageContext) {
                ...
        }
}
```

The method returns a Boolean value that can be used to prevent a transition when the result of its evaluation is false.

Validation methods have flexible signatures and can use different types of objects to register errors. They can use a ValidationContext object to register errors:

```
import org.springframework.binding.message.MessageBuilder;
import org.springframework.binding.validation.ValidationContext;
...
public void validateEnterPersonInfo(ValidationContext validationContext) {
  validationContext.getMessageContext().
    addMessage(new MessageBuilder().error()
    .source("person")
    .code("Size.person.firstName")
    .defaultText ("Length must be between 2 and 50").build());
}
```

Or a MessageContext object:

```
import org.springframework.binding.message.MessageBuilder;
import org.springframework.binding.message.MessageContext;
...
public boolean check(Person person, MessageContext messageContext) {
    messageContext.addMessage
        (new MessageBuilder().error().source("firstName")
            .code("Size.person.firstName").build());
        return true;
}
```

Or an Errors object:

```
import org.springframework.validation.Errors;
...
public boolean check(Person person, Errors errors) {
        errors.rejectValue("person",
                "Size.person.firstName",
                "Length must be between 2 and 50");
        return true;
    }
```

JSR-349 bean validation supports **partial validation** through validation groups.[6] A group defines a subset of constraints. Instead of validating all constraints for a given object graph, only a subset is validated. This subset is defined by the group or groups targeted.

```
@NotEmpty
@Size(min=2, max=50, groups=NameRule.class)
public String firstName;

@NotEmpty
@Size(min=2, max=50, groups=NameRule.class)
public String lastName;
```

Groups are represented by interfaces that are defined inside the model class or its parent.

```
package com.pr.validator;
public class PersonModelObject implements Serializable {
...
    public interface NameRule {
    }
}
```

---

[6]If you want more information about validation groups, the official documentation is a great start; it can be found at https://docs.oracle.com/javaee/7/tutorial/index.html.

In a flow definition, the equivalent of validation groups can be implemented using the validation-hints attribute on the `<view-state />`:

```
<!-- Flow definition file-->
<view-state id="enterPersonInfo" model="person" validation-hints="group1,group2">

    <transition on="submit" to="enterIdentityCardInfo">
      <evaluate expression="personValidator.check(person, messageContext)"/>
    </transition>
</view-state>
```

The validation groups are used to group together fields of the model object that are subjected to validation together.

```
@NotEmpty
@Size(min=2, max=50, groups={"group1,group2"})
public String firstName;

@NotEmpty
@Size(min=2, max=50, groups={"group1"})
public String lastName;
```

The validation-hints attribute is an expression that resolves to a comma-delimited string consisting of hints that are resolved by a ValidationHintResolver bean. By default, Spring uses a bean of type org. springframework.webflow.validation.

BeanValidationHintResolver matches the string values to class-based bean validation groups. In the preceding case, this bean looked for interfaces named Group1 and Group2 in the model or its parent. Fully qualified class names can also be provided.

A custom ValidationHintResolver can also be provided if necessary, but has to be set on the FlowBuilderServices in the web flow configuration. In the following, you can see an XML and Java Configuration sample:

```
  <!-- webflow-config.xml -->
<webflow:flow-builder-services id="flowBuilderServices"
            view-factory-creator="mvcViewFactoryCreator"
            conversion-service="conversionService"
            validation-hint-resolver="customValidationHintResolver" />

<!-- WebFlowConfig.class-->
@Bean
 public FlowBuilderServices flowBuilderServices() {
    return getFlowBuilderServicesBuilder()
                .setViewFactoryCreator(mvcViewFactoryCreator())
                .setValidator(this.mvcConfig.validator())
                .setConversionService(conversionService())
                .setValidationHintResolver(customValidationHintResolver())
                .setDevelopmentMode(true)
                .build();
}
```

```
@Bean
public CustomValidationHintResolver customValidationHintResolver(){
    return new CustomValidationHintResolver();
}

//CustomValidationHintResolver.java
import org.springframework.webflow.validation.BeanValidationHintResolver;
...
@Component("customValidationHintResolver")
public class CustomValidationHintResolver extends BeanValidationHintResolver {
        ...
}
```

---

■ ! If you want to test your understanding so far, check if you understand how view-states, actions, and transactions interact in the context of a flow. You can take a break from reading and try to solve the 11-pr-webflow-actions-practice practice project. This project contains all the classes necessary to implement a flow that creates a Person instance in two steps. The view templates are provided, and in the newPerson-flow.xml, the view-states and transaction elements are already in place. The only thing you have to do is to complete the web flow definition by adding actions and model objects. (TODO 40) Figure 7-13 shows the elements of the flow definition and some hints about which actions should be used and where.

---

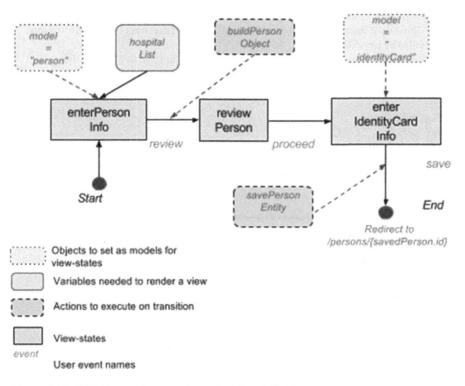

*Figure 7-13.* *Web Flow action practice project flow definition*

A PersonModelObject class is provided to use an instance of this type in the flow definition. A class called PersonBuilder is defined with helper methods that can be used to create a person model object and save the person that the flow will create. The following are the steps executed by the web flow:

1.  The enterPersonInfo view-state is entered and a form with the minimal data required to create a person is displayed. Almost all properties of the person model object for this form must be binded and are required, except for the middleName. When this view is rendered, the list of hospitals must be populated. In this example, the hospitalList is only needed to render the view. Keep this in mind when deciding which scope this variable should be assigned to. When leaving this state, the personal object model must be created from all the data introduced by the user. The personal numerical code is generated by the application. Just add an action to call the buildPersonObject of the personBuilder bean and save the result to a variable. This variable must be accessible to all view-states from this step on, so take this into account when choosing the scope for it. Figure 7-14 depicts the view specific to this view-state.

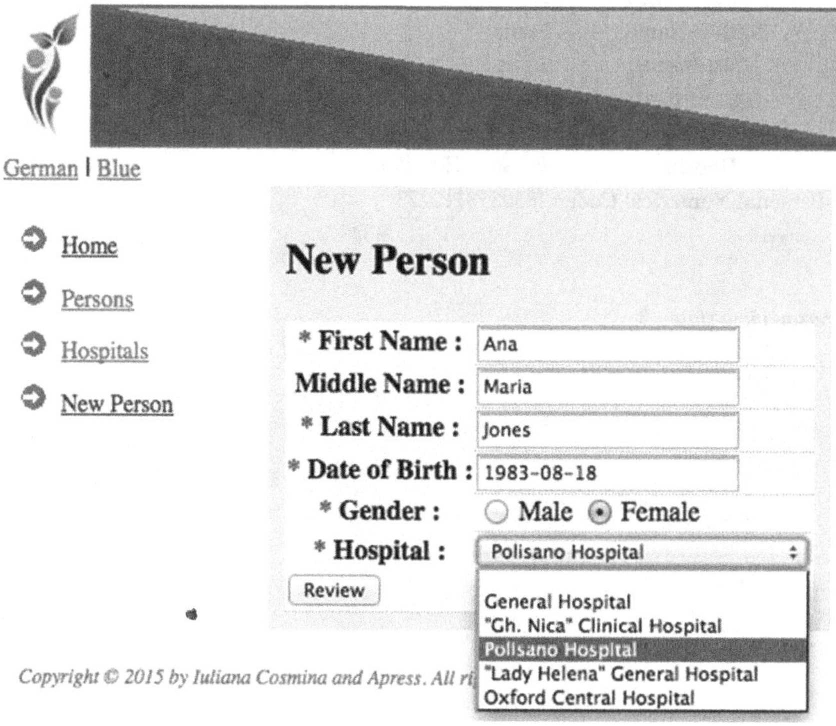

*Figure 7-14.* The enterPersonInfo view-state

2. Clicking the `Review` button must direct the user to the `reviewPerson` view-state, where the information introduced by the user and the application-generated personal numeric code is displayed. Only the transition element is missing from the configuration state. The next state to go to is `enterIdentityCardInfo`. Figure 7-15 depicts the view specific to this view-state.

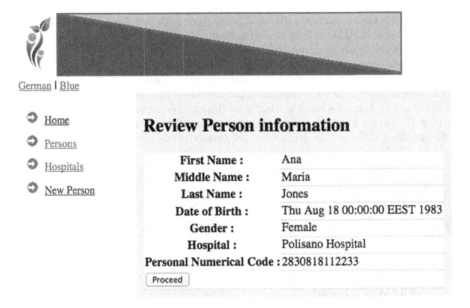

*Figure 7-15.* *The reviewPerson view-state*

3. The enterIdentityCardInfo is entered, and in this state, the personal details introduced and generated so far are displayed. The view specific to this view-state also contains a form that is used to insert data for the IdentityCard instance. A Person instance cannot be created without an IdentityCard. The personal numerical code cannot be edited; to change it, you have to go back to the first step of the flow and change the data there. All the properties of the identityCard object model for this form must be binded and all are mandatory. Figure 7-16 depicts the view specific to this view-state.

*Figure 7-16.* The enterIdentityCardInfo view-state

To save a person's data, just click the Save button. In the web flow definition, the `savePersonEntity` in the `personBuilder` bean call must be added when transitioning away to the end state. The `IdentityCardValidator` class defines a validator method that is applied automatically before saving an `IdentityCard` instance. The validation method is discovered and applied specifically when the flow is transitioning away from the `enterIdentityCardInfo` view-state, and checks if another person with the same personal numerical code already exists in the system. To try it out, just add a person born on January 8, 1942 at Oxford Hospital. You should get an error message like the one shown in Figure 7-17.

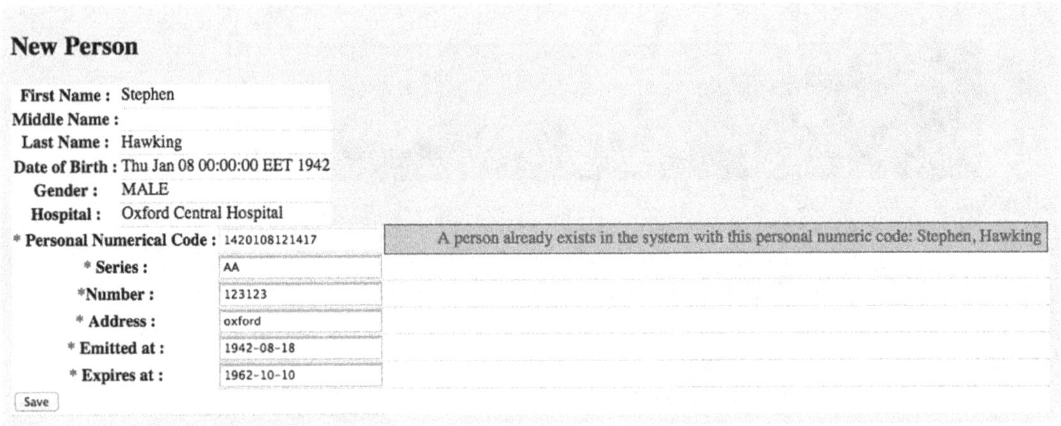

**New Person**

First Name : Stephen
Middle Name :
Last Name : Hawking
Date of Birth : Thu Jan 08 00:00:00 EET 1942
Gender : MALE
Hospital : Oxford Central Hospital
* Personal Numerical Code : 1420108121417    A person already exists in the system with this personal numeric code: Stephen, Hawking
        * Series :    AA
        *Number :    123123
        * Address :    oxford
        * Emitted at :    1942-08-18
        * Expires at :    1962-10-10
[ Save ]

*Figure 7-17. The enterIdentityCardInfo view-state when invalid data is inserted*

---

■ **Note**    As an exercise, you could try to make the validation more precise by testing for number and series duplication in an identity card.

---

# Action States

If you remember the first logical schema (see Figure 7-1) of the web flow execution that it is meant to be implemented after studying this chapter, you should remember that it had some decisional elements in the `if-then-else` style that made the navigation flow dynamic; because when transitioning based on the value of a variable, you can end up in different states. In the examples presented so far, this was not possible, because view-states and actions are not enough to do this. What can be done with view-states and actions, however, is preventing transitioning when an action fails, but not changing the state to transition to. To make this happen dynamically, two new state types are needed: action-states and decision-states.

An action state allows transition to a state that executes one or more actions using `<evaluate />` and `<set />` elements. The result of this action is raised as an event and a transition to another state is triggered. Different events can be raised to trigger different transitions dynamically, so an action state should be used when there is need of an action to be executed and the state to transition to is decided by the result of that action. Multiple `<evaluate />` are allowed inside an action-state, but the last one is used to control the transition. The `<set />` element can be used to define variables needed to execute that action and it is recommended for usage when transition control is not required.

The result of an action state can be any of the types in the following list, but it will always be converted to a string following the rules mentioned for each type, because to trigger a transition, the returned value must be mapped to an event:

- **Boolean**: Always evaluates to "yes" or "no".

- **String**: The name of the event to trigger.

- **Enumerated types**: The enumerated values is converted to String using the toString() method. The toString method must be defined in such a way that it returns acceptable values to transition on. Look at the following example; depending on the result of the evaluation of the getDecision(...) method, the transition is done to a different state.

```java
//ActionEnum.java
public enum ActionEnum {

    EDIT_ACCOUNT("accountEditState"),
    DELETE_ACCOUNT("accountDeleteState"),
    CREATE_ACCOUNT("accountCreateState");

    private String value;

    ActionEnum(String value) {
        this.value = value;
    }

    public String getValue() {
        return value;
    }

    @Override
    public String toString() {
        return value;
    }
}

//DecisionBean.java
@Component
public class DecisionBean implements Serializable {

    public ActionEnum getDecision(int decisionId) {
        switch (decisionId){
            case 0:
                return ActionEnum.EDIT_ACCOUNT;
            case 1:
                return ActionEnum.DELETE_ACCOUNT;
            case 2:
                return ActionEnum.CREATE_ACCOUNT;
        }
        throw new IllegalArgumentException("Option not supported!");
    }
}
```

```
//account-flow.xml
<flow...>
<action-state id="accountDecision">
    <evaluate
        expression="decisionBean.getDecision(requestParameters.decisionId)" />
    <transition on="EDIT_ACCOUNT" to="edit"/>
    <transition on="DELETE_ACCOUNT" to="delete"/>
    <transition on="CREATE_ACCOUNT" to="create"/>
</action-state>
<view-state id="edit" ... >
..
</view-state>

<view-state id="delete" ... >
..
</view-state>

< view-state id="create" ... >
..
</view-state>

</flow>
```

- `org.springframework.webflow.execution.Event`: The transition will use the id of the event object converted to String.

- Any other value that evaluates to `"success"`.

---

■ !   When using an `<evaluate />` expression inside a transition, a transition will occur if the result is any of the *true(Boolean)*, *"yes"*, *"true"(String)*, *"success"*. Enumerated types are converted to a `String` using its `toString()` method and the previous rule applies. Any other object is treated as *"success"*.

---

```
<view-state id="enterPersonInfo" model="person">
...

    <transition on="proceed" to="enterIdentityCardInfo" >
        <evaluate expression="personService.isNewPerson(person)"/>
        <!-- Must return "true", "yes",
            "success" or an object-->
    </transition>
</view-state>
```

So far, actions have been used in quite a simple manner and used to invoke methods on existing beans. These actions can be categorized as **No action** because they are used to invoke business services directly. The concept of "No action" might be confusing. The reason such a category exists is to categorize actions that are not defined by action classes.

```xml
<!-- newPerson-flow.xml-->
<action-state id="checkDuplicate">
    <evaluate expression="personService.isNewPerson(person)"/>
    <transition on="success" to="enterIdentityCardInfo"/>
    <!-- Transition always occurs -->
</action-state>
```

```java
// PersonService.java
@Service("personService")
public class PersonService {
    @Autowired
    PersonManager personManager;

    public boolean isNewPerson(Person person) {
        String pnc = PncBuilder.build(person);
        Person existingPerson = personManager.getByPnc(pnc);
        return existingPerson == null;
    }
}
```

But when the logic of an action becomes complicated, and even needs access to the flow context, actions can be implemented in different ways. The most simple way is to create a POJO (a bean), pass the flow context as an argument, and then invoke its methods by the flow. These are called the **POJO actions**.

---

■ ! To mark POJO actions, developers usually create their own annotation and set it to be component-scanned. In the Personal Records Manager project, the annotation is called @WebFlowAction.

```java
@Target({ElementType.TYPE})
@Retention(RetentionPolicy.RUNTIME)
@Documented
@Component
public @interface WebFlowAction {
 /**
  * The value may indicate a suggestion for a logical component name,
  * to be turned into a Spring bean in case of an autodetected component.
  * @return the suggested component name, if any
  */
 String value() default "";

}
```

For Spring to scan for this annotation, you have to add it to the configuration:

```
@Configuration
@EnableWebMvc
@ComponentScan(basePackages = {"com.pr, com.pr.persons,
  com.pr.hospitals, com.pr.validator"},
includeFilters = @ComponentScan.Filter(
  value = WebFlowAction.class,
  type = FilterType.ANNOTATION
))
@ImportResource({"classpath:spring/app-service-config.xml",
 "classpath:spring/db-config.xml"})
public class MvcConfig extends WebMvcConfigurerAdapter {
...
}
```

So, the following code can be written using a POJO action in the following manner:

```
  <!-- newPerson-flow.xml-->
<action-state id="checkDuplicate">
    <evaluate expression=
      "personAction.isNewPerson(requestContext)" />
      <transition on="success" to="enterIdentityCardInfo"/>
</action-state>

//PersonAction.java
import com.pr.WebFlowAction;
import org.springframework.webflow.execution.RequestContext;

@WebFlowAction
public class PersonAction {

    public String isNewPerson(RequestContext context) {
        Person person = (Person) context.getFlowScope().get("person");
        String pnc = PncBuilder.build(person);
        Person existingPerson = personManager.getByPnc(pnc);
        if (existingPerson == null) {
            return "success";
        } else{
            throw new DuplicatePersonException(existingPerson);
        }
    }
}
```

Notice how the context is declared as a parameter and set as an argument by the developer in the web flow action definition. They way that exceptions are handled in a web flow execution is covered later.

Another type of actions are the **plain actions**. For each action, a class is created that implements the org.springframework.webflow.execution.Action interface or extends the Spring-provided implementation, the org.springframework.webflow.action.AbstractAction class. The implementation provided by Spring provides some methods that can be used to generate events. For example, this class implements the org.springframework.beans.factory.InitializingBean interface (covered in Chapter 2) to receive an init callback when deployed within a Spring bean factory and exposes hooks to execute pre- (doPreExecute (RequestContext context)) and post- (doPostExecute(RequestContext context)) action execution.

The Action interface exposes only one method, named execute. Implementations of this interface are usually used to create singleton beans instantiated and managed by a Spring web application context. The request context is no longer declared as an argument in the flow definition, as an action defined this way is handled by Spring, which knows the argument to call the action method with. The advantages of using plain actions is that they can easily be parametrized with mocks and stubs in test environments. Also, action proxies may also be generated at runtime for delegating to POJO business operations that have no dependency on the Spring Web Flow API, which helps with decoupling components inside an application. They can be used to simplify a flow definition when an action is simple enough, because there is no need for a SpEL in the evaluate element or a method call; the name of the action component is enough for Spring to know what to do.

```
package org.springframework.webflow.execution;
public interface Action {
    public Event execute(RequestContext context)
        throws Exception;
}
```

The previous example can be written using a plain action too, and the code will look as follows:

```
<!-- newPerson-flow.xml -->
<action-state id="checkDuplicate">
    <evaluate expression="personAction" />
        <transition on="success" to="enterIdentityCardInfo"/>
</action-state>
//PersonAction.java
import org.springframework.webflow.execution.Action;
...
@WebFlowAction
public class PersonAction implements Action {

    @Autowired
    PersonManager personManager;

    @Override
    public Event execute(RequestContext context) throws Exception {
        Person person = (Person) context.getFlowScope().get("person");
        String pnc = PncBuilder.build(person);
        Person existingPerson = personManager.getByPnc(pnc);
        if (existingPerson == null) {
            return new Event(this, "success");
        } else{
            \\ how an exception is handled in webflow context is covered
            \\later in the chapter
             throw new DuplicatePersonException(existingPerson);
        }
    }
}
```

The context is automatically passed as an argument by Spring.

The most complex type of actions are the **MultiActions**. They are implemented by extending the org.springframework.webflow.action.MultiAction class, an extension of AbstractAction that provides multiple helper methods for returning events. All action methods must have the same signature as the execute method from the previous example; the context is also automatically passed as argument by Spring.

- success(), error(), yes(), no()

- result(), result(String), error(Exception)

The code in the previous example does not differ much when implemented with MultiAction, but it is added here to underline the differences between the two implementations:

```xml
<!-- newPerson-flow.xml -->
<action-state id="checkDuplicate">
    <evaluate expression="personAction.isNewPerson" />
        <transition on="success" to="enterIdentityCardInfo"/>
</action-state>
```

```java
//PersonAction.java
import org.springframework.webflow.action.MultiAction;
...
@WebFlowAction
public class PersonAction extends MultiAction {
    @Autowired
    PersonManager personManager;

    public Event isNewPerson(RequestContext context) throws Exception {
        Person person = (Person) context.getFlowScope().get("person");
        String pnc = PncBuilder.build(person);
        Person existingPerson = personManager.getByPnc(pnc);
        if (existingPerson == null) {
            return success();
        } else{
            throw new DuplicatePersonException(existingPerson);
        }
    }
}
```

In the previous examples, the same behavior was implemented using all types of actions, but technically, each type of action implementation is suitable to a certain case.

- **No action**: Easy to use: just plug in a business method call in the web flow definition. The main disadvantage here is the tight coupling between business logic and the flow definition, and the fact that business method calls can make your web flow definition look crowded. It is proper for usage in simple web flows in simple applications.

- **POJO action**: Can be used to glue the flow logic with the business login in a decoupled way and provides a flexible way to solve business layer exceptions; but the disadvantage is that the flow definitions might become more complex.

- **Plain action**: There are not many cases when this should be used, except of course, for explanatory exercises when teaching Spring Web Flow.

- **MultiAction**: Offers all the advantages of a POJO action, and the code for the implementation class might become quite complex.

It is recommended to use POJO actions and MultiActions, if possible, while taking into account the complexity of the flow definition vs. the complexity of the action class.

For any classes used to implement actions, the RequestContext is needed to obtain access to contextual information about the executing request. A new instance of this object is created every time there is a start, signalEvent(resume flow), or refresh to reconstruct the last viewed selection when the user requests a different response.

- getFlowScope(): Returns a map that can be used to get/set flowScope attributes.

- getRequestScope(): The same as getFlowScope(), but for the requestScope.

- getActiveFlow(), getCurrentState(), getFlowExecutionURL(): Access information about the flow itself; typically used for auditing and debugging applications.

- getMessageContext(): This can be used when an exception is thrown during an action execution on order to display an internationalized message regarding the error.

- getExternalContext(): Accesses information about the calling context.

# Decision States

The decision state type is an alternative for an action state type; when based on an evaluated expression, there are multiple possibilities of transitioning. As you have seen so far with action-state, the only outcome is the transition to a "success" view-state or the reload of the current view-state to display an error message. The decision state allows for branching of the transition process by using a practical if/then/else syntax, which allows an easier transitioning control. Similar to if/then/else statements in Java, the condition returns a Boolean value that determines the next state to go. When more conditions are required, an action state is more suitable.

```
<!-- newPerson-flow.xml -->
<decision-state id="checkDuplicate">
   <if test="personService.isNewPerson(person)" then="enterIdentityCardInfo"
                else="reviewExistingPerson"/>
</decision-state>
```

A new view-state has been introduced in this example, reviewExistingPerson; it allows the user to inspect the person already in the system to verify that the existing person is the one he tried to insert.

A decision state can be used in the final proposed flow to implement in this chapter, which is to check if a person's age is greater than 18 so that an account can be created; else, end the execution:

```
<!-- newPerson-flow.xml -->
<decision-state id="checkAdult">
   <if test="personService.isAdult(person)" then="enterAccountInfo"
                     else="end"/>
</decision-state>
```

```
//PersonService.java
import java.time.*;
...
@Service("personService")
public class PersonService {

    // using Java 8 classes to determine age
    public boolean isAdult(Person person){
        Date input = person.getDateOfBirth();
        Instant instant = input.toInstant();
        ZonedDateTime zdt = instant.atZone(ZoneId.systemDefault());
        LocalDate birthday = zdt.toLocalDate();
        long yearsDelta = birthday.until(LocalDate.now(), ChronoUnit.YEARS);
        return yearsDelta>=18;
    }
}
```

# Exception Handling

In the previous examples, the DuplicatePersonException exception class was mentioned. This class was introduced to throw an exception when the user tries to add an existing person to the system and to exemplify exception handling in the context of web flows.

```
public class DuplicatePersonException extends RuntimeException {

    private Person person;

    public DuplicatePersonException(Person person) {
        super("The person already exists in the system.");
        this.person = person;
    }

    public Person getPerson() {
        return person;
    }
}
```

When exceptions are raised in the context of a flow execution, they can be taken care of in a few ways:

- Let the exception propagate and define the web flow in such a way that an exception will cause a transition to an exception view-state.

    ```
    <transition on-exception="com.pr.problem.DuplicatePersonException"
                to="errorEndState" />
    ```

- Handle any exception globally; define a state in which any other state will transition into when an exception is thrown.

```
<flow>
    ...
    <global-transitions>
        <transition
            on-exception="com.pr.problem.DuplicatePersonException"
                to="errorEndState" />
    </global-transitions>
</flow>
```

- Use an `<exception-handler bean="flowExceptionHandler"/>` element as a child element to any state type. The bean set by the bean attribute of this element is a bean of type `org.springframework.webflow.engine.FlowExecutionExceptionHandler`. It is recommended to avoid this option, as it can leave the flow in an invalid state when used incorrectly. The most simple way to create a flow executor handler is to extend the `TransitionExecutingFlowExecutionExceptionHandler` class that extends the previously mentioned interface. The following code snippet is the equivalent of the `<global-transition />` element defined previously.

```
import org.springframework.webflow.engine.support.
        TransitionExecutingFlowExecutionExceptionHandler;

public class PersonFlowExceptionHandler
    extends TransitionExecutingFlowExecutionExceptionHandler {

    public PersonFlowExceptionHandler() {
        super.add(DuplicatePersonException.class, "errorStateId");
    }
}
```

- Catch the exception in an Action class and return an error event.

```
//PersonAction.java
@WebFlowAction
public class PersonAction extends MultiAction {

    @Autowired
    PersonManager personManager;

    public Event isNewPerson(RequestContext context) throws Exception {
        Person person = (Person) context.getFlowScope().get("person");
        String pnc = PncBuilder.build(person);
        Person existingPerson = personManager.getByPnc(pnc);
        if (existingPerson == null) {
            return success();
        } else {
            return error();
        }
    }
}
```

■ ! Before continuing further, take a look at the `12-pr-webflow-actions2-practice` module project. This project is expected to create a new `Person` instance, add all the details for it, and also insert a bank account into the system. To do this, all the elements presented until now are used: actions, action-states, decision-states, and also exception handling. The flow in Figure 7-18 requires a `Hospital` instance to be selected to create a `Person` instance. But what if the `Hospital` instance does not already exist in the system and has to be created first? Adding extra logic to do this will make the definition of the flow complicated and will connect the Person and Hospital logic. The proper way to do this is to add a subflow with the specific purpose of creating a new Hospital instance.

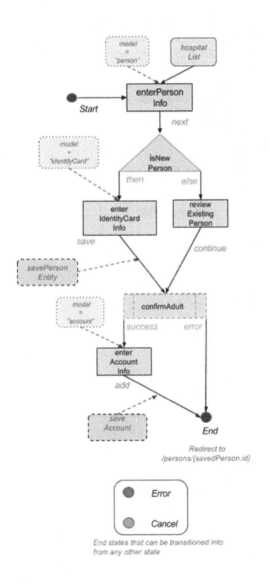

***Figure 7-18.*** *Add person and account flow definition*

Figure 7-18 depicts a logical schema of the web flow definition to be implemented in this project. All elements are required to be defined in the newPerson-flow.xml. The isNewPerson is represented as a triangle, a decision-state, and the confirmAdult is represented as a fancy rectangle, an action-state. The Cancel and the Error states can be reached form any other state using global transitions, so they are not connected to the schema because it would make it quite difficult to read.

In this example, some pieces of the flow definition are missing, but all the classes needed to wrap up the flow are fully developed and ready to use. The flow execution require three flow model objects: a PersonObjectModel instance, an IdentityCard, and an Account instance. The Account class was not used until now because every notion presented was covered without any complex logic being necessary. The Account class contains four fields that are populated by the user.

- The IBAN[7] field is mandatory and is considered to be 10 to 30 characters long, all digits. An exception is thrown if the data introduced by the user does not match this restriction.

- The bank field is mandatory and a string representing a bank name is required.

- The status field represents the status of the account and is also mandatory.

- The amount field is the amount of money being held by the banking account; this field is not mandatory.

In the following list, they steps of the execution and resources are presented to you, in the order you have to use them in the newPerson-flow.xml definition:

- The enterPersonInfo view-state is the same as in the previous code sample; the initial state of the flow where a form is displayed to the user for basic personal information to be provided. All fields but middleName are mandatory and must be validated; the hospital drop-down list must be populated when the view-state is rendered. The event name that causes the transition to the next step is called next and the next state is called isNewPerson.

- The contents of the view-state definition are missing and must be implemented to behave as described previously. (TODO 41) After the implementation is done you should see the view as in Figure 7-19.

---

[7]See https://en.wikipedia.org/wiki/International_Bank_Account_Number.

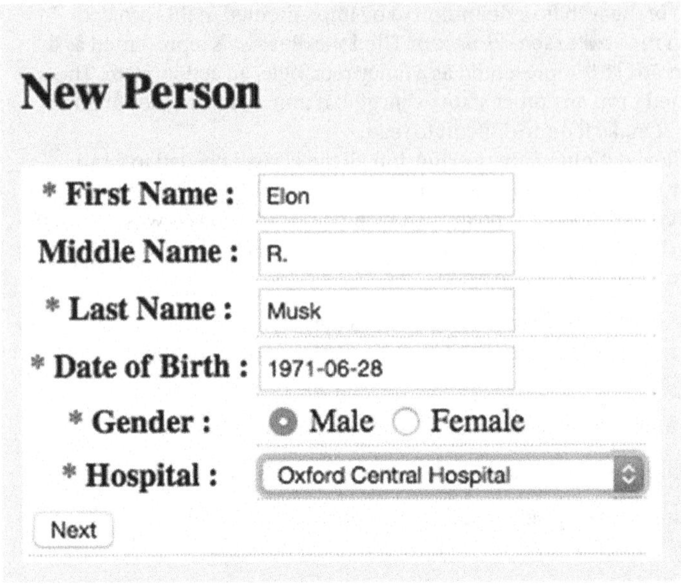

**Figure 7-19.**  *The enterPersonInfo view*

- The isNewPerson is a decision state using the result returned by calling the personService.isNewPerson(person) method as a condition. The method is defined in the com.pr.servicePersonService class, and a bean of this type named personService is already defined. If the evaluation returns true, transitioning is done to the enterIdentityCardInfo state, otherwise to the reviewExistingPerson state. To test the transition to the reviewExistingPerson state, insert a person born on October 1, 1935 at General Hospital.

  The content of this decision-state definition is missing and must be implemented to behave as described earlier. (TODO 42)

- The enterIdentityCardInfo is a view state that displays to the user a form requesting identification information: values for the fields in the identityCard object. All information is mandatory. The event to transition to the next state, confirmAdult, is called save. The transition is done after evaluation of the personBuilder.savePersonEntity(person, identityCard) method, and saving the result in flowScope.existingPerson, because this flow variable is later used to create an account.

- The content of this view-state definition is missing and must be implemented to behave as described earlier. (TODO 43) After the implementation is done you should see the view as in Figure 7-20.

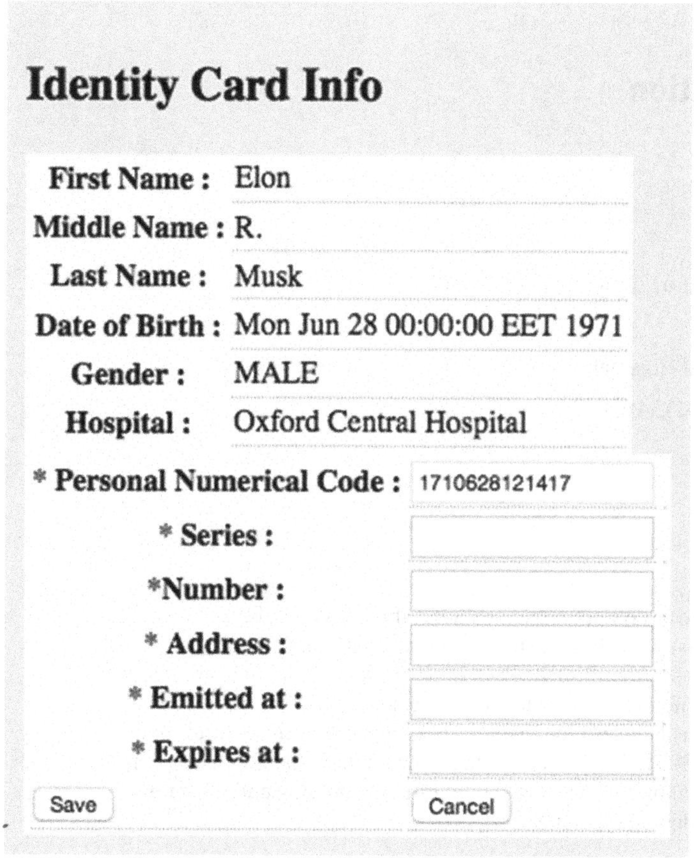

**Figure 7-20.** *The enterIdentityCardInfo view*

- The reviewExistingPerson is a view-state that displays the basic information of an existing person in the system, with the same personal numerical code as the Person instance that the user is trying to create. The data to populate the view is extracted at rendering time by calling personManager.getByPnc(person.pnc). The personManager id one of the data management beans presented in Chapter 2. It is defined in the 01-pr-service module project. The result of calling this method is saved in the flowScope.existingPerson, because this flow variable is later used to create an account. From this state, the user can transition to the confirmAdult state by using the event named continue.

- The content of this view-state definition is missing and must be implemented to behave as described earlier. (TODO 44) After the implementation is done you should see the view as in Figure 7-21.

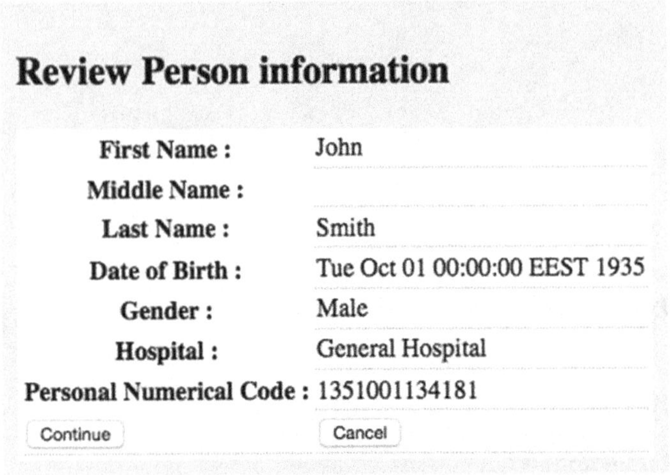

# Review Person information

| First Name : | John |
|---|---|
| Middle Name : | |
| Last Name : | Smith |
| Date of Birth : | Tue Oct 01 00:00:00 EEST 1935 |
| Gender : | Male |
| Hospital : | General Hospital |
| Personal Numerical Code : | 1351001134181 |

<kbd>Continue</kbd>  <kbd>Cancel</kbd>

*Figure 7-21.* *The reviewExistingPerson view*

- The confirmAdult state is an action-state that evaluates the personActions. isAdult expression. The class providing the implementation for this is com. pr.PersonActions; it is a class extending the MultiAction class presented earlier. On success, transition is done to the enterAccountInfo, and on error, transition is done to end, because obviously the Person instance does not represent an adult so a bank account cannot be added for this instance, thus this is where the flow execution ends. (TODO 45) The content of this action-state definition is missing and must be implemented to behave as described earlier.

- The enterAccountInfo is a view state that displays a form requesting minimum information for a bank account. The IBAN of the account must be unique in the system. If you want to test the validation for this field, just insert the value US13011012500000000012300695. Using the add event, if the information introduced is valid, a transition is done to the end state that displays the created person and banking information existing for it in the system.

- The content of this view-state definition is missing and must be implemented to behave as described earlier. (TODO 46) After the implementation is done you should see the view as in Figure 7-22.

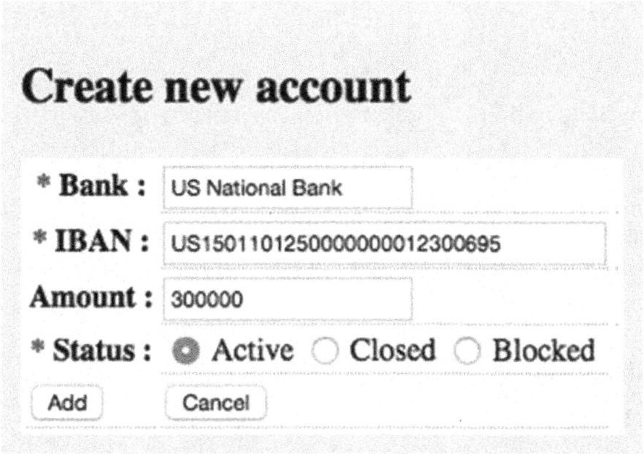

**Create new account**

| | |
|---|---|
| * **Bank :** | US National Bank |
| * **IBAN :** | US150110125000000000012300695 |
| **Amount :** | 300000 |
| * **Status :** | ● Active  ○ Closed  ○ Blocked |
| Add | Cancel |

*Figure 7-22.* *The enterAccountInfo view*

- error is a view-state used to display explicit content of the exceptions thrown in the application. It was implemented this way so that while resolving this exercise, you have a practical way to debug your problems, if you have any. In a real production application, the error view is simpler and more user-friendly.

- cancel is an end-state that the flow transitions into any time the user presses the Cancel button in any view.

- end is an end-state that redirects the user to a view with all the existing data for that person in the system.

- The <global-transaction /> element has two transition elements: one for the cancel scenario, when any the flow transitions to cancel, and one for any exception that is being thrown in the flow transition to the error state.

- When your implementation is correct and the data you inserted is valid, a new person should be created in the system and a new bank account should be added for it, and after the flow execution, you should be redirected to a view that displays the information, which looks similar to the one shown in Figure 7-23.

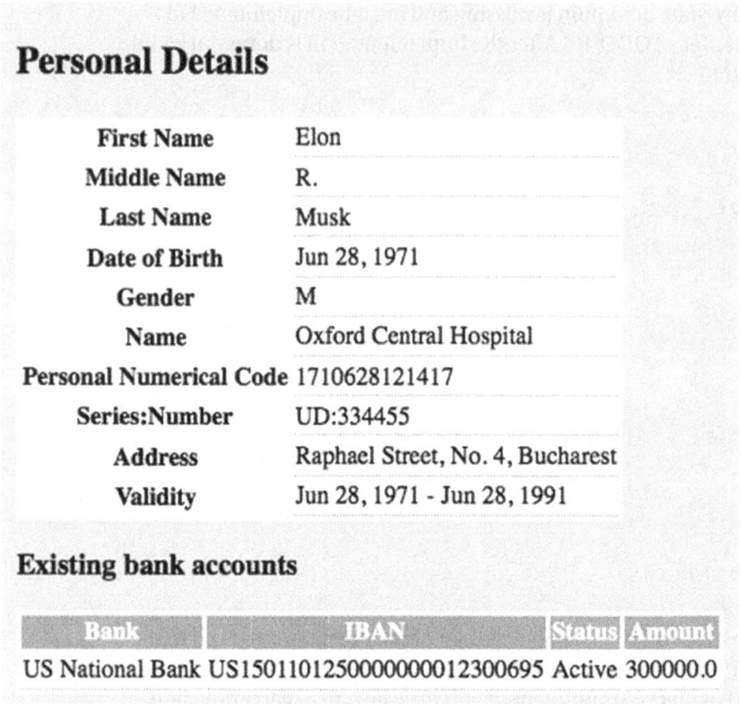

## Personal Details

| | |
|---|---|
| First Name | Elon |
| Middle Name | R. |
| Last Name | Musk |
| Date of Birth | Jun 28, 1971 |
| Gender | M |
| Name | Oxford Central Hospital |
| Personal Numerical Code | 1710628121417 |
| Series:Number | UD:334455 |
| Address | Raphael Street, No. 4, Bucharest |
| Validity | Jun 28, 1971 - Jun 28, 1991 |

### Existing bank accounts

| Bank | IBAN | Status | Amount |
|---|---|---|---|
| US National Bank | US15011012500000000012300695 | Active | 300000.0 |

*Figure 7-23.* *The view that the flow should redirect to after a successful execution*

## IMPORTANT OBSERVATIONS

The bind="false" attribute is needed, so the form is not validated before transitioning to the cancel state, as validation errors will prevent the transition.

```
<global-transitions>
    <transition on="cancel" to="cancel" bind="false" />
    <transition on-exception="java.lang.Exception" to="error" />
</global-transitions>
```

When using web flows, the exception handling is the most undocumented part of Spring Web Flow. Unless a web flow exception handler Is used, or action states that return error events and add the exception object to the flowScope, catching and treating exceptions is very tricky. Developers are basically forced into writing the code. That's why all web flow exceptions in this project cause a transition to the error view that uses JSP scriptlets to display a very detailed stacktrace that help developers reading this book to easily identify the mistakes in the code and configuration. The exception can be retrieved using the request. As mentioned, this view is only to be used for development purposes; for production, a more user-friendly view implementation should be used.

```
<!-- webapp/WEB-INF/error.jsp -->
<div class="error">
 <%
  Exception exception =
    (Exception) request.getAttribute("flowExecutionException");
  Exception cause =
    (Exception) request.getAttribute("rootCauseException");
 %>
...
 <%
   exception.printStackTrace(new java.io.PrintWriter(out));
 %>
...
 <% if (cause != null) { %>
  <h3>Cause: <%=cause.getMessage()%></h3>
   <p>
     <%
        cause.printStackTrace(new java.io.PrintWriter(out));
     %>
   </p>
   <%} %>
</div>
```

In case you insert data that is invalid, you can use the browser Back button to go back to the previous state and change the information. To prevent browsing back to a state previous to a transition with the Back button, the history attribute of the transaction element can be used:

```
<transition on="confirm" to="end" history="discard">
<!-- or invalidate all previous visited views in the browser history -->
<transition on="confirm" to="end" history="invalidate">
```

The default value for this attribute is preserve, which allows returning to a state before the execution of the transition and the data for the state is still accessible.

discard prevents backtracking to the state, meaning that all information related to the state is discarded and using the browser Back button results in a 500 HTTP internal server error.

invalidate prevents backtracking to the state, as well as any previously entered view-state, and pressing the browser Back button has the same effect as the previous case.

The proposed solution for this project can be found in the 12-pr-webflow-actions2-solution project.

# Subflows

A subflow is a flow that is being invoked by another flow. It has its own scope and the parent flow execution is suspended while the subflow is being executed. The conversation scope is the only scope that is shared between the parent flow and the subflows, as depicted in Figure 7-7. The subflow must be defined in the application in the same manner as any flow; it has its own views and language resources, because it is essentially a flow.

A subflow is launched from a special state in a parent flow called **subflow-state**. In the following example, the newPerson flow calls the newHospital subflow.

```
<!-- newPerson-flow.xml-->
<flow ...>
 <view-state id="enterPersonInfo" model="person">
     <binder>...</binder>
       <transition on="next" to="isNewPerson" />
       <transition on="addHospital" to="newHospital"/>
 </view-state>

 <subflow-state id="newHospital"
             subflow="hospitals/newHospital" >
         <output name="hospital"/>
       <transition on="saveHospital" to="enterPersonInfo">
         <evaluate expression="hospitalManager.save(hospital)"
                 result="flashScope.hospital" />
         <set name="flashScope.hospitalMessage"
                 value="hospital.msg.success" />
       </transition>
       <transition on="cancel" to="enterPersonInfo" />
   </subflow-state>
</flow>
```

The subflow in the previous example allows the user to insert a new Hospital instance in the system so that it can be used when the person is created, if the state transitioning into is saveHospital. The id of the subflow-state is the id of this state inside the newPerson flow definition. The subflow attribute is used to link this flow invocation with the flow definition, and contains the path inside the WEB-INF, where the flow definition and resources can be found. In the previous case, the flow definition file is located at /WEB-INF/ hospitals/newHospital/newHospital-flow.xml. Once registered with the FlowDefinitionRegistry, the subflow can be referred from any flow using its logical name, which is composed of the location and the flow name as a value for the subflow attribute:

```
\\WebFlowConfig.java
@Configuration
public class WebFlowConfig extends AbstractFlowConfiguration {
...

@Bean
public FlowDefinitionRegistry flowRegistry() {
  return getFlowDefinitionRegistryBuilder(flowBuilderServices())
      .setBasePath("/WEB-INF")
      .addFlowLocation("/persons/newPerson/newPerson-flow.xml")
      .addFlowLocation("/hospitals/newHospital/newHospital-flow.xml")
      .build();
      }
}
```

```
<subflow-state id="newHospital"
            subflow="hospitals/newHospital" >
<!-- hospitals = directory for Hospital specific resources -->
<!-- newHospital = flow name-->
```

The key values used for transitions inside the parent flow are the ids of end-states in the subflow:

```
<!-- newHospital-flow.xml-->
<flow ..>
    <var name="hospital" class="com.pr.ents.Hospital"/>

    <view-state id="enterHospitalInfo" model="hospital">
        <binder>
            <binding property="name" required="true"/>
            <binding property="code" required="true"/>
            <binding property="address"/>
            <binding property="location" required="true"/>
        </binder>
        <transition on="save" to="saveHospital"/>
        <transition on="cancel" to="cancel" bind="false" />
    </view-state>

    <end-state id="saveHospital">
        <output name="hospital" value="hospital"/>
    </end-state>

    <end-state id="cancel"/>

</flow>
```

The flashScope.hospitalMessage variable is used to display a message telling the user that the Hospital instance was saved correctly and can be used.

Although the conversation scope is accessible to the parent flow and subflows, global variables usage is discouraged, because it reduces the readability of the code, so that passing parameters between the parent flow and the subflow is more appropriate.

The <output name="hospital"/> is an output parameter designed to return the Hospital instance created by the newHospital flow to the parent flow; it is assigned the flashScope (see the evaluate element marked with (1) in the following code snippet).

There are also input parameters, required or not, to provide a parent flow variable value to the subflow. In the previous case, there is nothing needed, but assuming that you would need to send a Person instance as a manager for the hospital we are trying to create, the preceding definitions will change a little. The instance given as parameter has the flowScope in both of the flows because it is defined right under the <flow /> element.

```
<!-- newPerson-flow.xml-->
 <flow ...>
 <var name="person" class="com.pr.ents.Person"/>

  <view-state id="enterPersonInfo" model="person">
      <binder>...</binder>
        <transition on="next" to="isNewPerson" />
       <transition on="addHospital" to="newHospital"/>
  </view-state>

  <subflow-state id="newHospital"
              subflow="hospitals/newHospital" >
          <input name="manager" value="person"/>
          <output name="hospital"/>

        <transition on="saveHospital" to="enterPersonInfo">
          (1) <evaluate expression="hospitalManager.save(hospital)"
                 result="flashScope.hospital" />
            <set name="flashScope.hospitalMessage"
                value="hospital.msg.success" />
        </transition>
        <transition on="cancel" to="enterPersonInfo" />
    </subflow-state>
 </flow>

<!-- newHospital-flow.xml-->
 <flow ...>

   <input name="manager" required="true"/>
   <var name="hospital" class="com.pr.ents.Hospital"/>

   <view-state id="enterHospitalInfo" model="hospital">
   ...
   </view-state>

 </flow>
```

When subflows are involved, unit testing is quite tricky; that's why it is recommended to mock or stub them when the focus of the testing is on the parent flow. By overriding the configureFlowBuilderContext method from AbstractXmlFlowExecutionTests, a mock definition for the subflow can be added to the context:

```
import org.springframework.webflow.test.execution.AbstractXmlFlowExecutionTests;

public class NewPersonFlowTest extends AbstractXmlFlowExecutionTests {
...
@Override
    protected void configureFlowBuilderContext
            (MockFlowBuilderContext builderContext) {
```

```
    // setup newHospital subflow
    Flow newHospital = new Flow("newHospital");
    State start = new State(newHospital, "newHospital") {
        @Override
        protected void doEnter(RequestControlContext context)
                throws FlowExecutionException {
            // empty
        }
    };
    newHospital.setStartState(start);
    builderContext.registerSubflow(newHospital);
}
...
}
```

Unfortunately, even as this book is being written, testing subflows is still cumbersome and there are a lot of bugs opened and unresolved.[8]

When the scope is to test the subflows too, the getModelResources method of AbstractXmlFlowExecutionTests must be overridden. Add the subflow definition to the flow resources being tested:

```
import org.springframework.webflow.engine.Flow;
import org.springframework.webflow.test.MockExternalContext;
import org.springframework.webflow.test.MockFlowBuilderContext;
import org.springframework.webflow.test.execution.AbstractXmlFlowExecutionTests;

 public class NewPersonFlowTest extends AbstractXmlFlowExecutionTests {
...
  @Override
    protected FlowDefinitionResource
    getModelResources(FlowDefinitionResourceFactory resourceFactory) {
        FlowDefinitionResource flowDefinitionResources =
                new FlowDefinitionResource2;
        flowDefinitionResources0 = resourceFactory.createResource
                ("src/main/webapp/WEB-INF/persons/newPerson/newPerson-flow.xml");
        flowDefinitionResources1 = resourceFactory.createResource
                ("src/main/webapp/WEB-INF/hospitals/newHospital/newHospital-flow.xml");
        return flowDefinitionResources;
    }
    ...
}
```

---

[8]A bug related to mocking subflows; still open and unresolved since version 2.0.6. See
https://jira.spring.io/browse/SWF-1079.

■ ! Considering that the subflows are not a topic for the exam, there is no practice project with configurations missing, but a project was created that you can run and inspect to see the subflow to add a `Hospital` instance running:

`13-pr-webflow-subflow-solution.`

■ ? As a proposed exercise, if you want to test your understanding of subflows, you can try to turn the creating of an `Account` instance into a subflow.

# Flow Definition Inheritance

Flow definitions can be organized in hierarchies in a way similar way to bean definitions. Organizing them in hierarchies allows global transitions, common states, and actions to be shared among parent and children flows.

The child flow and the parent flow are both registered in the same flow registry.

There are a few things regarding flow definition inheritance that are interesting and worth covering. One of them is that multiple inheritance is supported, because inheritance between web flow definitions is more like a composition; basically, a child flow definition inherits all configuration elements form its parents, and elements with the same id are merged. Multiple parents are specified using comma as a separator:

```
<flow ... parent="parentFlow1, parentFlow2" />
 ...
</flow>
```

Parent flow definitions can also be abstract. In this case, these flows cannot be instantiated and executed; their purpose in the code is to wrap up common definition elements for multiple child flow definitions, to respect the DRY principle.[9]

```
<flow ... abstract="true" />
 ...
</flow>
```

Flow inheritance is analogous to bean definition inheritance. It is more a composition than inheritance, as parent and child are merged together to create a new flow.

Another interesting thing is that flow definition inheritance can be selective, meaning there is a way that only certain state definitions can be inherited, instead of the whole parent flow definition:

```
<flow ... parent="parentFlowName"/>
        <view-state id="childState" parent="parentFlowName#stateId">
</flow>
```

The restriction here is that the child flow can inherit only from one parent when restrictions are defined at the state level. Also, the child state definition type must be one and the same with the parent state definition. In the preceding example, the state element with `stateId` must be of type view-state in the parent too; otherwise, the web flow configuration is invalid.

---

[9]**D**on't **R**epeat **Y**ourself.

# Securing Web Flows

Before talking about how to secure web flows, a detailed introduction into Spring Security is necessary, because you need to understand core security concepts and how they can be configured with Spring Security.

## Introduction to Spring Security

Spring Security is a framework that can be used to secure web applications. It is very easy to use and highly customizable, providing access control over units of an application. When writing secure Spring web applications, this is the default tool that developers go to because configuration follows the same standard with all the Spring projects. Infrastructure beans are provided out of the box for multiple types of authentication and they are clearly compatible with other Spring projects. Spring Security provides a wide set of capabilities that can be grouped in four areas of interest: authentication, authorizing web requests, authorizing methods calls, and authorizing access to individual domain objects.

The following are Spring Security's core features:

- **Authentication** (user identification) and **authorization** (managing access to resources); comprehensible and extensible support is provided.

- It is easy to configure.

- It is highly customizable.

- Protection against session fixation, clickjacking, cross-site request forgery, and other type of attacks is provided via simple and flexible configurations.

- It can be integrated with the Servlet API.

Of course, there are more. You can read more about them on the official page of this project.[10]

There are five security concepts that you have to familiarize yourself with and understand to use Spring Security:

- **Credentials** are identification keys that an entity presents to the application to confirm their identity( a password or a token).

- **Principal** represents an authenticated entity that was recognized by the application based on its credentials.

- **Authentication** is the process that determines if the credentials of an entity are valid.

- **Authorization** is the process that determines if a principal is allowed access to a resource or performs a certain action. The decision process is often based on roles. The following are the most common roles:

  - GUEST, usually can just view data

  - MEMBER (or USER), can insert data

  - ADMIN, can insert and delete data

- **Secured item** is a resource that is being secured.

---

[10]Spring Security page at http://spring.io/spring-security.

The Spring Security version used in the book is 4.0.2.RELEASE and it is compatible with Spring 4. In the Gradle configuration of the 14-pr-web-security-practice module project, notice that the following libraries have been added:

```
springSecurityVersion = '4.0.2.RELEASE'
...
securityConfig : "org.springframework.security:spring-security-config:
                                $springSecurityVersion",
securityWeb    : "org.springframework.security:spring-security-web:
                                $springSecurityVersion",
securityTaglibs: "org.springframework.security:spring-security-taglibs:
                                $springSecurityVersion",
...
}
```

# Why Spring Security Is Awesome

The spring-security-config module provides security namespace parsing code and is needed when using XML configuration. As some developers still prefer to use XML configuration, the minimum configuration needed in XML is explained in the book alongside the Java Configuration. The spring-security-web provides filters and related web-security infrastructure beans. This library is needed for web-based authentication. The spring-security-taglibs provides security tags that can be used to secure elements in JSP pages.

The main reason why Spring Security is preferred when developing web applications is **portability**. Spring Security does not need a special container to run in; it can be deployed as a secured archive (WAR or EAR) and can run in stand-alone environments. For example, a secured web application archived as a WAR can be deployed on a JBoss or an Apache Tomcat application server. And as long as the underlying method of storing credentials is configured, the application will run exactly the same in any of these application servers.

When it comes to authentication and credential storage, Spring Security is very flexible. All common authentication mechanisms are supported (Basic, Form, OAuth, X.509, cookies, single sign-on). Regarding support storage for credentials databases, Spring Security supports anything—LDAP, properties file, custom DAOs, and even beans, among many others.[11]

Configuring Spring Security is easy. A common practice is to define a separate file when using XML and a separate configuration class when using Java Configuration. Infrastructure beans can be used to customize the following:

- How a principal is defined

- Where authentication information is stored

- How authorization decisions are made

- Where security constraints are stored

As we have seen so far when using Spring, anything can be done by keeping components as decoupled as possible. Spring Security respects the principle of **separation of concerns** (SoC). Restrictions are applied using an interceptor-based approach. It was mentioned at the beginning of the book that AOP is used when securing resources. Also, authentication and authorization are decoupled; changing the authentication method and credentials support does not affect authorization.

---

[11]A full list of authentication technologies that Spring Security integrates with; it can be found at http://docs.spring.io/spring-security/site/docs/current/reference/htmlsingle/#what-is-acegi-security.

Spring Security is consistent. The authentication purpose is to create a security context with the principal's information; it does not depend on the mechanism used. The authorization process has the same purpose, regardless of the resource type: consult resource properties, consult the principal's role, and decide to grant or deny access.

The way Spring Security works and the core components are depicted in Figure 7-24.

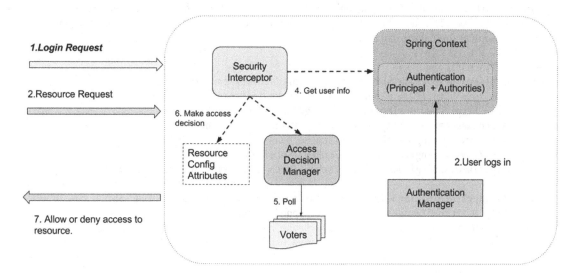

***Figure 7-24.*** *Spring Security anatomy*

The following explains the flow described in Figure 7-24:

1. The user makes a login request. (Introduces credentials in a login form and submits it.)

2. The user logs into the application and the **Authentication Manager** populates the security information of the user into the security context.

3. When the user makes resource requests (requests to view a page, starts a flow, requests a document) after logging in, the security interceptor intercepts them before they invoke a protected/secured resource.

4. The Security Interceptor then retrieves the user information from the context.

5. The **Access Decision Manager** polls a list of voters to return a decision regarding the rights the authenticated user has on system resources

6. The Spring Interceptor consults the resource attributes that are configured in the application.

7. Access is granted or denied to the resource based on the user rights (5) and the resource attributes (6).

# Spring Security XML Configuration

When using XML to configure Spring Security, any tag can be used by adding the security namespace to the Spring configuration file at http://www.springframework.org/schema/security/spring-security.xsd. The recommended practice is to have a separate configuration file that contains only the security-related configurations.

To log in to the Personal Records Manager application, a separate file should be created, named security-config.xml. This file should define the users and credentials needed to access the application and which resources these users can access:

```
<!-- security-config.xml -->
<beans xmlns:sec="http://www.springframework.org/schema/security"
      xmlns:xsi="http://www.w3.org/2001/XMLSchema-instance"
      xmlns="http://www.springframework.org/schema/beans"
      xsi:schemaLocation="http://www.springframework.org/schema/beans
       http://www.springframework.org/schema/beans/spring-beans.xsd
       http://www.springframework.org/schema/security
       http://www.springframework.org/schema/security/spring-security.xsd">

    <!-- styling&internationalization resources do not need to be secured -->
    <sec:http pattern="/images/*" security="none"/>
    <sec:http pattern="/styles/*" security="none"/>
    <sec:http pattern="/resources/*" security="none"/>

    <sec:http auto-config="true">
        <sec:intercept-url pattern="/auth*" access="permitAll"/>
        <sec:intercept-url pattern="/persons/newPerson"
                        access="ROLE_ADMIN"/>
        <sec:intercept-url pattern="/**"
                        access="ROLE_USER, ROLE_ADMIN"/>
        <sec:form-login login-page="/auth"
                        authentication-failure-url="/auth?auth_error=1"
                        default-target-url="/"/>
        <sec:logout logout-url="/j_spring_security_logout"
            logout-success-url="/home />
    </sec:http>

    <sec:authentication-manager>
        <sec:authentication-provider>
            <sec:user-service>
                <sec:user name="john" password="doe"
                        authorities="ROLE_USER"/>
                <sec:user name="jane" password="doe"
                        authorities="ROLE_USER,ROLE_ADMIN"/>
                <sec:user name="admin" password="admin"
                        authorities="ROLE_ADMIN"/>
            </sec:user-service>
        </sec:authentication-provider>
    </sec:authentication-manager>
</beans>
```

The configuration presented earlier uses basic authentication, without any password encryption. The `auto-config="true"` is a legacy attribute that automatically registers a login form, BASIC authentication, and a logout URL and logout services. It is not meant to be used for production applications, as the level of security required is higher than the default one provided by Spring Security out of the box for educational purposes.

The `<intercept-url />` elements are evaluated in the order they are listed into the configuration, so the most restrictive ones need to be at the top of the list; otherwise, the result might not be the expected one.

Three users are defined with different roles. Access to the `newPerson` flow has been restricted to users having the `ROLE_ADMIN` role, to test the configuration. This file is Spring Security 3.0-specific and it won't work in a Spring Security 4 environment, because this version has introduced a lot of changes.

The `<sec:logout />` logout element is used to customize logout details. The `logout-url` attribute specifies the URL that will cause a logout. Spring Security initializes a filter that responds to this particular URL. The `logout-success-url` attribute is used to define where the user is redirected after logging out.

In the `<sec:form-login />` the URL of the page used for authentication is set as a value for the `login-page` attribute. After successfully logging in, the user is redirected to the page set as a value for the `default-target-url` attribute. In case of failure, the user is redirected to the login view, and using the `auth_error` parameter, a proper value is displayed to the user. The `auth.jsp` template file presents to the user a login form looks like this for Spring Security 3:

```
<!-- auth.jsp -->
<form action="<c:url value='/j_spring_security_check'/>" method="post">
    <table>
        <tr>
            <td>
                <label for="j_username">
                  <spring:message code="login.username"/>
                </label>
            </td>
            <td>
                <input type='text' id='j_username' name='j_username'
                    value='<c:out value="${user}"/>'/>
            </td>
        </tr>
        <tr>
            <td>
                <label for="j_password">
                    <spring:message code="login.password"/>
                </label>
            </td>
             <td><input type='j_password' id='password'
                    name='j_password'/></td>
        </tr>
        <tr>
            <td colspan="2">
                <button type="submit">
                    <spring:message code="login.submit"/>
                </button>
            </td>
        </tr>
    </table>
    <c:if test="${not empty param.auth_error}">
```

```
        <div id="errors" class="error">
<!-- detailed security exception message is printed for development purposes -->
<!-- obviously, not recommended to be used in a production application -->
            <p><spring:message code="login.fail"/>:
                ${SPRING_SECURITY_LAST_EXCEPTION.message}
            </p>
        </div>
    </c:if>
</form>
```

There is another way to specify access by using Spring Security Expressions, but they must be enabled by declaring the use-expressions="true" attribute on the <sec:http /> configuration element. So, the access attributes under the <sec:http /> configuration element become this:

```
<sec:http auto-config="true" use-expressions="true">
    <sec:intercept-url pattern="/auth*" access="permitAll"/>
     <sec:intercept-url pattern="/persons/newPerson"
            access="hasRole('ROLE_ADMIN')"/>
    <sec:intercept-url pattern="/**"
            access="hasAnyRole('ROLE_USER, ROLE_ADMIN')"/>
    <sec:form-login login-page="/auth"
            authentication-failure-url="/auth?auth_error=1"
            default-target-url="/"/>
    <sec:logout logout-url="/j_spring_security_logout"/>
</sec:http>
```

---

■ !   Mixing expression style configuration with direct configuration is not permitted. You either use expressions or you don't. Mixing them will make your configuration file invalid.

---

Spring Security Expressions are quite easy to use and understand:

- hasRole('role') checks whether the principal has the given role.

- hasAnyRole('role1', 'role2', ?) checks whether the principal has any of the given roles.

- isAuthenticated() allows access for authenticated or remembered principals.

- permitAll allows unauthenticated users access to a resource. In the previous example, this is used to make sure that the login form is accessible so a user can insert his credentials for authentication to take place.

- Expressions can be aggregated hasRole('ROLE_ADMIN') and hasRole('ROLE_MANAGER').

The preceding configuration is relative to the beans namespace. Considering that the configuration file contains only security tags, the file could be created relative to the security namespace, and so the **sec** prefix would not be necessary, which makes the file more readable:

```xml
<?xml version="1.0" encoding="UTF-8"?>
<beans:beans xmlns="http://www.springframework.org/schema/security"
             xmlns:xsi="http://www.w3.org/2001/XMLSchema-instance"
             xmlns:beans="http://www.springframework.org/schema/beans"
             xsi:schemaLocation="http://www.springframework.org/schema/security
             http://www.springframework.org/schema/security/spring-security.xsd
                http://www.springframework.org/schema/beans
                http://www.springframework.org/schema/beans/spring-beans.xsd">

    <http pattern="/images/*" security="none"/>
    <http pattern="/styles/*" security="none"/>
    <http pattern="/resources/*" security="none"/>

    <http auto-config="true" use-expressions="true">
        <intercept-url pattern="/auth*" access="permitAll"/>
        <intercept-url pattern="/persons/newPerson"
            access="hasRole('ROLE_ADMIN')"/>
        <intercept-url pattern="/**"
            access="hasAnyRole('ROLE_USER, ROLE_ADMIN')"/>
        <form-login login-page="/auth"
            authentication-failure-url="/auth?auth_error=1"
                    default-target-url="/"/>
        <logout logout-url="/j_spring_security_logout"/>
    </http>

    <authentication-manager>
        <authentication-provider>
            <user-service>
                <user name="john" password="doe" authorities="ROLE_USER"/>
                <user name="jane" password="doe"
                        authorities="ROLE_USER,ROLE_ADMIN"/>
                <user name="admin" password="admin" authorities="ROLE_ADMIN"/>
            </user-service>
        </authentication-provider>
    </authentication-manager>
</beans:beans>
```

Spring Security 4 has introduced a few critical changes that need coverage in this book; because by the time this book is published, Spring Security 4 might be a subject on the exam.

■ !   Spring Security 4 has introduced the possibility of using CSFR tokens in Spring forms to prevent cross-site request forgery.[12] A configuration without a `<csrf />` element configuration is invalid, and any login requests direct you to a 403 error page stating:

```
Invalid CSRF Token 'null' was found on the request parameter
'_csrf' or header 'X-CSRF-TOKEN'.
```

To migrate from Spring Security 3 to version 4, you have to add a configuration for that element, even if all you do is disable using CSRF tokens.

```
<http auto-config="true" use-expressions="true">
    <csrf disabled="true"/>
    <intercept-url pattern="/auth*" access="permitAll"/>
    <intercept-url pattern="/persons/newPerson" access="hasRole('ADMIN')"/>
    <intercept-url pattern="/**" access="hasAnyRole('USER, ADMIN')"/>
    <form-login login-page="/auth"
                authentication-failure-url="/auth?auth_error=1"
                default-target-url="/"/>
    <logout logout-url="/logout"
                delete-cookies="JSESSIONID"
                logout-success-url="/"/>
</http>
```

The `delete-cookies` attribute can be used to specify a list of cookies to delete at logout time. In the previous configuration, only one is specified, named JSESSIONID; but if the application uses more cookies, they can be specified as a value for this attribute using their names separated by commas.

---

[12]This type of attack consists of hacking an existing session to execute unauthorized commands in a web application. You can read more about it at `https://en.wikipedia.org/wiki/Cross-site_request_forgery`.

■ ! Other critical changes are related to the login form **default** Spring resources, such as the login URL (that indicates an authentication request) and names of the request parameters (expected keys for generation of an authentication token).[13] These were changed to match JavaConfig. The login form in the `auth.jsp` view became the following:

```
<form action="<c:url value='/login'/>" method="post">
  <table>
    <tr>
      <td>
       <label for="username">
        <spring:message code="login.username"/>
       </label>
       </td>
      <td>
       <input type='text' id='username' name='username'
         value='<c:out value="${user}"/>'/>
      </td>
    </tr>
    <tr>
      <td>
        <label for="password">
          <spring:message code="login.password"/>
        </label>
      </td>
      <td><input type='password' id='password' name='password'/></td>
    </tr>
    <tr>
      <td colspan="2">
        <button type="submit">
          <spring:message code="login.submit"/>
        </button>
      </td>
    </tr>
  </table>
</form>
```

[13]The full list of configuration changes that were made to match Java Configuration is at https://jira.spring.io/browse/SEC-2783.

■ !  All previous examples used default values for the login URL and the authentication key names *j_spring_security_check, j_username, j_password* (in Spring Security 3), *login, username, password* (in Spring Security 4). Keep in mind that all of them can be redefined using Spring configuration.

If you are interested in keeping your form as secure as possible, you can configure CSRF usage and add the token generated by Spring to your form. The following are the required modifications:

- First you must enable CSRF generation in your security-config.xml file by adding a <csrf /> configuration element and a repository to generate the value for it. Modify the logout element appropriately; the third bullet in this list tells you why.

```
<beans:beans .../>
  <beans:bean id="tokenRepo"
class="org.springframework.security.web.csrf.HttpSessionCsrfTokenRepository">
      <beans:property name="sessionAttributeName" value="_csrf"/>
  </beans:bean>

  <http auto-config="true" use-expressions="true">
      <csrf token-repository-ref="tokenRepo"/>
      <intercept-url pattern="/auth*" access="permitAll"/>
      <intercept-url pattern="/persons/newPerson" access="hasRole('ADMIN')"/>
      <intercept-url pattern="/**" access="hasAnyRole('USER, ADMIN')"/>
      <form-login login-page="/auth"
          authentication-failure-url="/auth?auth_error=1"
                    default-target-url="/"/>
      <logout logout-url="/logout"
      delete-cookies="JSESSIONID"
      invalidate-session="true"
      logout-success-url="/"/>
  </http>
  ...
</beans:beans>
```

- Second, you must add a hidden parameter in every form that you are interested in protecting form cross-site request forgery.

```
<form action="<c:url value='/login'/>" method="post">
<input type="hidden"
    name="${_csrf.parameterName}" value="${_csrf.token}"/>
<table>
    <tr>
        <td>
          <label for="username">
            <spring:message code="login.username"/>
          </label>
            </td>
        <td>
          <input type='text' id='username' name='username'
              value='<c:out value="${user}"/>'/>
        </td>
```

```
        </tr>
        <tr>
            <td>
                <label for="password">
                    <spring:message code="login.password"/>
                </label>
            </td>
            <td><input type='password' id='password' name='password'/></td>
        </tr>
        <tr>
            <td colspan="2">
                <button type="submit">
                    <spring:message code="login.submit"/>
                </button>
            </td>
        </tr>
    </table>
</form>
```

- And last, logging out becomes a pain when CSRF is enabled, because you need to log out using a POST request. Thus, you cannot just use a link build like this (like in Spring Security 3):

```
<a href="<spring:url value="/j_spring_security_logout"/>">
    <spring:message code="menu.logout"/>
</a>
```

You need to add a logout form to the page and submit it using JavaScript:

```
<spring:url value="/logout" var="logoutUrl" />
    <form action="${logoutUrl}" id="logout" method="post">
        <input type="hidden" name="${_csrf.parameterName}"
            value="${_csrf.token}"/>
    </form>
<a href="#" onclick="document.getElementById('logout').submit();">
    <spring:message code="menu.logout"/>
</a>
```

Also, as we've been mentioning logout, you probably noticed the extra attributes of the `<logout />` element; their names are quite obvious, and if specified at logout, the specific resources are cleaned accordingly:

```
<logout logout-url="/logout"
            delete-cookies="JSESSIONID"
            invalidate-session="true"
            logout-success-url="/"/>
```

Also, a handler can be used instead of the `logout-success-url` that takes care of redirecting to the proper page and eventually cleaning up any resources:

```
<logout logout-url="/logout"
                delete-cookies="JSESSIONID"
                success-handler-ref="logoutSuccessHandler"/>
```

To view the token Spring Security has generated, you can use Firebug to view the contents of your login request. You should see something similar to what is depicted in Figure 7-25.

***Figure 7-25.*** *Spring Security CSRF token*

■ !    Another simplification change that can be done to this file is provided by a new feature introduced in Spring Security 4 that allows access expressions to be specified without the `ROLE_` prefix in front of them; thus, the preceding configuration becomes this:

```
<http auto-config="true" use-expressions="true">
  <csrf disabled="true"/>
  <intercept-url pattern="/auth*" access="permitAll"/>
  <intercept-url pattern="/persons/newPerson" access="hasRole('ADMIN')"/>
  <intercept-url pattern="/**" access="hasAnyRole('USER, ADMIN')"/>
    <form-login login-page="/auth" authentication-failure-url="/auth?auth_error=1"
            default-target-url="/"/>
    <logout logout-url="/j_spring_security_logout"/>
</http>
```

```
<authentication-manager>
  <authentication-provider>
    <user-service>
      <user name="john" password="doe" authorities="ROLE_USER"/>
      <user name="jane" password="doe" authorities="ROLE_USER,ROLE_ADMIN"/>
      <user name="admin" password="admin" authorities="ROLE_ADMIN"/>
    </user-service>
  </authentication-provider>
</authentication-manager>
```

Another part of configuration needs to be added in the web.xml file, if used. A security filter needs to be added to intercept all requests to the application. springSecurityFilterChain is a mandatory name and refers to an infrastructure bean with the same name. This bean is responsible for all the security within the application (protecting the application URLs, validating submitted usernames and passwords, redirecting to the log in form, etc.).

```
<filter>
        <filter-name>springSecurityFilterChain</filter-name>
        <filter-class>
            org.springframework.web.filter.DelegatingFilterProxy
        </filter-class>
    </filter>
    <filter-mapping>
        <filter-name>springSecurityFilterChain</filter-name>
        <url-pattern>/*</url-pattern>
    </filter-mapping>
```

## Configure Authentication

It was mentioned that authentication can be configured to work with almost any credential support technology. In this subsection, a few of them are covered. By default, in Spring Security the DAO authentication provider is used, as well as a specific UserDetailsService implementation to provide credentials and authorities. In the examples so far, the credentials were basically read from the configuration file and stored into memory. The credentials were not encrypted, so even if Spring Security is used, the application is not that secure. To encrypt credentials, the configuration must be modified to specify the encryption type:

```
<!-- spring-config.xml -->
<authentication-manager>
    <authentication-provider>
        <password-encoder hash="md5" >
                <salt-source system-wide="MySalt"/>
        </password-encoder>
        <user-service properties="/WEB-INF/users.properties" />
    </authentication-provider>
</authentication-manager>
```

```
#/WEB-INF/users.properties
john=a1c093d7a2742f0afef7720883a59016,ROLE_USER
#password: john

jane=a1c093d7a2742f0afef7720883a59016,ROLE_USER,ROLE_ADMIN
#password: jane

admin=5a693853b2958ecb256db46b808ac488,ROLE_ADMIN
#password: admin
```

In the preceding configuration, the md5[14] algorithm is used to encrypt the passwords and a method called password-salting is used to increase the security passwords by adding a well-known string to them. The string added to the password can be an application-wide string, like in the previous example where the String is "MySalt", or it can be a property of the entity—something that won't change, like its unique identifier in the system, for example. A combination of properties can be used as salt too, but all the properties must be constant for the duration of the entity; if any of the property values changes, the user won't be able to log in anymore because the authentication system won't be able to create the correct hash.

The preceding encrypted strings were generated using an instance of org.springframework.security. authentication.encoding.Md5PasswordEncoder:

```
import org.springframework.security.authentication.encoding.Md5PasswordEncoder;
public class PasswordGenerator {

    public static void main(String args) {
        Md5PasswordEncoder encoder = new Md5PasswordEncoder();
        String encrypted = encoder.encodePassword("doe", "MySalt");
        System.out.println(encrypted);
        encrypted = encoder.encodePassword("admin", "MySalt");
        System.out.println(encrypted);
    }
}
```

To use an entity property as salt, the previous configuration must be modified like this:

```
<authentication-manager>
    <authentication-provider>
        <password-encoder hash="md5">
            <salt-source user-property="id" />
        </password-encoder>
    </authentication-provider>
</authentication-manager>
```

The credentials were decoupled from the configuration by isolating them in a property file, which can be easily edited without needing to recompile the application. The credentials property file has a specific syntax:

```
[username] = [password(encrypted)]],[role1,role2...]
```

---

[14]Read more about MD5 at https://en.wikipedia.org/wiki/MD5.

But credentials in memory storage is not a solution for production applications; this is only suitable for very small and educational applications. For production application, the most common storage for credentials is a database. To provide these credentials to the authentication manager, a data source is needed:

```
<authentication-manager>
  <authentication-provider>
        <jdbc-user-service data-source-ref="authDataSource" />
    </provider>
</authentication-manager>
```

Two tables must be accessible using the authDataSource: one named users containing user credentials and one named authorities continuing user-role correspondences. The following queries are run by the authentication provider and must execute successfully:

```
SELECT username, password, enabled FROM users WHERE username = ?
SELECT username, authority FROM authorities WHERE username = ?
```

Another way to provide credentials is to write a custom implementation for an authentication provider:

```
  <authentication-manager>
    <authentication-provider user-service-ref="customCredentialsProvider" />
</authentication-manager>
```

The provider class can delegate to a DAO implementation to retrieve principals from a database using a data source and customized queries. The information is returned into a format recognized in the application. In the following example, an instance of type UserInfo is used as a principal in the application:

```
[commandchars=*
@Repository
public class CustomCredentialsProvider {
    private JdbcTemplate jdbcTemplate;
    @Autowired
    public void setDataSource(DataSource dataSource) {
        this.jdbcTemplate = new JdbcTemplate(dataSource);
    }

    public UserInfo getUserInfo(String username){
            String sql = "SELECT u.username name, u.password pass,"+
                    a.authority role FROM "+
                    "users u INNER JOIN authorities a" +
                    on u.username=a.username WHERE "+
                    "u.enabled =1 and u.username = ?";
            UserInfo userInfo =
            (UserInfo)jdbcTemplate.queryForObject(sql, new Object{username},
                    new RowMapper<UserInfo>() {
                    public UserInfo mapRow(ResultSet rs, int rowNum)
                      throws SQLException {
                        UserInfo user = new UserInfo();
                        user.setUsername(rs.getString("name"));
                        user.setPassword(rs.getString("pass"));
```

```
                        user.setRole(rs.getString("role"));
                        return user;
                    }
        });
            return userInfo;
    }
}
//UserInfo.java
public class UserInfo {
        private String username;
        private String password;
        private String role;
        //setter and getters for fields
}
```

## No web.xml Configuration

As the official documentation says, if Spring Security is used with Spring MVC, you
need an extra empty class that extends org.springframework.security.web.context.
AbstractSecurityWebApplicationInitializer, a class provided by Spring Security that ensures that
the springSecurityFilterChain gets registered. Also, you need to include the Spring Security XML
configuration file in the Java Configuration, as depicted in the following code sample:

```
import org.springframework.security.web.context.
        AbstractSecurityWebApplicationInitializer;
// Empty class needed to register the springSecurityFilterChain bean
public class SecurityInitializer extends AbstractSecurityWebApplicationInitializer {
}
public class WebInitializer extends AbstractDispatcherServletInitializer {

    @Override
    protected WebApplicationContext createRootApplicationContext() {
        XmlWebApplicationContext ctx = new XmlWebApplicationContext();
        ctx.setConfigLocation("/WEB-INF/spring/security-config.xml");
        return ctx;
    }

    @Override
    protected WebApplicationContext createServletApplicationContext() {
        XmlWebApplicationContext ctx = new XmlWebApplicationContext();
        ctx.setConfigLocations("/WEB-INF/spring/mvc-config.xml",
                "/WEB-INF/spring/app-config.xml",
                "/WEB-INF/spring/webflow-config.xml");
        return ctx;
    }
    ...
}
```

But as Java Configuration and web initializer classes were introduced to simplify configuration and get
rid of all XML, all the preceding configurations will soon be deprecated.

# Spring Security Java Configuration

The XML configuration style is close to its death, as Java Configuration gains popularity. So it was expected that Spring Security adapt, and they did. The Java Configuration is super-simple and intuitive. When working with Spring MVC and Spring Security to develop a working security configuration, you need to do the following:

1. Create an empty class extending AbstractSecurityWebApplicationInitializer to get the springSecurityFilterChain registered (as mentioned at the end of the previous section).

2. Create a security configuration class that extends WebSecurityConfigurerAdapter so that the developer can write the minimum amount of code for a valid security configuration. The security configuration class equivalent to the XML configuration presented in the previous section is depicted in following code snippet:

```
package com.pr.config;
...
import org.springframework.beans.factory.annotation.Autowired;
import org.springframework.context.annotation.Configuration;
import org.springframework.security.config.annotation
        .authentication.builders.AuthenticationManagerBuilder;
import org.springframework.security.config.annotation
        .web.builders.HttpSecurity;
import org.springframework.security.config.annotation
        .web.configuration.EnableWebSecurity;
import org.springframework.security.config.annotation
        .web.configuration.WebSecurityConfigurerAdapter;


@Configuration
@EnableWebSecurity
public class SecurityConfig extends WebSecurityConfigurerAdapter {

        @Autowired
        public void configureGlobal(AuthenticationManagerBuilder auth) {
            try {
                auth.inMemoryAuthentication()
                        .withUser("john").password("doe").roles("USER").and()
                        .withUser("jane").password("doe").roles("USER,ADMIN").and()
                        .withUser("admin").password("admin").roles("ADMIN");
            } catch (Exception e) {
                e.printStackTrace();
            }
        }
        @Override
        protected void configure(HttpSecurity http) throws Exception {
            http
                    .authorizeRequests()
                    .antMatchers("/resources/**","/images/**","/styles/**")
                        .permitAll()
```

```
                            .antMatchers("/persons/newPerson").hasRole("ADMIN")
                            .antMatchers("/**").hasAnyRole("ADMIN","USER")
                            .anyRequest()
                            .authenticated()
                            .and()
                        .formLogin()
                            .usernameParameter("username") // customizable
                            .passwordParameter("password") // customizable
                            .loginProcessingUrl("/login")  // customizable
                            .loginPage("/auth")
                            .failureUrl("/auth?auth_error=1")
                            .defaultSuccessUrl("/home")
                            .permitAll()
                            .and()
                        .logout()
                            .logoutUrl("/logout")
                            .logoutSuccessUrl("/")
                        .and()
                        .csrf().disable();
        }
    }
```

To enable CSRF usage, the preceding configuration must also define a CSRF provider bean and use it in the configuration:

```
...
import org.springframework.security.web.csrf.CsrfTokenRepository;
import org.springframework.security.web.csrf.HttpSessionCsrfTokenRepository;

 @Configuration
@EnableWebSecurity
public class SecurityConfig extends WebSecurityConfigurerAdapter {

@Bean
    public CsrfTokenRepository repo() {
        HttpSessionCsrfTokenRepository repo = new
HttpSessionCsrfTokenRepository();
        repo.setParameterName("_csrf");
        repo.setHeaderName("X-CSRF-TOKEN");
        return repo;
    }

    @Override
    protected void configure(HttpSecurity http) throws Exception {
      http.
        ...
        .and()
        .csrf().csrfTokenRepository(repo());
    }

}
```

# No web.xml Configuration

Add the Security configuration class to the root context in the class taking care of loading all the MVC environment components:

```
package com.pr.config;
...
import com.pr.config.MvcConfig;
import com.pr.config.SecurityConfig;
import com.pr.config.WebFlowConfig;
import org.springframework.web.filter.CharacterEncodingFilter;
import org.springframework.web.filter.HiddenHttpMethodFilter;
import org.springframework.web.servlet
      .support.AbstractAnnotationConfigDispatcherServletInitializer;
import javax.servlet.Filter;

public class WebInitializer
        extends AbstractAnnotationConfigDispatcherServletInitializer {
    @Override
    protected Class<?> getRootConfigClasses() {
        return new Class<?>{
                SecurityConfig.class
        };
    }

    @Override
    protected Class<?> getServletConfigClasses() {
        return new Class<?>{
                MvcConfig.class,
                WebFlowConfig.class
        };
    }
...
}
```

---

■ ! The SecurityConfig.class (and the Spring Security XML config file) were added to the root context because they define beans that can be used by other servlets and services in the same application. The getServletConfigClasses() is used only to instantiate the servlet-related beans.

---

## Spring Security Tag Library

Security tags can be used in JSP directly to secure elements in the page and prevent their rendering if the authenticated user is not allowed to see them. To use them, the Spring Security Tag library must be declared in the JSP page:

```
<%@ taglib prefix="sec" uri="http://www.springframework.org/security/tags" %>
```

In the examples attached to this chapter, two elements were secured in JSP:

- **The logout link** must be visible only when a user is authenticated; the following is the syntax to do this:

```
<!-- layout.jsp, tiles main template file -->
<sec:authorize access="isAuthenticated()">
  <li>
  <!-- we are using Security for with CSRF enabled -->
      <spring:url value="/logout" var="logoutUrl" />
        <form action="${logoutUrl}" id="logout" method="post">
          <input type="hidden" name="${_csrf.parameterName}"
              value="${_csrf.token}"/>
        </form>
        <a href="#" onclick="document.getElementById('logout').submit();">
          <spring:message code="menu.logout"/>
        </a>
  </li>
</sec:authorize>
```

So basically, the same expressions used when configuring Spring Security are used for the access attribute.

- **The NewPerson link** must be visible only to users with the ADMIN role:

```
<!-- templates/layout.jsp -->
<sec:authorize access="hasRole('ADMIN')">
    <li>
    <!--menuTab is a tiles attribute -->
        <c:if test="${menuTab eq 'newPerson'}">
          <strong>
            <a href="<c:url value="/persons/newPerson"/>"> .
              <spring:message code="menu.new.person"/>
            </a>
          </strong>
        </c:if>
          <c:if test="${menuTab != 'newPersons'}">
            <a href="<c:url value="/persons/newPerson"/>">
              <spring:message code="menu.new.person"/>
            </a>
          </c:if>
    </li>
</sec:authorize>
```

And another tag was used to display information about the user being logged in:

```
<!-- layout.jsp, tiles main template file -->
 <div class="footer">
        <sec:authorize access="isAuthenticated()">
            <p><spring:message code="user.loggedin"/>:
                <sec:authentication property="principal.username"/>
            </p>
        </sec:authorize>
            <p><spring:message code="footer.text"/></p>
    </div>
```

Using the Spring Tag library and intercept-url definitions, access to resources can be centralized in the Spring Security configuration file or class, because the access attribute can be replaced with the url attribute that is set with URLs that are intercepted by Spring Security.

```
<!-- layout.jsp, tiles main template file -->
<sec:authorize access="hasRole('ADMIN')">
                //New Person link
</sec:authorize>
// can be written as
<sec:authorize url="/persons/newPerson">
                //New Person link
</sec:authorize>
```

## Securing Methods

Spring Security uses AOP to secure method calls. The Spring Security namespace can be used to configure method security using XML. But the most commonly used and easy-to-understand way to secure methods is through annotations. Spring Security provides its own annotations, but JSR-250 annotations are supported too. Samples for all ways of securing methods are covered.

Assuming you want to secure all action methods involved in the newPerson flow, this is how it is done using XML:

```
<!-- security-config.xml -->
<security:global-method-security>
  <security:protect-pointcut
    expression="execution(* com.pr..*Actions.*(..))?
        access="hasRole('ROLE_ADMIN')" />
</security:global-method-security>
```

Of course, method security must be enabled, which can be done by adding the following element in the security configuration file:

```
<!-- security-config.xml -->
<beans:beans xmlns="http://www.springframework.org/schema/security"
            xmlns:xsi="http://www.w3.org/2001/XMLSchema-instance"
            xmlns:beans="http://www.springframework.org/schema/beans"
```

```
        xsi:schemaLocation="http://www.springframework.org/schema/security
        http://www.springframework.org/schema/security/spring-security.xsd
            http://www.springframework.org/schema/beans
            http://www.springframework.org/schema/beans/spring-beans.xsd">

<global-method-security
                secured-annotations="enabled" />
                ..
</beans:beans>
```

Securing an action method using annotations can be done using the @Secured Spring annotation, which is activated when the global-method-security element is present in the configuration.

```
//AccountActions.java
...
import org.springframework.security.access.annotation.Secured;

@WebFlowAction
public class AccountActions extends MultiAction {

    @Secured("ROLE_ADMIN")
    public Event saveAccount(RequestContext context) {
        ...
    }
}
```

The equivalent of the global-method-security XML configuration is @EnableGlobalMethodSecurity( securedEnabled = true), which can be placed on any configuration class annotated with @Configuration:

```
//SpringConfig.java
...
import org.springframework.security.config.annotation.
    method.configuration.EnableGlobalMethodSecurity;

@Configuration
@EnableWebSecurity
@EnableGlobalMethodSecurity(securedEnabled = true)
public class SecurityConfig extends WebSecurityConfigurerAdapter {
...
}
```

To enable JSR-250 annotations, and especially the @RolesAllowed annotation (that is an equivalent for Spring @Secured), the following configurations must be made:

```
<!-- security-config.xml -->
<beans:beans xmlns="http://www.springframework.org/schema/security"
            xmlns:xsi="http://www.w3.org/2001/XMLSchema-instance"
            xmlns:beans="http://www.springframework.org/schema/beans"
            xsi:schemaLocation="http://www.springframework.org/schema/security
```

```
                 http://www.springframework.org/schema/security/spring-security.xsd
                    http://www.springframework.org/schema/beans
                    http://www.springframework.org/schema/beans/spring-beans.xsd">

<global-method-security
                    jsr250-annotations="enabled" />


                        ..
  </beans:beans>
//SpringConfig.java
...
import org.springframework.security.config.annotation.
      method.configuration.EnableGlobalMethodSecurity;
@Configuration
@EnableGlobalMethodSecurity(jsr250Enabled = true)
public class SecurityConfig extends WebSecurityConfigurerAdapter {
...
}
```

Usage of @RolesAllowed is the same as @Secure, so the preceding code would become this:

```
//AccountActions.java
...
import javax.annotation.security.RolesAllowed;

@WebFlowAction
public class AccountActions extends MultiAction {

    @RolesAllowed("ROLE_ADMIN")
    public Event saveAccount(RequestContext context) {
        ...
    }
}
```

Spring Security also provides the @PreAuthorize annotation, which is used to set an expression that is evaluated to decide if the method is invoked or not. (Basically, the equivalent of the <intercept /> XML configuration element.) Being a Spring Security annotation, it supports SpEL. This annotation can be used if it has been enabled using the @EnableGlobalMethodSecurity annotation. The code snippet depicts the configuration and usage for this specific case:

```
//SpringConfig.java
...
import org.springframework.security.config.annotation.
      method.configuration.EnableGlobalMethodSecurity;
@Configuration
@EnableGlobalMethodSecurity(prePostEnabled = true)
public class SecurityConfig extends WebSecurityConfigurerAdapter {
...
```

```
//AccountActions.java
...
import org.springframework.security.access.prepost.PreAuthorize;

@WebFlowAction
public class AccountActions extends MultiAction {
  @PreAuthorize("hasAuthority('ROLE_ADMIN')")
  public Event saveAccount(RequestContext context) {
    ...
  }
}
```

## Securing Flow Definitions

Any component of a flow definition—states, subflows, transitions—can be considered resources and thus secured. So far, we have secured the web-flow link by using a `<sec:authorize />` element in the `templates/layout.jsp` tiles template and setting up authentication and authorization. But flow components can be secured using a `org.springframework.webflow.security.SecurityFlowExecutionListener` and by adding `<secured>` elements in the flow definition. Considering that authentication and authorization rules have been set up as described earlier, the next step is to configure a `SecurityFlowExecutionListener`. This can be done using XML configuration by adding the bean definition in the configuration file setting up the web flow environment, `webflow-config.xml`.

```
<!--webflow-config.xml-->
 <flow ...>
    <!-- Executes web flows -->
    <webflow:flow-executor id="flowExecutor" >
        <webflow:flow-execution-listeners>
            <webflow:listener ref="auditExecutionListener"/>
            <webflow:listener ref="securityFlowExecutionListener"/>
        </webflow:flow-execution-listeners>
    </webflow:flow-executor>

    <bean id="auditExecutionListener"
      class="com.pr.audit.AuditFlowExecutorListener"/>

<bean id="securityFlowExecutionListener"
    class="org.springframework.webflow.security.SecurityFlowExecutionListener"/>
    ... // other flow infrastrucure beans
</flow>
```

---

■ !  The `AuditFlowExecutorListener` bean is a developer helper bean: that is it prints information when a web flow event is triggered, when states are entered, and when exceptions are thrown. The class is present in the sample project for this chapter, but its code is not relevant for this topic.

---

This bean can be configured using Java Configuration by declaring it in the web flows configuration class:

```
//WebFlowConfig.java
...
import org.springframework.webflow.security.SecurityFlowExecutionListener;

@Configuration
public class WebFlowConfig extends AbstractFlowConfiguration {

    @Bean
    public SecurityFlowExecutionListener securityFlowExecutionListener(){
        return new SecurityFlowExecutionListener();
    }
    @Bean
    public FlowExecutor flowExecutor() {
        return getFlowExecutorBuilder(flowRegistry())
                .addFlowExecutionListener(new AuditFlowExecutorListener(), "*")
                .addFlowExecutionListener(securityFlowExecutionListener())
                .setMaxFlowExecutions(5)
                .setMaxFlowExecutionSnapshots(30)
                .build();
    }
    ...
}
```

Declaring this bean and setting it up as a flow execution listener ensures that any <secured /> elements in the flow definition are picked up and interpreted accordingly at flow execution time. This bean can define its own decision manager, which overrides the default AccessDecisionManager in the system, by setting up the desired bean reference to the accessDecisionManager property.

```
<!--webflow-config.xml-->
<bean id="securityFlowExecutionListener" class=
  "org.springframework.webflow.security.SecurityFlowExecutionListener">
    <property name="accessDecisionManager"
                ref="customDecisionManager" />
</bean>
```

```
//WebFlowConfig.java
org.springframework.security.access.vote.UnanimousBased;
...
@Bean
    public SecurityFlowExecutionListener securityFlowExecutionListener(){
        SecurityFlowExecutionListener sfel = new SecurityFlowExecutionListener();
        sfel.setAccessDecisionManager(customDecisionManager());
        return sfel;
    }

    @Bean
    AccessDecisionManager customDecisionManager(){
    //assume List<AccessDecisionVoter<? extends Object>> voterList is initialized
            return new UnanimousBased(voterList);
    }
```

The UnanimousBased is a simple concrete implementation of the AccessDecisionManager provided by Spring Security; it requires all voters to abstain or grant access.

The SecurityFlowExecutionListener bean throws AccessDeniedException when the user is not authorized to access a flow resource. The exception is caught by Spring Security servlet filter. Catching or suppressing this exception is not recommended. When extending SimpleMappingExceptionResolver, doResolveException should be implemented so that this exception is rethrown.

```
import
 org.springframework.web.servlet.handler.SimpleMappingExceptionResolver;

public class CustomExceptionResolver
             extends SimpleMappingExceptionResolver {

  @Override
  protected ModelAndView doResolveException
       (HttpServletRequest req, HttpServletResponse res,
        Object handler, Exception ex) {

     return super.doResolveException(req, res, handler, ex);
    }
}
```

The following example depicts the specific points where the secured element can appear in a flow definition:

```
<!--webflow-config.xml-->

<!-- 1. Under the flow element, securing the whole flow definition -->
<flow ...>
        <secured attributes="ROLE_ADMIN" />
</flow>

<!-- 2. Securing a view-state -->
<flow ...>
        <view-state id="enterPersonInfo" model="person">
                <secured attributes="ROLE_ADMIN" />
        </view-state>
</flow>

<!-- or a decision state -->
 <decision-state id="isNewPerson">
    <secured attributes="IS_AUTHENTICATED_FULLY"/>
        <if test="personService.isNewPerson(person)"
            then="enterIdentityCardInfo" else="reviewExistingPerson"/>
</decision-state>
```

```
<!-- 3. Securing a transition -->
<flow ...>
        <view-state id="enterPersonInfo" model="person">
                ...
                <transition on="next" to="isNewPerson" >
                <secured attributes="ROLE_ADMIN" />
                </transition>
        </view-state>
</flow>
```

The attributes attribute is a comma-separated list of Spring Security authorization attributes. Often, these are specific security roles. But, when using a custom access decision manager, the syntax can vary; for example, SpEL can be used when the custom access manager is a Spring bean that supports them.

Spring Security is a wide subject; if you intend to use it in your projects, there is a lot of good documentation available online. Often, complete code samples are provided to help the curious developer understand how it works and how to use it. And, of course, the starting point is the Spring Security Reference at http://docs.spring.io/spring-security/site/docs/current/reference/htmlsingle/. All that is covered in this book should suffice in helping a developer understand the basic concepts that might be in the certification exam.

## Spring Security with OAuth

OAuth[15] is an open standard for authorization. It is an open protocol to allow secure authorization in a simple and standard method for web, mobile, and desktop applications. It is designed to work with HTTP and basically allows access tokens to be generated by a server, which can then be used by the client to access resources on another server. It's like there is an authentication provider that guarantees that you are who you say you are (it vouches for you) to a different service provider.

When talking about OAuth2 (because it is the most commonly used at the moment), the following components need to be mentioned:

- **Resource owner**: An entity that grants or denies access to a protected resource.

- **Resource server**: The server that hosts protected resources; it is capable of accepting and responding to requests done with an access token.

- **Client**: The entity that requests protected resources on behalf of the owner. It can be a web application, a mobile application, or a client-side application (JavaScript).

- **AuthorizationServer**: A server that provides access tokens to the client after a successful authentication.

---

[15]The project's official page is at http://projects.spring.io/spring-security-oauth/.

For example, if you have a Google account, you can install Runtastic (a sport tracker application) on your phone and access that application using your Google account without exposing the Google password process, as shown in Figure 7-26.

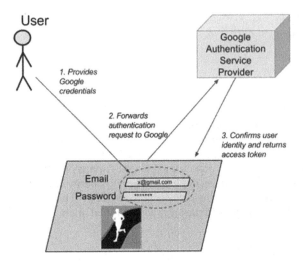

***Figure 7-26.*** *Google as authentication provider for Runtastic*

In the previous example, Google is the authorization server, the user is the client, the Runtastic application is the resource owner/resource server. But most applications—like Facebook, Twitter, LinkedIn, and GitHub—implement the authorization and resource server role.

Currently, Spring Security can be integrated with OAuth (1a) and OAuth2. A library is provided for each version; it needs to be included in the classpath of the application: `spring-security-oauth` for OAuth(1a) and `spring-security-oauth2` for OAuth2. OAuth is a simple way to publish and interact with protected data. A lot of information about OAuth and what it can be used for can be found by searching the Internet. The main idea is that using OAuth can give certain resources access without providing a username and password to the server.

To configure a Spring application as an authorization server, in a `@Configuration` class extending `org.springframework.security.oauth2.config.annotation.web.configuration.AuthorizationServerConfigurerAdapter`, the configure method must be overridden with an implementation that sets up the clients that can access the server. Extending the previously mentioned class provides empty method implementations for definitions inherited from the `AuthorizationServerConfigurer` interface (same package as the implementing class), making the job easier for the developer. The class must be annotated with `@EnableAuthorizationServer`, which is a convenient annotation provided by Spring to enable an authorization server.

Also, the Spring Security authentication manager (configured in the Spring Security configuration class annotated with `@EnableWebSecurity`) is injected here to secure the authorization end point.

```
import o.s.security.oauth2.config.annotation.web.configuration.*;
import o.s.security.oauth2.config.annotation.web.configurers.*;

@Configuration
@EnableAuthorizationServer
protected static class OAuth2Config extends AuthorizationServerConfigurerAdapter {
        @Autowired
        private AuthenticationManager authenticationManager;
```

```
    @Override (1)
    public void configure(AuthorizationServerEndpointsConfigurer endpoints)
        throws Exception {
        endpoints.authenticationManager(authenticationManager);
}

    @Override (2)
    public void configure(ClientDetailsServiceConfigurer clients)
        throws Exception {
      clients.inMemory()
          // client Id is used by OAuth to identify the client
          .withClient("client-with-secret")
          // grant types that are authorized for the client to use,
          //by default value is empty.
          .authorizedGrantTypes("password", "client_credentials")
          // roles that client must have in order to access the resource
          .authorities("ROLE_USER")
          //comma separated rights to the resource, by default none is specified
          .scopes("read", "trust")
          //The secret associated with the resource, by default, no secret is empty
          .secret("12#23$");
    }
}
```

The first configure method (1) injects the Spring Security authentication manager (set up in @EnableWebSecurity as in normal Spring Security), which is needed for the password grant defined tin the second method.

The second configure method (2) sets up the clients that can access the server, and their properties.

To implement the resource server, another configuration class is needed; this one must be annotated with @EnableResourceServer, which is a convenient annotation for OAuth2 resource servers, enabling a Spring Security filter that authenticates requests via an incoming OAuth2 token. The class is recommended to extend the org.springframework.security.oauth2.config.annotation.web.configuration. ResourceServerConfigurerAdapter, which provides empty implementation for methods inherited from the ResourceServerConfigurer interface (same package), making a developer's job easier.

```
import o.s.security.oauth2.config.annotation.web.configuration.*;
import o.s.security.oauth2.config.annotation.web.configurers.*;


@Configuration
@EnableResourceServer
protected static class ResourceServer extends ResourceServerConfigurerAdapter {

    @Override
    public void configure(HttpSecurity http) throws Exception {
        http
            .requestMatchers().antMatchers("/","/admin/beans").and()
            .authorizeRequests()
            .anyRequest().access("#oauth2.hasScope('read')");
    }
}
```

The `configure` method is used to set up resources for OAuth2 protection. Access to the resources is set up using the `HttpSecurity` bean, which is not something new, as it was used in previous examples to secure resources. But what is new here is the fact that access to resources can be configured using Spring Security Expressions that are applied on the `oauth2` security object. For example, the expression `#oauth2.hasScope('read')` tests the resource reading rights for the client the `oauth2` object is associated with. The expression handler is enabled by the `@EnableResourceServer` annotation.

The authorization and resource server application is usually an application that receives REST requests; there is really no need for an interface of any kind. The client application can be any type of application, but most of the time it is a web or mobile application.

When opening the Runtastic site or mobile application, a method of authentication can be selected. If authentication using a Google account is selected, the user must provide its Google credentials, which are sent to the Google authentication server to confirm their validity and send the confirmation to Runtastic. But Runtastic needs to access the user account information and use it to customize its interface to the user's preferences on the Google account. The confirmation received earlier is actually an access code that can be used to exchange for an access token that defines what information Google is willing to share about the user.

Technically speaking, the OAuth2 interaction between a web application and an authorization server implies the following steps:

1.    User accesses the web client application. The web client application redirects the user to the authorization server. The user logs in and the authorization server approves client access to the resource.

2.    Authorization redirects back to the web client with the access code

3.    The web client application exchanges the access code for the access token from the authorization server.

4.    The web client application uses the access token to get resources from the resource server.

Spring Security OAuth is not part of the certification exam as this book is being written, but most web and mobile applications require integration with popular social network applications and OAuth is the communication protocol that makes this interaction quite practical and easier for the end user. So it is best to have a basic idea on how this can be done. If you are interested in expanding your knowledge about it, there are some very good resources available at `projects.spring.io/spring-security-oauth/docs/oauth2.html`.

## Spring Social Projects

The beginning of this book presented a list of the Spring projects currently in development. By the time this book is published, that list will likely be deprecated: some of the projects were dropped, some were split into smaller projects, and some matured into solid frameworks. One the projects that matured into a solid framework is Spring Social, which provides an API to connect Spring applications to third-party APIs for social networks like Facebook, Twitter, and others. In the century of Web 2.0 and Big Data, connecting applications and sharing information in a practical way is a necessity. So Spring decided to start this project to help web applications developed in Spring integrate with SaaS (Software as a Service) API providers such as Facebook, Twitter, and LinkedIn. Currently under work, there are also integration modules for GitHub and Tripit. The communication is done using the service type provided by any of the mentioned applications. Most of them use REST. Facebook uses its own type of communication called the Facebook Graph. Figure 7-27 depicts all Spring Social projects, the application they communicate with, and with which protocol.

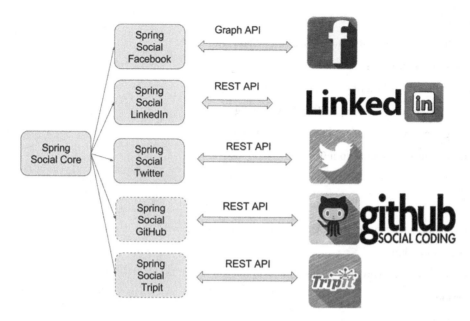

**Figure 7-27.** *The Spring Social projects*

Spring Social provides a lot of features designed to make the process of connecting local user accounts to hosted provider accounts easy to implement: a controller that handles authorization between the Java/Spring application and the service provider, a controller that enables user authentication by signing into a service provider, connection factory classes, real-time callback handlers, and much more.

More information on how Spring Social can be used is on the official page of this project at `http://projects.spring.io/spring-social/`.

# Summary

After completing this chapter, you should be able to

- Describe what Web Flow is and what problems it solves.
- Describe the Web Flow architecture.
- Understand how Web Flow processes a request.
- Configure Web Flow with Spring MVC.
- Describe the typical flow implementation guidelines.
- List the elements of a flow definition.
- Define flows using the XML language.
- Test flow execution outside the container.
- Flow definition best practices.
- Describe branching.
- Describe an action-state and how it should be used.

- Describe a decision state.
- Describe how exceptions are handled in Spring Web Flow.
- Describe and use subflows.
- Describe and use flow inheritance.
- Configure Spring Security using XML and Java Config.
- Use Spring Security to secure parts of JSP pages and methods.
- Use Spring Security to secure your flows.

# Quick Quiz

**Question 1:** What problems can be avoided using flows for web navigation?

- duplicate submissions
- state collisions between browser windows
- stale session state
- none of the above

**Question 2:** How do the DispatcherServlet and Spring MVC Flow Controller work together?

- Spring MVC Flow Controller intercepts and resolves all requests
- DispatcherServlet intercepts all requests and forwards the flow requests to the Flow Controller

**Question 3:** What are the main components that need to be configured to have a working Web Flow environment?

- a flow executor
- a flow registry
- a SecurityFlowExecutionListener bean
- a flow adapter
- a flow mapping
- an MvcViewFactoryCreator creator

**Question 4:** Which of the following affirmations is true about FlowExecutor?

- It is the central facade and entry-point service interface into the Spring Web Flow system.
- It does not need a FlowRegistry to function properly.
- It handles managing flow executions.

**Question 5:** Which of the following affirmations is true about FlowDefinitionRegistry?

- To configure a Spring Web Flow environment, a bean of this type is not mandatory.
- It requires a mandatory FlowBuilderServices bean as an argument so it can be instantiated.
- It is a container of flow definitions.

**Question 6:** What can you say about the following code snippet?

```
<button id="newPersonButton" name="_eventId_proceed" type="submit">
        <spring:message code="command.proceed" />
</button>
```

- It is the JSP definition of a button used to resume a flow that has an event named proceed associated with it.
- It is a simple JSP definition of a button that is named _eventId_proceed.
- It is a simple JSP definitiod of a button used to submit a form.

**Question 7:** How many requests does a flow interaction imply?

- one
- two
- three
- none, because it uses session

**Question 8:** What can be said about the following web flow configuration class?

```
@Configuration
 public class WebFlowConfig {
   ...
}
```

- To be valid, the @EnableWebFlows is necessary.
- The class could extend the AbstractFlowConfiguration class that is provided by Spring Web Flow to provide access to builders for the Web Flow environment.

**Question 9:** What can be said about the FlowController?

- It is the controller that intercepts and resolves flow requests.
- It is the adapter between the Spring MVC Controller layer and the Spring Web Flow engine
- It should be configured by the developer to define how flow requests are handled.

**Question 10:** Which of the following are elements of a flow definition?

- beans
- states
- transitions
- converters
- data

**Question 11:** Which of the following are valid states types in a flow definition?

- start state
- action state
- decision state
- view state
- persistence state
- end state
- conversion state

**Question 12:** Which of the following affirmations is true about a flow definition?

- It must have exactly one end state.
- It must have at least one decision state.
- It can have as many end states as the logic requires.
- It is a flow defined in a single XML file.

**Question 13:** What triggers a transition?

- user events in view states
- user events in any kind of state
- the result of evaluation an expression in an action and decision state

**Question 14:** Which of the following is true?

- A flow definition has its own internationalization resources.
- Each view state has a corresponding view.
- Decisions states are more complex view states.

**Question 15:** Consider the following flow definition:

```
<view-state id="enterIdentityCardInfo" model="identityCard">
    <binder>
        ...
    </binder>
    <transition on="save" to="confirmAdult">
      <evaluate expression="personBuilder.savePersonEntity(person, identityCard)"
        result="flowScope.existingPerson" />
    </transition>
</view-state>
```

Which of the following is true?

- The view template logical name is the same with the view state id, enterIdentityCardInfo in this case.

- The view template logical name can be anything as long as it is linked in the web flow configuration file or class to the state id.

- Transitioning to the confirmAdult can be prevented by an exception being thrown when executing the personBuilder.savePersonEntity expression.

**Question 16:** What can you say about global transitions?

- Only one can be declared in a web flow definition

- One or more can be declared in a web flow definition

- It is a transition type that can be used to cancel the flow execution at any point in the execution

**Question 17:** Choose the proper order of the following steps in creating a flow:

1. Add the actions and states behavior.

2. Create mock views to test the connection of the states.

3. Define view states and end states.

4. Define transition between states.

    - 4, 1, 3, 2

    - 3, 4, 2, 1

    - 3, 4, 1, 2

    - 1, 3, 4, 2

**Question 18:** Which of the following affirmations are true about testing web flows?

- The test class must be annotated with @RunWith(SpringJUnit4ClassRunner.class).

- The test class must extend the AbstractXmlFlowExecutionTests.

- Mock views can be used to test the flow navigation during development.

**Question 19:** Which of the following is true about flow scope?

- This scope is shared between parent flows and subflows.

- This scope lasts until the flow ends.

- Flow scoped variables can be declared by evaluate elements in the following manner:

```
<evaluate expression="service.computeResult()"
    result="flowScope.result" />
```

**Question 20:** Which of the following is true about view scope?

- View scoped variables are available to all view states.

- View scoped variables can only be defined inside a `view-state` element.

- View scoped variables are created when entering the view state and destroyed when transition to the next flow occurs.

**Question 21:** Which of the following is true about request scope?

- Request scope lasts for only one request.

- This scope is useless; it exists just for compatibility with request-response mechanisms on the Web.

- Variables in this scope can be used for view initialization.

- Variables in this scope are fetched only once, and subsequent browser refresh button-pressing won't affect the initial fetched value.

**Question 22:** Which of the following is true about flash scope?

- This scope lasts for the entire flow.

- This scope lasts for the entire flow, but is cleared every time a view is rendered, making it perfect for exchanging data between flow execution steps.

- This scope involves two requests.

**Question 23:** Which of the following is true about conversation scope?

- This scope is the widest web flow scope.

- Variables defined in this scope are available to subflows too.

- Variables defined in this scope introduce a dependency between subflows and parent flows.

**Question 24:** Considering the following two code snippets:

```
1. <flow ...>
      <on-start>
         <evaluate expression="hospitalManager.findAll()"
             result="flowScope.hospitalList" />
      </on-start>
   <view-state id="enterPersonInfo" model="person">
         ...
   </view-state>
   </flow>
```

```
2. <flow ...>
     <view-state id="enterPersonInfo" model="person">
         <on-render>
           <evaluate expression="hospitalManager.findAll()"
               result="requestScope.hospitalList" />
         </on-start>
     </view-render>
   </flow>
```

Which of the code snippets is recommended to initialize a hospital list when the enterPersonInfo view is rendered?

- 1, because the hospitalList should be initialized only once

- 2, because the hospitalList should be refetched every time the enterPersonInfo view is rendered, so the most recent information is available in the flow execution

- either of them

**Question 25:** At which points in the flow can actions be executed?

- on flow start

- on state entry

- on view render

- on transition execution

- during transition execution

- on state exit

- on flow end

- after flow end

**Question 26:** Which of the following Spring expressions are valid?

- <evaluate expression="searchService.suggestHospital(externalContext.sessionMap.mostUsed)"result="viewScope.hospitals" />

- <set name="flowScope.personName" value="sessionScope.name" />

- <set name="flashScope.successMessage" value="resourceBundle.successMessage" />

**Question 27:** Which of the following are valid types for an action state?

- Boolean, true or false

- Boolean, always just "yes" or "no"

- Any value that evaluates to "success"

- Any String that can be matched to a trigger event name

**Question 28:** Select the way in which a developer can define an action.

- Extend the `Action` class

- Extend the `MultiAction` class

- Add call business methods directly in the web flow definition

**Question 29:** What can be said about authentication and authorization?

- They are tightly coupled, changing configuration for authentication will require changes in the authorization configuration as well.

- They are fully decoupled; changing configuration for authentication will not affect authorization.

- They are both synonyms for application security.

**Question 30:** What is needed to configure Spring Security with Spring MVC using Java Configuration?

- The security beans `AuthenticationManager` and `HttpSecurity` have to be defined in a class annotated with `@Configuration`.

- Create a class that extends `AbstractSecurityWebApplicationInitializer` to register the `springSecurityFilterChain`.

- Create a configuration class that extends `WebSecurityConfigurerAdapter` that is annotated with `EnableWebSecurity`.

- Add the Security configuration class to the root context.

# Practical Exercise

The practical exercise for this chapter involves configuring Spring Security. The project you have to complete is named `14-pr-web-security-practice`. The project contains a view named `login.jsp`, which is a custom login form designed to work with Spring Security 4. There are a few TODO tasks that you must be able to complete if you have been paying enough attention when reading the Security section.

The first one, (TODO 47) requests you to add a new filter of type `org.springframework.web.filter.DelegatingFilterProxy` with the filter name `springSecurityFilterChain`. The class that will do this is already in place and is called `com.pr.init.SecurityWebApplicationInitializer`; you just have to modify it to register the filter. Afterward, you can start the application using the `appStart` Gradle task for this submodule project; for reference, see Figure 7-28.

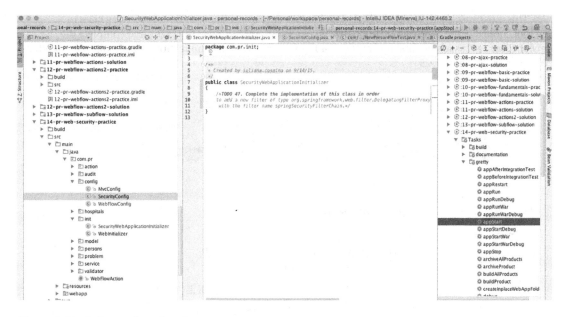

**Figure 7-28.** *Reference for subproject*

You are not done yet, though. When starting the application, you see in the console that there was some trouble creating your security context and your login page is not visible. This is what you should see in the console:

```
00:35:40 WARN Failed startup of context o.a.g.JettyWebAppContext@2da59753
{/security,file:
/.../personal-records/14-pr-web-security-practice/build/inplaceWebapp/,STARTING}
...
Caused by: java.lang.IllegalArgumentException: An AuthenticationManager is required
        at org.springframework.util.Assert.notNull(Assert.java:115) ~na:na
...
```

If you remember, the security section well, you already suspect what is missing. The previous task just defines the filter. Now you need to create a Spring Security configuration class to provide your users their roles and overall details such as the location of the login form, if a CSRF token is used. All this is marked as TODO 48. A part of the class is already set up for you, providing the bean that generates a CSRF token. You can find the partial implementation in com.pr.config.SecurityConfig. The comments in the TODO task instruct you on what is further needed. After all the configuration is in place, you can try to start the application again. And unfortunately, it won't start. This is what you see if you try to open http://localhost:8080/security/.

```
HTTP ERROR 500
Problem accessing /security/auth. Reason:
    Server Error
Caused by:
org.springframework.web.util.NestedServletException:
Request processing failed; nested exception is java.lang.IllegalStateException:
No WebApplicationContext found: no ContextLoaderListener registered?
```

This is because there is still one little detail to take care of: adding the SecurityConfig class to the root context of the application. To do this, go to com.pr.init.WebInitializer and complete the getRootConfigClasses method body (TODO 49). After restarting the application, you should see something really similar to Figure 7-29.

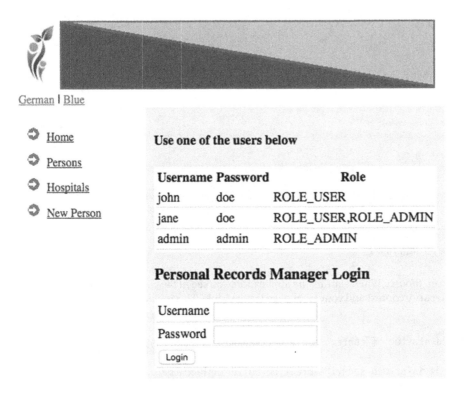

***Figure 7-29.*** *The login form displayed when Spring Security is properly configured*

If the previous task is resolved correctly, the login form should be visible. But wait, the New Person menu option is visible. You want only users with the ADMIN role to see that menu item. Something is clearly missing. So go to 14-pr-web-security-practice/src/main/webapp/WEB-INF/templates/layout.jsp and secure that menu item. Do not forget to reference the proper taglib!

After solving the last TODO item, the New Person menu item should not be visible on the main page when a user is not logged in. Log in using *john*. If you see the New Person link, something is wrong in the configuration of the HttpSecurity, because *john* has a USER role, and only users with an ADMIN role can view and access that menu item. Log in with *jane* or *admin*. If you see that option, then your configuration is correct and you have completed this lab.

As a bonus exercise, try playing with the security tag library and use the URL to configure access. Or remove the tag altogether and secure the flow.

The proposed solution can be found in subproject 14-pr-web-security-solution. Try not to look before developing your own solution, and use it only for comparison.

## CHAPTER 8

# Spring Boot and WebSocket

Although they are not yet part of the certification exam, Spring Boot and Spring WebSocket are included in this book because of the potential that these two projects have in the future development of Spring Web applications.

## What Is Spring Boot?

Spring Boot is a promising Spring project that makes it really easy for developers to create Spring-powered, production-grade applications and services. It makes configuration less of a hassle, offering complete, but easy-to-use defaults bits and pieces that you can stack up together like LEGO bricks. (Yes, the LEGO analogy again.) Spring Boot can be used to create stand-alone Java applications or web applications and its primary goals are to do the following:

- Provide a faster, practical, and more accessible way to start development with Spring

- Provide a default set of customized infrastructure beans, which can be easily overridden if a specific configuration is required

- Provide a large set of features common to large classes of projects (embedded servers, security, metrics, etc.)

- Offer the option of dropping any XML configuration or the necessity of generating code

When developing web applications, a container is necessary. Usually, an application server or a web server is necessary to run a web application.

A web server like Apache HTTP, for example, is dedicated to sending HTML to the client and forwarding requests to application servers. It handles only static resources.

An application server, like Apache Tomcat is built around a web server and is dedicated to the efficient execution of program and routines; it supports different types of applications, load balancing, transaction demarcation, and so forth; and it is specifically designed to handle dynamic resources.

Apache TomEE is a full-blown Java EE container and an application server based on Apache Tomcat. This type of application server is also called an enterprise server because it is designed to support complex applications like ERPs.[1]

---

[1]Enterprise resource planning (ERP) is business-management software. It is typically a suite of integrated applications (see https://en.wikipedia.org/wiki/Enterprise_resource_planning).

The Jetty server was used in the examples in this book. Jetty is an embedded server. Application/web servers are separate applications that you install, start up, maybe customize the configuration, and deploy your artifact on. An embedded server does not need all that. An embedded HTTP server is software that implements the HTTP protocol; it can be embedded into the application that you are developing. It is limited to handling HTTP requests and can be plugged in with the default configuration, or it can be customized. Up until now, the Jetty embedded server was plugged in at runtime by using the Gradle Gretty plugin. Using Spring Boot, this is no longer needed. All that is needed is to configure the `spring-boot-starter-jetty` as a compile-time dependency for the application.

# Usage and Configuration

A simple sample for this case is the `08-chapter-01-solution` project, a module of `book-code`. If you open the project, you will notice the following:

- A new version element was added in the ext element of the Gradle configuration of the `build.gradle` file (the `book-code` parent project):

```
springBootVersion = '1.2.7.RELEASE'
```

- In the same file, a new dependencies array named boot was added:

```
boot = [
    springBootPlugin: "org.springframework.boot:spring-boot-gradle-plugin:
                                            $springBootVersion",
    starterWeb      : "org.springframework.boot:spring-boot-starter-web:
                                            $springBootVersion",
    starterJetty    : "org.springframework.boot:spring-boot-starter-jetty:
                                            $springBootVersion",
    actuator        : "org.springframework.boot:spring-boot-starter-actuator:
                                            $springBootVersion",
    yaml            : "org.yaml:snakeyaml:1.16"
]
```

- The Gradle configuration file for `08-chapter-01-solution` has the following contents:

```
apply plugin: 'spring-boot'

buildscript {
    repositories {
        mavenCentral()
    }
    dependencies {
        classpath boot.springBootPlugin
    }
}

dependencies {
    compile (boot.starterWeb){
        (*)exclude module : "spring-boot-starter-tomcat"
    }
    compile boot.starterJetty, boot.actuator, boot.yaml

    testCompile misc.junit
}
```

And this is all. The Gradle Gretty plugin, was replaced by the Spring-Boot plugin that is needed for running Spring Boot applications. The default web runtime that Spring Boot uses (Tomcat) was excluded, and `spring-boot-starter-jetty` was added as a dependency using the variable assigned to the `boot.starterJetty library`. This is enough to develop and run a simple web application.

---

■ ! The **spring-boot-starter-actuator** added using the **boot.actuator** variable is not really necessary in the examples for the book, but you need to know that this library exists. It should be used when you want to add production-ready features like metrics and monitoring to your application. Also, if you look in the log after the application starts, you will see a few lines that look like this:

```
Mapped "{[/]}" onto public java.lang.String com.book.web.
    HelloWorldController.index()
Mapped "{[/error],produces=[text/html]}" onto public o.s.web.servlet.
    ModelAndView
Mapped "{[/beans],methods=[GET]}" onto public java.lang.Object
Mapped "{[/trace],methods=[GET]}" onto public java.lang.Object
Mapped "{[/metrics/{name:.*}],methods=[GET]}" onto public java.lang.Object
o.s.boot.actuate.endpoint.mvc.MetricsMvcEndpoint.value(java.lang.String)
apped "{[/health]}" onto public java.lang.Object
o.s.boot.actuate.endpoint.mvc.HealthMvcEndpoin
    t.invoke(java.security.Principal)
```

These are a set of RESTful endpoints added to the application to provide access to management services provided by Spring Boot. Try accessing `http://localhost:8080/metrics` or `http://localhost:8080/health` after the application starts with the default configuration (otherwise, the port and the `contextPath` might be different) and check out the data returned to you by Spring Boot.

The YAML dependency is covered later.

---

The core class of this application is the `com.book.Application` class:

```
[commandchars=+
package com.book;

import org.springframework.boot.SpringApplication;
import org.springframework.boot.autoconfigure.SpringBootApplication;
import org.springframework.context.ApplicationContext;

@SpringBootApplication
public class Application {

    public static void main(String args) {
        ApplicationContext ctx = SpringApplication.run(Application.class, args);
        assert(ctx!=null);
    }

}
```

If you run this class, you get a web application run on Jetty that is available at `http://localhost:8080/`. The most important element in this class is the `@SpringBootApplication` annotation. Spring Boot code is available to the public, and if you look for the annotation code on GitHub, this is what you will find:

```
package org.springframework.boot.autoconfigure;

...// import statements

@Target(ElementType.TYPE)
@Retention(RetentionPolicy.RUNTIME)
@Documented
@Inherited
@Configuration
@EnableAutoConfiguration
@ComponentScan
public @interface SpringBootApplication {
    /**
     * Exclude specific auto-configuration classes
       such that they will never be applied.
     * @return the classes to exclude
     */
    Class<?> exclude() default {};

}
```

When placed on a class, this annotation has the following effect:

- It indicates that this a configuration class that can be used to instantiate beans via @Bean annotated methods (because this annotation is itself annotated with @Configuration).

- It triggers component scanning on the package in which the class is defined (because of the @ComponentScan annotation).

- It automatically adds @EnableWebMvc when spring-webmvc is in the classpath. This is ensured by the spring-boot-starter-web being a dependency of this project. This marks the application as a web application, so Spring Boot knows to set up a DispatcherServlet.

- The @EnableAutoConfiguration annotation does exactly what the name of the annotation says: it enables the autoconfiguration of a Spring context. So Spring Boot wraps up a configuration by basically guessing which beans are necessary, given the little configuration there is. Autoconfiguration is quite intelligent and if some custom configuration is provided, the provided beans override the default ones that Spring Boot comes with.

The scope of this annotation is enriched, starting with Spring Boot 1.3.0, which wasn't yet released when this book was written, but the code is available on GitHub.[2]

The preceding main method uses the `SpringApplication.run` convenient method to launch an application. Thus, no XML was needed anywhere to create this web application. This method returns the created ApplicationContext instance. The created context is autowired into the HelloWorldController,

---

[2]View the code at https://github.com/spring-projects/spring-boot/blob/master/spring-boot-autoconfigure/src/main/java/org/springframework/boot/autoconfigure/SpringBootApplication.java

which is a simple REST controller used to display all the beans in the context. In the spirit of keeping things simple, a complex configuration involving a view resolver was avoided, because the scope of this module is to show the power of Spring Boot and what exactly it does in the background. The autowired context is used to create an HTML string that is rendered when accessing http://localhost:8080/ and shows the name of all the beans created by Spring Boot or defined in the application; thus, you can analyze what Spring Boot is doing in the background. The simple controller looks like this:

```
@RestController
public class HelloWorldController {
    @Autowired
    ApplicationContext ctx;

    @RequestMapping("/")
    public String index() {
        StringBuilder sb = new StringBuilder("<html><body>");

        sb.append("Hello there dear developer,
            here are the beans you were looking for: </br>");

        String beanNames = ctx.getBeanDefinitionNames();
        Arrays.sort(beanNames);
        for (String beanName : beanNames) {
            sb.append("</br>").append(beanName);
        }
        sb.append("</body></htm>");
        return sb.toString();
    }
}
```

This is roughly what you see in the browser:

```
Hello there dear developer, here are the beans you were looking for:

actuatorMetricRepository
application
applicationContextIdFilter
auditEventRepository
auditListener
autoConfigurationAuditEndpoint
basicErrorController
beanNameHandlerMapping
beanNameViewResolver
beansEndpoint
characterEncodingFilter
configurationPropertiesReportEndpoint
counterService
...
healthEndpoint
healthMvcEndpoint
helloWorldController
...
```

Of course, the list is incomplete here—just a small snippet is depicted. You have to run the application yourself to see the complete list.

---

■ ! And you can view the same list of beans in JSON format if you access the actuator service available at `http://localhost:8080/beans`.

---

Also, if you want to know where the implementation for these beans comes from, just look at the dependencies for your project in Gradle view in IntelliJ IDEA. You should see something similar to what is depicted in Figure 8-1, but the list will be way bigger.

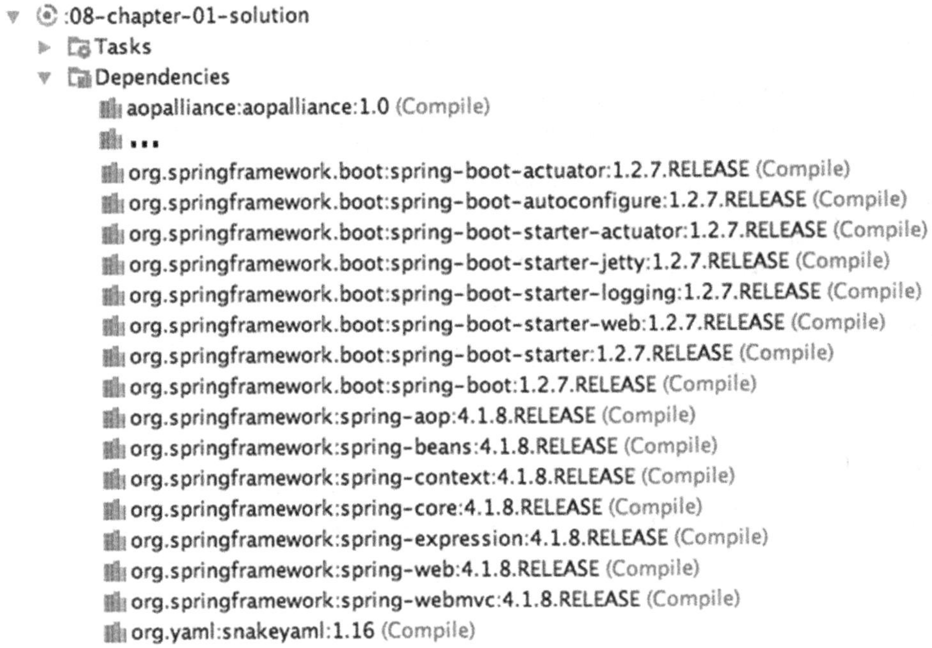

▼ ⊙ :08-chapter-01-solution
   ▶ ⌂ Tasks
   ▼ ⌂ Dependencies
      ▦ aopalliance:aopalliance:1.0 (Compile)
      ▦ ...
      ▦ org.springframework.boot:spring-boot-actuator:1.2.7.RELEASE (Compile)
      ▦ org.springframework.boot:spring-boot-autoconfigure:1.2.7.RELEASE (Compile)
      ▦ org.springframework.boot:spring-boot-starter-actuator:1.2.7.RELEASE (Compile)
      ▦ org.springframework.boot:spring-boot-starter-jetty:1.2.7.RELEASE (Compile)
      ▦ org.springframework.boot:spring-boot-starter-logging:1.2.7.RELEASE (Compile)
      ▦ org.springframework.boot:spring-boot-starter-web:1.2.7.RELEASE (Compile)
      ▦ org.springframework.boot:spring-boot-starter:1.2.7.RELEASE (Compile)
      ▦ org.springframework.boot:spring-boot:1.2.7.RELEASE (Compile)
      ▦ org.springframework:spring-aop:4.1.8.RELEASE (Compile)
      ▦ org.springframework:spring-beans:4.1.8.RELEASE (Compile)
      ▦ org.springframework:spring-context:4.1.8.RELEASE (Compile)
      ▦ org.springframework:spring-core:4.1.8.RELEASE (Compile)
      ▦ org.springframework:spring-expression:4.1.8.RELEASE (Compile)
      ▦ org.springframework:spring-web:4.1.8.RELEASE (Compile)
      ▦ org.springframework:spring-webmvc:4.1.8.RELEASE (Compile)
      ▦ org.yaml:snakeyaml:1.16 (Compile)

***Figure 8-1.*** *Transitive dependencies added by Spring Boot to a web application project*

So far, only the default configuration inferred by Spring Boot has been presented. This application is roughly similar to the one in the official tutorial at `https://spring.io/guides/gs/spring-boot/`; but in this book, things are spiced up a little.

# Customizing Spring Boot

There are a few ways that Spring Boot configuration can be externalized"

- use properties files

- use YAML files

- use environment variables

- use command-line variables (when a Spring Boot command-line interface is installed)

In the previous example, the controller and the configuration class were in the same package, and by default, the configuration class annotated with SpringBootApplication scans only the current package and its subpackages. This can be changed by annotating the same class with @ComponentScan and specifying different package groups.

In the 08-chapter-02-solution module, the Application was moved to the com.book.init package, and HelloWorldController was moved to com.book.web, as depicted in Figure 8-2.

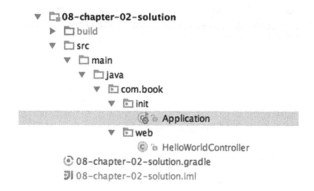

***Figure 8-2.*** *Spring Boot with beans and configuration in different packages*

The new configuration class code looks like this:

```
package com.book.init;

import org.springframework.boot.SpringApplication;
import org.springframework.boot.autoconfigure.SpringBootApplication;
import org.springframework.context.ApplicationContext;
import org.springframework.context.annotation.ComponentScan;
import org.springframework.context.annotation.Import;
```

```
@SpringBootApplication
@ComponentScan(basePackages = {"com.book.*"})
//or @ComponentScan(basePackages = {"com.book.init", "com.book.web"})
public class Application {

    public static void main(String args) {
        SpringApplication.run(Application.class, args);
    }
}
```

But what if you want the application to be available on a different port and in a different context path? There are a few ways to do this.

The simplest way is to create a customized bean class that implements the org.springframework. boot.context.embedded.EmbeddedServletContainerCustomizer interface and provides a concrete implementation for the customize method:

```
package com.book.init;

import org.springframework.boot.context.embedded.ConfigurableEmbeddedServletContainer;
import org.springframework.boot.context.embedded.EmbeddedServletContainerCustomizer;
import org.springframework.stereotype.Component;

/**
 * Created by iuliana.cosmina on 9/23/15.
 */
@Component
public class CustomizationBean implements EmbeddedServletContainerCustomizer {
    @Override
    public void customize(ConfigurableEmbeddedServletContainer container) {
        container.setPort(8083);
        container.setContextPath("/boot");
    }
}
```

By adding this bean to the configuration, the application can now be accessed at http://localhost:8083/boot.

Another way to do this is by using a customized factory bean for JettyEmbeddedServletContainerFactory. Aside from *port* and *contextPath*, some settings for the optimization of the embedded Jetty server used to run the application can be provided. The @Bean annotated method that declares this bean can be added to any configuration class that is taken into consideration by Spring Boot.

```
package com.book.init;

import org.eclipse.jetty.server.Server;
import org.eclipse.jetty.util.thread.QueuedThreadPool;
import org.springframework.beans.factory.annotation.Value;
import org.springframework.boot.context.embedded.jetty.
        JettyEmbeddedServletContainerFactory;
import org.springframework.boot.context.embedded.jetty.
        JettyServerCustomizer;
```

```java
import org.springframework.context.annotation.Bean;
import org.springframework.context.annotation.Configuration;

/**
 * Created by iuliana.cosmina on 9/27/15.
 */
@Configuration
public class JettyFactoryConfig {

@Bean
 public JettyEmbeddedServletContainerFactory
     jettyServletContainerFactory(@Value("${server.port:8085}") final String port,
         @Value("${jetty.threadPool.maxThreads:200}") final String maxThreads,
         @Value("${jetty.threadPool.minThreads:8}") final String minThreads,
         @Value("${jetty.threadPool.idleTimeout:60000}") final String idleTimeout) {
         final JettyEmbeddedServletContainerFactory factory =
             new JettyEmbeddedServletContainerFactory(Integer.valueOf(port));
         factory.setContextPath("/boot");
         factory.addServerCustomizers(new JettyServerCustomizer() {
             @Override
             public void customize(final Server server) {
                 // Customize the connection pool used by Jetty to handle
                 //incoming HTTP connections
                 final QueuedThreadPool threadPool =
                     server.getBean(QueuedThreadPool.class);
                 threadPool.setMaxThreads(Integer.valueOf(maxThreads));
                 threadPool.setMinThreads(Integer.valueOf(minThreads));
                 threadPool.setIdleTimeout(Integer.valueOf(idleTimeout));
             }
         });
         return factory;
     }
}
```

By adding this bean to the configuration, the application can now be accessed at
http://localhost:8085/boot.

Values for the customizations can be provided, directly as done before, but they also can be provided
using properties files or YAML files. In order to provide the configuration via a properties file, a file named
application.properties has to be created and applied to the application from the outside, or it can be
packaged in the jar. If multiple profiles are used, multiple files can be added. Their naming matches the
application-{profile}.properties template.

SpringApplication looks for an application.properties file in the following locations, and adds them
to the Spring environment:

- a /config directory under the current directory

- the current directory

- a classpath /config package

- the classpath root

Being a resource file, application.properties must be located during development under src/main/resources.

The preceding list is ordered by precedence, so Spring Boot looks for property files by traversing the list from top to bottom. The first properties file found is taken into consideration, and it does not matter if the subsequent locations have a properties file defined.

The default name of the properties file is application.properties. Spring Boot looks for it, unless it was changed by setting the environment variable named spring.config.name.

The location of the file can also be provided as the value for the environment variable named spring.config.location.

So if the 08-chapter-02-solution application is packaged into a runnable jar called boot.jar, the application could be run from the command line with the following arguments:

```
#Spring Boot will search in the classpath for a file named boot.properties
$ java -jar boot.jar --spring.config.name=boot

#Spring Boot will read the properties the specified file
$ java -jar boot.jar --spring.config.location=/Users/myuser/config/default.properties
```

In the preceding example, the file is saved under book-code/08-chapter-02-solution/src/main/resources and has the following contents:

```
#application.properties
app.port=8084
app.context=/boot
```

These property values are injected using the @Value annotation into a customization bean that is picked up and used by Spring Boot. The application is then accessed at http://localhost:8084/boot.

```
package com.book.init;

import org.springframework.beans.factory.annotation.Value;
import org.springframework.boot.context.embedded.ConfigurableEmbeddedServletContainer;
import org.springframework.boot.context.embedded.EmbeddedServletContainerCustomizer;
import org.springframework.stereotype.Component;

@Component
public class PropertiesConfBean implements EmbeddedServletContainerCustomizer {

    @Value("${app.port}")
    private Integer value;

    @Value("${app.context}")
    private String contextPath;

    @Override
    public void customize(ConfigurableEmbeddedServletContainer container) {
        container.setPort(value);
        container.setContextPath(contextPath);
    }
}
```

The `EmbeddedServletContainerCustomizer` interface is used for customizing autoconfigured embedded servlet containers. Any beans of this type are instantiated and used to initialize the configuration of the embedded server before the container itself is started.

Without an `EmbeddedServletContainerCustomizer` bean, the contents of `application.properties` look different, because they must match the standard property names[3] that Spring Boot looks for, as follows:

```
#application.properties
server.port=8084
server.context-path=/boot
```

When the `snakeyaml` library is in the classpath, YAML files can be used instead of properties files. YAML is a well-known format within the Ruby community. It is a superset of JSON, and as such, it is a very convenient format for specifying hierarchical configuration data. In the previous example, if the `application.properties` file is replaced by `application.yml`, with the following contents, the behavior will be exactly the same, because the internal `org.springframework.beans.factory.config.YamlPropertiesFactoryBean` converts the contents of the YAML file into the properties in the initial `application.properties` file.

```
#application.yml
app:
  port:8082
  context:/boot
```

---

■ ! Both `application.properties` and `application.yml` can be used in the same project, because for bigger projects, the configuration list could be quite large and migration could be a long duration process; it is convenient to be able to do the migration gradually. Be careful not to have the same properties defined in both files, because if this happens, properties defined in `application.properties` take precedence.

---

YAML properties can be used in a different way. A class can be designed to have its fields initialized from a YAML file. The following `AppSettings` class is such a class.

```java
package com.book.init;

import org.slf4j.Logger;
import org.slf4j.LoggerFactory;
import org.springframework.boot.context.properties.ConfigurationProperties;
import javax.annotation.PostConstruct;
import javax.validation.constraints.NotNull;
@ConfigurationProperties(prefix="app")
public class AppSettings {

    private static Logger logger = LoggerFactory.getLogger(AppSettings.class);

    @NotNull
    private Integer port;
```

---

[3]The property names standard list for `application.properties` or `application.yml` is at http://docs.spring.io/spring-boot/docs/current/reference/htmlsingle/#common-application-properties.

```
    @NotNull
    private String context;

    public Integer getPort() {
        return port;
    }

    public void setPort(Integer port) {
        this.port = port;
    }

    public String getContext() {
        return context;
    }

    public void setContext(String context) {
        this.context = context;
    }

    public AppSettings() {
    }

    @PostConstruct
    public void check() {
        logger.info("Initialized {} {}", port, context);
    }
}
```

The annotation that allows this is @ConfigurationProperties, which marks a class to be used for initialization with property values by the Spring DataBinder utilities. The advantage here is that usage of the @Value annotation and hard-coding the property names is avoided. Validators can also be added on the fields (notice the @NotNull annotations).

The prefix attribute is used to refer to the parent element in the YAML file. This bean is then autowired into the YamlConfBean, which uses its properties as needed.

```
package com.book.init;

import org.springframework.beans.factory.annotation.Autowired;
import org.springframework.boot.context.embedded.ConfigurableEmbeddedServletContainer;
import org.springframework.boot.context.embedded.EmbeddedServletContainerCustomizer;
import org.springframework.stereotype.Component;

@Component
public class YamlConfBean implements EmbeddedServletContainerCustomizer {

    @Autowired
    private AppSettings appSettings;
```

```
    @Override
    public void customize(ConfigurableEmbeddedServletContainer container) {
        container.setPort(appSettings.getPort());
        container.setContextPath(appSettings.getContext());
    }
}
```

For Spring Boot to know to create and initialize a bean of type AppSettings, a modification must be made to the Application class. The @EnableConfigurationProperties (AppSettings.class) annotation must be added to the class definition at the same level as @SpringBootApplication. If the class name (AppSettings in this case) is not specified in the annotation, Spring Boot will scan, create, and initialize beans of all classes annotated with ConfigurationProperties.

```
package com.book.init;

import org.springframework.boot.SpringApplication;
import org.springframework.boot.autoconfigure.SpringBootApplication;
import org.springframework.boot.context.properties.EnableConfigurationProperties;
import org.springframework.context.annotation.ComponentScan;

@SpringBootApplication
@ComponentScan(basePackages = {"com.book.init", "com.book.web"})
@EnableConfigurationProperties(AppSettings.class)
public class Application {

    public static void main(String args) {
        SpringApplication.run(Application.class, args);
    }

}
```

When using Spring Boot, a Spring ASCII banner is printed in the console at application startup, like the one shown in Figure 8-3.

***Figure 8-3.*** *Spring Boot console banner*

This too can be customized. The instructions can be found in the official documentation at http://docs.spring.io/spring-boot/docs/1.2.6.RELEASE/reference/htmlsingle/#boot-features-banner. A banner.txt file needs to be created under the resources directory; a text-to-ASCII generator should be used to create the desired banner. The one presented in module 08-chapter-03-solution is shown in Figure 8-4.

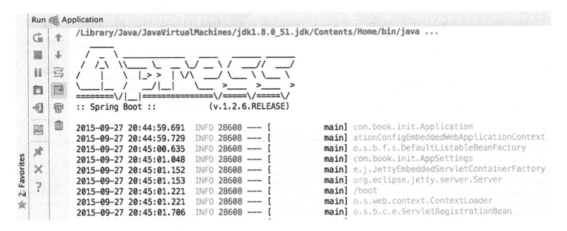

*Figure 8-4. Apress Spring Boot console banner*

## Importing Additional Configuration Elements

If an application is migrated to Spring Boot, a lot of the configuration classes and even XML configuration elements can be imported into the Spring Boot configuration class. Additional configuration classes can be imported using the @Import annotation or by adding a @ComponentScan to the Spring Boot core initialization class (the one with the main method in it) and setting the basePackages attribute value with the package name where the class can be found, which ensures that Spring automatically picks up all Spring components, including @Configuration classes.

XML configuration can be imported using the @ImportResource annotation, as the Spring Boot initialization class is nothing more than a more complex @Configuration class.

---

If you are using a Unix system, you can also test the examples attached to the chapter using the curl command. Just open a console and execute:

```
curl localhost:8080/boot
#modify port or contextPath accordingly
```

In the console, you should see an output similar to what you see in the browser.

---

# Running Spring Boot Applications

The main difference between using Spring Boot and developing web applications in the typical way is that when the Gradle spring-boot plugin is used, a web archive (*.war) is no longer created, because there is no need for it. The war file is strictly a deployable file that needs to be run using a web server or an application server. Spring Boot can be used to have an embedded server in the application. So when the Gradle spring-boot plugin is used instead of a war, an executable Java archive (*.jar) is created.

The created archive can be found under the [project_root]/build/libs and can be executed just like any jar. In the 08-chapter-03-solution.gradle configuration file, there is the line jar.archiveName = "boot.jar", which is used to specify the name of the final archive. Without it, the name of the resulting jar would be 08-chapter-03-solution.jar, which is long and unpractical.

To build the project, create the jar and then execute the application. The following lines can be executed in the console (shell or command prompt):

```
#this will work only if you have Gradle installed on the system
$ gradle clean build
$ java -jar build/libs/boot.jar
```

But what if we want the result to be a web archive that should be deployed on an application server or a web server? That can be done too, in three simple steps:

1. Modify the application to provide a Servlet initializer for the servlet environment. This is done by making the class annotated with @SpringBootApplication to extend the Spring Boot convenient class org.springframework.boot.context. web.SpringBootServletInitializer and overriding its configure method:

   ```
   @SpringBootApplication
   @ComponentScan(basePackages = {"com.book.init", "com.book.web"})
   @EnableConfigurationProperties(AppSettings.class)
   public class Application extends SpringBootServletInitializer {

       @Override
       protected SpringApplicationBuilder
           configure(SpringApplicationBuilder application) {
           return application.sources(Application.class);
       }

       public static void main(String args) {
           SpringApplication.run(Application.class, args);
       }
   }
   ```

2. Leave all the Spring Boot components as dependencies, but use the Gradle war plugin. (Basically, replace apply plugin: 'spring-boot' with apply plugin: 'war'.)

3.　Set the embedded server dependency as provided:

```
apply plugin: 'war'
war.archiveName = "boot.war"

buildscript {
    repositories {
        mavenCentral()
    }

    dependencies {
        classpath boot.springBootPlugin
    }
}

dependencies {

    compile (boot.starterWeb){
        exclude module : "spring-boot-starter-tomcat"
    }
    compile boot.actuator, boot.yaml
    providedCompile boot.starterJetty
    //previous 2 lines replaced:
    //compile boot.starterJetty, boot.actuator, boot.yaml

    testCompile misc.junit, misc.hamcrestCore,
        misc.hamcrestLib, boot.starterTest
}
```

After these changes, if the project is built under the build/libs directory, a boot.war should be created that can be deployed on any web or application server.

---

■ !　Try to modify the configurations for the 08-chapter-03-solution to create a deployable war, as described before. You can use Jetty to run the war on by adding the Gretty plugin that was used in the examples for this book until Spring Boot was introduced, by adding

```
apply from:
  'https://raw.github.com/akhikhl/gretty/master/pluginScripts/gretty.plugin'
```

in the 08-chapter-03-solution.gradle file, and then running the appStart Gradle task.

When deploying the war to an application server or a web server, keep in mind that the relevant embedded server settings read from the application.yml file are ignored (because they are relevant only to Spring Boot) when a class annotated with @SpringBootApplication is used to run the application; so the application is available on the port and location that you set for that server. When using Gretty, the location that your application can be accessed is printed in the console log.

```
...
INFO Jetty 9.2.10.v20150310 started and listening on port 8080
INFO 08-chapter-03-solution runs at:
INFO   http://localhost:8080/08-chapter-03-solution

...
```

---

## Testing Spring Boot Applications

Applications built with Spring Boot can be tested using **unit tests**. Spring Boot provides a library to do just that in the most practical manner possible. It is called `spring-boot-starter-test`. It must be added as a dependency of the project to use it.

As for common Spring Web applications, the servlet context must be mocked, and only the controller behavior is tested. The `HelloWorldController` is too simple to test, so a proper one is needed.

```java
@RestController
public class MessageController {

    @Value("${app.message:Hello World}")
    private String message = "Hello World";

    @RequestMapping("/message")
    public String message(){
        return message;
    }
}
```

The default value for the `message` property is set to *Hello World*, if it is not present in the `application.yml` file:

```yaml
app:
  port: 8084
  context: /boot
  message: Testing, is this thing on?
```

The class to instantiate and test this controller in a mock environment looks like this:

```java
import static org.hamcrest.Matchers.equalTo;
import static org.springframework.test.web.servlet.result.
    MockMvcResultMatchers.content;
import static org.springframework.test.web.servlet.result.
    MockMvcResultMatchers.status;

import org.junit.Before;
import org.junit.Test;
import org.junit.runner.RunWith;
import org.springframework.boot.test.SpringApplicationConfiguration;
import org.springframework.http.MediaType;
import org.springframework.mock.web.MockServletContext;
import org.springframework.test.context.junit4.SpringJUnit4ClassRunner;
import org.springframework.test.context.web.WebAppConfiguration;
import org.springframework.test.web.servlet.MockMvc;
import org.springframework.test.web.servlet.request.MockMvcRequestBuilders;
import org.springframework.test.web.servlet.setup.MockMvcBuilders;

@RunWith(SpringJUnit4ClassRunner.class)
@SpringApplicationConfiguration(classes = MockServletContext.class)
@WebAppConfiguration
public class MessageControllerTest {
```

```java
    private MockMvc mvc;

    @Before
    public void setUp() throws Exception {
        mvc = MockMvcBuilders.standaloneSetup(new MessageController()).build();
    }
    @Test
    public void getMessage() throws Exception {
        mvc.perform(MockMvcRequestBuilders.get("/message")
          .accept(MediaType.APPLICATION_JSON))
                .andExpect(status().isOk())
                .andExpect(content().string(equalTo("Hello World")));
        // testing the default value for this field
    }
}
```

The MockServletContext is used as argument for the @SpringApplicationConfiguration annotation, which provides a mock context where the MessageController can be instantiated. The MockMvcBuilders utility class is used to instantiate the controller instance that is to be tested.

In Chapter 3, MockitoJUnitRunner.class was used to test a controller, but the Spring Test library offers more appropriate and intuitive methods, especially for REST controllers.

The MockMvc should be familiar from Chapter 3. It is used here for the same purpose: to send HTTP request to the DispatcherServlet, and the status and content methods come into place to help test the results.

---

■ !  Notice that the value returned by the content method is expected to be *HelloWorld*, and this is because the mock context does not include the application.yml. To include the YAML file in the context and test the value configured there, integration testing is needed.

---

Applications built with Spring Boot can be tested using integration tests. These can be written easily for REST controllers because of a class provided by Spring Boot named org.springframework.boot.test. TestRestTemplate that extends the classical RestTemplate. The extra feature of this class is that secured resources can be tested too.

```java
import com.book.init.AppSettings;
import com.book.init.Application;
import org.junit.Before;
import org.junit.Test;
import org.junit.runner.RunWith;
import org.springframework.beans.factory.annotation.Autowired;
import org.springframework.boot.test.IntegrationTest;
import org.springframework.boot.test.SpringApplicationConfiguration;
import org.springframework.boot.test.TestRestTemplate;
import org.springframework.http.ResponseEntity;
import org.springframework.test.context.junit4.SpringJUnit4ClassRunner;
import org.springframework.test.context.web.WebAppConfiguration;
import org.springframework.web.client.RestTemplate;
```

```java
import java.net.URL;
import static org.hamcrest.Matchers.equalTo;
import static org.junit.Assert.assertThat;

@RunWith(SpringJUnit4ClassRunner.class)
@SpringApplicationConfiguration(classes = Application.class)
@WebAppConfiguration
@IntegrationTest
public class MessageControllerIT {

    @Autowired
    AppSettings appSettings;

    private URL base;
    private RestTemplate template;

    @Before
    public void setUp() throws Exception {
        this.base = new URL("http://localhost:" + appSettings.getPort() +"/" +
                appSettings.getContext() + "/message");
        template = new TestRestTemplate();
    }
    @Test
    public void getMessage() throws Exception {
        ResponseEntity<String> response =
                template.getForEntity(base.toString(), String.class);
        assertThat(response.getBody(),
                equalTo("Testing, is this thing on?"));
    }
}
```

Because real configuration classes are used to create the context in integration tests, beans can be injected and used inside the test class. In the previous example, the AppSettings bean is used to load the configuration details from the application.yml file, so the resulting endpoint for the MessageController is exactly the same as when the application is run with Spring Boot, and so is the content returned by the message method.

The @IntegrationTest annotation is another convenient feature provided by Spring Boot to start the embedded server on which the test will be run. It is designed to be used in conjunction with @SpringApplicationConfiguration. The server is started on the port value and it is injected using the AppSetting.port property value.

# WebSocket Introduction

Interaction between a user and a software service implies some type of communication. In the Web 2.0 era, software services are provided via web or mobile application, and communication is done over different protocols, the most common being HTTP. HTTP is a request-response model, with the client making the request (initiating a transaction) and the application providing the request service sending a response.

But more and more is needed from web applications, and the HTTP request-response model is becoming insufficient because information can be transmitted from the server to the client only after a request is received; the server cannot send data in between requests or without being asked for it by the client first.

Think about a shopping application. Users need to insert personal data into a form to place an order. But while a user fills the form, the service that receives and processes orders might become inaccessible because of an internal issue. Wouldn't it be nice if the server could send a message to the browser to inform the user that his order cannot be processed, saving him from wasting time inserting data into the form?

There are workarounds that can be implemented to implement this type of behavior, such as HTTP long polling, which is a technique involving the client to poll the server for new information and the server to keep that request open until new data is available. But this technique might cause trouble when the connection between the client and the server gets interrupted frequently (like when switching between Wi-Fi and cellular networks); messages get lost and the server might keep requests open that no longer need to be. To overcome these situations, a communication management system must be implemented—so things get even more complicated.

To provide a proper and practical solution, the WebSocket protocol was standardized in 2011 as RFC 6455.[4] Most web browsers now implement a client API that supports it. As the official documentation says: "The goal of this technology is to provide a mechanism for browser-based applications that need two-way communication with servers that does not rely on opening multiple HTTP connections."

# Spring WebSocket Implementation

Oracle has released JSR 356 as part of the JEE7 standard. It is the Java API for WebSocket that should be implemented to integrate WebSocket into web applications on the Java client and server sides. Client applications can be developed in any technology, and as long as they are compliant with the RFC 6455, they will be able to communicate with the server. The situation and the possibilities are depicted in Figure 8-5.

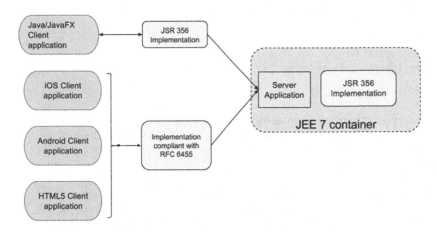

***Figure 8-5.*** *A client-server application leveraging WebSocket schema*

In Spring 4.1, a module named `spring-websocket` was introduced to provide support for WebSocket-based, two-way communication between the client and the server in web applications. The implementation is a JSR-356-compatible Java WebSocket API and it also includes SockJS-based fallback options. The SockJS is a JavaScript library that provides a WebSocket-like object (WebSocket behavior is emulated). It is most suitable when the application needs to be supported in older browsers that do not support the WebSocket protocol.

The Spring Framework WebSocket infrastructure is based on the Spring Messaging Foundation. Infrastructure beans like `MessageChannel` and `MessageHandler` are used as building blocks for the WebSocket environment.

---

[4]https://tools.ietf.org/html/rfc6455

In the `spring-messaging` module, support for STOMP[5] was added, providing an annotation programming model for routing and processing messages from WebSocket clients. This means that controller methods can be used to process HTTP requests (when methods are annotated with `@RequestMapping`) and can also be used to process WebSocket messages when methods are annotated with `@MessageMapping`, an annotation that was introduced in Spring 4.0.

The complementary operation, sending the result of the method back to the client, is implemented using the `@SendTo` annotation, which is used to mark a subscription endpoint to which all the potential clients are registered; this way, they are identified as receivers of messages from the server. The communication between clients and the server application using the WebSocket protocol is asynchronous, and when the server is overloaded, it can have delays in sending the messages.

The WebSocket protocol is streaming, and messages can be sent to/received from a WebSocket at the same time, so a connection and a `WebSocketSession` implementation is needed to provide the infrastructure through which the messages will be exchanged.

The following are the steps to create a WebSocket-compliant application using Spring WebSocket:

1. Define the format for the STOMP message and the POJO to model it.

2. Define the format for the server reply message and the POJO to model it.

3. Create a message-handling controller.

4. Configure Spring for WebSocket communication handling.

5. Create a client application.

6. Create an executable server application.

To get familiarized with WebSocket Spring components, you'll follow steps to create a mIRC[6]-like application that uses the WebSocket protocol. The application will be quite simple: it will require a username to allow connection to the server, but no authentication will be implemented. The server will receive messages from users and redistribute them to all connected clients. The server will communicate the time every 60 seconds and it will censor bad words, like *bomb* and *murder*. The source code to do this is explained later in the section.

**[STEP 1]** The STOMP message is a JSON representation containing the username and a message that the sends to the server:

```
{
    'name' : 'jules',
    'content' : 'Hello World!'
}
```

The POJO is quite simple and contains two properties (the JSON key names from the previous snippet) and getters.

```
package com.book.ws;

import com.fasterxml.jackson.annotation.JsonProperty;
import com.fasterxml.jackson.annotation.JsonPropertyOrder;

@JsonPropertyOrder({ "name", "content"})
public class ChatMessage {
```

---

[5]STOMP is an acronym for Simple Text-Orientated Messaging Protocol. It defines a message format that any available STOMP clients can use to communicate with any STOMP server application. Basically, it represents a standard communication unit independent of languages and platforms.

[6]A popular Internet Relay Chat (IRC) used extensively in the 1990s (see http://www.mirc.com).

```java
    @JsonProperty("content")
    private String content;

    @JsonProperty("name")
    private String name;

    public String getName() {
        return name;
    }

    public String getContent() {
        return content;
    }
}
```

JSON-specific annotations can be used, so POJO fields can be named differently than the key names in the JSON message and can also be used to customize the serialization. For example, the @JsonPropertyOrder is used here to define ordering of properties at serialization time. In the previous code, the annotation ensures that the resulting JSON object will always have "name" as the first property and "content" as the second.

---

■ ! The JSON annotations are used abusively in the previous example, simply for demonstration purposes. As the field names of the class are one and the same with the JSON property names, the @JsonProperty can be removed because it doesn't have any effect on the code. The same goes for the @JsonPropertyOrder, which can be removed because the order of the properties in the resulting JSON object is not really important in this case.

---

[STEP 2] Upon receiving a ChatMessage and extracting the information, the server application processes it and responds with a ServerMessage instance that is sent to a separate queue that the client is subscribed to. The response is serialized to a JSON representation. Defining a format for the server is easy in a mIRC application; all that is needed is a JSON representation with one property:

```json
{
        'content' : 'It is 18:13'
}
```

The POJO class that will be serialized could look like this:

```java
package com.book.ws;

public class ServerMessage {
    private String content;

    public ServerMessage(String content) {
        this.content = content;
    }

    public String getContent() {
        return content;
    }
}
```

Spring uses the Jackson JSON library to serialize and deserialize instances used for WebSocket communication.

**[STEP 3]** Creating a message-handling controller is also quite easy when using the @MessageMapping @SendTo annotations.

```
package com.book.ws;

import org.springframework.stereotype.Controller;
import org.springframework.messaging.handler.annotation.MessageMapping;
import org.springframework.messaging.handler.annotation.SendTo;
import java.util.Random;

@Controller
public class ChatController {

    @MessageMapping("/mirc")
    @SendTo("/topic/chat")
    public ServerMessage process(ChatMessage message) throws Exception {
        //generate random lag
        Random rn = new Random();
        Thread.sleep((rn.nextInt(5) + 1) * 1000);
        return MessageProcessor.build(message);
    }
}
```

The MessageProcessor is a utility class used to build the ServerMessage instances, which is serialized and sent to the client. The implementation is not really relevant for this section, as it only contains a static method used to build a ServerMessage instance based on a ChatMessage instance.

```
package com.book.ws;
public class MessageProcessor {
    public static ServerMessage build(ChatMessage message) {
        if (message.getContent() != null && !message.getContent().isEmpty()) {
            if (message.getContent().contains("bomb")) {
                //censoring using string.replace(...)
                 return new ServerMessage
                 ("[" + message.getName() + "]: "
                    + message.getContent().replace("bomb", "****"));
            } else if (message.getContent().contains("murder")) {
              //censoring using string.replace(...)
                 return new ServerMessage
                 ("[" + message.getName() + "]: "
                    + message.getContent().replace("murder", "****"));
            }
            return new ServerMessage
              ("[" + message.getName() + "]: " + message.getContent());
        }

        return new ServerMessage("[server]: Welcome " +message.getName());
    }
}
```

In the preceding code snippet, the process method is mapped to the destination "mirc", so if a message is sent to this destination, the method is called. This behavior is provided by annotating the method with @MessageMapping("/mirc"). Any message received from the client application(s) is deserialized, resulting in a ChatMessage instance that is used as an argument for the process method call.

The Thread.sleep call is used to simulate a delay. The Random instance is used to generate a random duration for the delay with a maximum of 5 seconds. This artifice was added to demonstrate that communication between the client application and the server is indeed asynchronous.

# Spring WebSocket Configuration

[STEP 4] To configure Spring for WebSocket communication handling with STOMP messages, a configuration class needs to be created.

```
package com.book.init;

import org.springframework.context.annotation.Configuration;
import org.springframework.messaging.simp.config.MessageBrokerRegistry;
import org.springframework.web.socket.config.annotation.
    AbstractWebSocketMessageBrokerConfigurer;
import org.springframework.web.socket.config.annotation.EnableWebSocketMessageBroker;
import org.springframework.web.socket.config.annotation.StompEndpointRegistry;

@Configuration
@EnableWebSocketMessageBroker
public class WebSocketConfig extends AbstractWebSocketMessageBrokerConfigurer {

    @Override
    public void configureMessageBroker(MessageBrokerRegistry config) {
        config.enableSimpleBroker("/topic");
        config.setApplicationDestinationPrefixes("/app");
    }

    @Override
    public void registerStompEndpoints(StompEndpointRegistry registry) {
        registry.addEndpoint("/mirc").withSockJS()
            .setStreamBytesLimit(512 * 1024)
            .setHttpMessageCacheSize(1000)
            .setDisconnectDelay(30 * 1000);
    }
}
```

Each of the elements in the previous class declaration has a specific responsibility. The following describes each of them.

- @EnableWebSocketMessageBroker enables WebSocket message handling using a message broker.

  AbstractWebSocketMessageBrokerConfigurer is a Spring convenient class implementing the WebSocketMessageBrokerConfigurer interface to provide empty method bodies for optional methods that are now needed for a minimal configuration of a WebSocket application.

- The `configureMessageBroker()` method implementation is used to configure a message broker. The `config.enableSimpleBroker("/topic")` enables a simple memory-based message broker used to filter destinations prefixed with "/topic" targeting the broker. The `config.setApplicationDestinationPrefixes("/app")` method designates the prefix for messages that need to be handled by methods annotated with @MessageMapping.

- The `registerStompEndpoints()` registers the "/mirc" STOMP endpoint, and enables and configures the SockJS fallback options. The subsequent chained method calls are used to configure streaming details.

  Streaming transports save responses on the client side and do not free the memory occupied by delivered messages, so the connection needs to be recycled from time to time. WebSocket communication is based on HTTP Streaming, which works by pushing content continuously to browser. The memory usage is kept accumulated in browser. Basically, the browser needs to close and reconnect the streaming channel to release memory. So there are a limited number of bytes that can be sent before the HTTP streaming connection is closed. The default value set by SockJS is 128K; the `.setStreamBytesLimit(512 * 1024)` call sets it to 512K.

  The number of server-to-client messages that can be cached in a session waiting for the next HTTP request polling is also limited. The default is 100 and it is set by the web server; the `.setHttpMessageCacheSize(1000)` call sets it to 1000.

  The number of milliseconds after an inactive client is disconnected is 5 seconds and it is set by the web server, but the `.setDisconnectDelay(30 * 1000)` call sets it to 30.

To use all of these elements, the `spring-websocket` and `spring-messaging` libraries must be added as dependencies. When using Spring Boot, only the `spring-boot-starter-websocket` dependency is necessary. Spring Boot adds all the necessary dependencies.

Aside from this, the entry point of the application is the `com.init.Application` class, which is a typical boot-up Spring Boot class.

```
package com.book.init;

import org.springframework.boot.SpringApplication;
import org.springframework.boot.autoconfigure.SpringBootApplication;
import org.springframework.context.annotation.ComponentScan;

@SpringBootApplication
@ComponentScan(basePackages = {"com.book.init, com.book.ws"})
public class Application {

    public static void main(String args) {
        SpringApplication.run(Application.class, args);
    }
}
```

# WebSocket Client Application

As depicted in Figure 8-5, client applications for a Spring WebSocket server application can be written in any programming language for which a WebSocket implementation or Socket-compatible implementation exists. For the example in this section, the simplest way to create a client application is the plain old HTML and JavaScript pair.

[STEP 5] Creating a browser client application is easy, and for the scope of this book, it is part of the same application and deployed on the same embedded container. The application is a JavaScript client that sends and receives messages from the server.

The module project for this section can be found under the book-code project and it is called 08-chapter-04-solution. The module is a Spring Boot WebSocket project organized as follows:

- The sources for the WebSocket server-application can be found under src/main/java. The configuration classes are placed in the com.book.init package. All classes involved in WebSocket communication are placed under the com.book.ws package.

- The sources for the JavaScript client application can be found under src/main/resources/static. The client application can be accessed at index.html. The functions that get called on specific HTML events are all gathered in the index.js file. The JavaScript external libraries used in the project are under the static/ext directory.

- jQuery is used to simplify the development of the JavaScript code used to handle HTML user events.

- SockJS is used to emulate WebSocket and provides a WebSocket-like API.

- The STOMP library is used to help create STOMP messages.

The structure of the full Spring Boot WebSocket project is depicted in Figure 8-6.

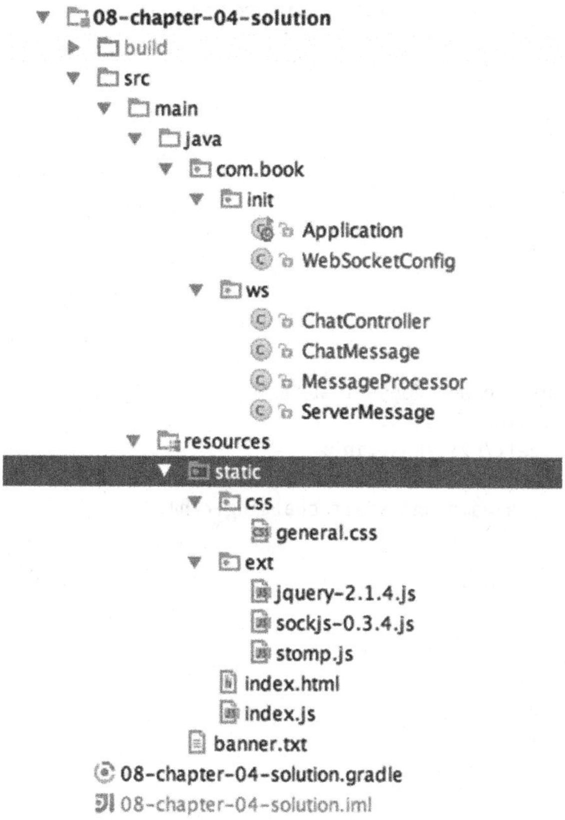

```
▼ 🗀 08-chapter-04-solution
    ▶ 🗀 build
    ▼ 🗀 src
        ▼ 🗀 main
            ▼ 🗀 java
                ▼ 🖻 com.book
                    ▼ 🖻 init
                        🔹 ⓑ Application
                        © ⓑ WebSocketConfig
                    ▼ 🖻 ws
                        © ⓑ ChatController
                        © ⓑ ChatMessage
                        © ⓑ MessageProcessor
                        © ⓑ ServerMessage
            ▼ 🗀 resources
                ▼ 🖻 static
                    ▼ 🖻 css
                        🖼 general.css
                    ▼ 🖻 ext
                        📄 jquery-2.1.4.js
                        📄 sockjs-0.3.4.js
                        📄 stomp.js
                    📄 index.html
                    📄 index.js
                📄 banner.txt
    ⓒ 08-chapter-04-solution.gradle
    🗾 08-chapter-04-solution.iml
```

*Figure 8-6.* *The 08-chapter-04-solution project structure*

The client application when no client is connected is depicted in Figure 8-7.

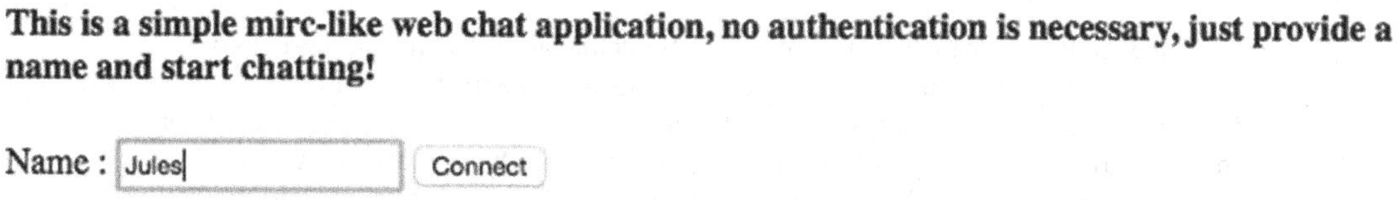

**This is a simple mirc-like web chat application, no authentication is necessary, just provide a name and start chatting!**

Name : [ Jules| ]  [ Connect ]

*Figure 8-7.* *The client application before connection*

Here is the static front-end that is written in HTML and represented by the index.html file:

```html
<!DOCTYPE html>
<html>
<head>
    <title>WebSocket mIRC-like sample application</title>
    <script src="ext/sockjs-0.3.4.js"></script>
    <script src="ext/stomp.js"></script>
    <script src="ext/jquery-2.1.4.js"></script>
    <script src="index.js"></script>
    <link rel="stylesheet" href="css/general.css">
</head>
<body>
<noscript><h2 style="color: #ff0000">Seems your browser doesn't support
    JavaScript! Websocket relies on Javascript being enabled.
    Please enableJavascript and reload this page!</h2></noscript>
This is a simple mirc-like web chat application,
    no authentication is necessary, just provide a name and start chatting!</h4>

<div class="header">
    Name : <input id="name" type="text"/>
    <input id="connection" type="button"/>
</div>
<div class="chatDiv">
    <textarea class="chat"></textarea>
</div>
<div class="footer">
    <input id="content" type="text"/>
    <input id="send" type="button" value="Send"/>
</div>

</body>
</html>
```

The following describes the four JavaScript functions in index.js:

- setConnected(boolVal): The argument is a boolean value. The method is called with true when connecting to the server application and with false when disconnecting. The same button is used for connecting and disconnecting. The label on the button changes depending on the current state of the application. When the application is accessed for the first time, a name is required to connect to the application.

```javascript
function setConnected(connected) {
    \\ set label for the connect/disconnect button
    connected ? $("#connection").attr("value", "Disconnect") :
            $("#connection").attr("value", "Connect");

    \\ disable name textfield so the name cannot be modified
    \\ after connecting
    $("#name").prop("disabled", connected);
```

```
    \\hide the chat window
    connected ? $(".chatDiv").show() : $(".chatDiv").hide();

    \\hide the insert message textfield
    connected ? $(".footer").show() : $(".footer").hide();

    \\empty the chat window
    $(".chat").html("");
}
```

- The function attached to the Connect/Disconnect button. When the application is accessed for the first time, a name is required to connect to the application.

```
$("#connection").click(function () {
        name = $("#name").val();
        if (name != "") {
            if ($("#connection").val() == "Connect") {
                //connecting
                var socket = new SockJS("/mirc");
                stompClient = Stomp.over(socket);
                stompClient.connect({}, function (frame) {
                    setConnected(true);
                    stompClient.subscribe("/topic/chat", function (message) {
                        showMessage(JSON.parse(message.body).content);
                    });
                    stompClient.send("/app/mirc", {},
                        JSON.stringify({"name": name, "content": ""}));
                });
            } else {
                //disconnecting
                stompClient.disconnect();
                setConnected(false);
            }
        }
    });
```

If a *name* is provided, SockJS and STOMP are used to open a connection to /mirc, that has the ChatController waiting for messages. After the connection has succeeded, the client subscribes to the "/topic/chat" destination where messages from the server application are published. When a server message is published to that destination, it is added to the chat text area.

- The showMessage(message) function appends the message received from the server application to the chat text area. The "&#xA;" character set represents a new line in HTML.

```
function showMessage(message) {
    $(".chat").append(message + "&#xA;');
}
```

- The function attached to the Send button is used to read the name and the message inserted by the user. The STOMP client is used to send the data to the "/app/mirc" destination (where the ChatController is waiting for messages).

```
$("#send").click(function () {
        var name = $("#name").val();
        var content = $("#content").val();
        stompClient.send("/app/mirc", {},
                JSON.stringify({"name": name, "content": content}));
        $("#content").val("");
});
```

To test the application, it first has to be built with Gradle by running the build task in the command line or in Intellij IDEA. This results in the creation of a jar archive under build/libs named ws-mirc.jar. The application can be run from a terminal by executing

```
java -jar ws-mirc.jar.
```

Or the com.book.init.Application class can be executed with an Intellij IDEA launcher, as depicted in Figure 8-8.

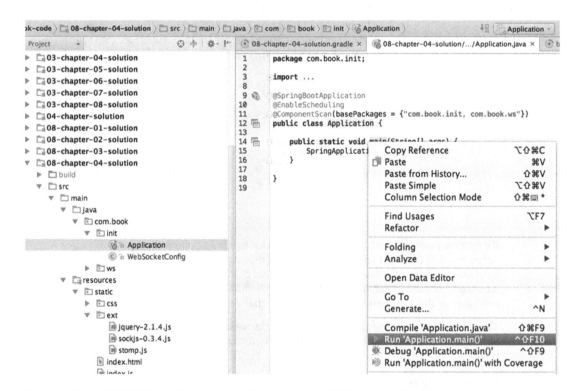

***Figure 8-8.*** *Intellij IDEA launcher can be used to run a Spring WebSocket application*

The application can support multiple clients. In Figure 8-9, the application is accessed from a Firefox browser by a user named *Jules* and it is accessed from a Safari browser by a user named *John*.

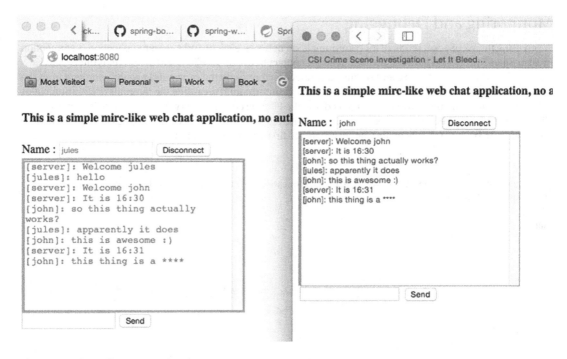

**Figure 8-9.** *Two clients accessing the same server*

## Configure the Server Application to Send Scheduled Messages

The server application should be able to send messages that tell the time to clients every 60 seconds. This can be done using a @Scheduled annotated method that publishes messages to the destination where clients expect messages from the server to be published. This method can be added in any class annotated with a stereotype annotation on it (@Component, @Controller, @Service, etc.), but in the book samples, it is added in the ChatController to keep related components together.

```java
//ChatController.java
  @Autowired
  SimpMessagingTemplate template;

  @Scheduled(fixedDelay = 60000)
  public void setNotification() throws Exception {
      LocalTime now = LocalTime.now();
      this.template.convertAndSend("/topic/chat", new ServerMessage
        ("server: It is " now.getHour() ":" now.getMinute()));
  }
```

The SimpMessagingTemplate bean is initialized by Spring Boot when the WebSocket support is enabled by having a configuration class annotated with @EnableWebSocketMessageBroker. But there is another thing to do—declaring a scheduled method is not enough. Scheduling must be enabled for the method to be picked up. As expected, there's an annotation for that: @EnableScheduling, which can be used on any @Configuration class in the application. When using Spring Boot, the most obvious way is to place it on the Application class.

# Monitoring and Debugging

When using the WebSocket protocol for communication between a client and a server application, a connection must exist and be opened between the two. The first contact between the client and the server is often called a **handshake**, which involves the client sending a connection request to the server and a reply being sent from the server, confirming the connection. When using stomp.js, information regarding the internals of communication between the client and the server can be tracked into the Firebug console. Every time a message is sent from the client and one is received from the server, you can see it in the console, as depicted in Figure 8-10. Notice that the handshake between the client and the server are the first two messages in the list.

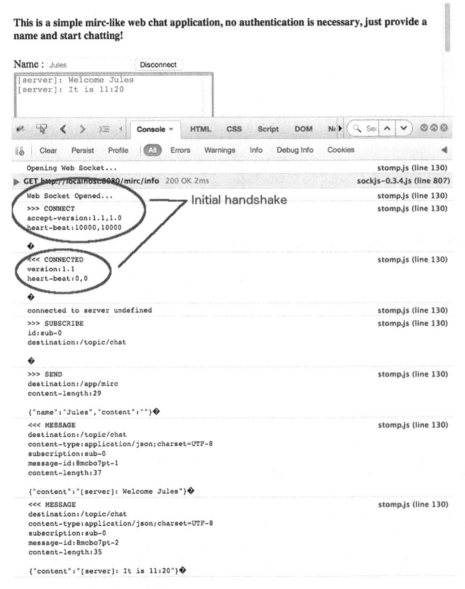

**Figure 8-10.**  *stomp.js monitoring*

Debugging a JavaScript client application can be done by using `console.log()` messages in the JavaScript code and/or by using the `debugger;` statement to set the breakpoint in the JavaScript code and control execution from there.

Debugging a server-side Java application can be done easily during development, especially with a smart development tool like IntelliJ IDEA. All that you have to do is start the application as usual, but instead of a normal launcher, choose the debugging launcher. Figure 8-11 shows the debugging launcher on the menu.

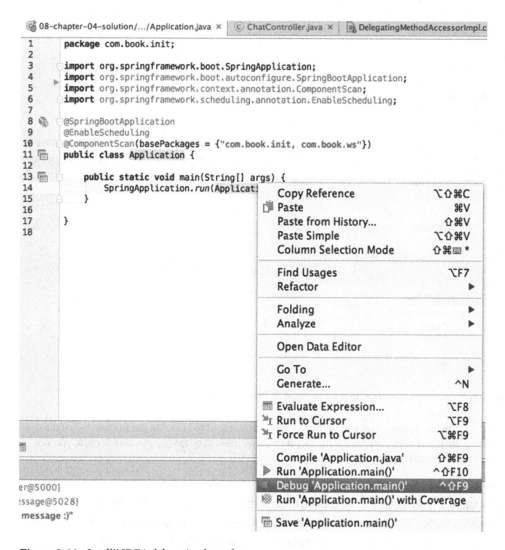

*Figure 8-11. IntelliJ IDEA debugging launcher*

Then place a breakpoint in the `ChatController.process()` message and send a message from the client to test it. Execution is paused, so you can inspect Spring beans and objects involved in the communication. A debug snippet using Intellij IDEA is shown in Figure 8-12.

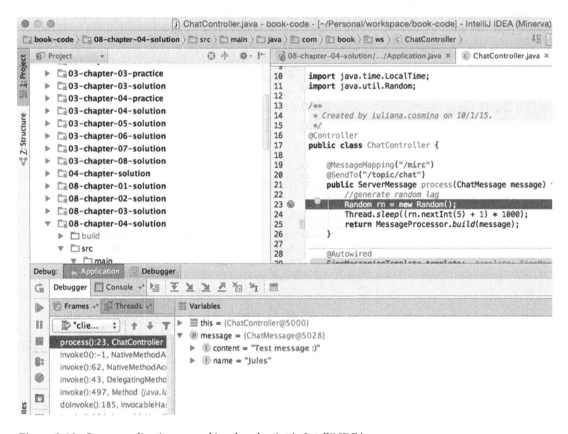

**Figure 8-12.** *Server application paused in a breakpoint in Intellij IDEA*

In Figure 8-12, the breakpoint is placed in line 23 of class `ChatController`. On the bottom left of the figure, you can see the name of the method currently being executed, `process()`, and on the right, you see the contents of a `ChatMessage` instance.

---

■ **!**   Since the topics in this chapter are not covered in the certification exam, there is neither a quiz section nor a practice section. But if you want to test your knowledge and understanding of Spring Boot, a recommended exercise is to try switching the Personal Records manager project to Spring Boot.

---

# APPENDIX

# Resources and Quiz Answers

The purpose of this appendix is to help you set up the development environment that you will use to write, compile, and execute the Spring applications specific to this book and to provide detailed responses for the questions in the quiz attached to each chapter.

## Study Guide Projects

The appendix for this book is quite small because it was written in such a way that you are guided through the normal succession of steps that you would have to through every time you start development of an application.

1. Choose your tools

2. Install your tools

3. Verify installation

4. Design the application

5. Develop and test

At the end of Chapter 1, I presented the tools and instructed you how to install them and how to verify the correct installation. The code samples for the book were written on an Apple Mac computer. One of the strong points of Java is that it is multi-platform, so the code can be run on any operating system. The tools recommended (Gradle, Intellij IDEA, Liferay, and Tomcat) are Java based, and are available at their official sites. The installation instructions are almost identical for any operating system, the only difference is in how an environment variable is set. Information about doing this on different operating systems is widely available on the internet and considering this book is for developers with a little experience, this should not be a problem for you.

The code for this book is split in two projects: `personal-records` and `book-code`. The `personal-records` project follows the evolution of a Spring web application. It was built incrementally and module names were prefixed with a number; if traversed in the ascending order of their prefixes, you will notice that every module contains the code of the previous one and something extra. It simulates the evolution of the configuration, exchanging and adding libraries until the final form of a complete web application is reached, when security and evolved components such as web flows are in place.

Using this study guide you will learn not only how to build Spring web applications, but also how to design a workflow for you and your team and how to design a multi-layered application from scratch.

The code was split in two because some topics such as alternative configurations and alternative view technologies needed to be presented separately without overcrowding the `personal-records` project. So really small modules covering these were created and wrapped up in a different project called `book-code`.

For `book-code`, the name of each module is constructed using the chapter number in which the module is covered and an index number. The modules are referenced in a chapter in ascending order of their indexes.

Both projects are Gradle multi-module projects and are configured in a similar manner. The project structures can be seen side by side in Figure A-1.

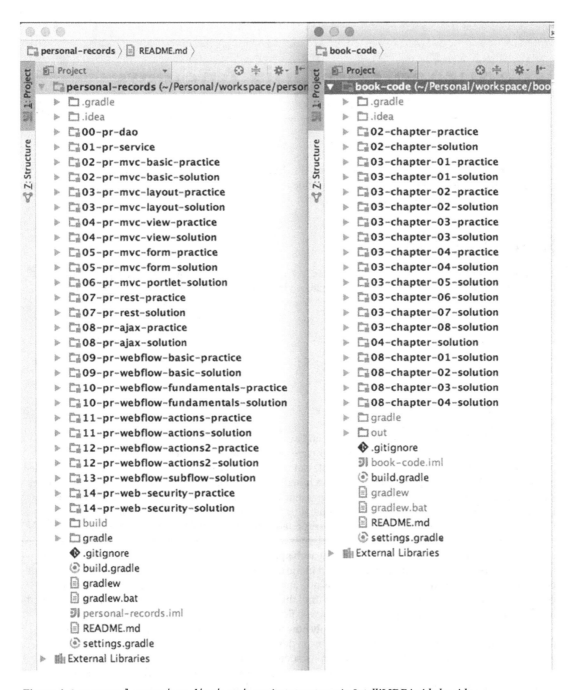

*Figure A-1.* `personal-records` *and book-code project structures in IntelliJ IDEA side by side*

# Gradle Configuration Explained

project-records and book-code are parent projects that define a set of libraries available for the child modules to use. As the configurations are very similar, from this point on only the configuration of the person-records project will be covered. person-records has the Gradle configuration in a file named build.gradle.

All the modules have the Gradle configuration file named after the module: [module_name].gradle. Also, there's a closure element in personal-records/settings.gradle that verifies at build time if all modules have their configuration file present.

```
rootProject.children.each {
  project -> project.buildFileName = "${project.name}.gradle"
  assert project.projectDir.isDirectory()
  assert project.buildFile.exists()
  assert project.buildFile.isFile()
}
```

This was a development choice; the components of a module are also more visible in an editor this way. Plus, if you want to modify the configuration file for a module you can easily find the file in IDEA using a unique name. Imagine the pain if you use the Command+Shift+N to search for a specific build.gradle file and you have 20+ matches.

Another approach for a multi-modular project would have been to have only one build.gradle file for the whole project and use Gradle-specific closures to customize configuration for each module. But in the spirit of good development practices, I decided to keep configurations for the modules as decoupled as possible and in the same location as the module contents.

# Building and Troubleshooting

After you download the source code you need to import the project in the IntelliJ IDEA editor:

1.  Select from the IntelliJ IDEA menu File ➤ New ➤ Project From Existing Sources (the menu options are depicted in Figure A-2).

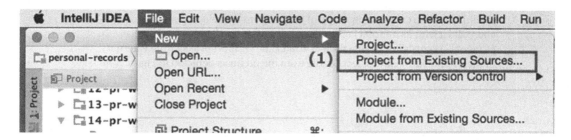

*Figure A-2.* *Project import menu options in IntelliJ IDEA*

2. A popup window will appear requesting the location of the project (Figure A-3). Select the personal-records directory.

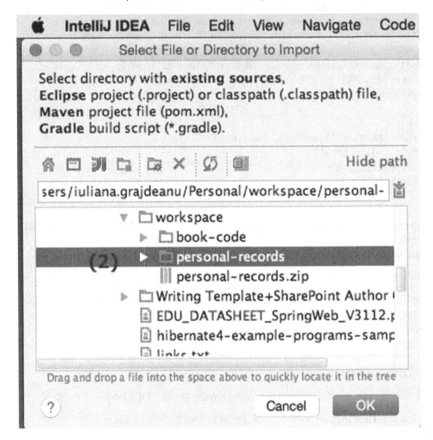

***Figure A-3.*** *Project import popup in IntelliJ IDEA*

3. IntelliJ IDEA can create its own type of project from the selected sources and build it with its internal Java builder, but this option is not useful here as personal-records is a Gradle project. Check the "Import project from external model" radio button and select Gradle from the menu as depicted in Figure A-4.

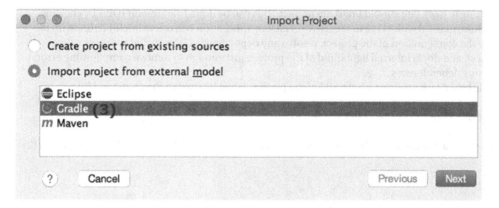

*Figure A-4.* *Selecting the project type in IntelliJ IDEA*

4. The last popup will appear and ask for the location of the build.gradle file and the Gradle executable. The options will be already populated for you. If you have Gradle installed you might want to use it (Figure A-5).

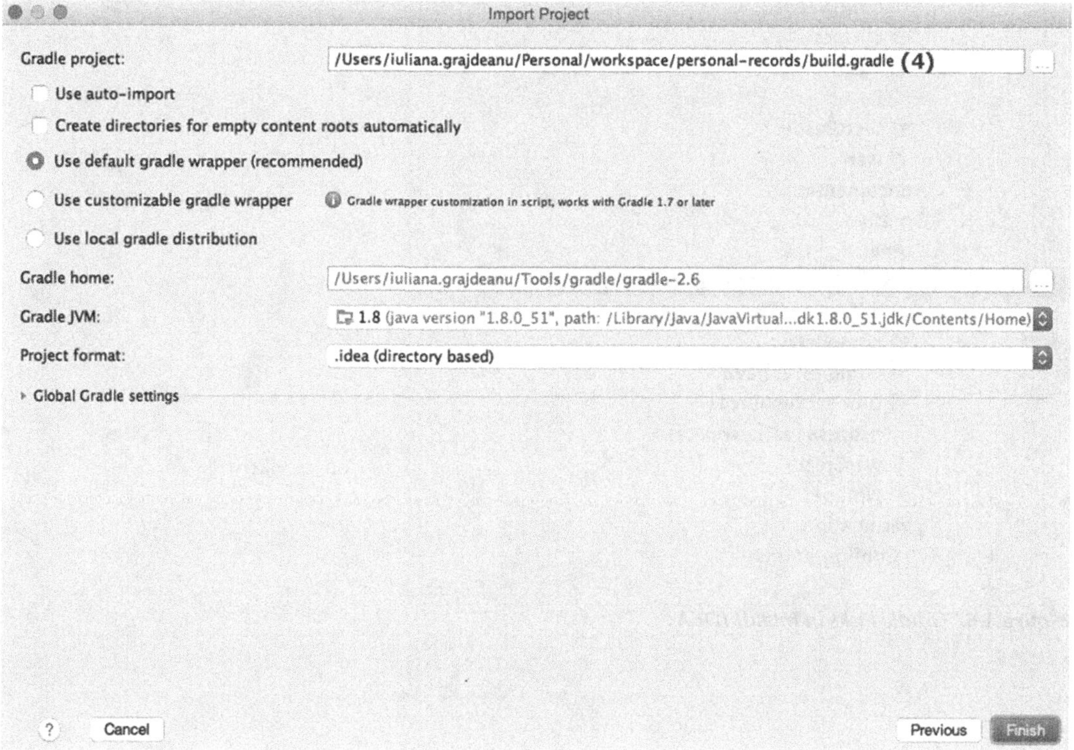

*Figure A-5.* *Last popup for project import in IntelliJ IDEA*

Before getting to work you should build the project. This can be done from IntelliJ IDEA by clicking the Refresh button, marked with (1) in in Figure A-6. Clicking this button will cause IntelliJ IDEA to do the following: scan the configuration of the project, resolve any dependencies (this includes downloading missing libraries), and do an internal light build of the project, just enough to remove compile-time errors caused by missing dependencies.

The Gradle build task executes a full build of the project. It can be used in the command line:

```
.../workspace/personal-records $ gradle build
```

Alternatively, you can use it in IntelliJ IDEA as depicted in Figure A-6, where the task is marked with (2).

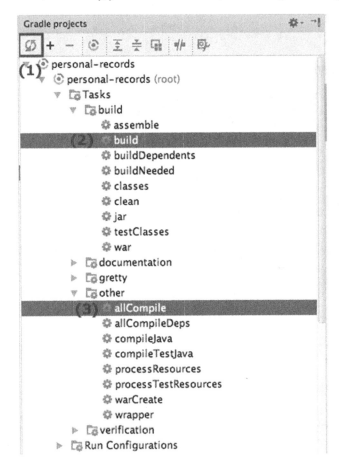

**Figure A-6.** *Gradle tasks in IntelliJ IDEA*

It will execute the following set of tasks on every module:

```
:00-pr-dao:compileJava UP-TO-DATE
:00-pr-dao:processResources UP-TO-DATE
:00-pr-dao:classes UP-TO-DATE
:00-pr-dao:jar UP-TO-DATE
:00-pr-dao:assemble  UP-TO-DATE
:00-pr-dao:compileTestJava  UP-TO-DATE
:00-pr-dao:processTestResources UP-TO-DATE
:00-pr-dao:testClasses  UP-TO-DATE
:00-pr-dao:test  UP-TO-DATE
:00-pr-dao:check UP-TO-DATE
:00-pr-dao:build  UP-TO-DATE
```

The tasks depicted here are only for the 00-pr-dao module. The Gradle build task will execute all the tasks it depends on. As you can see, it does not run the clean task, so you need to make sure to run this task manually when building a project multiple times, to make sure the most recent versions of the classes are used.

As the project contains incomplete sources that you will have to complete (in modules post fixed with -practice), executing this task will fail. You could just execute tasks clean and compile Java, but there's a better way. I have created a custom task in the project called allCompile. This task executes the clean and compileJava tasks for all modules. It is marked with (3) in Figure A-6. It is defined in build.gradle and inherited by the child modules, so it can be executed for a module separately.

# Deploy on Apache Tomcat

Every web application in this project is run with the Jetty embedded web server to keep things simple. But there are certain advantages in using an external container such as Apache Tomcat server. Starting the server in debug mode and using breakpoints to debug an application is much easier to do is one advantage. An external container can run multiple applications at a time without the need to stop the server. Plus embedded servers should be used only for testing and educational purposes; in practice application servers are preferred, because of reasons explained in Chapter 8.

Here is what you have to do if you are interested in doing this. First download the latest version of Apache Tomcat 8.x from the official site[1] and unpack it somewhere on your system. Then configure an IntelliJ IDEA launcher to start the server and deploy the chosen application. This is quite easy to do, but there are a number of steps to be executed and they are listed below:

1.  From the runnable configuration menu choose Edit Configurations (1). A popup window will appear listing a set of launchers. Click on the + and select the Tomcat Server option. The menu will expand: select Local (2) because you are using a server installed on your computer. Figure A-7 depicts these menu options.

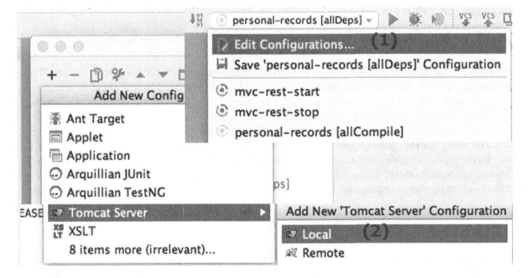

*Figure A-7.*  *Menu options to create a Tomcat launcher in IntelliJ IDEA*

---

[1]http://tomcat.apache.org/

2. A popup window like the one in Figure A-8 will appear and will request some information.

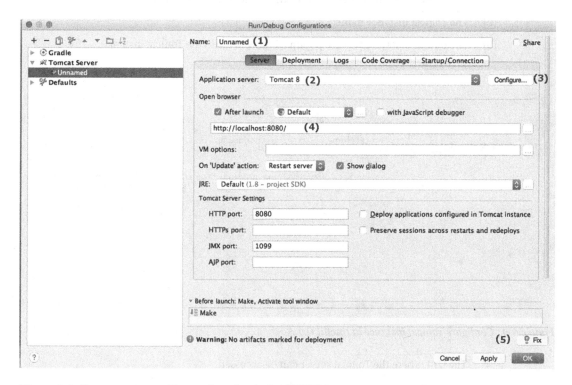

**Figure A-8.** *Popup to create a Tomcat launcher in IntelliJ IDEA*

In the previous figure, some items are numbered and their meaning is explained in following list:

(1)   The launcher name; you can insert a more obvious name in there.

(2)   The Tomcat instance name.

(3)   The button that will open the popup window to insert the Tomcat instance location (Figure A-9).

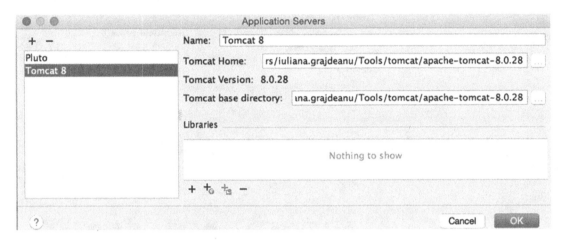

***Figure A-9.*** *Configure Tomcat instance in IntelliJ IDEA*

(4)   The URL where the Tomcat server can be accessed.

(5)   The choose artifact button. Unless there is no war set to be deployed to Tomcat, this button will be displayed with the red light bulb icon on it.

3.   Click the Fix button and select an artifact. IntelliJ IDEA will detect all artifacts available (Figure A-10) and present them to you in a list you can choose from. If you intend to open the server in debug mode and use breakpoints in the code, select an artifact with the name post-fixed with (exploded); this way IntelliJ IDEA manages the contents of the exploded war and can link the actions in the browser with the breakpoints in the code.

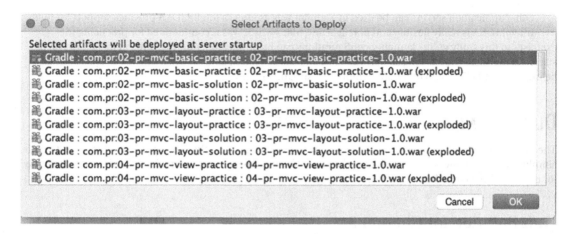

*Figure A-10.* *Deployable artifact list in IntelliJ IDEA*

4. Complete the configuration by clicking the OK button. You can specify a different application context by inserting a new value in the Application Context text field. Choosing a different application context will tell Tomcat to deploy the application under the given name and the application will be accessible via the following URL: `http://localhost:8080/[app_context_name]/`. In Figure A-11, the application will be accessible via `http://localhost:8080/mvc-basic/`.

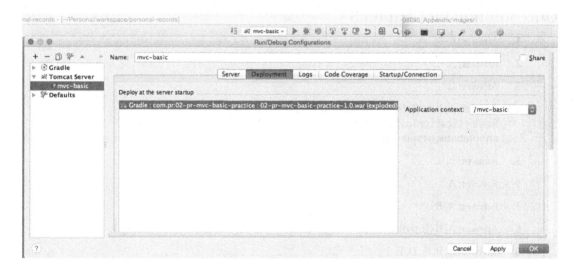

*Figure A-11.* *Inset a new application context in IntelliJ IDEA*

Other application servers can be used in a similar way as long as IntelliJ IDEA provides support for them.
IntelliJ IDEA is really flexible and practical and that's why it was recommended for practicing the exercises in this study guide: launcher configurations can be duplicated, multiple Tomcat instances can be started at the same time as long as they function on different ports, and so on. The Gradle projects can also be imported in Eclipse and other Java editors that support Gradle.

# Quiz Answers

The following sections contain answers to the quiz questions for every chapter. Answers to questions that are simple enough to remember after reading the chapter will not be detailed. Extra details will be provided only for questions that could be considered tricky.

## Quiz Solution for Chapter 2

1. Answer: A, B, C

2. Answer: B

3. Answer: A, B, D (C, interface-based injection, is not supported in Spring. D, field-based injection, is supported by annotating fields with @Autowired, @Value, or related annotations; JSR-250 @Resource, JSR-330 @Inject.[2])

4. Answer: A, B, C (as stated in Chapter 2.)

## Quiz Solution for Chapter 3

1. Answer: C

2. Answer: A

3. Answer: C

4. Answer: A, B, C (D is incorrect because classes implementing WebApplicationInitializer or extending its subclasses do not require any annotations, as stated in Chapter 3.)

5. Answer: B, C

6. Answer: A.[3]

7. Answer: A, B

8. Answer: A, B (Interface ViewConfigurer is not part of any Spring Web library.)

9. Answer: A, B, C, D, E

10. Answer: A

11. Answer: C (B is not correct because multiple view types can be supported using ViewResolver chaining too.)

---

[2]http://docs.spring.io/spring/docs/4.2.3.RELEASE/spring-framework-reference/
htmlsingle/#beans- annotation-config
[3]http://docs.spring.io/spring/docs/4.2.3.RELEASE/spring-framework-reference/
htmlsingle/#mvc- servlet-special-bean-types

12. Answer: B, C (D is not true, because it is an incomplete answer. Indeed it can be taken into consideration by setting a value for the `ignoreAcceptHeader` property, but that must be true, which is not mentioned here.)

13. Answer: A, B, C, D

14. Answer: A, B, C

15. Answer: B

16. Answer: B (The path variable name (`id`) is different than the method argument name (`number`) and in this case the annotation `@PathVariable` should define in which argument the path variable value should be injected by using the path variable name as an argument: `@PathVariable("id")`.)

17. Answer: E (All others are valid return types that can be matched to a view representation. A null value will crash the application.[4])

18. Answer: B, C (D is incorrect because `@ModelAttribute` can also be used on methods. Look at the next question option A to see what for.)

19. Answer: A, B (C is not true because the statement is ambiguous.)

20. Answer: B

21. Answer: A, B (C is not true because the two implementations covered by A and B could suffice. If the word "must" is replaced with "might" then this statement would be true too.)

22. Answer: A

23. Answer: B

24. Answer: A, B, D, G (C is used on handler arguments, E is used on validation annotations, and F is used on setter methods to enforce that a dependency is mandatory.)

## Quiz Solution for Chapter 5

1. Answer: C

2. Answer: A, B, D

3. Answer: C

4. Answer: A

5. Answer: A, B, C

6. Answer: B

7. Answer: A, B(C does not exist)

8. Answer: A, C, D

9. Answer: D

---

[4]`http://docs.spring.io/spring/docs/4.2.3.RELEASE/spring-framework-reference/htmlsingle/#mvc- ann-return-types`

# Quiz Solution for Chapter 6

1. Answer: B, C (Ajax is a technique for building interactive applications for the Web and an acronym. It is not a set of standards or technologies and that is why B and D are not valid options.)

2. Answer: C

3. Answer: A, B, C

4. Answer: A

# Quiz Solution for Chapter 7

1. Answer: A, B, C

2. Answer: B

3. Answer: A, B, D, E, F

4. Answer: A, C

5. Answer: B, C

6. Answer: A

7. Answer: B

8. Answer: B

9. Answer: A, B

10. Answer: A, B, C (Converters are present in the Spring WebFlow environment, but they are not defined explicitly in a flow definition, which is why answer D is not valid. Data is only handled when a flow is executed, which dismisses answer E.)

11. Answer: B, C, D, F (A start state is a concept and is the first state that is entered when the flow starts its execution and is always a view state, so answer A is dismissed. There is no such thing as a persistence state type, so answer E can be dismissed. But as an observation, there is a special attribute in the end-state set to persist data in the flow before completion of the flow process. G can be dismissed, too; there is no conversion state type.)

12. Answer: C, D

13. Answer: A, C

14. Answer: A,B (C is false because a decision state does not have a view associated with it.)

15. Answer: A, C

16. Answer: B, C

17. Answer: B

18. Answer: B, C

19. Answer: B, C

20. Answer: B, C

21. Answer: A, C

22. Answer: B, C

23. Answer: A, B, C

24. Answer: B

25. Answer: A, B, C, D, F, G (E makes no sense: during transition execution, no action can be executed because any result of the action would be lost. F is also invalid because an action can be executed only in the context of a flow execution.)

26. Answer: A, C

27. Answer: B, C, D

28. Answer: A, B, C

29. Answer: B

30. Answer: A, B, C, D

# Index

## A

Action phase, 154
AJAX (asynchronous JavaScript and XML), 229
  communication flow, 230
  components, 156
  custom tags, 250
  functions, 229
  GET and POST requests, 233
  jQuery, 233, 236
    AJAX calls, 243
    features, 239
    HTML DOM manipulation, 240
    Spring MVC, 245
  JSON format
    done and fail callback methods, 250
    @RestController, 246
  quiz solution, 414
  requests
    XMLHttpRequest methods, 233
  @Valid annotation, 230
All-in-one configuration, Spring Web MVC, 56
AOP (aspect-oriented programming)
  advices, 41
  aspects, 41
  @TransactionConfiguration, 43
  transaction-manager attribute, 44
  UML diagram, 41
Apache Tiles, 111
Apache TomEE, 367
Autodiscovery, 26
Autowiring, 26

## B

Base tile, 112–113
Bean factory post processors, 30

## C

Combined lifecycle strategy, 31
@ComponentScan annotation, 63
@ControllerAdvice, 93
ContentNegotiatingViewResolver, 78

## D

Data binding process, 129
Data transfer object (DTO), 122
Data validation
  annotations, 133
  JEE @Constraint annotation, 135
  Hibernate Validator, 132, 134
  hibernate-validator.jar contents, 134
  message keys, 134–135
Domain objects, 122

## E

@ExceptionHandler, 92
External Libraries, 251

## F

Flash attributes, 102
Flow. *See* Web flow

## G

Guide projects
  Apache Tomcat server
    application context inset, 411
    artifact list, 411
    configuration, 410
    deployment, 407

Guide projects (*cont.*)
  lists, 410
  menu options, 408
  popup menu, 409
  steps, 408
 build.gradle file, 403
 Gradle configuration, 403
 installation, 401
 personal-records and book-code, 401
 project structures, 402
 spring web applications, 401
 steps, 401
 troubleshooting
  gradle tasks, 406
  import popup, 404
  IntelliJ IDEA editor, 403
  menu options, 403
  module execution, 407
  popup menu, 405
  project type, 404
  task executes, 407

## H

HAL, 196
Hamcrest, 105
HandlerAdapter interface, 71
HandlerExceptionResolver, 90
Handler interceptors, 106
HandlerMapping, 68
Handshake, 398
HATEOAS, 195–196
Hibernate Validator, 132, 134
hibernate-validator.jar contents, 134
HospitalFormatter, 128
HTTP request-response model, 385
Hypermedia driven REST web service, 216, 219

## I

Infrastructure beans, 1
InternalResourceViewResolver, 75
Internationalization process, 85
Inversion of control (IoC), 18

## J, K

Jetty server, 368
JSON View Resolver, 84
JSP tags, 251
JSTL (JSP Standard Tag Library), 251

## L

LocaleResolver interface, 87

## M, N, O

MessageSource interface, 85
@Mock annotation, 104
Mockito, 103
@ModelAttribute annotated method, 137

## P, Q

Plain old Java objects (POJOs), 17
Pivotal, 2

## R

ReloadableResourceBundleMessageSource, 86
Render phase, 154
Repositories, 13
ResourceBundleMessageSource, 85
REST (REpresentational State Transfer), 189
 Accept HTTP header, 194
 advantages, 197
 basic authentication, 198
 cache, 190
 client-server architecture, 190
 code on demand, 190
 compliance levels, 195
 Content-Type HTTP header, 194
 DELETE request and response, 194
 GET request and response, 192
 HATEOAS, 195
 layered system, 190
 message converters, 190
 OAuth 1.0a and OAuth 2.0, 198
 POST request and response, 192
 PUT request and response, 193
 quiz solution, 413
 Spring MVC, 199
  @Async annotated methods, 213
  AsyncRestTemplate methods, 203
  consumes and produces
   properties, 210
  exception handling, 208
  execute and exchange methods, 200
  filter interceptor, 203
  handler methods, 205
  HATEOAS, 216
  hidden methods, 203
  HttpServletRequest/
   HttpServletResponse, 211
  HTTP status codes, 207
  interceptor, 214
  message converters, 201
  resources, 204
  @RestController, 206
  RestTemplate methods, 199

states, 190
transport layer, 190
transport protocols, 190
uniform interface, 189
Richardson Maturity Model, 195

## ■ S

Separate configuration, Spring Web MVC, 57
Separation of concerns (SoC), 328
SimpleMappingExceptionResolver, 91
Spring, 27
    accessing beans
        annotated beans, 40
        bean identification by id, 40
        bean identification by name, 39
        bean identification by type, 38
    AOP (see AOP (aspect-oriented programming))
    bean scopes, 35
    classes, 17
    configuration, 21
        annotations, 25
        mixed approach, 26
        prefixes and corresponding paths, 24
    convention over configuration paradigm, 1
    core container, 19
    dependency injection, 1
    development environment, 8
        build tools, 9
        IDE, 10
        Personal Records Manager application, 11
    frameworks, 1
    infrastructure beans, 1
    integration testing, 45
    library, 1
    lifecycle and instantiation, 27
        advantages, 29
        bean factory post processors, 30
        bean initialization and destruction, 30
        BeanPostProcessors, 34
    Pivotal, 2
    PlainPersonRepository class, 20
    quiz answers, 412
    Spring Certification section, 5
    spring-context modules, 19
    spring-core and spring-beans modules, 19
    spring-expression modules, 19
    Spring-released projects, 2
    study guide, 7
        application developer, 5
        code downloads, 8
        conventions, 8
        objectives of, 4
        Spring Framework's support, 4
        structure, 7

unit testing, 44
XML configuration, 21
Spring Boot
    application server, 367
    execution, 381
    goals, 367
    testing
        @IntegrationTest annotation, 385
        integration tests, 384
        spring-boot-starter-test, 383
    usage and configuration
        ApplicationContext instance, 371
        AppSettings class, 377
        @Bean annotated methods, 370
        command-line variables, 376
        @ComponentScan annotation, 370
        @ConfigurationProperties, 378
        EmbeddedServletContainer
            Customizer, 377
        @EnableAutoConfiguration
            annotation, 370
        @EnableConfigurationProperties, 379
        environment variables, 376
        Gradle configuration, 368
        @Import annotation, 380
        prefix attribute, 378
        properties files, 373
        @SpringBootApplication
            annotation, 370
        Spring Boot console banner, 380
        transitive dependencies, 372
        YAML files, 375
    web server, 367
Spring Framework Reference, 5
Spring portlets
    configuration, 156
    definition, 151
    MVC framework, 153
    portlet application
        admin menu, 173–174
        App Manager installation, 182
        Command Prompt, 170
        download process, 170
        Finish Configuration, 171
        Hello World Portlet, 179
        Liferay installation, 170
        Liferay Password, 172
        Person database, 187–188
        Site configuration page, 185
        site templates, 173–175
        Site URL, 186
        start Liferay, 170
        uninstall option, 184
    recommendations, 168
    web application, 152

Spring portlets (*cont.*)
workflow, 154
XML
and annotations, 164
app-config.xml, 158
App Manager, 159
configuration, 158
definition, 157
liferay-display.xml, 159
liferay-portlet.xml, 161
message converter, 158
mvc-config.xml, 158
portlet controller bean, 161
site template, 160
syntax, 160
ViewRendererServlet, 163
web.xml, 163
SpringServletContainerInitializer, 64
Spring Web Certification Exam, 5
Spring Web MVC
behavior, 53
description, 53
DispatcherServlet, 54
form object management, 137
forms
data binding, 129
data formatting, 125
data transfer object, 122
data validation, 132
domain object, 122
editing a person, 119–120, 122
JSP c taglib, 124
to search a person, 123
functional flow, 54–55
infrastructure beans, 67–68
ContentNegotiatingViewResolver, 78
HandlerAdapter interface, 71
HandlerExceptionResolver, 90
HandlerMapping, 68
JSON View Resolver, 84
localeResolver, 87
MessageSource, 85
personalization beans, 85
ThemeResolver, 88
ViewResolver, 73
ViewResolver chaining, 74
infrastructure components, 54
libraries, 54
practice application welcome page, 61
quiz solution, 412–413
user-provided components
Accessing Model data, 100
controllers, 94
handler interceptors, 106
redirect requests, 101

selecting a view, 101
testing controllers, 103
user-provided web components, 54
view technologies
data-delivery views, 109
display views, 109
file-generating views, 109
Thymeleaf, 115
Tiles Layouts, 110
XML configuration, 56
all-in-one configuration, 55–56
<mvc\:annotation-driven/> element, 60
<mvc\:default-servlet-handler/>, 60
mixed configurations, 63
separate configuration, 55, 57
using annotations, 61
without using web.xml file, 64
Spring WebSocket
ChatMessage, 388
client application
JavaScript functions, 394
module project, 392
client-server application, 386
HTTP request-response model, 385
JSON-specific annotations, 388
MessageProcessor, 389
mIRC, 387
monitoring and debugging, 398
process method, 390
Random instance, 390
@SendTo annotation, 387
server application, 397
SockJS-based fallback, 386
STOMP messages, 390
WebSocket-compliant application, 387
StaticMessageSource, 85
Stubs, 103

## ■ T, U, V

ThemeResolver, 88
Thymeleaf
selection/asterisk expressions, 116
Spring integrations, 118
standard dialects, 116
template page, 117–118
text externalized expressions, 116
URL expressions, 116
variable expressions, 116
Tiles Layout
Apache Tiles, 111
configuration files, 111
defining page templete, 111
reusable page template, 110
TilesViewResolver bean, 114

# ■ W, X, Y, Z

WebAppConfiguration annotation, 105
Web flow
    actions, 282
        EL expressions, 288
        environment-specific variables, 289
        findAll method, 288
        on flow end, 288
        on flow start, 286
        HTTP session cotents, 289
        RequestContext, 289
        requestParameters, 290
        scope-specific variables, 289
        on state entry, 287
        on state exit, 287
        on transition execution, 287
        on view render, 287
    action state, 272
        boolean, 305
        definition, 304
        enumerated types, 305
        getActiveFlow(), 311
        getCurrentState() method, 311
        getExternalContext() method, 311
        getFlowExecutionURL() method, 311
        getFlowScope() method, 311
        getMessageContext() method, 311
        getRequestScope() method, 311
        MultiActions, 310–311
        No action, 307, 310
        plain actions, 309, 311
        POJO actions, 307, 310
        string, 305
    annotations, 267
        MvcConfig class, 268
        New Person link, 272
        WebFlowConfig class, 268
        WebInitializer class, 270
    architecture
        backing class, 259
        configuration file, 261
        DispatcherServlet, 260
        FlowController class, 260
        FlowDefinitionRegistry, 260
        FlowHandlerMapping maps, 260
    decision state, 311
    exception handling
        account flow, 315
        amount field, 315
        backtracking, 321
        bank field, 315
        cancel, 319
        confirmAdult state, 318
        end state, 319

        enterAccountInfo, 318
        enterIdentityCardInfo, 316
        enterPersonInfo, 315
        error, 319
        flow execution, 312
        IBAN field, 315
        JSP scriptlets, 320
        reviewExistingPerson, 317
        status field, 315
    flow definition
        components, 273
        contextRelative prefix, 276
        decision state, 272
        end states, 272, 277
        inheritance, 326
        Mock views, 278
        redirect prefixes, 277
        schema, 273
        scope, 272
        subflow state, 272
        testing, 279
        transitions, 272, 277
        user event, 275
        view-state id, 274
        view states, 272, 277
infrastructure beans, 262
internal logic, 261
model object, 291
    conversion, 293
    data binding., 292
    enterIdentityCardInfo
        view-state, 303
    enterPersonInfo
        view-state, 301
    formatting, 294
    IdentityCardValidator
        class, 304
    JSR 349 bean validation, 294
    partial validation, 298
    programmatic
        validation, 296
    reviewPerson view-state, 302
problems, 259
quiz solution, 414
scope
    conversation scope, 282, 284
    explicit variables, 284
    flash scope, 282, 285
    flow scope, 282–283
    request scope, 282, 285
    standard EL expression, 284
    template EL expression, 284
    view scope, 282–283
scopes, 282
Spring Security

Web flow (*cont.*)

    access decision manager, 329

    advantages, 328

    authentication, 327

    authorization, 327

    configure authentication, 339

    credentials, 327

    features, 327

    flow definition, 350

    Java configuration, 343

    logout link, 346

    NewPerson link, 346

    OAuth, 353

    portability, 328

    principal, 327

    secured item, 327

    secure methods, 347

    Social projects, 356

    XML configuration, 330

    states, 258

    subflow

        conversation scope, 323

        definition, 322

        flashScope.hospitalMessage
variable, 323

        getModelResources method, 325

        input parameters, 323

        key values, 323

        output parameter, 323

        unit testing, 324

    XML configuration, 263

        conversionService, 267

        flowBuilderServices, 266

        flowExecutor, 265

        FlowHandlerMapping, 264

        flowRegistry, 266

        max-executions property, 266

        mvcViewFactoryCreator, 267

# Get the eBook for only $5!

Why limit yourself?

Now you can take the weightless companion with you wherever you go and access your content on your PC, phone, tablet, or reader.

Since you've purchased this print book, we're happy to offer you the eBook in all 3 formats for just $5.

Convenient and fully searchable, the PDF version enables you to easily find and copy code—or perform examples by quickly toggling between instructions and applications. The MOBI format is ideal for your Kindle, while the ePUB can be utilized on a variety of mobile devices.

To learn more, go to www.apress.com/companion or contact support@apress.com.

Printed in the United States
By Bookmasters